Some of My Best Friends Are Books

Second Edition

Guiding Gifted Readers from Preschool to High School

Judith Wynn Halsted

Great Potential Press, Inc.
Scottsdale, Arizona
www.giftedbooks.com

Some of My Best Friends Are Books, Second Edition
Guiding Gifted Readers from Preschool to High School

Cover Design: ATG Productions, Inc.
Interior Design: The Printed Page

Published by
Great Potential Press, Inc.
(formerly Gifted Psychology Press, Inc.)
P.O. Box 5057
Scottsdale, AZ 85261

Library of Congress Cataloging-in-Publication Data

Halsted, Judith Wynn, 1940-
    Some of my best friends are books : guiding gifted readers from preschool to high
school / Judith Wynn Halsted.--2nd ed.
        p. cm.
    Includes bibliographical references and index.
    ISBN 0-910707-51-0
    1. Gifted children--Books and reading--United States. 2. Gifted
children--Education--United States. 3. Children's literature--Bibliography. 4. Young
adult literature--Bibliography. 5. Bibliography. I. Title.

Z1039.G55 H35 2002
025.5'5--dc21
                                                        2001058578

Dedication

*This book is dedicated with love
and gratitude to the next generations—*

David and Keely   *Mark and Barbara*
Christopher and Caroline   *Chloe and Benjamin*

Preface

This book is for parents, teachers, librarians, and counselors of children and young people who are different from the norm by reason of giftedness or intense interests—intellectual, artistic, or musical.

For many of these children, at least for a portion of the time, it is quite true that some of their best friends are books. It is with them in mind that this second edition of *Some of My Best Friends Are Books* has been written. Here we outline the reasons books are so important to gifted and capable students, and we offer suggestions for the best use of books to enhance their growth.

This book proposes that by reading and discussing books with children, teachers and parents can encourage optimum development in two areas—emotional and intellectual—in one pleasurable activity.

Emotional: Books can provide a focus for discussions (*non-threatening* discussions, since, after all, they are about someone else) that touch not necessarily on plot and characterization but instead on feelings, values, and decision-making. Parents who have tried this tell me that they find books to be wonderful bridges for communication with their youngsters.

Intellectual: Reading is a natural ally in the effort to provide our students with intellectual challenge. With the judicious use of books, parents or teachers can create an individualized program for any youngster. A practical measure of the benefit of reading is the higher scores earned on college entrance exams by students who have spent more time reading—fiction as well as nonfiction—compared with those who have read less; but a more fundamental benefit of reading is its ability to keep intellectual curiosity alive.

As with the previous edition, this book is addressed not only to those who work with young readers who are formally identified as gifted, but also to those who work with the many others who may not be included in that category, especially:

> ➤ the many gifted students who have not been identified;

> ➤ the bright and eager learners who are not placed in a gifted program because they do not quite meet the criteria of the local schools;

> ➤ the many highly able children in rural areas of our country or in larger schools where no gifted program is provided; and

> ➤ children who have special ability or intense interests, and for that reason feel "different," whether or not they could be identified as gifted.

Therefore I encourage any adult who senses a special spark in a child, even if "gifted" seems not quite the right word, to read this book. My hope is that parents and teachers will find that the ideas presented here benefit any child who is interested in reading and talking about challenging books.

The first version of this book, *Guiding Gifted Readers* (1988), was written to provide background information and book lists for adults who wished to help gifted children understand and cope with their differing emotional needs. Recognizing that intellectual challenge is an emotional need for many of these youngsters, I included in the first edition of *Some of My Best Friends Are Books* (1994) a fuller discussion of intellectual needs than in the 1988 book. In this second edition, I have intended a balance between emotional and intellectual needs in the first seven chapters. In Chapter 8, the annotated bibliography, no such balance is intended. Books that encourage discussion of emotional developmental issues still predominate, while the category "Drive to Understand" has been expanded to offer more books to meet intellectual interests. As in previous editions, this book is addressed both to educators—teachers, counselors, and librarians—and to parents, with more awareness in this edition that many parents are looking for creative ways to use books as they homeschool their children.

Teachers who wish to provide challenge for gifted children in the face of funding cuts and curricular change may find a reading program to be the answer. They will find updated suggestions for using book discussion in school settings. Counselors who work with gifted children and their families may be aware that recent textbooks in counseling the gifted recommend bibliotherapy as one approach to meeting these children's psychological needs. Detailed information is listed here on the process of bibliotherapy. Librarians who assist them will find new books listed along with old treasures in the annotated bibliography, which comprises about half of this book.

Parents who wish to monitor their children's education, or even to teach their children themselves, will find information and support. As teachers, counselors, and school librarians continue to struggle with massive challenges, conscientious parents recognize that they must become more involved in their children's education by being more active at home and, if possible, by volunteering at school, where they are certainly needed. How will parents find the time? How will they use that time to make the greatest impact? And how can parents who have no background in teaching enhance their children's educational experience with the confidence that they are doing it well? This book provides some answers.

The home is an ideal setting for both types of book discussion—instructional and bibliotherapeutic—encouraged in this book. For all parents, reading and discussing books with their children is a dynamic way to supplement the school's curriculum. For those parents who homeschool, this book offers a great deal of information to help them use books as primary resources for promoting the intellectual and emotional development of their children.

Some of My Best Friends Are Books, 2nd Edition has three parts and is divided into eight chapters. Part One, "The Children," is comprised of two chapters that offer updated background information on the emotional and intellectual developmental needs, respectively, of children of high ability. Chapter 2 also includes information to assist parents in keeping up with educational trends.

Part Two, "The Process," begins with a chapter about typical reading patterns and the need for reading guidance. Then, the two subsequent chapters each suggest methods for an approach to discussing books with young readers: enhancing *emotional* development through bibliotherapy in Chapter 4, and promoting *intellectual* growth through discussion of ideas in Chapter 5. Chapter 4 can be used as a primer on developmental bibliotherapy in general, with giftedness offered here as the example of one domain in which this technique can be used to meet the developmental needs of young people, while Chapter 5 offers a variety of methods for discussing books on an intellectual level.

Part Three, "The Books," offers in the first two chapters criteria for selecting challenging books and a brief overview of children's literature, with special emphasis on gifted readers. The final—and longest—chapter is an expanded annotated bibliography listing over 300 books carefully selected for their usefulness in promoting the intellectual and emotional development of gifted children and young people. The Index of Categories guides the reader to categories of concern for gifted students, aiding in the selection of good books that relate specifically to the various emotional and intellectual characteristics outlined in the first part of the book.

There is nothing new about the idea that children need good books or that books can be used to help children build coping skills. The response to *Guiding Gifted Readers* suggested that there was something new and welcome in the ideas it presented for using books with *gifted* children to help them develop optimally. The first edition of *Some of My Best Friends Are Books* offered broader goals, improved organization, and an enlarged bibliography. My hope is that this third book will prove as useful as the first two. As in the two previous books, the stories of children are composites of children I have known, with fictional names.

I want to thank the staff of the Traverse Area District Library in Traverse City, Michigan, particularly Bernadette Gropusso, Youth Services librarian; Katheryn Carrier, Sandy Robey, and their colleagues at the reference desk; Vicki Jones of the library's Public Computing Center; and Marly Wyckoff for her help with interlibrary loan requests. Dawn Farley and Liz Messing, librarians in the Traverse City Area Public Schools, made time to read and comment on sections of this book; their suggestions help to ensure the validity of this new edition and are deeply appreciated.

I am grateful for quick and thoughtful responses to requests for information from Linda Silverman, whose book *Counseling the Gifted and Talented* has been helpful to many; to Sharon Lind, whose work on Dabrowski's theory of overexcitabilities is quoted in Chapter 4; and to Margaret Gosfield, editor of the *CAG (California Association for the Gifted) Communicator*. Kit Finn, a graduate student at the Center for Gifted Education at the College of William and Mary, provided information on the Center's literature curriculum, and Jamie Johnson, librarian at the Center for Application of Type, sent information on research on the Myers-Briggs Type Indicator. Their interest and assistance was timely and very welcome.

I am grateful, too, to James T. Webb, Ph.D., for the original idea that led to this book and its earlier versions, and to editor Audie L. Alcorn, for his fresh reading of the manuscript and perceptive questions.

Ideas for books to consider for inclusion in Chapter 8 have come from many people who love to read and talk about books.

In addition to the students whose reading I have guided through the years, I thank Todd Ramlo and David and Mark Halsted. Their stories add life and meaning to the theories presented here. I also want to thank all those who have used *Guiding Gifted Readers* or the first edition of *Some of My Best Friends Are Books* and have written letters or stopped me on elevators and in the halls at conferences to tell me what the book has meant to them. Without their assurance that the ideas presented here are adaptable to many settings and are a contribution to the understanding and education of our brightest children, this edition would not have been written.

I welcome the opportunity to thank my husband, David; our sons, David and Mark; and our daughters-in-law, Keely and Barbara, for many conversations and vital encouragement. Thanks also to our grandchildren, now Christopher, Chloe, and Caroline, much-loved companions in our continuing exploration of children's books.

—Judith Wynn Halsted

Table of Contents

Preface v

Introduction xv

Part I: The Children 1

Chapter 1. The Heart of the Child: Emotional Development . . . 3

Establishing an Identity 7

Being Alone 16

Relationships with Others 23

Using Abilities 29

How Books Can Help 37

References 38

Chapter 2. The Mind of the Child: Intellectual Development . . 41

The Need for Intellectual Development 42

The Child in Charge 46

Obstacles in the Way 52

The Importance of Parents 61

How Books Can Help 63

References 64

Part II. The Process 67

Chapter 3. Reading Guidance 69

Fundamentals of Reading Guidance 70

Reading Patterns: What to Expect 73

Special Characteristics of Gifted Readers 87

Reading Aloud 89

Avid Readers and Resistant Readers 91

References 102

Chapter 4. Emotional Development through Books **105**
    Bibliotherapy 106
    Literature for Bibliotherapy 120
    Logistics: Organizing Discussion Groups at School . . . 122
    Logistics: Organizing Discussions at Home 128
    Planning for Discussion 131
    Goals of Bibliotherapy at Different Stages 141
    An Author's View 145
    Bibliotherapy: An Affirmation of Strengths 146
    References 148

Chapter 5. Intellectual Development through Books **151**
    What Books Can Do for Intellectual Development . . . 152
    What Schools Are Doing with Books and Reading:
    A Primer for Parents 161
    Reading Programs for Gifted Students 166
    Discussing Books at School 168
    Discussing Books at Home 178
    Using the Library 183
    References 192

Part III. The Books **195**

Chapter 6. Choosing Books that Challenge **197**
    Books for Older Children 206
    Suggested Book Lists 211
    References 212

Chapter 7. All the Wealth: Children's Literature **213**
    Fiction 216
    Nonfiction 220
    Biography 225
    Traditional Literature 229
    Fantasy and Science Fiction 236
    Poetry 244
    Books about Children's Literature 251
    Reference Books about Children's Literature 252
    References 256

Chapter 8. Annotated Bibliography **257**
    Categories 258
    Preschool 262
    Two and Three Years Old 267
    Four Years Old 276
    Early Elementary (K–Grade Two) 289
    Upper Elementary (Grades Three – Five) 325
    Middle School (Grades Six – Eight) 376
    Senior High (Grades Nine – Twelve) 431

Subject Index **489**

Index of Categories **503**

Index of Authors **515**

Index of Titles **521**

About the Author **527**

Introduction

Steven is a joy! A cheerful, curious, friendly, bright preschooler, he talks easily with adults and seems quite mature. In fact, his teacher relies on him as the most responsible child in his group. But other children are sometimes puzzled by him. Steven gets frustrated when his friends can't follow what he's saying, and it bothers him that they don't share his amazed interest in the insects he brings to class. Adults, though, help him find out about insects in books, and he is beginning to read about them himself.

Marcelo is a smart, sullen high school junior. Social difficulties have left their marks on him, most obviously in the discrepancy between his ability and his performance. His PSAT scores qualify him to compete for a National Merit Scholarship, but his grades will keep him out of the better colleges. Teachers say that he doesn't measure up to his potential, that he refuses to do homework, and that he just doesn't study, particularly for courses that require consistent daily effort such as French and math.

Marcelo is defensive about his school record and confused about his future. He's so tired of hearing that he's "not measuring up to his potential" that he has stopped listening. He wants to be part of the high school social life but he doesn't feel like he fits in;

he feels no one understands him. He knows he has mental ability that he does not use, at least not at school, but he has no idea how to "realize his potential." He is depressed about his lack of direction, but the teachers see Marcelo, who a few years ago was passionately concerned about national and international politics, as merely cynical and disinterested. They're concerned, but they don't know how to help him.

Tamika is also a high school junior. She is active in sports, student government, and the school newspaper, and she keeps her grades at an honors level. Her special interest is biology, and she has arranged with the biology teacher to do an independent study as a supplement to the regular classwork. Tamika is quiet about her own excellent grades and is ready to help others who don't understand as quickly. In the summer, she's a counselor at a day camp where the campers love her. She's always available to them for ping-pong or a quiet talk.

Despite her full schedule and many friends, Tamika feels truly alone sometimes. Her concerns about the future are so much more intense than her friends' that she has never attempted to discuss them with anyone. Although she worries about the future of the world, Tamika's plans for her own future are taking shape. She wants to go to a university with a strong biology curriculum and is looking forward to visiting campuses.

If we were to ask both Marcelo's and Tamika's parents what their children were like as preschoolers, they would describe someone remarkably like Steven. What determines whether a Steven will, in 12 years, turn into a Marcelo or an Tamika?

Steven, Marcelo, and Tamika are all gifted. This giftedness adds an extra dimension to their lives, imposing on them certain developmental and intellectual tasks in addition to those all children face. Little has been written about the steps that lead a gifted child from being a bright and curious preschooler to being a well-adjusted high school student with a promising future. Based on a background of experience with gifted children and adults, this book attempts an answer to this question: If I'm fortunate enough to start with a child like Steven, what can I do to help him or her develop into a confident, productive young adult who remains as happy and responsive as Steven is now?

Consider now a fourth student. Beth is a conscientious ninth grader whose organization, discipline, and genuine interest in learning help her to maintain an A-minus average. Requirements for the gifted program at her school are unusually high, and her test scores have not qualified her to join. But her intellectual curiosity and her voracious reading habit set her apart from those of her classmates who are too busy for books. Sometimes Beth wonders why she has not been selected for special classes, but she is confident that she has a bright future nevertheless. To be honest, she is often relieved not to have the pressure of being labeled a "gifted" student.

In another school district, Beth might be eligible for the gifted program. But with or without the label, she is a bright, intellectually curious girl whose development depends in part on nurturing adults who recognize and encourage these qualities.

Each stage of childhood and adolescence brings a different challenge for children of high ability. Preschoolers need to develop a positive self-concept and grow toward a strong sense of self. In the early grades of elementary school, such youngsters begin to understand that people have different levels of abilities, and they must learn to value abilities that differ from their own. Although bright children need friends who share their own capabilities, they must learn to get along with all children.

In the later elementary grades, talented students often choose whether to acknowledge and follow their natural eagerness to learn, or to hide their abilities in order to fit in. This is one reason why it is so important for preschoolers to develop a strong sense of self—a confidence in their own worth.

Well-adjusted gifted children enter middle school able to withstand the turmoil that typifies that age. If giftedness and intellectual curiosity are part of their self-concept, these aspects will remain intact—if temporarily submerged—as these youngsters try on various personae. Ideally, they emerge from this stage knowing their capabilities, being at ease with their classmates, and having a few close friends.

Senior high students with this background—more aware of their individuality and of their responsibility for their own future—have a chance to accept and use their abilities without self-consciousness. If we were able to follow Steven to this point, we would find him still happy but far more self-aware, conscious of both his abilities and his shortcomings. We would find that he enjoys his intelligence and his curiosity and that he feels a sense of responsibility to himself—and to others—to fulfill his promise, although he doesn't know where his mind will lead him. He realizes that even though he is different, he is accepted by family and friends. He accepts and values others as well. He has the confidence to take risks, to allow himself to fail, and to pick up the pieces and try again when he does. Steven's healthy development is more likely to occur if his parents, teachers, friends, and school system value and nurture giftedness, whether or not they *formally* identify it.

In fact, many exceptionally bright youngsters are not identified as gifted. Instead they are labeled "difficult" or "emotionally immature" or "too talkative" or "withdrawn"—or even ADHD. The unique, often intense, emotional and intellectual needs of such children may never be accepted and understood—let alone met—either by the children themselves or by the adults around them. Other children—those who aren't intellectually gifted but who are talented or creative in ways that aren't easily identified or for which no programs are available—may also be underappreciated and underserved.

In *Growing Up Gifted* (1983, p. 6), Barbara Clark defines gifted individuals as "those who are performing, or who show promise of performing, at high levels of intelligence." It is important to note that this definition includes those who show promise but, because of environmental conditions that can be changed, may not show the fulfillment of it yet.

Unfortunately, "gifted" is a value-laden word, inviting charges of elitism that make students, parents, and teachers uncomfortable. But it is the best word we have to label a phenomenon that we know exists—and we have plenty of Marcelos to remind us that giftedness is no guarantee of a happy, productive life.

To the contrary, it is estimated that 20% to 25% of gifted children have social and emotional difficulties (Janos & Robinson, 1985). This is especially true of the highly gifted. A teacher of one such child consoled his parents by saying, "Some people aren't so good at being children. But they will be good adults." One reason for this is that children of school age typically cannot choose their milieu; they are forced to try to fit in or to give up in defeat, often at great cost to self-esteem. In contrast, adults who have succeeded in their educational path usually have some control over their daily work environment; they can choose to work where they are likely to find friends among their colleagues.

That work is very important to gifted children is one of the ways they differ from the norm, according to Winner (1996), who points out that, in contrast to the culture around them, they are motivated to achieve mastery, they derive pleasure from challenge, and they often have an early sense of what they want to do as adults. In addition, Winner goes on, they are independent and nonconforming, and they are often more introverted than average children, both because they are so different and because developing their talent requires time alone. Clearly, they are different. And "the social and emotional problems faced by the gifted are caused not by their being gifted but by the consequences of their being so different from others," summarizes Winner (1996, p. 233).

The differences gifted children experience require them to take different paths toward optimal emotional and intellectual development. This book recommends that the adults most concerned with the development of gifted, talented, creative children consider very seriously the potential that books and reading have for helping these children understand themselves and become all that they can be.

Books for children are plentiful, and most bright children are good readers who find them easily. It may seem, then, that *planning* to use books is unnecessary—but surprisingly often, where there is no planning, even good readers are not introduced to the pleasures of leisure reading. Teachers struggling to meet basic requirements have little time to suggest and follow through with extra reading for brighter students. Parents may find it difficult to keep track of what their children are reading. Guiding children's reading appears to be one more unaffordable luxury in an increasingly busy world.

Yet books offer compelling advantages to parents and teachers who want to nurture the minds and hearts of highly able children. *Excellent books* are abundant, inexpensive, and are accessible sources of challenge and understanding. In fact, books should be the first choice of enrichment for these bright youngsters.

Merely providing books is not enough, however. A knowledge of gifted children, discussion techniques, and children's literature is necessary to make maximum use of the benefits books offer. By filling the gaps in their knowledge, parents, teachers, counselors, and librarians can bring gifted children and books together more effectively. In so doing, they can help gifted children be themselves—comfortable in their present world and poised to grow into happy, productive adults.

References

Clark, B. (1983). *Growing up gifted: Developing the potential of children at home and at school.* 2nd ed. Columbus, OH: Merrill.

Janos, P. M. & Robinson, N. M. (1985). Psychosocial development in intellectually gifted children. In F. D. Horowitz & M. O'Brien (Eds.), *The gifted and talented: Developmental perspectives* (pp. 149-195). Washington, DC: American Psychological Association.

Winner, E. (1996). *Gifted children: Myths and realities.* New York: Basic Books.

Part One:

The Children

Chapter 1

The Heart of the Child: Emotional Development

It often goes unrecognized that gifted children can have trouble with emotional and social development. It is assumed that, even if they do have problems, they also have the intelligence to deal with them. Sensitive adults who work with gifted children realize that this is not true—that gifted children often are burdened with *extra* emotional and social needs and difficulties. In fact, being gifted can truly complicate the usual problems of growing up.

In addition to the general psychosocial needs of all adolescents, the following were identified by Buescher (1985, in Frey 1991) as specialized *additional* needs of gifted students:

➤ recognizing and owning their giftedness;

➤ resolving the dissonance between their expectations of themselves and their actual performance (they must learn to accept the fact that they cannot always perform at a high level in every area);

➤ taking risks (the reluctance of gifted adolescents to take risks can hamper their willingness to take appropriate but difficult courses);

➤ determining how much to respond to others' expectations and how much weight to give to their own needs;

➤ coping with their impatience with the frequent lack of clear-cut answers, especially in personal relationships and career choices; and

➤ meeting their inner demand for an identity, while avoiding the temptation to make premature decisions (usually regarding college and career) which would limit future access to their full potential.

While Buescher's work highlights the difficulties of giftedness for teenagers, his point holds true for gifted people of all ages— that is, to understand their emotional needs, it is necessary to recognize the extra developmental tasks they face.

In this book, five broad areas in which giftedness affects development will be discussed. One area, intellectual development, is reserved for the next chapter. In this chapter, we will look at the following four aspects of emotional development as they pertain to gifted children:

➤ establishing an identity,
➤ needing time alone,
➤ relationships with others, and
➤ learning how to use one's ability.

After a brief introduction to each of these concerns, we will consider them again in greater detail.

First, while every child must establish his or her own identity, the gifted child must recognize and accept an identity that is different from the norm and that may not be popular or acceptable to peers or family.

Take a look at Marcelo, the unhappy high schooler described in the Introduction, when he was younger.

4

As a seventh grader, Marcelo has already figured out that his ideas seem weird to his classmates and even to his parents and teachers. Entering a new school, he's determined to be quiet and to keep his hand down. No more frantic arm waving when the answer is so very clear! Stifle, stifle, stifle. Stifle is the name of the game. At an age when he should be establishing his sense of identity, he is denying a large part of himself. He is attempting to lose himself in the crowd called "normal." If he had been helped to understand and accept his differences when he first became aware of them, he would be freer to acknowledge them now.

Second, while all children must learn to be alone at times, gifted children may actually *require* time alone, and they may need more of it than most people need or can understand. They may have to learn to cope with mixed feelings about their own need for time alone—aware that they also need time with other people, and uncertain how to balance these divergent needs with the expectations of others.

Hannah loves to read, play the piano, and sew—all solitary activities. After a day crowded with people at school, she enjoys coming home to these quiet pursuits. Her parents are worried, however, because she seldom invites friends home with her. Although Hannah is happy with her friends at school and content with her activities at home, she senses her parents' concern and wonders whether there is something wrong with her. Her worries would be relieved if her parents recognized her need for time alone and encouraged her to take it.

Third, all children must learn how to get along with others; gifted children must find a few good friends and learn to value and respect others, even though they themselves may be rejected. Rejection sometimes results from the unusual intensity of many gifted children, a characteristic that is difficult for other children to understand. Gifted people also have heightened sensitivity to the comments and actions of others, so that being misunderstood or rejected is a more painful experience for them than for most. For gifted children, the issues of friendship, so important to their healthy development, are much more complex than they are for most children.

> *Eleven-year-old Brian talks with enthusiasm to high school students and adults, but he can find no other grade school children who share his interest in biology. His sixth grade classmates are puzzled by the intensity that marks his oral science reports, and he mistakes their lack of understanding for rejection. In response, he is building a protective wall around himself, neither giving nor expecting friendship from people his own age. If he can be helped to respect his classmates' social or athletic skills as well as his own knowledge of biology—and if he can find just one or two friends his age who share his interest, perhaps at a community science center—he will avoid years of social isolation. Otherwise, Brian may not learn to make friends of his own age until he enters college.*

Fourth, while all adolescents must make career and college decisions, gifted youngsters often have so many possibilities that choice paralyzes them. Unwilling to give anything up and unable to choose, gifted teenagers and young adults may find it difficult to take the steps that will enable them to make full use of their abilities.

> *Wei, a superior student in math and science, is considering a career in medicine. He also plays piano and guitar in a band that has performed at high school proms for the last three years. Music is so important to Wei that he wants to delay entering college while he tests his chances of finding work as a*

professional musician. But he's afraid that too much time away from science and math will dull his skills and ruin his chances of getting into medical school. As he weighs the decision, college application deadlines are passing by. He's beginning to panic about his future. Attention paid to preliminary college and career planning, beginning in the early adolescent years, would have helped.

This chapter considers the emotional development of gifted children by further exploring each of these four aspects of development. Since this discussion serves as background for later sections, only brief mention will be made here of ways in which books can enhance that emotional development.

Establishing an Identity

A major task of growing up is the search for one's identity. Gifted children, in order to be wholly themselves, *must* recognize and accept their own giftedness. But since the history of education in our country reveals a persistent strain of anti-intellectualism (Ravitch, 2000), intellectual giftedness can often seem like more a burden than a blessing. Gifted children learn early—sometimes before they enter kindergarten—that many people are annoyed by and resentful of the precocious and verbal child whose abilities are above the norm. And so to fit giftedness willingly and comfortably into one's self-concept takes a degree of maturity that must develop over time.

Who They Are

Establishing an identity is a matter of discovering who one is, of learning what it is that makes each one of us, like the Little Prince's rose, "unique in all the world." And what gifted children discover may be a self that they know will not be popular. They may then feel that they must choose between being themselves and being liked. Out of this conflict and the ways they choose to deal with it will emerge their identity. Several characteristics of typical bright children contribute to this conflict.

Difference. Gifted children realize fairly early not only that they are different, but also that there is something vaguely unacceptable about this difference. Our society is ambivalent about difference as well as intelligence, and children can easily develop the uncomfortable feeling that something is "wrong" with them. Usually, they do not know what it is or even why they are different. They only know that when they exercise their creativity or knowledge, they do not fit in. They then feel alone, wrong, even freakish; ironically, they may feel inferior to those around them.

At the same time, especially if their environment provides enough stimulation, they may experience the elation of the insights and awareness their giftedness makes possible. They can know the joy of discovering new ideas, new people with whom they can use their vocabularies fully, and new stimuli such as museums, music or films that excite them.

They live with this paradox, and they must learn, in the "down" times when they are feeling different and alone, to trust that the "up" times, when they can enjoy the benefits of their extra measure of perception, will come again. Some of them must learn to make a little "up" time last over a long "down" period. One friendship established at summer camp may be what carries a child through the next school year; one understanding and stimulating teacher may keep another child going through two or three years with indifferent teachers.

> *Attending a high school that places more emphasis on sports than on academic achievement, Melissa finds her work with a statewide youth organization more stimulating than school. Although meetings occur only twice a year, the friendships she has made with other natural leaders, the creative energy she puts into planning conferences, and the experience of traveling to large cities around the state have*

compensated for her feeling of not fitting in at school. Gradually she is learning to integrate the sense of being different and alone at school with the sense of inner delight and satisfaction that her giftedness brings in another setting. Her identity includes both.

Ambivalence about the label. Middle-elementary children, just becoming aware of the concept of giftedness, may be ambivalent about having the label applied to them. If parents and teachers react positively and matter-of-factly to the idea of giftedness, children will probably do the same, accepting their abilities and learning to use them with enthusiasm. If anything in their environment causes them to be uncomfortable with the term, however, their responses may range from what appears to be showing off to denying their gifts and the responsibilities they imply.

Self-conscious about his lack of athletic ability, Derrick seeks approval by offering answers in class eagerly and frequently. However, the other children think he is boasting about how much he knows. Meanwhile, Tandi answers questions only when the teacher calls on her and even uses a doubtful tone of voice to give the impression that she knows no more than anyone else. Both responses indicate that these children need help in accepting who they are. Establishment of a healthy identity depends on that acceptance.

Overexcitabilities. It is often noted that gifted children, especially the highly gifted, have extraordinarily high degrees of sensitivity and intensity. Piechowski's (1991) outline of Dabrowski's concept of "overexcitabilities" helps to explain this. Some people experience heightened degrees of excitement in any of five areas: psychomotor, sensual, intellectual, imaginational, and emotional.

Offering snapshots of the positives and negatives that characterize each overexcitability, Lind (2000) states that psychomotor overexcitability, which is demonstrated by those who love physical activity, may look to some like hyperactivity, thus contributing to the possibility that some gifted children may be mislabeled ADHD (Webb, 2001). Sensual overexcitability brings a heightened pleasure in music, language, and art, as well as the potential of discomfort from too much sensory stimulation. Students who are intellectually overexcitable are intensely curious and often avid readers; they may appear impatient with others who cannot keep up with their ideas. Children who have imaginary playmates and love to hear stories rich in fantasy display imaginational overexcitability, which can also mean that they grow restless in classrooms where literal thinking is favored over imagination. Very young children may demonstrate emotional overexcitability in their intense reactions, reaching beyond what is normal even for the "terrible twos." But as they grow older, these children are also capable of strong empathy and deep relationships.

Any of these overexcitabilities can make a child stand out as different and can present a challenge to teachers, parents, and the child himself, who all must make an effort to understand and cope with this difference. See Lind's article for a more detailed discussion of overexcitability, including helpful coping strategies.

The concept of overexcitability sheds light on the observation that gifted people are often super-sensitive—sharply aware of their own and others' feelings. In fact, a heightened sensitivity may be the first trait of giftedness parents see in a very young child (Silverman, 1994). In addition, they are often intense, not only in their depth of feeling but also in their commitment to an interest or a cause and in their manner of expressing that commitment. In the adult world, the sensitivity and intensity of the gifted usually meet some degree of tolerance, but children are not always so understanding. Gifted children who exhibit emotional overexcitability need the support of an adult who takes Dabrowski's view that *the emotional extremes that these children experience are not a sign of neurosis but an indication of potential for growth.*

Awareness of moral issues. Gifted children read the newspapers and watch television news with comprehension earlier than most children. At an early age, they become aware of adult concerns about war, the environment, racial issues, and other social concerns. They may become deeply worried about the future of the world at a time when other children their age are unaware and uninterested—another difference between them and their classmates.

> *Richard will never forget hearing of the assassination of Martin Luther King, Jr. The five-year-old was watching television when the news bulletin interrupted. He wasn't traumatized by the event, but he still remembers it as the awakening of the political awareness that is a major focus of interest for him still.*

All of these characteristics of gifted youngsters—and the additional ones discussed elsewhere in this book—are aspects of the self that a high-potential child must learn to understand, accept, and balance as he or she develops a sense of identity.

Who They Will Become

The search for identity raises some complex issues for gifted people. Can they successfully explore all of the possibilities open to them? Will they accept and develop their ability, or deny its existence and leave it unused? Will they use their leadership potential in positive ways? With many choices open to them, how will they select a challenging and satisfying career? There are many ways in which gifted people confront these issues—some of them healthier and more productive than others.

Exploring possibilities. Establishing an identity means more than merely discovering who we are. It also means creating who we will become through imagination, risk-taking, and exploring available identities and choosing from among them. Gifted youngsters may (and should) experiment with more identities than

11

most children, displaying more imagination and less convention-ality. Books offer possibilities that they would otherwise not encounter and permit them to experience vicariously various roles and ways of living as they move through the process of creating a personal identity.

Developing potential. In order to feel accepted and to fit in with their social group, some children deny the gift and avoid developing it fully. They may become restless adults, moving without a clear sense of direction from one pursuit to another. Because they have not trained themselves to use their abilities, they are often dissatisfied with the limited opportunities avail-able to them. We are happiest when we know that our talents are being stretched and used; we feel best about ourselves when we know we are being useful. To reach that point, gifted children must develop the potential that lies within them.

> *Jabrae was identified as gifted in junior high. Although he loved to read and talked glibly about ideas, he never learned to focus his thoughts suffi-ciently to complete written assignments on time. After graduation, he held a number of restaurant jobs, intending to save money for college but delay-ing his application because he feared that his lack of study skills would lead to failure. Within two years, he married a woman who met many of his emo-tional needs but did not share his intellectual interests. Soon, supporting a wife and children took precedence over his education. Jabrae might have become an excellent teacher—his original goal— but his lack of training now confines him to work that offers no security and does not require him to think. With less time for reading now and no one with whom to discuss his ideas, Jabrae is lonely and resentful—an outcome that could have been pre-vented by early information about his ability and encouragement to use it well.*

12

Other children feel that superior ability implies a responsibility. They see a gift as something to be developed so that they can pass it on by giving to others. These youngsters can learn to rejoice in their gifts and to use them with humility and productivity.

> *Joyce grew up in a well-to-do family and enjoyed an excellent education. After her marriage, there was no financial need for her to work. However, from her late elementary years she knew that she wanted a career that would serve other people in some way. She stayed home with her young children, but she continued her education as a part-time student while gaining experience as a volunteer in several community organizations. Fifteen years later she was ready to begin a career as a psychologist. Her present work includes helping gifted girls make appropriate educational and vocational decisions.*

Leading others. Another issue facing these children is their potential for leadership. Many of them are natural leaders, and developing a sense of identity means finding ways to explore and use their leadership ability. In some, the talent for leadership is so strong that if it finds no positive outlets, it will express itself in negative ways. These children need adults who can see past the negative expressions and offer guidance in the constructive use of leadership ability. Since books provide examples of both negative and positive leaders, book discussion is one way of providing such guidance.

> *Unchallenged by his high school courses, Ibrahim not only refuses to do his assignments but also loudly proclaims to other students his low opinion of the teachers, the curriculum, and the school's requirements. Because Ibrahim's voice carries some weight in his small high school, other students are beginning to neglect their work, too, influenced by Ibrahim's natural leadership ability. Ibrahim and*

> *the others will all be happier if an adult can see what*
> *is happening and help Ibrahim plan ways of redi-*
> *recting his abilities.*

Choosing a career. After exploring different roles for themselves, gifted students often discover that they can do so many things well that career choice is extremely difficult. Hence they need to develop superior self-knowledge and excellent decision-making skills. Multi-talented young adults must face the fact that they will not have time to bring all of their strengths to full flower. Again, books can help, enabling them to explore various options without spending months or years on each, helping them to establish priorities and to make vocational and avocational choices.

Asynchrony

While gifted youngsters deal with these issues, they may also face the enormous task of integration. Different parts of themselves may develop at different rates, with academic interest and achievement sometimes far outstripping other areas of growth. The disparity between rates of intellectual, emotional, and physical development has been called asynchrony (Morelock, 1992), an apt term for what happens with children whose various developmental schedules are not in tune with one another. It simply expresses the fact that in gifted children, intellectual development can move rapidly, while social, emotional, and physical growth remain tied to chronological age.

Asynchrony makes it difficult to know whether a child should skip a grade level in school. It is exemplified by a third grade boy who joined an enrichment class of fifth and sixth graders in the junior high library to work on a research project, but who had to tape record his report because his fine motor skills were not advanced enough to write all he had learned. Asynchrony causes surprise when the unusually tall, unusually verbal 10-year-old does not behave like the 12-year-old she appears to be. We must consider asynchrony in choosing appropriate books for the second grader who is reading at the sixth grade level.

If a young child's intellectual growth has far surpassed emotional and social development, there may later come a necessary time of academic latency that allows social and emotional growth to catch up. This can happen during the high school years, after college, or any time in between.

> *Ibrahim began kindergarten at four, was accelerated another year in high school, and entered college at 16. When he graduated from college at 20 he was sure of two things: he wanted to go to graduate school, and he did not want to go to graduate school that fall. He spent two years working at various jobs, learning to be self-supporting while consolidating his career plans. Now in graduate school, for the first time he is studying with his agemates—still occasionally restless at the pace of coursework, but adapting to it with a new measure of maturity and self-understanding.*

Indeed, it may not be until the early twenties or later that the different aspects of a very complex person—the intellectual, emotional, social, and physical—begin to come together. It will help the person living through this asynchrony if he and his parents recognize what is happening and know that the prognosis is good.

A Healthy Self-Image

Establishing a healthy identity means discovering and accepting who one is and creating the person one will become. For the gifted, this includes acknowledging and using giftedness unselfconsciously. In addition, the gifted person needs to develop a protective attitude toward her abilities. On the one hand, she must integrate giftedness into her self-concept, and on the other, she must be able to see it, with humility, as a unique part of herself that needs special nurturing. Only when she can do this has she fully accepted herself as a gifted person.

How does a gifted youngster reach this point? By admitting that she has many of the characteristics of gifted people, including some that are unpopular or misunderstood, such as being hyper-critical or talking too much in class or wanting more time alone than most people do; by understanding the positive and useful sides of those unpopular characteristics; by forgiving herself for having them and by bringing them under control to make good use of them; by recognizing the advantages of being gifted and learning to enjoy them; and by realizing that high intelligence is useless without training and self-discipline.

These attitudes cannot easily be taught by precept. Example is far superior, and examples can come from role models—gifted people whose lives are based on these understandings. Such role models can be alive or imaginary: parents, teachers, and friends— or characters in books.

Of course, some gifted children have so many barriers in their way that developing a healthy identity may be beyond their reach. The fortunate ones will have a good chance of becoming what Abraham Maslow (1962) called self-actualized adults: giving, productive people who make full use of their potential and gain deep satisfaction from doing so.

Being Alone

"Being alone" is an ambiguous term. It can mean being alone and liking it, being alone and feeling lonely, or being alone by being different. A gifted child can experience all of these and can also develop conflicting emotions about being alone. The child's confusion is compounded by the reactions of other people to those who appear to be "loners." Human beings are social ani-mals, suspicious of those who choose to be less social than the norm. The gifted child is aware of this, and his own feelings about being alone are colored by his assumptions of the feelings of others. He needs understanding from adults around him that he must be alone part of the time.

Being Alone and Liking It

While gifted children appreciate the warmth of friendship as much as others, they also need time to develop their talent. Children—and adults—who are talented in math, science, music, art, athletics, or some other highly specialized field, all spend unusual amounts of time alone. However, they do not suffer from being alone as much as others do; they know how to be alone and how to use time alone productively (Winner, 1996).

It has long been recognized that gifted people tend more toward introversion, needing more time alone, than does the general population. In a review of research, Williams (1992, p. 33) states that "...in the gifted and talented population the majority appear to be introverts, while the general population contains from 25%–35% introverts." Characteristics of introversion include the following:

➤ restoring depleted energy by being alone, while extroverts restore energy by being with people;

➤ forming deep and loyal relationships with a few best friends rather than needing many friends;

➤ being slow to respond to people and situations;

➤ thoughtfulness, needing time to reflect before speaking;

➤ preferring some of the time to read rather than to be with others;

➤ focusing on concepts and ideas; and

➤ possessing an ability to work on complex problems and a willingness to work uninterrupted for long periods of time.

Introverts of any age must spend some of the time acting like extroverts and then need time alone to regain lost energy. Introverted adults, for the most part, can find compatible work settings, but for the introverted student, the requirement that he act like an extrovert for the entire school day exacts a toll.

None of these characteristics is "wrong," yet introversion may worry parents and teachers who are not aware of its prevalence among the gifted. Kiersey and Bates (1984) suggest that introverted children are often vulnerable in school, misunderstood, and expected to change. Their need for time alone after school should be respected as well.

> *In the question period after a parents' meeting on stress in gifted children, a mother expressed concern because her son resisted her attempts to sign him up for a full schedule of after-school programs. "Maybe he's an introvert," the speaker suggested. "Oh, no," the mother responded. "He gets along very well with people!" The speaker explained that many introverts do, only they need to do so for less time than extroverts. In fact, the speaker revealed, she herself was an introvert, and yet here she was, voluntarily speaking to a group. Once the mother realized that introversion is not a negative and certainly does not preclude getting along with people, she was ready to accept her son's need for alone time after school.*

While gifted children, and adults too, may need what seems to be an inordinate amount of time alone, they can use it productively; in fact, they may well be far less productive if they do not have it. Those who gather large amounts of information require more time to assimilate it; those who are more creative require more incubation time for their ideas. However, the gifted child who enjoys being alone may feel an underlying sense of guilt, secretly believing that something is wrong with her. Is she really alone by preference, she wonders, or did she somehow send potential friends away? And yet it is so delicious, she feels, to have quiet time to read, or build, or plan, or dream. Maybe tomorrow she will invite someone over. But she would really rather have this time to herself. Is that all right?

It *is* all right, of course, and she should be reassured about that. Caring adults should support this legitimate need to be alone. Parents must learn to be patient with a child who spends hours apparently doing nothing, playing with blocks, taking things apart, daydreaming seemingly without purpose while chores remain undone. One such child later, as a college junior, worked on a medical research project at a major teaching hospital, contributing his ability to "play" freely with computers as he developed new ways to graph test results. He linked this ability to the hours he spent happily alone in a garage filled with treasures, experimenting to learn how things worked—"useless" alone time that fathered his present productivity.

Gifted people who have developed a sense of inner-directedness and a protective attitude toward their own abilities may sense that time spent with other people can hold them back. Their characteristic intensity may keep them at their work for long periods of time, and time spent socializing can seem to them to be wasted. It may take years for them to recognize the value of relaxed time with other people, and they may always struggle for a satisfactory balance between time alone and time with others.

> *Jesse came home from school every day to lose himself in books. For him, this was replenishment for his soul; for his mother it was a source of concern. Usually she was silent, reflecting that after an hour or so of reading, Jesse was glad to go outside and play, and he was a welcome friend both at school and in his neighborhood. One afternoon, however, she ventured, "Jesse, you're always reading. Why don't you invite a friend over tomorrow?" Looking up in surprise from his book, Jesse said, "But Mom— some of my best friends are books!"*
>
> *Pondering his words later, she realized that Jesse was right. In books he communed with authors whose interests and intensity matched his own—*

> *something he found in no child in the neighbor-*
> *hood. In coming home to read after school, Jesse was*
> *seeking his own balance.*

In *The Magic Bookshelf* (1999), Janie and Richard Jarvis relate the story of an elderly man who looks back over the interesting people he has known—and suddenly realizes that many of them were characters in books. They point out that while reading, a solitary activity, may seem lonely to non-readers, to avid readers it is one of the pathways to an enriched life.

Being Alone and Feeling Lonely

Adults who watch a child spend time alone often fear that the child is lonely. However, gifted children who are busy with books, collections, music, or other favorite pursuits may not *feel* lonely. They may, however, sense that they do not fit in with other children, and it is their response to this feeling of not belonging that adults must monitor and try to guide. The following are some typical coping behaviors.

Fitting in. Gifted youngsters may respond by trying to fit in. Without guidance, however, these attempts often do not work. Some try, often successfully, to hide their ability by producing mediocre work in school. By the time they complete sixth grade, this can become a pattern—one that becomes difficult to change as time goes on. Girls are likely to lower their aspirations during the junior high years in ways that will profoundly affect their futures (Kerr, 1997). Gifted boys may hide their academic abilities in order to appear sufficiently masculine (Kerr & Cohn, 2001).

Drawing attention. Children who wish to belong to the group sometimes use another ploy: attracting attention to themselves. Capitalizing on their differences may be the only way they know to do this. For gifted children, this can mean showing off their knowledge or using sarcasm or condescension with other children—behavior that can backfire and cause real rejection.

Kirsten was a mature second grader with the highly critical nature gifted children sometimes develop. Feeling insecure when she entered a new school, she adopted the role of class police officer, letting her classmates know when they did not measure up to her standards and too often informing the teacher, too, of their failings. What began as her own fear of rejection led quickly enough to actual rebuff from her new classmates. A sympathetic adult can help lead Kirsten toward self-understanding, and help her enhance her social skills.

Arrogance. In a few cases, a gifted child will display a sense of elitism or arrogance toward others who are not as able. Such an inappropriate response to a feeling of not belonging is more likely to occur in gifted children who do not understand giftedness. Self-acceptance must precede acceptance of others. If parents and teachers cannot help gifted children to understand themselves, the children are hampered in developing self-acceptance, and an *appearance* of arrogance may result. It is in truth a defense, of course; the child is really feeling uncertain of how to relate to others.

Withdrawal. Other gifted children make no attempt to fit in, but withdraw instead. They may spend much time reading, which causes concern for adults. (The negative aspects of reading too much are discussed in Chapter 3.) However, spending large amounts of time reading is not necessarily unhealthy for gifted youngsters. They may use this time as part of their identity search, reading for various role models, identifying with different characters, working out the basic question: Who am I? They may identify with undesirable characters some of the time, but usually this is only temporary.

The need to learn friendship skills. Children who do not feel part of a group may need to develop social skills. This can be especially difficult for those who were rejected by other children or by parents when they were young, and who learned to protect themselves by getting along on their own. It is hard for these children to recognize that they do indeed need others and that they can take the first steps toward being a friend. However, they can be helped by school gifted programs that devote time to discussion of friendship skills, and by parents who teach the concepts at home. The books listed under "Relationships with Others" in the bibliography are recommended because they portray children learning how to be friends or, in the case of nonfiction, they directly teach about friendship.

Being Alone by Being Different

Being alone and different—that is, standing apart, being alone because one is different and because one is quite deliberately being oneself—is something that almost all gifted children will have to accept at some time. They know that they are different, but they may not know, unless a trusted adult tells them, *why* they are different. As has been said earlier, knowledge of their giftedness and acceptance of their differences are very important steps in the search for identity.

It takes courage to be oneself, though—to be different and to like oneself despite the difference. This courage takes time to develop, and it must be done during that stage in life when conformity seems most important. Some gifted children need a great deal of support from parents, teachers, and other adults to move through this period successfully. Their independence and autonomous style must be incorporated into their identities, while at the same time they must learn to get along with others. Fortunately, the importance of standing alone is a common theme in literature, and books can easily be found to promote discussion and guidance.

Relationships with Others

For all of us, one key to emotional well-being is to strike a balance between seeing ourselves as individuals and seeing ourselves as members of a society. While the latter can be harder for gifted people, they as much as anyone need the nurturing warmth of good relationships.

Gifted children often see things from unusual points of view that others cannot share, and so they are misunderstood. They are even different from other gifted children; people at the upper ranges of intelligence differ from one another far more than do people in the middle and lower ranges. This makes it even more difficult for gifted people to find and develop friendships.

At the same time, friends are extremely important to most gifted children. The eagerness to communicate with others can show itself very early. One gifted toddler would stand up in his stroller, wave his arms, and crow in delighted greeting whenever he saw another baby being pushed toward him—the very picture of emotional overexcitability. The response was usually a languid glance from the other child, yet until he outgrew his stroller, he continued his enthusiastic greetings.

Parents often worry that their gifted child will have trouble fitting in socially, and they sometimes encourage educational decisions that are detrimental academically in order to favor social development. However, according to Pendarvis, Howley, and Howley (1990, p. 234), there is:

> ...no empirical evidence to support the belief that gifted children are socially incompetent. Rather, it seems that they are socially competent but that some gifted children, because of their preference for activities that engage their intellect, avoid social interaction with age-mates. They may prefer the company of older children or adults; or they may prefer solitary activities, such as reading. These preferences do not indicate emotional problems,

nor do they appear to have a detrimental effect on
gifted children's emotional well-being.

It seems, then, that parents should not worry, but should
accept the child's pattern of friendship, which may differ from
parents' expectations but may suit the child very well.

Finding Peers

Parents can play an important role in helping a gifted child
accomplish the two most important tasks he faces in building
relationships with others: finding peers, and getting along with
people of widely varying abilities.

The special problem gifted children have in finding friends is
not that they are loners, but that they need at least a few friends
who can function on their level, with whom they can speak as
equals. As Kerr (1991, p. 125) points out:

> whenever verbally gifted students find themselves
> in conversations with individuals of lower verbal
> ability, they may be constantly trimming their
> conversation to fit the group. Particularly tactful
> verbally gifted students may conscientiously avoid
> using long words and discussing topics about
> which their agemates are ignorant. However, years
> of attempting to relate to people of lesser verbal
> ability may transform the talkative and friendly
> gifted student into a sarcastic cynic.

Most of all, they need a friend who can listen with understanding.

Therefore, although they differ markedly from one another,
their greatest social need is for friendships with other gifted children. Given the opportunity, gifted children may choose friends
of their own mental age, rather than their own chronological age.
Without such friendships, they may shrivel emotionally and intellectually; with them, they can thrive.

Getting along with others, then, means first finding appropriate others. The stratified grading arrangement in most schools makes it difficult for gifted children to find one another unless special arrangements are made by their parents or teachers. A gifted child may need to belong to several different groups—not necessarily of her own age—that will challenge her intellectually and introduce her to people with whom she can share her passionate interests.

This can be demanding and exhausting for parents. For one junior high student to join an adult astronomy group, his mother drove him to weekly meetings at a planetarium an hour away, driving home between one and two in the morning. Another family drove a daughter five hours each way, every other week for two years, to allow her to play in a university youth symphony. These parents understood their children's need to share their interests with other youth, and they were willing to sacrifice in providing for that need.

Other Children

Getting along with others also means getting along with those who don't share, let alone understand or respect, one's abilities and interests. In classrooms where there are only one or two gifted students, the gifted child is likely to alienate his classmates because he can do schoolwork so easily.

A subtler cause of resentment may be the intense interest gifted children have in topics that do not interest their classmates. If they talk too long about their shell collections, or use words that are too big, they can bore and finally turn away other students without understanding why. A lack of interest in seashells can quickly become a lack of interest in Tim, who talks about seashells all the time. And even before this happens, Tim may feel that it has happened—that the rejection of seashells is a rejection of him.

Gifted children are usually extremely sensitive, and remarks that most children toss off and forget can truly hurt them. They do not understand how lightly other children may make a cruel remark, and others have no idea how long and deeply the gifted child may brood over what is said. But the gifted child, if hurt, even if he was once as eager for friends as the baby in the stroller, begins to build a wall of defense, making it even harder to develop friendships.

Moreover, team sports are not interesting to some gifted children, and if they've been academically accelerated, their physical coordination doesn't match that of their classmates. In most schools, a lukewarm attitude toward team sports or a lack of athletic ability can serve as further wedges between gifted children and their peers.

So gifted children can begin to feel rejected for a variety of reasons. And since giftedness does not necessarily include social maturity, these youngsters react in the same ways that most children do to feelings of rejection: they withdraw or act out. Either choice brings further rejection, and a downward cycle begins.

To reverse this cycle, children must take several steps that require maturity as well as adult guidance: they must develop empathy with those who are not as quick as they are, they must learn to cope with being misunderstood and teased, and they must recognize and modify the behavior that leads to rejection and teasing—all of this while retaining their own identities.

Parents and Teachers

Getting along with peers is the most obvious problem of getting along with others; however, gifted children can find themselves in other situations that may cause emotional problems, both at home and at school. These youngsters are vulnerable, and the attitudes they perceive in significant adults can make a tremendous difference in their attitudes toward themselves and their giftedness.

Parents. Parents who accept their child's giftedness may be relieved to have the school confirm what they have suspected, especially if a suitable program is available, and they may join other parents to support programs for the gifted students in the community.

Undeniably, parenting a gifted child properly places an extra strain on the parents' time, energy, and money. If parents have enough of these resources, their support can make all the difference. In some cases, memories of their own gifted childhoods can add richly to the support they offer to their child. If a gifted child has difficulty in finding peers, his parents may be his best friends for a time.

A child in such a family sees that giftedness is worthy of the effort needed to develop it. But there's a fine line between encouragement and pressure.

> *Raphael has studied piano for six years and his teacher is pleased with his progress. When he enters ninth grade, however, homework, soccer, and the ski team will all demand more time, and he is considering dropping piano lessons. His parents are proud of his musical talent, which they believe is greater than his athletic ability, yet if they urge him to continue with piano, are they pressuring him to work beyond his endurance? Or are they encouraging him to develop a talent that could be a satisfying source of pleasure, relaxation and artistic expression throughout his adulthood? To find an answer, they must take time for careful discussion with Raphael— discussion that includes plenty of listening to Raphael's ideas and reassurances to him of their support.*

By contrast, some parents want their child to be just like everyone else, and they try to ignore the evidence that she is gifted. Such parents may refuse to place their child in a gifted program, preferring to believe that the school has made a mistake. Or parents may acknowledge signs of giftedness in their child but still refuse appropriate educational programs, in the hope that avoiding a special program will help the child to be "normal."

Either of these responses amounts to rejection of the child as she is and insistence that she be someone else. It can also mean failure to provide opportunities for enrichment or for college. The effect on the child's life can be devastating.

Giftedness may appear to some to be a "high-class problem," but parents of gifted children know that it is also exhausting, sometimes frightening, and always challenging. As awareness of giftedness grows, more books for parents are published. One in particular that helps parents meet the emotional needs of their gifted children is *Guiding the Gifted Child* by Webb, Meckstroth, and Tolan (1982). This seminal book has been significantly updated in a 1993 chapter by Webb in the *International Handbook of Research and Development of Giftedness and Talent*.

Teachers. Gifted children can make themselves unpopular with teachers, especially with those who do not know about or are not sympathetic to the special characteristics and needs of the gifted. One middle-aged woman still recalls with an inner cringe the scorn in her second-grade teacher's voice when she naively gave an answer from a few pages beyond the assigned reading. "You read ahead!" the teacher accused. She had, but she hadn't learned yet that in some classrooms it is necessary to conceal such out-of-bounds curiosity.

Teachers whose energies are stretched as they try to meet the needs of a wide range of students may not always appreciate bright children who come up with many creative responses instead of the one "right" answer. Such students can see to the heart of a lesson plan while the teacher slowly presents it to the rest of the class, and their enthusiasm—or lack of tact—makes it hard for them to keep their insights to themselves.

Consider the fifth grader who announced that the book the class had read was so simple it would be easy to write a sequel. He then proceeded, on the spot, to outline a very plausible plot, making both the original and the sequel sound ridiculously trite. How could a teacher lead a serious discussion after that? By laughing with the group and waiting until everyone had enjoyed the spontaneous humor before going on to a productive discussion.

Even teachers who seek out and encourage gifted students find them frustrating at times. An excellent teacher told a gifted fourth grader's mother about a field trip. "He was at my elbow talking the whole day. I wanted to listen because everything he says is worth hearing, but I have to listen to the others, too!" she said in exasperation the mother could well understand.

Many gifted children are analytic thinkers, highly critical of the status quo and only too willing to express an opinion about how things are being run. It is especially important for them to learn early how and when to question authority and how effective politeness and respect can be. Parents' early efforts to teach these lessons to preschoolers will pay off when school starts. If both parents and teachers can enjoy giftedness yet can also under-stand—and gently modify—the negative traits that can go along with it, the child's self-acceptance and ability to get along with others, both adults and children, will be greatly enhanced.

Using Abilities

Humanistic psychologist Abraham Maslow (1962) developed a framework he called the hierarchy of needs, which is especially relevant in understanding gifted people. Maslow arranged human needs in five levels, from those so basic that life depends on them to those so advanced that only a few can feel and meet them. He makes the point that these needs must be met in a certain order; until the lowest ones are met, we are not free even to sense the higher ones.

Physiological needs are the most fundamental. Safety and security needs come next. Only if we feel that we are safe and secure can we experience the next needs, belonging and love. When we are sure that we belong and are loved, we are ready to sense the need for self-esteem. Those who achieve a healthy self-esteem are able to move to the highest level of need, self-actualization—the full use of one's resources and the fulfill-ment of potential.

Gifted children, as already mentioned, are especially prone to feelings of not belonging. After all, they're "different," and a sense of fitting in and being appreciated can be hard to come by. So the need to belong can sometimes be difficult to meet. Self-esteem can also be a problem, since much of our self-esteem is based on how we sense we are perceived by others. Yet if, despite obstacles, the needs at these levels are met, the gifted person may still have great difficulty with self-actualization, the full use of abilities— a paradox, since in the gifted person the store of talents and skills is so great. These issues have a profound impact on the gifted child's ability to lead a satisfying life as an adult. The foundations for self-actualization must be laid in childhood.

In reaching toward full use of their abilities, gifted students may find that some of their personal characteristics can paralyze them, making progress difficult. The following are some barriers that may hinder them.

Reluctance to Take Risks

To become a self-actualized adult, the high-ability child must make decisions that enable him to develop his potential. Often, especially among young children, the child is not aware that he is making life-shaping decisions. But choices made at an early age, seemingly minor at the time, have a cumulative effect on how well prepared a person will be to take advantage of opportunities in his college years and beyond.

> *As an eighth grader attending his first statewide church youth meeting, Nels felt out of place and wanted to leave early. A counselor spent an hour talking with him about his concerns and finally per-suaded him to stay through the weekend. By the next day, he was comfortable enough even to volunteer for a minor position in the organization.*

After a year of involvement at the state level, he was chosen to attend a national meeting, where he was selected to serve on the national council. Holding leadership positions at two annual meetings gave him the confidence and experience to win a scholarship for a summer program in Japan before his senior year in high school. This experience helped him gain a merit scholarship at a highly-ranked university.

Although much of this might have happened in any case, Nels still traces his rich experiences to a Saturday afternoon in junior high when he was persuaded to see the weekend through, and he still makes risk-taking decisions with that example in mind. These decisions have kept options open for him and have put him in a position to become a self-actualized adult.

Whether or not to use all of one's potential becomes an issue early in the educational process. Gifted children often feel society's ambivalence toward those of high intellectual ability, and they may decide to understate their ability in order to get along (Pendarvis, 1990). The second grader who read ahead was faced with a decision: would she read ahead again? The fifth grader who becomes aware that she answers too many questions in class and begins rationing how many she will answer per day is dealing with this issue, although she does not see it that way. The middle school student who lets his grades slide because he feels that fitting into a certain social group is more important than achieving academically is facing decisions that will ultimately affect self-actualization. All of these children are making choices based on their reluctance to take the risk of social failure, giving little or no thought to the long-range consequences.

Perfectionism

A related problem is perfectionism, another common characteristic of gifted people. While a balanced perfectionism manifests itself as a healthy pursuit of excellence, when added to the intensity that also characterizes gifted students, perfectionism easily becomes unbalanced and has a negative effect on their lives.

In these cases, perfectionists have unrealistically high standards for their performance and may feel worthless if they do not meet these standards. Hearing consistent accolades from parents and teachers about their accomplishments, they equate flawless performance with self-worth, and they're afraid to attempt a task that they might not perform well from the start. Their perfectionism puts them under severe stress.

Eventually they may try only those activities they know they will do well. To counteract perfectionism and learn to risk, they must see that failure is not disastrous. They must think of themselves not as perfect, but as experimenters.

Ursula has always been a superb student, but now in the eleventh grade, she has to work harder than she has in the past to maintain her A average. She spends extra hours on her homework, leaving little time for social activities. She's become tense and has frequent headaches. The debate coach has been looking forward to Ursula's joining the team this year, but now Ursula is reluctant; she's never spoken in public and isn't sure how she'll do. If she doesn't join the team, she'll be narrowing her experiences when she should be broadening her outlook and options. If she joins, she probably will make valuable mistakes, and she can learn that life goes on after a defeat. And having to manage her time more carefully will force her to establish priorities. She may also realize that she is valuable to the team, even when she doesn't win.

One possible cause of perfectionism offered by Kerr (1991) is that it is an inborn tendency in the child's personality. This explanation provides relief to parents who have wondered if they are responsible and adds to the frustration of parents who wish to help their child achieve a better perspective. A music teacher relates this story:

> *One of my most talented violin students tied himself up in knots over studying, staying up till midnight to finish homework he said none of the other sixth graders ever did. He felt extraordinarily pushed at science fair time and said the pressure was just too much, but he nevertheless placed second in his entire middle school! Knowing that in the next few years, both music and studies will require more time, his parents worry about helping their son balance his musical aspiration and his academic goals.*

Another cause, according to Kerr, may be that the child is unaware of her giftedness and so believes that her superior performance is based entirely on her own efforts. Perfectionism may also be due to an overemphasis by parents or schools on systems of rewards or "points" for achievement, rather than on doing well for the pure pleasure of it.

To change perfectionism from a destructive paralysis to a positive pursuit of excellence, Kerr suggests that students need to learn to set priorities, recognizing that they cannot be perfect in all areas at once. Parents and teachers can encourage them to choose by asking them whether the science report or the math test is more important, or perhaps even whether it would be better to take time for a long relaxing walk rather than re-writing tomorrow's essay yet again.

In one of the books suggested in Chapter 8, *Perfectionism: What's Bad about Being Too Good?*, Adderholdt and Goldberg (1999) speak directly to teenagers about the effects of perfectionism and ways to manage it. Among their many suggestions is to read for pleasure as a reward to oneself for work well done.

Underachievement

Another problem directly related to the full use of ability for gifted and intellectually curious students is underachievement, which has several possible causes. One is a lack of challenge in the curriculum. It is probably true that in classrooms where teachers struggle with a wide range in ability levels among 30 children, many children are not appropriately challenged—and for the gifted and the highly gifted, this is almost certainly the case unless a special program is in place for them.

A second, and pervasive, cause of underachievement among the gifted is the fear of rejection because of their high intelligence. They can decide surprisingly early to hide their abilities in order to conform. Adolescent girls are especially at risk, feeling they must choose between academic excellence and intimacy (Winner, 1996).

Some find that after several years of not performing, they have missed some basic skills. Suspecting and fearing that they are no longer able to perform at a high level, they resist trying. For them, underachievement has become a pattern that will be hard to break.

There are other, far more complex reasons for under-achievement. For more information on this difficult problem, see Davis and Rimm (1998), Kerr (1991), Rimm (1986, 1991), and Whitmore (1980).

Multipotentiality

According to Kerr (1991), multipotentiality first shows up in elementary school, when students who perform well in many or all school subjects have great difficulty choosing a topic from several options, and then have trouble finishing a project.

This pattern of excellence in school subjects combined with difficulty in making choices and following through continues through middle school. In senior high, multipotential students may have problems with college and career decisions, as well as "high flat profiles" on aptitude and interest tests. These profiles lack the peaks and valleys of most students' profiles, offering no areas of relative strength or weakness to guide them in life decisions, and they lead adults to make the obvious but unhelpful statement, "You can do anything you want to do!"

"Multipotentiality is most commonly a concern of students with moderately high IQs (120-140), those who are academically talented, and those who have two or more outstanding but very different abilities such as violin virtuosity and mathematics precocity" (Kerr, 1990). Choosing among areas that offer equal promise of different success experiences is surely painful, but one lifetime does not provide time for excellence in several demanding fields of endeavor.

If these students resist the narrowing of their activities which is required in order to make a choice, they jeopardize their chances of achieving significantly in any area. The result can be poor career decision-making and, ultimately, dissatisfaction with career choice.

Low External Expectations

Finally, gifted youngsters may fail to make full use of their abilities because they are never given a chance to appreciate their own potential. A gifted student in a typical classroom can make "A"s without much effort, and both the student and his parents may believe that the grade means the student is doing as well as he can. In fact, the grade may mean only that the student has met the highest expectations set by that teacher or has performed at the top of what may be an average class.

Lack of Appropriate Internal Expectations

Earning the best grade available does not necessarily equate with doing the best work a gifted student is capable of doing, but what that "best" would be is never pointed out to some students. Since high grades and other measures of external expectations are not a reliable guide, it is desirable for a gifted student at an early age to learn to assess his or her own potential and then to be the judge of whether it has been realized. This is a complex process, requiring guidance from adults who recognize high ability, even if latent. With such guidance, the student can learn to recognize the feeling—the joy—of doing well for its own sake.

Why is it important that a gifted person use all of his resources? One answer, of course, is that we need all the talent we have available to help us solve the world's problems. For the gifted individual, it is more to the point to recognize that he will simply be happier and more satisfied—life will be much more interesting—if he learns to understand and manage his intensity and creativity. Little research has been done on the gifted adult, so we have no clear idea of the long-term impact of failing to make full use of one's abilities. But Maslow's hierarchy, affirming that self-esteem and self-actualization are needs, points to the importance of being accepted, useful, valued, and free to use whatever talent one has.

To do this, the gifted child must identify his talents, accept them, and then make a decision about whether or not to use them. The first steps in this decision can be made in the early elementary years. At this point, the child begins to see some of the disadvantages of being gifted, some of the conflicts it brings him. He may also run into barriers, external limitations like the absence of educational opportunities, and make a decision (consciously or not) about how hard he will work to overcome them.

Whether a gifted child will use her abilities depends to a large extent on how successfully she establishes her identity, learns to be alone, and learns to get along with peers, family, and teachers. This is the crux of the matter: Can this person, who has the potential to become a self-actualized, fully-functioning, and contributing member of society, be content with herself and giving to those around her? Can this person actually do it? How can we guide our gifted children to grow up happy with themselves and prepared to give to others?

How Books Can Help

Books—that is, fiction—can help us guide the emotional development of our gifted children precisely because stories touch the emotions. A skillful author can make us care about characters who have the same problems presented in this chapter. If a book can "hook" a child emotionally, he may be far more receptive to ideas than if they are presented in a lecture by a concerned adult.

A child who is unwilling or unable to talk about things that are bothering him, or perhaps even to admit them to himself, often can identify with a character in a book ("*He's* bored in school, too!") strongly enough to experience an emotional release, a catharsis, when that character undergoes an emotional experience. He can also acquire some insights into his own situation. This is the process—often called bibliotherapy—that is discussed in detail in Chapter 4.

References

Adderholdt, M. & Goldberg, J. (1999). *Perfectionism: What's bad about being too good?* Minneapolis: Free Spirit.

Buescher, T. M. (1985). A framework for understanding the social and emotional development of gifted and talented adolescents. *Roeper Review, (8)*, 10-15.

Davis, G. A. & Rimm, S. B. (1998). *Education of the gifted and talented* (4th ed.). Boston: Allyn and Bacon.

Frey, D. E. (1991). Psychosocial needs of the gifted adolescent. In M. Bireley & J. Genshaft (Eds.), *Understanding the gifted adolescent: Educational, developmental, and multicultural issues* (pp. 35-49). New York: Teachers College Press.

Jarvis, J. & Jarvis, R. (1999). *The magic bookshelf: A parents' guide to showing growing minds the path to the best children's literature.* Atlanta: Lorica.

Kerr, B. A. (1997). *Smart girls: A new psychology of girls, women, and giftedness.* Scottsdale AZ: Great Potential Press (formerly Gifted Psychology Press).

Kerr, B. A. (1991). *A handbook for counseling the gifted and talented.* Alexandria: American Association for Counseling and Development.

Kerr, B. A. (1990). Career planning for gifted and talented youth. In Berger, S. (Ed.), *Flyer files on gifted students.* Reston, VA: ERIC Clearinghouse on Handicapped and Gifted Children.

Kerr, B. A. & Cohn, S. J. (2001). *Smart boys: Talent, manhood, and the search for meaning.* Scottsdale, AZ: Great Potential Press.

Kiersey, D. & Bates, M. (1984). *Please understand me: Character and temperament types* (5th ed.). Del Mar, CA: Prometheus Nemesis.

Lind, S. (2000). Overexcitability and the highly gifted. *CAG Communicator, 31 (4)*, 19, 45-48.

Maslow, A. (1962). *Toward a psychology of being.* Princeton: VanNostrand.

Morelock, M. J. (1992). Giftedness: The view from within. *Understanding our gifted, 4 (3)*, 1, 11-15.

Pendarvis, E. D., Howley, A. A., & Howley, C. B. (1990). *The abilities of gifted children.* Englewood Cliffs, NJ: Prentice Hall.

Piechowski, M. M. (1991). Emotional development and emotional giftedness. In N. Colangelo & G. A. Davis (Eds.), *Handbook of gifted education* (pp. 285-306). Boston: Allyn and Bacon.

Ravitch, D. (2000). *Left back: A history of failed school reforms.* New York: Simon & Schuster.

Rimm, S. (1991). Underachievement and superachievement: Flip sides of the same psychological coin. In N. Colangelo & G. A. Davis (Eds.), *Handbook of gifted education* (pp. 328-343). Boston: Allyn and Bacon.

Rimm, S. (1986). *Underachievement syndrome: Causes and cures.* Watertown, WI: Apple Publishing Co.

Silverman, L. K. (1994). The moral sensitivity of gifted children and the evolution of society. *Roeper Review, 17 (2),* 110-116.

Webb, J. T. (2001). Mis-diagnosis and dual diagnosis of gifted children: Gifted and LD, ADHD, OCD, Oppositional Defiant Disorder. *Gifted Education Press Quarterly,* 15(1) 9-13.

Webb, J. T. (1993). Nurturing social-emotional development of gifted children. In K. A. Heller, F. J. Monks, & A. H. Passow (Eds.), *International handbook of research and development of giftedness and talent* (pp. 525-538). Oxford: Pergamon Press.

Webb, J. T., Meckstroth, E. A., & Tolan, S. S. (1982). *Guiding the gifted child: A practical source for parents and teachers.* Scottsdale, AZ: Great Potential Press (formerly Ohio Psychology Press).

Whitmore, J. R. (1980). *Giftedness, conflict, and underachievement.* Boston: Allyn and Bacon.

Williams, R. (1992). Personality characteristics of gifted and talented students as measured by the Myers-Briggs Type Indicator and the Murphy-Meisgeier Type Indicator for Children. (Doctoral dissertation, East Texas State University, 1992). Dissertation Abstracts International, 53 (03), 762A. (University Microfilms No. AAC92-22511).

Winner, E. (1996). *Gifted children: Myths and realities.* New York: Basic Books.

Chapter 2

The Mind of the Child: Intellectual Development

The first version of this book went to press in 1987, the year Diane Ravitch and Chester E. Finn, Jr. published *What Do Our 17-Year-Olds Know? A Report on the First National Assessment of History and Literature.* Their book was one of the first calls to action regarding our nation's school system. Since then, we have seen such major new developments as mainstreaming, the rise of the homeschool movement, charter schools, and a growing interest in vouchers. The increasing awareness of a crisis in our educational system has generated a storm of studies, programs, and efforts to reform and restructure the schools—all amid priority setting and budget cuts.

With no clear resolution to this crisis in sight, any consideration of the intellectual needs of high-potential youngsters must be set within the context of the world in which they currently live and go to school. What do these children need for optimum intellectual development? What obstacles face teachers and school administrators as they try to meet those needs? How can parents identify gaps and compensate for them at home? And what is the role of books and reading?

The Need for Intellectual Development

While concern for the *emotional* development of bright and gifted children is a relative newcomer to the educational scene, efforts to help them meet their *intellectual* potential have long been discussed, researched, and implemented. In many school districts, tests and inventories help determine students' IQs and learning characteristics, and universities throughout the country have developed programs to prepare teachers in gifted education. Curricula designed to tap the reasoning powers of high-potential students appear in professional journals, and centers for gifted education, such as the one at the College of William and Mary, provide curricula in science, language arts, and social studies for high-ability learners. Programs such as Future Problem Solving and Odyssey of the Mind have sprung up to provide enrichment activity for gifted students.

Still, our high-potential students face increasing odds as they attempt to find their place in the sun. According to *National Excellence: A Case for Developing America's* Talent (Office of Educational Research and Improvement, 1993, p. 13)—the first national report since 1972 on the education of gifted children— these students receive mixed messages from the world around them. Pointing to the current of anti-intellectualism in American society, the report states:

> As a culture, we admire and reward the brilliant, creative mind after it has invented something practical or produced tangible results. Yet we are not inclined to support those who want to pursue an artistic or intellectual life, and we find ways of discouraging those who wish to do so.... [Responding to this discouragement,] students say they want to do well, but not exceptionally well, because it is more important to be accepted by the "in crowd (which) is not the brain crowd."

Regardless of their inborn motivation, our most able students need encouragement to resist the cultural message.

The highly able child, like other children, is a blend of emotions and intellect—with artistic, physical, social, and spiritual dimensions. Because the intellectual aspect stands out (as does the physical with athletes), school programming for these students has typically been designed to meet only intellectual needs. But if, in the past, gifted programs erred in ignoring other facets of children's lives, much has been done in recent years to correct this. This book is part of that attempt, taking the approach that intellectual development is just one fraction of the total person.

It should be noted that intellectual development is an emotional need for some intellectually gifted people, especially the highly gifted. In fact, Webb (1992, p. 12) states that "profoundly gifted children are ones for whom intellectual stimulation and/or creative expression are clearly emotional needs that may appear to be as intense as the physiological needs of hunger or thirst." Silverman (1993, p. 10) concurs, stating that the neglect of appropriate educational opportunities for gifted children "affects their morale, motivation, social relationships, aspirations, sense of self-worth, and emotional development." For these students, meeting intellectual needs is not a purely intellectual task; there is deep feeling behind it. Adults who seek to promote the intellectual development of their children will be more effective if they acknowledge and reinforce this driving need to learn.

To have curiosity satisfied; to experience a wealth of diversity of ideas, places, and people; to explore all the world and find a place in it—all of this is truly a *survival is*sue for these youngsters. They must be able to grow, to learn, and to develop their capacities, or they will wither intellectually and emotionally.

Intellectual Needs as Emotional Needs

A bright or gifted child has extraordinary abilities, each accompanied by needs: a need for the ability to be developed and used, and a need for the child possessing it to become creative and eventually able to produce something of value to himself or others. For unusually talented people, the impetus is not merely that where there is an ability, it is best to develop it. Rather, an intellectually gifted child will not be happy or complete, and certainly not self-actualized, until he is using his intellectual ability at a level approaching his full capacity.

Imagine the frustration of an athlete who isn't allowed to run, jump, or move. This gives some inkling of the frustration of a bright child denied the chance to challenge her mind. Underachieving gifted students may not display such restlessness as obviously as an athlete would, but this doesn't mean they don't need intellectual stimulation.

It is important that parents and teachers see intellectual development as a requirement for these children, and not merely as an interest, a flair, or a phase they will outgrow. A painting student is quoted as saying, "I have a hard time *not* painting. I paint about 10 hours a day. Painting is my life" (Piechowski, 1979). Another student says simply, "I read because I can't help it." Gifted adults who relax by playing a musical instrument, by reading in a foreign language, or by experimenting with computer programming are expressing the same drive for mental stimulation. These activities are not work for them; they are paths to being fully alive.

Recognizing intellectual development as a need can help parents cope with the inevitable frustration caused by a child who reads or tinkers or practices an instrument for "too many" hours per day. And it can help teachers find patience when a child insists on working endlessly on a project or report, threatening to hold up the progress of the rest of the class.

Intellectual Overexcitability

Another way of thinking about the drive to understand comes from Kazimierz Dabrowski's intriguing ideas about developmental potential, which were introduced in Chapter 1. In this section, we take a look at Piechowski's work with Dabrowski's concept of intellectual overexcitability and how it can help adults appreciate not only the need for intellectual development, but also the strength of feeling behind it.

In 1979, Piechowski listed characteristics of intellectual over-excitability that may be familiar to those who deal with gifted youngsters: probing questions, problem solving, curiosity, concentration, capacity for sustained intellectual effort, voracious reading and starting on difficult books at a young age, a wide variety of interests, theoretical thinking (thinking about thinking, moral thinking, development of a hierarchy of values), independence of thought (often expressed in criticism), and processes of self-monitoring and self-evaluation. All of these characteristics are part of the drive to learn, to know, to understand.

Piechowski (1979, p.34) also states that intellectual over-excitability has more to do with "striving for understanding, probing the unknown and love of truth than with learning per se and academic achievement." More recently, he describes it as "an avidity for knowledge and the search for truth—expressed as discovery, questioning, and love of ideas and theoretical analysis" (1991, p. 287).

It is this extra sense of urgency about knowing that underlies the need of some gifted children for intellectual development—i.e., that causes them to say, "I read because I can't help it."

Intellectual overexcitability, like the others Dabrowski lists, is not always understood or valued by those who may not discern how it contributes to the development of gifted individuals. Thus, gifted students quickly realize that it is often best to dampen their enthusiasm for learning. Reading and book discussion with other gifted students, then, provide a welcome venue for expressing their intellectual interests where they can be accepted.

"Can you tell your readers how awful it feels when you have to go for two days without reading?" said one young man when he knew I was writing this book. A 19-year-old German student described why he was drawn toward a career in university teaching: "When I read about culture, then I am happy!" Both of these young men exhibit the unusual intellectual intensity Piechowski describes.

Not everyone who has the potential for high intellectual achievement also possesses a passionate interest in intellectual pursuits. For those who do have such strong interests, though, learning about the work of Dabrowski and Piechowski often brings a reassuring shock of self-recognition.

The Child in Charge

Some bright children seem to lose touch with their drive to understand. Although as preschoolers they may have been as eager to learn as Steven, who was described in the Introduction, by the middle elementary grades, their intellectual curiosity appears to be dulled and they are willing to settle for half-hearted efforts in school. What makes the difference between those who gradually reject and those who continue to be nourished by the pleasures of learning?

Just as gifted children must achieve a sense of identity that incorporates their unusual abilities, so must they recognize early that the drive to understand is part of who they are (Halsted, 1998). At the preschool and primary levels, parents and teachers should help talented children know this about themselves; learning is a source of pleasure for them. The knowledge that they enjoy learning should be integrated into their developing self-concepts.

Whatever steps adults take to satisfy the child's curiosity and enrich her experience, their underlying attitude that learning is important—for its own sake and to the child—is critical and must gradually be adopted by the child. Ultimately, the responsibility for keeping curiosity both satisfied and piqued must shift to the child, as she makes decisions that enable her to continue learning. The knowledge that she *needs* to learn and that it is up to her to meet that need is part of her survival kit.

This largely intellectual challenge can be added to the four emotional needs presented in the first chapter. For satisfactory development, then, gifted and talented children must accomplish the following five tasks as they grow up:

➤ achieve a sense of identity which includes their giftedness,

➤ understand and make positive use of their need for time alone,

➤ learn to get along with others of all ability levels,

➤ determine how to make use of their abilities, and

➤ acknowledge and learn how to satisfy their drive to understand.

Because reading and talking about books can help children cope with these five broad developmental tasks, many books that show characters dealing with these tasks are recommended in the bibliography, Chapter 8, in this book. But for now, we will focus specifically on the intellectual characteristics of gifted students and on necessary conditions for their optimal development.

Optimal Intellectual Development

Parents may notice signs of high ability in very young children, but if they are inexperienced observers, it may be some time before they grasp the meaning of these behaviors. A long list of such traits is provided by Smutny, Veenker, and Veenker (1989). Below are a few that relate to verbal development and reading. The young gifted child:

➤ likes to play with words,

➤ uses proper grammar and structure earlier than agemates,

➤ uses rich language, with metaphor and analogy,

➤ asks about new words; learns and practices them,

➤ learns to read without instruction before starting school, and/or

➤ makes up stories and songs.

Once these children start school, it becomes clear that their abilities set them apart from their classmates. Because they have different abilities, they learn differently—not only more and faster, but also "in different modes and at greater depth" (Kerr, 1991, p. 23). Kerr points out that "capable learners learn most effectively when appropriately challenged and tend to become bored and frustrated when the *pace* and *complexity* of material is below their ability" (p. 22, emphasis mine).

Their intellectual abilities, then, dictate their intellectual needs. What are other needs related to their intellectual characteristics?

They need to be with others of their own ability level. Grouping gifted children together is controversial, but research indicates that it provides the optimum learning situation for them. Kerr (1991, p. 23) cites research concluding that "ability grouping has minimal effects, either positive or negative, on the achievement of average or below-average students. Substantial evidence shows, however, that ability grouping has a positive effect on the achievement of gifted students."

In addition, they need teaching techniques that rely on the higher levels of thinking (Amidon, 1991)—that is, on analysis, synthesis, and evaluation, rather than primarily on knowledge, comprehension, and application. Using the higher levels of thinking as a method of talking about books is discussed in Chapter 5.

If just these four general intellectual needs—pace of learning, complexity of material, being with other bright learners, and higher levels of thinking—are considered, we can see how books and book discussion can meet the special needs of bright and gifted children. A reader can choose her own pace of reading, books are available at every degree of complexity, a discussion group can bring together learners of like ability (just two, a child and an adult, are enough), and the questions can elicit higher levels of thinking.

Many lists describe the intellectual characteristics of gifted children at all ages. These lists are typically used in conjunction with intelligence and achievement test scores to determine eligibility for school gifted programs. They offer more than that, however, if the intellectual characteristics are used as a spring-board for identifying the intellectual *needs* they imply.

The following is a compilation of three of these lists (from Clark, 1983; Ehrlich, 1985; and Webb, Meckstroth, & Tolan, 1982). The listing below eliminates overlap and groups intellectual characteristics of gifted youngsters into three categories: verbal, thought-processing, and performance characteristics.

Following each list of characteristics is a list of related intellectual needs, derived in part from Clark's examples of problems that may appear in work patterns or in getting along with others if the needs are not met.

Verbal Characteristics and Needs

Gifted children in general:

➤ have a large vocabulary and are able to use advanced terminology correctly,

➤ read early and may be self-taught; read enthusiastically and widely, often above grade level; select reading material purposefully and enjoy challenging books,

➤ understand language subtleties and use language for humor,

➤ write words and sentences early, and produce superior creative writing (poetry, stories, plays), and

➤ display verbal ability in self-expression, choice of colorful and descriptive phrasing, and ease in learning a second language.

To challenge verbal abilities, gifted students need to do the following:

➤ use their full vocabulary and develop it further with intellectual peers,

➤ read books at an appropriate intellectual and emotional level,

➤ be introduced to books that represent a variety of literary conventions and styles and that use language gracefully, and

➤ express ideas verbally and in depth by writing or speaking with others who challenge and thus refine their views and concepts.

Thought-Processing Characteristics and Needs

As a group, gifted children display the following traits in thought processing:

➤ they enjoy experimenting and can generate original ideas and solutions;

➤ they give evidence of divergent thinking, offering responses that are atypical, rather than the convergent answers expected from most children and found in the teacher's answer book;

➤ they accept open-ended situations and questions at an early age and do not require immediate solutions; they can accept ambiguity (and thus can enjoy novels that do not have clear-cut endings);

➤ they enjoy complexity and may try to create it—for example, by adding rules to games;

➤ they have unusual power to process information using logic, abstract thinking, and symbolic thought;

➤ they show flexibility of thought and seek alternatives; they are able to see all sides of an issue; and

➤ they synthesize well, seeing relationships others miss; they transfer past learning to new situations and draw generalizations.

To develop thought-processing potential, gifted students need to do the following:

➤ consider alternatives and possible consequences of choices in an accepting environment,

➤ be exposed to a great variety of vicarious experiences,

➤ test new ideas without required conclusions or products,

➤ discuss ideas with intellectual peers,

➤ be exposed to many ideas at different levels, and

➤ take plenty of time for incubation of ideas.

Performance Characteristics and Needs

In their performance, gifted children:

➤ show great curiosity and unusual persistence in efforts to gain answers,

➤ possess a wide range of interests and information,

➤ comprehend new concepts rapidly at an advanced level; they have little or no need for drill,

➤ display creativity and imagination, enjoy fantasies and science fiction, may have an imaginary playmate in their preschool years, can develop a variety of solutions to problems, and generate original ideas,

➤ are persistent and goal-directed; they have a long attention span and may want to spend more than the time allotted to complete a project, and

➤ show unusual intensity regarding school projects, political or environmental issues, religion, world events, intellectual inquiry into an area of special interest, interpersonal relationships, and abstract values.

To enhance performance characteristics, gifted students need to do the following:

➤ have curiosity met with exposure to varying styles of life, values, and approaches to problems,

➤ be exposed to new information and new issues,

➤ be presented with material at their own rate of learning,

> ➤ develop skills in creative thinking and problem solving,

> ➤ pursue interests beyond the time desired by most students, and

> ➤ learn skills for dealing with intensity by exploring ways by which others cope with it.

Reading such a list of ideal conditions should not lull us into the comfortable assumption that all of our bright and gifted children have these experiences at school. While many of them do, it is safe to assume (since it is estimated that only half of our gifted children are identified) that most do not, and the programs now in place are threatened by budget cuts. What stands between our brightest children and the full realization of their potential?

Obstacles in the Way

Most educators want to do all they can to meet the educational needs of every student, and in many schools there is awareness that this should include the special needs of gifted children. However, regardless of their desire to provide an appropriate educational environment for everyone, teachers and administrators are often thwarted by economic barriers, by trends in education, and by social conditions (including television and video games) that stand in the way of their efforts to meet the needs of all students equally. Above average students often lose out.

Economic Barriers

The Federal Office of Gifted and Talented, which had been dissolved in 1981, was re-established in 1988 in a period of increasing interest in gifted education. In 1994, however, funding was cut in half as the resolve to provide special programs for gifted students weakened. It has increased since, but still is not back to the 1988 level.

"In the late 1990s the gifted movement remains strong," according to Colangelo and Davis (1997, p. xiii), "but 'ebbing' is taking place because of budget difficulties..." (and, they add, because of the detracking movement, which is discussed later in this chapter). Budget difficulties are caused in part by the lack of governmental mandates requiring that gifted students be served. Since programs for mentally and physically handicapped youngsters are mandated by federal and state governments, they cannot be cut, leaving gifted programs open and vulnerable as one of the few ways to reduce costs. Parents and teachers have seen gifted programs trimmed or eliminated as state aid designated for them is frozen or dropped entirely. Sometimes the children who are highly able but not identified as gifted suffer the most from budget cutting and increased class size (Nordheimer, 1992).

The outlook is not good for the early reinstatement of lost support, since the level of funding for gifted programs varies with political and educational trends (Clark, 1997). Interest and funding surged after Sputnik, when the nation needed scientists who would help us compete in space exploration. The urge to be competitive is still paramount, but now the perceived need is different: to build a workforce with sophisticated technological skills. Money can be expected to flow in that direction until computer literacy is fully integrated into our schools.

Parents who watch gifted children move rapidly through their school years during a time of financial retrenchment occasionally resort to legal action, as they attempt to force school systems to meet their children's special needs. To help such parents save both time and money, Karnes and Marquardt (1991a) discuss the advantages of mediation and due process over litigation. A companion volume (1991b) presents parents' stories of their efforts to use the legal system to ensure appropriate education for their youngsters. In 1992, the authors founded The Institute for Law and Gifted Education as part of The Center for Gifted Studies at the University of Southern Mississippi, and in 2000, they published a new book, *Gifted Children and Legal Issues: An Update*, which supplements the first two, discussing recent developments in legal issues regarding gifted education.

Trends in Education

Education is a creature of trends, in part resulting from our efforts to teach many different kinds of learners in public schools. Since no one approach reaches all students, educators continually revise teaching methods. A long look at the history of education in the United States, such as the one offered by Ravitch (2000), reveals that often, revision is accomplished by returning to older methods, once rejected but now seen in new light. Educational reform can be seen as a pendulum, swinging from one theory to an opposing theory, and then when it has gone too far, moving back again.

An example of the effect of this on gifted education is the response to the 1983 report of the National Commission on Excellence in Education, *A Nation at Risk*, which resulted in efforts not merely to reform, but to restructure the public school system in this country. Echoes of this restructuring include a swing of the pendulum toward two classroom strategies that adversely affect gifted students. "Detracking is one recent damaging reform movement; cooperative learning is the other," according to Colangelo and Davis (1997, p. 4).

These practices threaten ability grouping, a mainstay of gifted education and a strategy that meets the very real need of gifted children to spend time with others of like ability. Davis and Rimm (1998), stating their belief that the movement to eliminate ability grouping has "bad consequences for gifted children," cite several authors in the field of gifted education who share concern about the change. Rogers (2002) in her provocative book entitled *Re-Forming Gifted Education: Matching the Program to the Child*, provides substantial research supporting the benefits of various types of ability grouping, along with other educational alternatives.

Detracking. The detracking movement is designed to answer charges against tracking, which assigns students to full-time instructional groups that may persist from one year to the next. Opponents of tracking fear that it may permanently lock students out of settings where they might be appropriately taught.

Although ability grouping is different from tracking, it is threatened by detracking. Ability groups place students with similar learning needs together for the length of time needed for instruction (Fiedler, Lange, & Winebrenner, 1993). This enables teachers to provide specific instruction aimed at a common level, as in homogeneous reading or math groups in a heterogeneous elementary school classroom.

Unfortunately, ability grouping may be perceived as tracking. Detracking is therefore increasingly accomplished by eliminating programs which group gifted students together even for brief periods of time.

Cooperative learning. Often used to replace tracking and gifted programs, cooperative learning places children in small short-term groups that include students of all ability levels; the group is responsible for the learning of all its members. Thus the top learner in each group typically leads the others, without the opportunity for expanded learning of his own. In an article on the needs of highly gifted children, Kearney (1993) states that "certain popular educational strategies, such as cooperative learning, can exploit these [gifted] children, especially if they are permitted no time with intellectual peers and no regular, daily access to curriculum at an appropriate level of difficulty."

Research indicates that cooperative learning is not academically beneficial to gifted and talented students (Robinson, 1990; Rogers, 2002). In fact, if used excessively, it may be resented by gifted students who prefer to work individually and to be responsible for their own learning (Robinson, 1997).

It is not surprising that the loss of ability grouping in favor of cooperative learning is strongly disliked by gifted students and is of serious concern to leaders in gifted education. This concern offers guidance to parents in evaluating their children's schools: Is there a balance between cooperative programs and time allowed with intellectual peers, in groups of top students studying appropriately difficult material?

Parents who are not well versed in educational change may have to become active investigators to learn what has happened or is planned for gifted children in their home community. Those who wish to advocate for their children would do well to ask how secure the funding for the gifted program is, and to inquire gently and politely—but persistently—about provisions for students of high ability.

If the educational needs of gifted students are to be met, alternative methods of working with them in a heterogeneous classroom must be developed. Parents of bright and gifted children should watch to make sure, if the gifted program in their school is diminished or eliminated, that compensating programs are put into place that will continue to challenge their students. In *Helping Gifted Children Soar: A Practical Guide for Parents and Teachers*, Strip and Hirsch (2000) offer a clear discussion of options available to accomplish this, as does *Re-Forming Gifted Education: Matching the Program to the Child* by Rogers.

Social Conditions

Alarming statistics revealing disturbing social trends in our children's lives and schooling are reported so relentlessly that we may become numb to them. Without question, children's potential for intellectual development is affected by divorce, poverty, malnutrition, a lack of health care, struggling single parents, frazzled parents in two-income families, and other social problems, including safety in schools.

In her book, *Endangered Minds: Why Children Don't Think—And What We Can Do about It*, Jane M. Healy (1999) looks behind these factors to two others that also characterize our children's world: the rapid pace of living, and reliance on instant sensory gratification. She expresses deep concern that the stresses and deprivations our children experience are actually changing their brains and their capacity for sustained analytical thought.

Citing research into physical changes that occur in the brain as a result of learning, Healy suggests that our processing of language is an important part of the development of our ability to think. It is at risk if appropriate language experiences are not available—and are not reinforced through practice—at the optimum moment in the brain's developmental schedule. Among her concerns is the interplay between the developing brain and reading.

With this in mind, let's look at how two major contemporary forces, television and video games, affect our children's reading and thinking—and the implications for their intellectual growth.

Television and video games. Without even considering the questionable *content* of many television programs, two compelling objections are immediately obvious to many experts: watching television is passive, and it steals time in which a child could be active. By contrast, reading is active, requiring the brain's involvement to interact with the words and to create the pictures that television provides for us.

Healy (1999, p. 208) quotes a personal communication from M. Russell Harter, a researcher in reading and the developing brain at the University of North Carolina:

> Reading triggers certain experiences in the brain that just don't happen if you don't read. I think our brains are designed to symbolize and represent information in the way that we call language. If we don't exercise it, we lose it. Television, even *Sesame Street*, is not very symbolic. It makes things very tangible and easy to understand, but reading is the kind of exercise that causes the brain to develop differently because it uses that symbolic capability.

Jerre Levy, a biopsychologist at the University of Chicago, states:

> The main thing that worries me about TV is not even its intellectual level. To the extent that children commit time looking at TV, they're not

spending time reading. When a child reads a novel, he has to self-create whole scenarios, he has to create images of who these people are, what their emotions are, what their tones of voice are, what the environment looks like, what the feeling of this environment is. These self-created scenarios are important, and television leaves no room for that creative process. I think brains are designed to meet cognitive challenges. It's just like muscles; if you don't exercise them they wither. If you don't exercise brains, they wither (in Healy, 1999, p. 214).

Reading is not the only activity preferable to watching television. Vivian Paley, teacher of young children at the University of Chicago Laboratory Schools, points out that:

none of the [television] programming—simply by virtue of what the medium is—suits the way a child learns. The child is simply not a passive creature. If you leave a child just sitting alone in his room with his toys, there's an active monologue going on there....The more opportunities for the child to play, and to play with other children, the better—and also to have open-ended conversations between parents and children about everything that's on a child's mind. And of course to be read to, just to be read to from all the wonderful prose and poetry that is available for children (in Obermiller, 1989, p. 16).

The lack of reading skills, and the lack of the critical and analytical thinking they support, should be recognized as a danger to our nation equal to a lack of technological skills, but more insidious. "The survival of our kind of democracy requires the...active mind that the print culture produces and that [the] television spectator habit does not," according to Librarian of Congress James H. Billington (1990).

The controlling element of the electronic culture is television...and this represents a threat of passivity that can block the effective functioning of an active citizenry that our democracy requires. Both our educational and political institutions and traditions are imperiled over the long run.

Thoughtful parents have been concerned for years about the amount of time children are exposed to television, even in well-regulated homes. Children whose television time is limited when they are toddlers tend to watch more and more television as they grow older, and reading time decreases. Parents interested specifically in weaning children from television to books can begin with the suggestions in *The Magic Bookshelf* (Jarvis & Jarvis, 1999).

Video games demand more participation than television, but parents are justifiably uneasy about them nevertheless. The activity required is narrowly focused and without creativity, and, as Winn (1991) worries, "children accustomed to the quick gratification of video games may not be willing to put up with the arduous efforts necessary to learn to play a musical instrument well, or to excel at tennis, even though their manual dexterity may indeed have been improved by all those hours steering little figures around on the video screen."

Addressing the question of whether there is any value in video games—such as good hand-eye coordination—Sylvia Rimm (1992, p. 5), a child psychologist who specializes in underachievement, suggests that while video games may improve visual-motor integration, the same benefit, as well as many others, is gained by working on a computer. She goes on to list disadvantages: "Some games are violent and seem to encourage aggressive behavior in children. Furthermore, children spend so much time playing these games, that it may seem difficult to lure them away for healthier outdoor play, their chores and responsibilities, reading, and/or homework." She recommends limiting video-game play to weekends and allowing no more than 45 minutes to an hour, to "minimize any damage."

In a chapter titled "TV, Video Games, and the Growing Brain," Healy (1999, p. 206) states:

> It seems fairly safe to say that much of children's experience with such games will have little, if any, transfer value to traditional school tasks.... We do know that lack of use can definitely affect potential for brain connections. If a child spends an inordinate amount of time on video games (or television, or even other types of computer use) instead of playing and experimenting with many different types of skills, the foundations for some kinds of abilities may be sacrificed. These losses may not show up until much later, when more complicated kinds of thinking and learning become necessary. Tender young brains need broad horizons, not overbuilt neural pathways in one specific skill area.

All of these experts, and many others, are concerned not only about the direct negative effects of television and video games, but also about the time they take from reading. Healy (1999) reports that a study of fifth graders indicated that they watch television for an average of two hours and ten minutes a day. Of these same children, 50% read four minutes a day or less outside of school, 30% read two minutes or less, and 10% do not read at all outside of school. For older students, these percentages are no doubt lower, as will become clear in the next chapter.

The key seems to lie in a combination of several factors, including:

➤ how much time the child spends with television or video games,

➤ the content and quality of the shows she watches or the games he plays,

➤ whether the reading habit has already become well established, and

➤ whether the child's activities incorporate a balance that includes mental, physical, and social activities unrelated to television or video games.

Reading seems so simple that it can easily be taken for granted. In fact, we may need to worry less about illiteracy than about aliteracy—citizens who know how to read at a functional level but who do not choose to read, thereby avoiding the mental demands of reading and losing the benefits of the mental exercise, as well as the information they could gain by reading. This trend begins in our middle schools (Beers, 1998). Gifted students as well as average ones are at risk. The difference can be in their awareness of their need to learn and of their responsibility for their own education.

The Importance of Parents

Regardless of economic barriers, swings of the education pendulum, and social changes, gifted and intellectually curious students are still the people described in these first two chapters, with the same emotional and intellectual characteristics and needs. There will always be some who learn faster than others and some for whom knowledge in academic content areas—the sheer joy of learning about the arts and sciences—is an end in itself. Parents and teachers concerned with meeting such students' special needs must continue to be vigilant to ensure that provisions are made for them.

Unfortunately, tighter school budgets and curricular change threaten even long-standing gifted programs, so children identified as gifted are in danger of losing the special curricular offerings they need. Their parents, knowing how much their children have benefited from programming designed for them, must find ways to compensate at home for the loss.

Some of these parents turn to home schooling. This is particularly true of parents of highly gifted children, whose unique needs may well not be met in even a strong school gifted program.

Although it can be abused, when home schooling is offered to enthusiastic learners by parents who are skilled teachers and who have access to rich community resources, it can be a very successful alternative (Clark, 1997; Rivero, 2002). In fact, the average scores of homeschooled students on standardized tests range from the 65th to the 80th percentile, 15 to 30 points above the norm (Ray & Wartes, 1991). College admissions officers receive so many applications from homeschooled students that they have established criteria by which to judge their non-traditional resumes. As home schooling presents a reasonable option for a growing number of families and more resources become available to them, books remain a core component of any home schooling plan.

Whether or not home schooling is being considered, parents should be active in seeking three pieces of information:

➤ a description of the kind of educational program that is best for their child,

➤ how much of the desired program he or she is receiving in school, and

➤ what the parents can do to compensate for any missing elements.

Developing complete answers to all three may be a long-term project. This chapter provides a brief discussion of the first item and some information to help parents evaluate school programs— more is found in Chapter 5. The remaining chapters offer one response to the last item. While books are not a panacea, using them effectively is one of the best ways to fill gaps left in the school program or to counteract distracting social influences.

How Books Can Help

A glance back over the list of intellectual characteristics and needs found earlier in this chapter should confirm that reading and book discussion are ideal ways to respond to the characteristics and to meet the related needs.

Many bright and gifted people suppress awareness of their need to learn. Teaching these children to use books is one way of demonstrating that learning is important to them and that books can be a significant part of their lives. When teachers go to the trouble of establishing book discussion groups, or when parents take the time to read what their children are reading and talk to them about it, it becomes clear that significant adults value and encourage reading. If reading and book discussions are happy and successful experiences, children learn to love books.

Especially where programs designed for gifted children are unavailable, a vigorous use of books can be a real contribution to a child's growth. Few activities are as available, as inexpensive, and as richly rewarding. No wonder some of their best friends are books!

References

Amidon, S. R. (1991). Encouraging higher level thinking in the gifted adolescent. In M. Bireley & J. Genshaft (Eds.), *Understanding the gifted adolescent: Educational, developmental, and multicultural issues* (pp. 91-103). New York: Teachers College Press.

Beers, K. (1998). Choosing not to read: Understanding why some middle schoolers just say no. In Beers, K. & Samuels, B.G., *Into focus: Understanding and creating middle school readers* (pp. 37-63). Norwood, MA: Christopher-Gordon.

Billington, J. H. (1990, September). The electronic erosion of democracy. Inaugural C. Walter and Gerda B. Mortenson Lecture, Urbana, IL.

Clark, B. (1997). *Growing up gifted: Developing the potential of children at home and at school.* 5th ed. Upper Saddle River, NJ: Merrill.

Clark, B. (1983). *Growing up gifted: Developing the potential of children at home and at school.* 2nd ed. Columbus, OH: Charles E. Merrill.

Colangelo, N. & Davis, G. A. (1997). Preface. In N. Colangelo & G. A. Davis (Eds.), *Handbook of gifted education* (pp. xii-xiv). Boston: Allyn and Bacon.

Davis, G. A. & Rimm, S. B. (1998). *Education of the gifted and talented.* 4th ed. Boston: Allyn and Bacon.

Ehrlich, V. Z. (1985). *Gifted children: A guide for parents and teachers.* New York: Trillium.

Fiedler, E. D., Lange, R. E., & Winebrenner, S. (1993, September). In search of reality: Unraveling the myths about tracking, ability grouping and the gifted. *Roeper Review, 16,* 4-7.

Halsted, J. W. (1998). Keeping curiosity alive. In J. F. Smutny (Ed.), *The young gifted child: Potential and promise, an anthology.* Cresskill, NJ: Hampton Press.

Healy, J. M. (1999). *Endangered minds: Why children don't think—and what we can do about it.* New York: Simon & Schuster.

Jarvis, J. & Jarvis, R. (1999). *The magic bookshelf: A parents' guide to showing growing minds the path to the best children's literature.* Atlanta: Lorica.

Karnes, F. A. & Marquardt, R. G. (2000). *Gifted children and legal issues: An update.* Scottsdale, AZ: Great Potential Press (formerly Gifted Psychology Press).

Karnes, F. A. & Marquardt, R. G. (1991a). *Gifted children and the law: Mediation, due process and court cases.* Scottsdale, AZ: Great Potential Press (formerly Ohio Psychology Press).

Karnes, F. A. & Marquardt, R. G. (1991b). *Gifted children and legal issues in education: Parents' stories of hope.* Scottsdale, AZ: Great Potential Press (formerly Ohio Psychology Press).

Kearney, K. (1993, November/December). Discrimination against excellence. *Understanding Our Gifted, 6 (2),* 16.

Kerr, B. (1991). *A handbook for counseling the gifted and talented.* Alexandria: American Association for Counseling and Development.

Nordheimer, J. (1992, November 29). Gifted education, seen as a luxury in hard times, encounters cutbacks. *New York Times.*

Obermiller, Tim. (1989, Summer). All in a day's play. *The University of Chicago Magazine,* 81 (4), 14-19.

Office of Educational Research and Improvement. (1993). *National excellence: A case for developing America's talent.* Washington, DC: U.S. Government Printing Office.

Piechowski, M. M. (1991). Emotional development and emotional giftedness. In N. Colangelo & G. A. Davis (Eds.), *Handbook of gifted education* (pp. 285-306). Boston: Allyn and Bacon.

Piechowski, M. M. (1979). Developmental potential. In N. Colangelo & R. T. Zaffrann (Eds.), *New voices in counseling the gifted* (pp. 25-57). Dubuque, Iowa: Kendall/Hunt.

Ravitch, D. (2000). *Left back: A history of failed school reforms.* New York: Simon & Schuster.

Ravitch, D. & Finn, C. E. (1987). *What do our 17-year-olds know? A report on the first national assessment of history and literature.* New York: Harper & Row.

Ray, B. & Wartes, J. (1991). The academic achievement and affective development of home-schooled children. In J. Van Galen & M. A. Pittman (Eds.), *Home schooling: Political, historical, and pedagogical perspectives* (pp. 43-62). Norwood, NJ: Ablex.

Rimm, S. (1992, Autumn). Sylvia Rimm on raising kids. Grandville, MI Public Schools: *IMAGE Informer,* p. 5.

Rivero, L. (2002). *Creative home schooling for gifted children: A resource guide.* Scottsdale, AZ: Great Potential Press.

Robinson, A. (1997). Cooperative learning for talented students: Emergent issues and implications. In N. Colangelo & G. A. Davis (Eds.), *Handbook of gifted education.* 2nd ed. (pp. 243-252). Boston: Allyn and Bacon.

Robinson, A. (1990). Point-counterpoint: Cooperation or exploitation? The argument against cooperative learning for talented students. *Journal for the Education of the Gifted, 14,* 9-27.

Rogers, K.B. (2002). *Re-Forming gifted education: Matching the program to the child*. Scottsdale: Great Potential Press.

Silverman, L. K. (1993). The gifted individual. In Linda Kreger Silverman (Ed.), *Counseling the gifted and talented* (pp. 3-28). Denver: Love.

Smutny, J. F., Veenker, K., & Veenker, S. (1989*). Your gifted child: How to recognize and develop the special talents in your child from birth to age seven*. New York: Facts on File.

Strip, C & Hirsch, G. (2000). *Helping gifted children soar: A practical guide for parents and teachers*. Scottsdale, AZ: Great Potential Press (formerly Gifted Psychology Press).

Webb, J. T. (1992). Assessing gifted and talented children. *Illinois Council for the Gifted Journal*, 11, 10-21.

Webb, J. T., Meckstroth, E. A., & Tolan, S. S. (1982). *Guiding the gifted child: A practical source for parents and teachers*. Scottsdale, AZ: Great Potential Press (formerly Ohio Psychology Press).

Winn, M. (1991, December 22). Nintendo and the challenges of life. *New York Times Book Review*, p. 2.

Part Two:

The Process

Chapter 3

Reading Guidance

One of the changes my husband and I noticed when our younger son departed for college, along with how long it takes the dishwasher to fill up and how often the trash has to be taken out, was the loss of the sense of urgency about each day that we had felt when we had children in residence. Almost always now, whatever doesn't get done today really can be put off until tomorrow.

With growing children this is not so. Especially in the early years, each day is important, and if the needs at a given stage are not met at that time, the child cannot conveniently make up for the loss later on. The child's changing developmental requirements march on, regardless of parents' commitment, energy, patience, presence, income, and whatever else makes the difference between good and inadequate parenting. Thus the sense of urgency—the need, the readiness is *now*, and the attentive parent senses the demand for an immediate response.

The principle extends to children's reading. Each stage of childhood lasts a breathlessly short time, and so also does the period of peak response to the literature appropriate to that stage.

As adults we feel a certain leisure about our reading, assuming that two or five years from now we can read a given book and expect much the same emotional and intellectual response we would have if we read it this week. Not so with children. They can, of course, read Mother Goose rhymes much later, but after the age of four or five, the emotional response to the rhythms and the intellectual response to the word play are dulled. They can read fairy tales even as adults, but after the middle elementary years, the intense interest—the magic—is gone, and with it the power of the tales to enrich the growing imagination of the child. There are far too many excellent books available for the late elementary and junior high reader to have time to read them all. No wonder the thoughtful school librarian feels a sense of urgency, trying to expose children to the best of the wealth before they are too old—that is, before they are 14 or 15!

Using books with bright and curious children requires knowledge of the needs of these youngsters (Part One), the books available to them (Part Three) and the processes of change, presented here in Part Two. We begin with reading guidance—how to help them seek out the best books *for them* among the wide range of literature available.

Fundamentals of Reading Guidance

Reading guidance may be defined as offering "the right book for the right child at the right time." It means being aware of what a child is reading in terms of quality, age-appropriateness, content, and being ready to offer suggestions for further reading that will move that child along with good literature at each stage of development.

By observing the reading patterns of children, we can see that the types of literature they enjoy alters as they grow—from nursery rhymes to a wide range of adult fiction and nonfiction. While this change in their *interests* occurs naturally, it does not follow that a maturing of their *literary taste* is just as natural. The steps from grocery store picture books to well-written, insightful fiction and sophisticated, demanding nonfiction almost always require guidance.

Practicing reading guidance means watching a child read through the Hardy Boys series and being ready at the right time with a suggestion that he might also enjoy Alfred Hitchcock's short stories, and a few years later a Leon Garfield novel and then Edgar Allan Poe—all filled with suspense but moving up the ladder of age appropriateness and literary quality. Or it may mean noticing that a third grader who has reread Laura Ingalls Wilder a number of times is ready to be introduced to *Caddie Woodlawn*, and then later to the historical fiction of Elizabeth George Speare, Avi, and Scott O'Dell. Later still, she may enjoy *Johnny Tremain* or *Across Five Aprils*, and eventually Willa Cather's novels of the American West. In addition, she could be encouraged to branch out horizontally, with biography or fiction about the history of other countries.

Parents are in the best position to offer such long-range reading guidance. Teachers and librarians usually see only one to six or seven years of a child's development, so they must work harder early in their relationship with a child to learn what he has enjoyed reading. This will provide the background information needed to suggest books that will interest and delight him and keep him coming back for more good literature.

Reading guidance involves stretching a child's mind and spirit—always trying to suggest a book that meets her where she is in the hope that when she has read it, she will have grown a little. Those who guide reading do not deny the use of escape literature, but they want the child to learn to use it appropriately. This means the child must learn to recognize when she wants to read something easy and when she wants to be challenged—and then be able to find each type at the right moment.

Adult influence on the priority a child places on reading seems to be limited to about four years, roughly from second grade to fifth. Our influence on the *quality* of children's reading lasts perhaps two more years—through the important middle school years (longer for those who continue leisure reading). Thus, time is precious indeed, and there isn't very much of it to introduce them to the wealth of children's literature. These are crucial years to stimulate imaginative thinking, to ensure that they will know some of the classics when they enter college, and to help them establish a pattern of reading that will last a lifetime. These early years are a time for subtle intervention, for suggestions, for sharing and passing on the enjoyment of reading. It is no time for well-intentioned adults to watch passively as mediocre reading habits unfold and stabilize.

Reading guidance takes many forms. It can be as informal as the casual mention of a title or an author a parent has enjoyed, or the "floor work" librarians do—talking with students as they browse the shelves. Or it can be more formal—a book talk carefully planned by a librarian or a teacher, or a list of books from which students are required to select five to read each semester for an English class. Reading guidance can also be subtly woven into the fabric of family life:

> *Although she is now the mother of teenagers, Ginny has warm memories of summers spent reading when she was a child and adolescent. Her mother had always enjoyed reading, and she was ready each year with suggestions of books Ginny might enjoy that summer. They were books she might otherwise have missed:* Cry, the Beloved Country; Too Late the Phalarope; My Name is Aram; Madame Curie; Wind, Sand and Stars; A Death in the Family. *Some were in her mother's library; she found others in the public library at her mother's suggestion. She has less time now, but reading is still a source of immense pleasure for Ginny, in part a result of her mother's gentle reading guidance.*

The relationship between the student and the guiding adult is important for the success of reading guidance, as is the genuine love of the adult for books and the natural wish to share this pleasure. If these are present, then an adult can establish a reading guidance relationship with students even without a formal program. Any adult who listens to a student talk about books she is reading and is ready with suggestions for more good reading at appropriate times is offering reading guidance.

Reading Patterns: What to Expect

As they grow from preschoolers to high school seniors, from nonreaders to independent and voluntary readers and perhaps even to mature readers, children's interest in reading as a leisure activity ebbs and flows in predictable patterns. Through research in children's reading, we also see a clear pattern in the types of literature and topics that appeal at different ages, so that it is possible to say, for example, that students in the early grades enjoy fairy tales, while sixth graders prefer mysteries.

The best way to learn what any child likes to read is to ask, but a direct question may not elicit clear information. A bit of probing may be necessary. What does he do with his leisure time? What are his favorite television programs? What was the last good book he read? Forming his own reading interests is part of each child's learning who he is, and that takes time. The third grader doesn't have a complete answer to questions about what she likes to read. The ninth grader will, and if she is lucky enough to have been introduced to a variety of good books and has had some intelligent, perceptive reading guidance, her answer will include good adult literature.

When using an informal interview to determine a child's reading interests, it is important to remember that he cannot be interested in literature he hasn't been introduced to yet. It does not mean much if a fourth grader says that he doesn't like fantasy if he hasn't read or heard anything that he recognizes as fantasy. It is necessary to learn not only what he has enjoyed, but also what kinds of books he has in his background.

As children grow older, the reading interests of boys and girls diverge as one would expect, with girls more responsive to relationships and boys to facts. Boys in the primary grades (kindergarten through grade two) prefer nonfiction, while girls prefer fiction, although boys are more flexible—more willing to try fiction than girls are to try nonfiction (Langerman, 1990). The greatest gender difference is evident between ages 10 and 13, when boys want action, adventure, and sports, while girls read fantasy, animal stories, and stories about people (Haynes, 1988).

Reading studies have shown this divergence for a long time, fostering the belief that while girls would read "boys' books" (books in which boys are the main characters), boys would not read "girls' books." However, teachers who read girls' books to a class—Jean Fritz' *Homesick: My Story*, Jane Langton's *The Fledgling*, or Avi's *The True Confessions of Charlotte Doyle*, for example— report that boys and girls sustain interest equally well. Building on this response, teachers and parents may encourage some boys to read on their own some of the fine literature about girls. Adults choosing books to use for discussion with gifted children should not worry too much about the gender of the main character.

Preschool

Because few school districts provide programs for gifted preschoolers, the characteristics and needs of these children are not as carefully documented as those of school age children. Yet more people are becoming aware of their special needs—and of the immense importance of reading and talking about books to preschoolers.

Recent research indicates that between the ages of one and a half and four years, children's brains are especially open to learning language (Clark, 1997). During this time they gain language skills more easily than they ever will again. It is a critical period for parents to provide rich language experiences for their child by talking directly to him and reading aloud. This is especially so for unusually bright and curious children who respond eagerly to the stimulation and the exposure to new ideas that reading aloud can provide.

Nothing in a preschooler's life can quite match the warmth of being held and read to, and if the one who is reading loves not only the child but also the literature and the experience of sharing it, so much richer are both reader and child. Since the child's attention span is short at this age, it is best if there can be several brief "story hours" a day.

It is impossible to overemphasize the importance of reading aloud to children of any age, but especially to preschoolers. Any parent who doubts this, or who cannot find time for reading aloud, should read *Babies Need Books* (Butler, 1998), an eloquent statement of the pleasures and advantages of growing up in a family where reading aloud is valued. Butler can make a believer of anyone, and she gives plenty of suggestions for books to help those unfamiliar with children's literature.

Numerous studies document the fact that children who are read to as preschoolers are better prepared for learning to read when they enter school. Since their language skills are superior, they are prepared to do well in any area that depends on language, and what area does not? Some parents read to their preschoolers specifically to build language and pre-reading skills. Books such as *Reading Begins at Home* (Butler & Clay, 1991) and *Straight Talk about Reading* (Hall & Moats, 1999) offer suggestions for pre-reading activities.

In addition, parents may read to their preschoolers simply to enrich the children's store of knowledge. An ever-increasing supply of information books for young children makes this an easy project, one that is sure to interest the parents as well as the child. In the process, the child learns that books are an infinitely varied source of fascinating information. Good nonfiction for preschoolers offers text only as a starting point and invites discussion: children asking questions, parents answering, and vice versa. Parents should feel free to depart from the text and talk about details on each page. How does the machinery run? Why are they doing this? Let's draw a picture of what is not on the page. Gail Gibbons' books, such as *Farming*, offer an example: How does the hay arrive through the door in the haymow on the second floor of the barn? Draw the exterior view, with the elevator.

But a more fundamental reason for making time to read to a preschool youngster, several times a day if possible, is to instill the sense that reading is a source of pleasure. By sitting with a child, cuddling, enjoying a good story and lovely illustrations, talking about the pictures and characters and imagining what would happen if this child were in the story or had the same choices to make, adults lay the foundations for a lifetime of reading for pleasure and information. Reading at its best, even for adults, is an emotional response to the art of literature. The openness to the emotional response begins here, in a loving environment, when the child's imagination is most accessible and flexible. Children who miss books at this age will never be able to make up entirely for the loss, because never again will they be so receptive.

In addition to having loving adults who enjoy reading to them, preschoolers should attend a library story hour where they can experience literature with other children. The children's librarian knows the range of children's literature and understands how to make it live. Skilled librarians use music, puppets, and storytelling as well as reading aloud, and they involve the children as participants, making the literature an immediate experience.

This approach is perfect for toddlers, who are delighted with the sheer joy of language and who respond well to cumulative tales such as "The House that Jack Built" or the nonsense syllables in Mother Goose or the rhythms in Dr. Seuss. For three- and four-year-olds, stories that allow the children to join in the repetition are favorites, as are books without words that allow them to tell the story themselves.

For content, young preschoolers enjoy stories with simple plots about everyday experiences and about "things that go," such as trucks, trains, and cars. They like stories with talking animals or toys, or with characters their own age. Older preschoolers are ready to begin hearing tales from folklore, such as "The Three Billy Goats Gruff," "The Little Red Hen," and "The Gingerbread Boy," and they are eager listeners to anyone who will read from the rich trove of nonfiction available for them.

Teaching preschoolers to read. Some gifted children of this age teach themselves to read, often to the alarm of parents who have been told not to push. If the children have indeed only been encouraged and not forced, but have learned spontaneously from being read to and asking questions about letters and words on signs, there is no cause for alarm. As many parents have learned, there is not much a parent can do to prevent a child from teaching herself to read if she is ready.

The harder question is whether parents should respond to the obvious interest of a gifted child by teaching him to read. This is one of the unresolved issues in education—teaching preschoolers to read is frowned upon by some educators and encouraged by others. Clark (1997, p. 120-121) goes so far as to write, "I am convinced that reading is a natural, happy event if introduced during this...period [18 months to four years of age]. What we do at 6 years of age may be remedial reading." While she is not suggesting that parents engage in formal teaching, she goes on to say that:

> if allowed the opportunity to play with words, if read to or shown any of the ways letters can be used to represent sound, children find their own way to learn. In an environment that responds *as the children direct* [emphasis mine], that is rich in good language experiences, children enjoy learning in their own way. Learning to read is no exception.

The parent of a gifted child may reason that knowing how to read could keep the child occupied in school while the teacher works with slower learners, preventing the disruptive behavior that accompanies boredom. Certainly, it is difficult to withhold information from a child who clamors for it.

A mother who reluctantly admits that she taught her two children to read when they were three and four recently asked her younger son, now in college, how he felt about his reading lessons at the time. His

> *surprising answer was that it was confidence-building for him, not because he would start school already reading, but because the time she spent teaching him was proof that "I was worth being taught to read." For him, learning to read was a rite of passage, a welcome into the circle of his reading family.*

It is possible for parents to teach their own gifted children to read without undue pushing. The question to answer before making this decision is that of motivation: Are the parents truly hoping to meet the child's need, or is a secret need of their own being met? For most parents, answering this question honestly will require some soul searching. One clue to parental need is this: Have they imagined telling a friend or relative that Jennifer is now reading? The brief pleasure of that conversation is surely not worth risking the possibility of turning reading into a chore for Jennifer.

Yet even when parents conclude that their motives are pure, if they then begin to teach their child to read, they should continue to monitor their own behavior. Lessons should be very brief, and if there is any hint of impatience or stridency in their voices or in the child's, they should stop.

Sensible guidance is available in *Reading Begins at Home*, by Butler and Clay (1991). Pointing out the importance of parental sensitivity to any anxiety on their part or their child's, Butler and Clay suggest a method of teaching that can be used by parents who decide it is appropriate for their family. Another book, *Straight Talk about Reading*, by Hall and Moats (1999), urges parents to prepare preschoolers for reading instruction by going beyond the alphabet song to promoting letter recognition and phonemic awareness, so that the child recognizes the separate speech sounds in a word. Although the goal is *preparation* for learning to read in school, rather than teaching preschoolers to read, some children may learn to read before they begin school with this much instruction at home.

Joy is the only really good criterion for judging the value of preschool reading lessons at home. Is there joy in doing it for the child and the parents? If not, it would be better not to bother. Continue to enjoy reading aloud, continue weekly trips to the library, and wait for nature to take its course.

Early Elementary (Grades K-2)

These are the years when most children learn to read—that is, learn the techniques of interpreting the words on a page. As they gain reading skills in the classroom, they eagerly come to the library. A group of first or second graders swarms over the shelves of easy-to-read books. They select a wide range of books, some of which they can read themselves but most of which they will have to find an adult to read. Whatever the library's limit on books per child, they will come to the circulation desk with that number or more.

As they become independent readers, they become more selective. They learn to use the "five finger test," reading a page and putting one finger down for each word they do not know. If by the end of the page fewer than five fingers are down, probably the book is close enough to their reading level for comfort. They begin to recognize authors' names and may want to read all of the Encyclopedia Brown books or everything written by Beverly Cleary.

Gifted children, and those most enthusiastic about reading, often become independent readers earlier than most. When they do, they should have free access to books at their reading level in the school library. If library policy limits access to the collection by grade level, the policy should bend as soon as students are ready for more challenging books. It was a proud day when a second grader in such a school came home to announce, "I can read chapter books now!" He was finally, and appropriately, allowed to walk past the picture books to where the chapter books were kept, although not every child in his class had achieved this level of reading expertise.

As they become independent readers, primary children choose realistic animal and nature stories as well as adventure and mystery. They continue to enjoy folklore of increasing complexity, and they love fairy tales, especially at about third grade.

Their enthusiasm for the library story hour is undiminished, and as important as it is for parents to continue to read aloud at home, it is also important for teachers to find time to read aloud daily to the class. One primary teacher greets the children as they return from their library time and selects one book that has been checked out for immediate reading to the entire class. Then, all the children have quiet time to read their library books. These children look forward to library hour as one of the most important times of the week.

Upper Elementary (Grades 3 – 5)

A surge in reading begins at about fourth grade and carries through into middle school. Most children's reading is done between fourth and sixth or seventh grade, and these few years are vital in forming the reading patterns that will continue in adulthood. If at this time they have access to good books, time to read, and an enthusiastic adult, gifted children in particular have an excellent chance of joining that fortunate group of adults whose lives are immeasurably enriched by the pleasure they find in reading.

By third or fourth grade, readers have usually identified their favorite authors and ask for their books in the library. Most young readers become interested in fantasy and science fiction at this age, often introduced to it through C. S. Lewis's Narnia series or, more recently, through the Harry Potter books. A few children at this age begin to show an interest in biographies or historical fiction. One study (Swanton, 1984) indicates that gifted students are more likely than their classmates to select fantasy, science fiction, and history.

By the fifth grade, the reading habit is becoming well fixed. Fifth graders may add the Greek and Roman myths and the legends of King Arthur and Robin Hood to their list of interests.

Adventure, mystery, and fantasy remain on the list for gifted and average students alike.

Problem novels. At this late elementary stage, children begin to read contemporary realistic fiction, including the "problem novels"—books about problems they or their friends may be experiencing. There are books for this age group about young people coping with physical or mental disability, divorce, drugs, aging, and death, as well as books that deal with the typical questions and concerns of growing up—finding friends, moving through puberty, and developing a sense of one's own identity. An excellent source for such reading is *The Best of Bookfinder* (Dreyer, 1992), which lists books for children and young adults, summarized and cross-referenced according to topic and feelings exemplified in the books' stories.

Young people know that they can read about someone their age coping with problems they themselves face, and this may cause gifted students to turn more readily to books for an understanding of difficulties related to being gifted. Ironically, however, there is some evidence that gifted students do not perceive books as a source of problem solving as much as average students do (Martin, 1984). It is possible that because they choose books at a higher reading level, they don't see those that deal with the problems of people their own age. Reading guidance can point them to useful books that they would otherwise miss.

Unfortunately, some gifted children lose interest in reading as a leisure activity sometime during these years (Martin, 1984). There seem to be two major reasons for this. One is that some youngsters become deeply involved in computers, video games, or sports and do not want to spend time reading; the other is that gifted students may resent being forced to read material not of their own choice. They want "interesting" and "exciting" reading, and their opinion of what is interesting and exciting often does not coincide with the material found in elementary reading texts.

For this reason, a literature-based reading curriculum emphasizes reading from a collection of trade books so students can choose. Open-ended assignments encourage them to read books and also allow them some choice, and reading guidance to help students find appropriate books can also help. The freedom to choose their reading, even if within a group of books pre-selected by an adult, adds greatly to their motivation to read.

For those who are drawn from reading to computers or sports, it's a good idea to suggest books about these topics, so that reading can complement their areas of major interest rather than compete with them. And it is still important, difficult as it may be, for the teacher to find time in the school day to read aloud and for the students to read silently.

Middle School (Grades 6-8)

At the beginning of this period, youngsters may still be at the peak of interest in reading, exploring every field of literature. By the end of it, however, other activities and interests take over, and many young people find less time for unassigned, leisure reading. What happens to young adolescents in other aspects of their lives occurs in their reading lives too—they are leaving childhood and the literature appropriate to it. They move to the Young Adult section in bookstores and libraries, perhaps looking for genre fiction and reading only romance or only fantasy (Herald, 1997).

At this age, boys are less flexible than girls in their reading choices. They will read about female characters as long as the plot provides suspenseful action in an outdoor setting. Girls prefer internal action focused on what a character thinks and feels, not just on what she does, and they are willing to experiment with a wider range of reading (Carlsen, 1980).

Although reading tapers off for most students in these years, gifted students are more likely to continue reading avidly. One study (Carter, 1982), designed specifically to determine leisure reading interests of gifted students at this age, reports that the gifted students read more than twice as much as the students in the control group, choosing more science fiction and fantasy, fewer problem novels, and a wider range of historical fiction than students in the comparison group. Of the students in the study, only the gifted showed the pattern of moving toward reading adult fiction; this shift began to occur at the end of the eighth grade.

As middle school gifted students come to grips with their differences from others, reading begins to serve social and psychological needs as well as academic needs. Although they are *able* now to read adult literature, Baskin (1998) suggests that they may still need to read about people their own age. She points out that as reading interests mature, advanced readers may select books on the same topics average readers choose, but with more sophisticated treatment—and they may seek not only novels, but also drama, poetry, biography, and autobiography.

As they begin the transition to adult literature, young people need reading guidance more than at any other time. Perhaps surprisingly, gifted students are no more skilled than others at selecting excellent literature without adult help. Girls are likely to discover the more simplistic, sentimentalized romantic adult novels, while boys tend toward sensationalized, violent adventure. Without direction, they may never find the superb adult literature that can fill their present need for romance and adventure, while at the same time developing their taste for good literature. If they don't learn the difference between sentimental or sensational novels and good literature at this age, chances are slim that they will eventually develop into mature readers. Adults guiding them can use both the fiction and nonfiction that is available for this age group.

Fiction. Although they are very important for middle school readers, novels written for and about young adults may be overlooked for a surprising reason: many teachers have little knowledge of this fast-growing body of literature (Samuels, 1998). Young adult literature has been an important genre for decades, but college students preparing to teach English, studying the classics of the English language, may never have a course in young adult literature. Therefore, English classes for middle school and high school students—especially for advanced readers—are more likely to focus on the classics. The protagonists may be in their teen years, but the issues are not those of teens today. Samuels suggests using young adult novels to help students develop into lifelong readers, and introducing classics later on.

In doing so, she echoes the advice of middle school teacher Susan Rakow (1991), who notes that gifted adolescents experience the same emotional and social problems that their peers do. Rakow presses for the use of young-adult literature to help them understand and discuss their experiences, yet points out that honors courses frequently offer them only the classics, cutting them off from the opportunities for self-discovery that are made available to their classmates. "When teachers and parents discourage gifted adolescents from reading young-adult novels, they fail in their responsibility to provide appropriate reading guidance," she writes (p. 49).

Earlier, Carlsen (1980, p. 34) put it succinctly this way: "Accelerating the intelligent child by giving him or her the adult classics of literature will not increase enjoyment of reading." The classics should not be ignored entirely, of course—but neither should they be overdone with young students. In the middle school years, mixing a few classics with several young adult novels would be advisable, leaving heavier use of classic literature for the later senior high years.

Nonfiction. Nonfiction is far more important to middle school readers than teachers have recognized, according to Carter and Abrahamson (1998). Not only do these young readers choose to read nonfiction for pleasure, they need plenty of experience with it to prepare for standardized tests, which require skill in interpreting expository prose rather than fiction material.

These authors show that the range of nonfiction topics middle school students choose is as diverse as the range for adults—and there is a wealth of nonfiction books available to them. As with fiction, the problem with nonfiction is one of choosing the best among the abundance that is available. Chapter 6 offers some suggestions for guidance.

In seeking suitable literature, parents who homeschool their children would do well to read the articles cited above: Baskin on gifted readers, Samuels on young adult novels, and Carter and Abrahamson on nonfiction for middle school youngsters. Their next step would certainly be a trip to the library to follow up on the suggestions of these experienced teachers.

Senior High (Grades 9-12)

At some point in the senior high years, students leave the YA (Young Adult) section and move to adult reading. Their interests are unsurprising: mysteries, science fiction and fantasy, biographies of celebrities, and how-to books. Escapist reading helps them deal with the angst of this time in their lives, believes Herald (1997). But they also glean suggestions for books to read from parents and friends, from book covers and movie-related titles, and by following favorite authors (Milliot, 1998).

As they grow older, their interests will become so individualized that general statements no longer apply. Anyone hoping to guide or influence their reading will have to know them as individuals, and know their reading background as well.

For some, their motivation is likely to be related to their interest in philosophical issues and their attempts to formulate their own opinions and value systems. For gifted high schoolers, this may raise special considerations that are discussed in Chapter 4 under "Goals of Bibliotherapy with Gifted Students."

Senior high readers prefer protagonists who are making the same transition they face, from adolescence to adulthood; they are not interested in books with middle-aged characters, but do enjoy stories about the elderly, who face some of their problems: a changing peer group and adjustment to physical and mental changes (Carlsen, 1980).

Some senior high students, serious about preparing for college beyond their high school courses, become interested in reading more of the classics on their own. If such a student is fortunate enough to work with a mentor who possesses a broad knowledge of books as well as a sympathetic understanding of the student, this can be an extremely rewarding endeavor.

Another approach for these intellectually curious students is provided by *Reading Lists for College-Bound Students* (Estell, Satchwell, & Wright, 2000). This book gathers suggested reading lists from over 100 colleges—lists of classics the colleges would like their first-year students to have read before they arrive on campus. Reading these books ahead of time is not required, but it does provide a background to give new students a head start on college assignments.

In my work as an educational consultant, I recommend that students work with *Reading Lists for College-Bound Students* during their high school summers. One reason is that it provides some information about the colleges. For example, the list for each college is introduced with comments about reading requirements on that campus. For some colleges, the authors also include essay questions from the application that draw on the applicant's response to literature.

In addition, the book offers help with planning a serious reading program. Rather than assuming anyone will try to read all of the books on even one college's list, the authors provide suggestions for creating a personal reading list. To help with this project, one chapter lists the 10 most-recommended authors and the 100 most-recommended works. As an aid to purposeful reading, there is a section on keeping a reading diary. Finally, recognizing that not every college-bound student is a potential literature major, the authors provide titles related to majors in a variety of subjects—science, political science, business, the fine arts, and others. The list for those planning to take Advanced Placement English is a good pre-college reading list in itself.

For the most fortunate, the reading experience at this age is one of long, leisurely discovery. In the autobiographical book *Self-Consciousness*, John Updike (1989, p. 109) writes, "...certain kinds of novels, especially 19th-century novels, should be read in adolescence, on those dreamily endless solitary afternoons that in later life become so uselessly short and full of appointments, or they will never be read at all."

Special Characteristics of Gifted Readers

Alison, a nine-year-old growing up in a Midwestern university town, exemplifies the characteristics of gifted readers (Swinger, 1989, p. 51):

> *Alison read before she entered kindergarten, and according to school and home records she read at least 73 books in the third grade, including* Little Women. *She has also read* Charlotte's Web, Anne of Green Gables, Peter Pan, Heidi, *and* Alice's Adventures in Wonderland, *most of them recommended to her by her mother or a teacher.*

> *Alison looks for books by her favorite authors: Patricia MacLachlan, Patricia Reilly Giff, and L. M. Montgomery. When she discovered the Babysitters Club Series, she read several in a row, then immediately reread* Charlotte's Web.

> *At school she reads constantly, even during math and spelling tests.*

> *Everyone in Alison's family reads, including all the grandparents and her great-grandmother, who uses talking books for the blind. Alison still enjoys having bedtime stories read to her, and she sometimes reads the bedtime story to her younger brother. She "appears to belong to that group of people for whom reading is as natural and necessary as breathing."*

Only a few studies, including those mentioned under the age groupings above, consider the points at which gifted readers differ from the average, but they provide information that may apply equally to intellectually curious children, whether or not they are identified as gifted.

Gifted children read earlier, better, and more than most children. In what they choose to read, however, differences are not so great. Gifted youngsters read a greater variety of books, and they may be more adventurous in exploring different types of literature, but in general, their reading interests closely parallel those of other children their age. For example, Hawkins (1983) found that in the upper elementary years, gifted girls prefer biography, fairy tales, and animal stories, while gifted boys prefer science and science fiction. They want to read about the same subjects as other students do, although the specific books they read may vary.

Gifted children read three or four times as many books as most children, and some continue to do a great deal of reading after the time when children's reading typically tapers off (Russell, 1961; Whitehead, 1984).

> When Gretta was in fifth and sixth grades, she typically read a book each day. In junior high, reading longer and more demanding books, her reading diminished to an average of three books a week. Now in senior high, when most of her friends find no time for unassigned reading, Gretta still reads a book every week or two; in the summer she systematically lists the books she plans to read, and she finds time to read 16 to 20 adult books in addition to working.

Recent studies of the reading interests of gifted children—especially gifted high school students—are rare. However, Romey (2000) interviewed eight gifted girls in an Alabama high school, grades 9-12, about their reading patterns. These girls preferred historical romance, mystery/horror, and science fiction; of primary importance to them was fiction with a strong female character. In interviews, they discussed how being avid readers set them apart from their classmates, so that the opportunity to talk with others who enjoyed reading was validating in itself.

A summary of reading patterns of gifted youngsters indicates the importance of guiding their reading early and consistently, as:

➤ they may teach themselves to read before they start school;

➤ whether or not they are reading in kindergarten, they are probably independent readers by second grade at the latest;

➤ by third grade, they may have identified their favorite authors;

➤ by fifth grade, the habit of reading is well established, if it is going to be;

➤ by sixth grade, their reading may diminish if they are among the many gifted youngsters who become involved in sports, computers, or video games;

➤ by eighth grade, extracurricular reading may well have disappeared for some, although it may reappear later;

➤ others spend extraordinary amounts of time reading, but need guidance to identify good literature; and,

➤ capable of reading sophisticated literature, they have the potential to gain a great deal from the best books if they are directed to them.

For the adult who works with such children, reading guidance is especially rewarding, because the children are likely to respond with great enthusiasm and develop a close relationship with the adult who talks about books with them.

Reading Aloud

When their children learn to read, parents should give some family reading time over to hearing the children read aloud—but they should also continue reading aloud to children.

Unhappily, most parents stop this practice by the time youngsters are eight or nine. In November of 1992, the Associated Press reported the findings of a study by the American Federation of

Teachers: soon after parents stopped reading aloud, their children began to spend more hours in front of the television set. The study showed that 52% of parents read daily to children under eight, but only 13% continued to read every day to children aged nine to 14—and that children under 10 spent more time reading than watching television, while older children reversed these priorities.

In addition to promoting a continued interest in reading, parents who read aloud can introduce their children to literature they might not find on their own, such as classic children's stories, folklore, poetry, and mythology.

Children will happily listen to adults read not only more advanced literature than they can read themselves, but also books they can read but would not choose. Slower-paced books of real quality lend themselves to reading aloud. *Old Ramon*, by Jack Schaefer, is a quiet book about a wealthy boy's relationship with a shepherd as they take the sheep to the high ground one summer— a trip arranged by the boy's father precisely so he could learn from the wise, unlettered older man. This is not initially an exciting book, and children who want adventure will not choose to read it themselves; however, fifth graders will sit silently day after day and listen, coming to love the book and to identify with the boy, and they will be sorry to have the story end.

The story hour at home remains important for the warmth provided by the luxury of reading in a frenetic world, and it can answer a crucial need: unhurried, quiet time for reflection. The longer parents keep up the tradition of story hour, the better— both for the quality of family life and for the intellectual development of their children. Some families continue reading aloud until the children are in middle school. How much would have been missed if they had stopped when the children learned to read!

Books listing literature for reading aloud (and suggestions for choosing books especially for this purpose) include *More Books Kids Will Sit Still For* (Freeman, 1995), and *The Read-Aloud Handbook* (Trelease, 1995).

Avid Readers and Resistant Readers

As readers, gifted children can be considered in two groups: those who pick up a book in their free time, and those who find something else to do. Members of the first group seem to have copious reading as a life goal. Reading comes naturally to them, and when tasks must come first, they feel distracted and annoyed. Those in the second group usually *can* read quite adequately (unless there is a learning disability); they simply do not choose to read *much*.

Avid Readers

Voracious in the pursuit of books, avid readers often keep several going at once.

> *For a period of several years, Kevin could be traced through the house by the open books spread face down on the floor of each room he had left. He exemplifies those who learn early how to use the local library and the school library, becoming personal friends of the librarians who, in turn, are delighted with such enthusiastic patrons.*

Such children may read with amazing speed and comprehension, or they may pore over a passage, savoring the beauty of words. They know how to skim and when to study. These are often the early readers, teaching themselves before they start school or being taught by parents who respond to their interest.

In working with avid gifted readers, there are three potential problems: the impulse of some children to read books that are emotionally too advanced for them; the challenge of finding books at the right level, both emotionally and intellectually; and the child who reads too much.

Reading too far ahead. It is important to remember that "read" in the early stages can mean something closer to "decode"— children can understand the words, pronounce most of them, and glean meaning from the sentences and paragraphs. They may be able to read a book of a hundred or more pages and summarize the story at a time when most of their classmates are still reading early readers with controlled vocabularies. But even avid young readers are probably not emotionally ready to comprehend what they read—to understand the symbolism, or grasp everything the author says about human relationships.

Some children push themselves, or are pushed by their perception of the pride others take in their reading, to read whatever they can decode before they have developed the emotional readiness to comprehend. Then they may later not read a book when they are emotionally ready for it because they have already "read" it. They do not realize, of course, that it would be an entirely different experience for them at the right time. Such children in the sixth grade sometimes choose books normally read by third graders, perhaps trying to catch up on what they missed three years ago, when they were in such a hurry.

> *Seven-year-old Yun-Fei is reading at the sixth grade level. Therefore, she can read* The Witch of Blackbird Pond. *While she can follow the story line and answer fact questions about the plot, Yun-Fei is not ready to understand why the old Quaker woman who lives at the pond is feared as a witch, nor can she appreciate the courage shown by Nat and Kit in befriending her.*

Children like Yun-Fei, especially those who know how proud their parents are of their reading ability, need guidance to help them find appropriate reading. In some cases, it seems that more than anything else, they need permission not to stretch too far— permission to enjoy the books that are appropriate for their level of emotional development.

Finding the right books. The resulting problem for the guiding adult is to know what books to suggest. It is without doubt a challenge to find a book for a second grader who reads at the sixth grade level. In general, it seems best to match fiction with his emotional level, while guiding him toward nonfiction at his reading level.

> *In the second grade, Doug is reading Mary Norton's* The Borrowers, *E. B. White's* Trumpet of the Swan, *and George Selden's* The Cricket in Times Square. *At the same time, he is pursuing his interest in computers and lasers by reading books on these topics written for middle school children. By the time he is in the upper elementary grades, he will be able to find more challenging fiction.*

Good sources for recommendations of intellectually challenging books are *Books for the Gifted Child* (Baskin & Harris, 1980; Volume 2, Nelson & Hauser, 1988) and books listed under "Drive to Understand" in Chapter 8 of this book.

Reading too much. A third concern for those who work with gifted readers is to recognize that constant and prolific reading may not always be desirable. Occasionally, the motive is not thirst for information or deep interest in fiction, but simply the need of a gifted child to fill time he would prefer to spend playing with neighborhood children—if only he knew how to be accepted.

It is best to respond to this situation positively. The child should not be told he is reading too much or playing with others too little, but he should subtly and persistently be led to increase time with other children to achieve a better balance. It's quite likely that this child sees himself as a "reader"—that is, "I am a reader" is a positive part of his self-concept. Anything that makes him feel guilty about the time he spends reading may convince him that reading is somehow wrong; he may also begin to believe that he himself is not quite acceptable as the reader he is. In other words, no connection should be made between time spent with other children and time spent reading. Each should be valued independently.

How much is too much time spent reading? That varies with the child. Those who tend toward introversion may spend more time alone than adults anticipate—and they enjoy it. Remembering that reading is a productive and restorative way to spend time alone, parents and teachers must determine how much is appropriate for an individual child. Their evaluation should be based on how much time she spends with other children, how content she seems to be with herself, and how happily she spends time alone. If reading is an escape because interpersonal skills are lacking or because of depression or fear, then some intervention—perhaps professional—should be considered.

However, in our socially oriented society, it is quite possible that adults are overly zealous to see children relate to others. If a child relates well with other children when she does play with them and seems happy with herself in general, then it probably should not be of great concern if she spends less time with other children than adults think is necessary.

Resistant Readers

Some highly intelligent and able children simply don't choose to spend their leisure time reading. They may be quite capable of reading to gain information, and they certainly have the potential for success in college and career, but they aren't people who enjoy literature as an art form. In the long run, this is no more alarming than the fact that some children never learn to enjoy music or dance or theater, or participate in sports or cooking. No matter how much we want our children to be well-rounded, they retain the right to develop their own interests. All we can do is expose them to the world around them and then accept the total package the child represents—without unduly imposing our values upon them as we watch them make their choices.

Nevertheless, in the short run, it is to the child's advantage to read—both to hone the skill and for the vast amount of information he can gain. Therefore, adults should avoid the tendency to view the middle-grade child—and to allow him to see himself—

as a non-reader. It may help to understand what is going on if adults recognize that the roots for his resistance to reading may have been established long ago, in the preschool years, especially if an older sibling has pre-empted the reading role.

Consider the plight of the two- or three-year-old younger child growing up in a reading family. It is known, of course, that parents who are readers are good models for their children. Children growing up in homes where reading is valued are more likely to be good readers themselves than those in homes where little reading is done. But for this child, whose older siblings are also reading, there is a negative side: everyone in her world takes pleasure from an activity not yet available to her, inevitably ignoring her in the process. Frequent read-aloud sessions can only partially atone for this, and if the older children read when she wants to play with them—as they will if they are avid readers—it seems natural that she will resent reading to some degree. She learns to capitalize on what she *can* do, and so may begin her self-image as one who *does* rather than one who reads. Regardless of this child's ability to read by the time she is a third grader, the doer identity will have had a significant head start over the reader identity, and the reader may never catch up.

> *Jessica's parents and her older brother, Michael, had open books in every room. She, too, was included in the reading orgy, having been read to in the womb and the crib long before she could pick out her own books in the library. But if she wanted Michael to play with her, his invariable response was, "Jessica, I'm* READing*." When she wanted her mother's attention, it was, "When I'm through with this chapter," and Dad's was an absent-minded, "That's nice, dear," as he turned a page.*
>
> *So Jessica began to draw. Her wallpaper still shows evidence of her early interest in art. Then she turned to clay and from there, as a teenager, to beads.*

While her family read, she sat among them working with tiny crystals and wires. Her giftedness found its outlet in the handiwork of her fingers as she created beautiful, intricate designs for necklaces and earrings. At 20, she has already sold her work at local art fairs and has planned a career in jewelry design. While she enjoys reading, she spends leisure time with beads, not books.

Jessica is proof that gifted nonreaders can be productive and happy. Nonetheless, because reading is such an important skill for success in school, it is important that adults in reading families not give up on their young children as potential readers, particularly during the peak reading period in the elementary grades.

At school. Because some bright children who do not choose to read in leisure time are conscientious about completing assignments, it is critical that teachers include full books in the curriculum as well as fragments of literature. If this is not happening, it may help if parents ask the teacher to do what they cannot do at home—assign a book.

The assignment may be all the incentive necessary, and it need not add to the teacher's burden. A simple notebook for recording titles of books read may be enough to keep them going if the teacher has no time for reading logs or more elaborate book-reporting procedures; in fact, this is something that not every child in the class would have to do. The book assignments should be free choice, from a list of recommended titles for quality control. Suggestions for the list can come from the school librarian, from Chapter 8 in this book, from Silverman and Lovecky's list (1993) of books featuring gifted children, or from *Books for the Gifted Child*, Volume 2 (Nelson & Hauser, 1988).

There are many ways for a teacher, with the help of the school librarian, to bring children's literature into the classroom. However, when there are too many children but not enough time to meet the pressing curriculum requirements in every subject, literature may seem like a luxury. In these classrooms, it is especially important that reading be assigned to resistant but competent readers.

At home. Parents can also gently build reading time into the family's schedule. One common way of doing this is to set bedtime a half-hour earlier than necessary, with optional reading time. Limiting television is commendable for a variety of reasons; reading at bedtime is an excellent substitute. Many more suggestions for working with resistant readers are found in *The Magic Bookshelf* (Jarvis & Jarvis, 1999).

If parents are aware of the child's reading—occasionally reading one of his books and talking with him about it, asking his opinion, and listening well—he will benefit in several ways. He will begin to think of himself not only as a reader, but as one who can respond to books and make judgments about them, judgments that others value. Parents usually find themselves truly enjoying children's books, giving the child something of importance to share with them. Most important, books can become a bridge for more real communication than would otherwise occur. The elementary years are the ideal time to build these bridges— they will be needed in the adolescent years!

Finally, parents as well as teachers can help keep gifted children from prematurely deciding that they do not enjoy reading by continuing to read aloud.

Older resistant readers. As these children reach middle school, they may yet begin to enjoy reading, even if not as much as avid readers do. It will help if reading continues to be assigned. When these youngsters understand that a background in literature is part of a good education, some highly motivated and curious students, whether avid readers or not, will read from lists of classics or suggested pre-college reading during the summers simply to gain that background. Some will not turn to reading until even later—her mother reports that Jessica (the beadworking artist mentioned earlier) is now, as a young adult, reading Dostoevski.

Some children will never be avid readers, and those of us whose business or interest it is to push books will do better if we can accept that gracefully. They can grow into happy, productive adults anyway, and there is nothing to be gained if they feel guilty about their lack of interest in reading. If our goal is simply their joy in the literature that we have been able to introduce to them, and if we achieve that, it is enough.

Mature Readers

Gifted and intellectually curious children have an opportunity to develop into what is known as a "mature reader." Mature readers consider reading an integral part of life. It is not something they do only to relax or to escape or if there is nothing good on television. It is something they plan for in each day, and if the day develops so that they have no time for it, they may become restless, rather like joggers who miss their run. Some—busy parents, for example—stay up late at night to read their daily quota after the house is quiet, acknowledging that having balance in their lives is more dependent on reading time than on sleep.

The time spent reading each day may not be measurable in hours, especially for individuals leading active family and professional lives; however, the reading material will be carefully chosen with a long-range goal in mind, if only vaguely so. Reading will be a fairly important part of their pursuit of needs or interests they have identified, and the material they read will be appropriate to that pursuit.

Mature readers read about a variety of subjects, but with particular depth and perception in one or more interest areas. The gender gap has closed by now, and individual interests predominate. Seen as a tool for individual growth, their reading is purposeful, not random or accidental.

Reading is enjoyed not only for the characterization and story line of a novel or the information gained from well-chosen nonfiction, but also for the aesthetic pleasure found in language presented as the art form it can be. Mature readers may read slowly, savoring sentence structure and descriptive passages. While not everything they read is written on a high level, much of it is, and their competence in the skill of reading is superior at all levels.

Among mature readers, differing patterns emerge, reflecting personalities and life stages. A 16-year-old who would begin his freshman year in college in the fall showed his idiosyncratic tastes in his summer reading list. Not following any of the college-bound lists but pursuing reading that he had not had time to complete in a shortened high school career, he read *The Idiot*, *1984*, *Jude the Obscure*, *Tom Jones*, *Tales of the Mabinogi*, *The Journey through Wales* and *The Description of Wales* by Gerald of Wales, *Macbeth*, and Bulfinch's *The Age of Chivalry* and *The Legends of Charlemagne.*

An older but less focused reader, a graduate student in anthropology, wrote a series of letters to his sister and brother-in-law, both medical students, during a period when he was deliberately expanding his reading range:

> "Perhaps I could pursue [French] as a form of personal entertainment [rather than as a course of study]. My other three courses are extremely interesting to me, so I spend a lot of time reading related books and articles, recommended by the professor or those I find on my own. If I only stuck to the course syllabus, I'd have enough time for French, etc....

> "In this week's *U.S. News and World Report* is a biographical article on an architectural historian, Vincent Scully.... He recently published *Architecture: The Natural and the Manmade*.... I mention it in case architecture is/becomes one of your reading interests.

> "I'm excited that you find *The Limits of Art* useful. Though it is often quickly buried beneath a pile of

other books and papers in my room, it is never 'lost.' I always know where it is—unlike most other books I have, excepting the dictionary, of course.

"Thinking about the major influences during the last few years, I realized that several lead back to the bookshelf in [his brother-in-law's] parents' home…. At the time…I was beginning to feel…a rebirth of interest in reading. I spent a couple of nights before falling asleep reading the house copy of T. S. Eliot…. I asked your mother about a book she had called *Good Reading*…. I still occasionally refer to it. Books like *The Limits of Art*…have now assumed some of the responsibility (for older Western lit, anyway)."

A different style of mature reading belongs to the brother-in-law in medical school. Seeking a balance to the daily diet of science, he pursues music avocationally. Without a musical instrument available at present, he has begun a planned program of reading and listening, reading about the structure in Bach's music, for example, and then listening with an informed ear. He also consults an art history text, adding "his" composers to the time line in the book to aid in placing them chronologically in his mind. At one time a resistant reader, he now uses reading systematically, as a tool to enrich his intellectual life.

In a small town near a river known to fly fishermen around the world lived a mature reader in his mid-40s. He gave up an academic career in order to have time for the outdoor activities he loved and found work compatible with a sportsman's schedule. His reading interests encompassed modern fiction, nonfiction, and poetry, and he and his wife belonged to a book club for over 10 years. Books they discussed that were particularly meaningful to him included Moon's *Blue Highways*, Freud's *Future of an Illusion*, Kerouac's *On the Road*, *The Sportswriter* by Richard Ford, Joseph Campbell's *The Power of Myth*, *Christabel* and *This Boy's*

Life (which is annotated in Chapter 8), and *The Last Lion*, the second volume of Manchester's biography of Winston Churchill.

The list reveals the breadth and depth of interests of a thoughtful, open-minded adult—characteristic not only of this fly fisherman, but also of the friends with whom he and his wife met to discuss the books they read. The unexpected existence and longevity of the group in this remote town testifies to the value of reading in an enriched adult life—a possible future for students who list books among their best friends and who may worry that their love of books sets them apart. In the tiny town near the river, a love of books brought friends together.

Furthermore, the concept of mature reading as an adult can be useful in guiding the careers of multi-talented teens. Such gifted students must make a choice among interests, keeping one as a vocation and the others as avocations. It can be easier to give up the full-time pursuit of a favorite interest if one understands that he can continue to follow it through reading. In fact, he may make a career choice partly on the basis of which interests are most accessible through a program of planned and deliberate reading.

Therefore, the possibility of becoming a mature reader should be introduced in high school, so students can consider how to make use of it in their lives. It will be helpful if they realize that mature reading is an acceptable and enjoyable life pattern. With this reassurance, dedicated readers who have reached the age when few of their peers still enjoy leisure reading can avoid any concern about their own continuing interest in books.

References

Baskin, B. (1998). Call me Ishmael: A look at gifted middle school readers. In K. Beers & B. G. Samuels (Eds.), *Into focus: Understanding and creating middle school readers* (pp. 65-79). Norwood, MA: Christopher-Gordon.

Baskin, B. H. & Harris, K. H. (1980). *Books for the gifted child*. New York: Bowker.

Butler, D. (1998). *Babies need books: Sharing the joy of books with our child from birth to six.* (Rev. ed.). Portsmouth, NH: Heinemann.

Butler, D. & Clay, M. (1991). *Reading begins at home: Preparing children for reading before they go to school.* (2nd ed.). Portsmouth, NH: Heinemann.

Carlsen, G. R. (1980). *Books and the teenage reader: A guide for teachers, librarians and parents.* (2nd ed.). New York: Harper & Row.

Carter, B. (1982, Summer). Leisure reading habits of gifted students in a suburban junior high school. *Top of the News, 38*, 312-317.

Carter, B. & Abrahamson, R. F. (1998). Castles to Colin Powell: The truth about nonfiction. In K. Beers & B. G. Samuels (Eds.), *Into focus: Understanding and creating middle school readers* (pp. 313-332). Norwood, MA: Christopher-Gordon.

Clark, B. (1997). *Growing up gifted: Developing the potential of children at home and school.* (5th ed.). Upper Saddle River, NJ: Prentice-Hall.

Dreyer, S. S. (1992). *The best of bookfinder: A guide to children's literature about interests and concerns of youth aged 2-18.* Circle Pines, MN: American Guidance Service.

Estell, D., Satchwell, M. L., & Wright, P. S. (2000). *Reading lists for college-bound students* (3rd ed.). Stamford, CT: Thomson.

Freeman, J. (1995). *More books kids will sit still for: A read-aloud guide.* (2nd ed.). New York: Bowker.

Hall, S. L. & Moats, L.C. (1999). *Straight talk about reading: How parents can make a difference during the early years.* Lincolnwood, IL: Contemporary Books.

Hawkins, S. (1983). Reading interests of gifted children. *Reading Horizons, 24*, 18-22.

Haynes, C. (1988). Explanatory power of content for identifying children's literary preferences. *Dissertation Abstracts International, 49-12A*, p. 1317 (University Microfilms No. DEW8900468).

Herald, D. T. (1997). *Teen genreflecting.* Englewood, CO: Libraries Unlimited.

Jarvis, J. & Jarvis, R. (1999). *The magic bookshelf: A parents' guide to showing growing minds the path to the best children's literature.* Atlanta: Lorica.

Langerman, D. (1990, March). Books and boys: gender preferences and book selection. *School Library Journal,* 132-136.

Martin, C. E. (1984). Why some gifted children do not like to read. *Roeper Review, 7,* 72-75.

Milliot, J. (1998, September 14). PW/BEA survey finds some good news about reading habits. *Publishers Weekly, 245 (37),* 10.

Nelson, G. A. & Hauser, P. (1988). *Books for the gifted child, Volume 2.* New York: Bowker.

Rakow, S. R. (1991, January). Young-adult literature for honors students? *English Journal, 80 (1),* 48-51.

Romey, E. A. (2000). *A study of common themes in reading selections of gifted girls: Implications for bibliotherapy.* Unpublished master's thesis, University of Georgia, Athens.

Russell, D. (1961). *Children learn to read.* Boston: Ginn.

Samuels, B.G. (1998). Creating lifetime readers: A novel idea. In K. Beers & B. G. Samuels (Eds.), *Into focus: Understanding and creating middle school readers* (pp. 347-362). Norwood, MA: Christopher-Gordon.

Silverman, L. K. & Lovecky, D. (1993). Books for children featuring gifted children. In L. K. Silverman (Ed.), *Counseling the gifted and talented* (pp. 337-345). Denver: Love.

Swanton, S. I. (1984, March). Minds alive: What and why gifted students read for pleasure. *School Library Journal, 30,* 99-102.

Swinger, A. K. (1989, Winter). Portrait of a gifted reader: Alison. *Ohio Media Spectrum, 41,* 46-51.

Trelease, J. (1995). *The read-aloud handbook.* (4th ed.). New York: Penguin.

Updike, J. (1989). *Self-consciousness.* New York: Knopf.

Whitehead, R. J. (1984). *A guide to selecting books for children.* Metuchen, NJ: Scarecrow.

Chapter 4

Emotional Development through Books

O n the surface, it often appears that most eager learners have everything going for them and that they can handle any difficulties on their own. They themselves help to perpetuate this myth—they are quick to perceive what is expected of them and to produce it, so that even alert adults may not be aware of these children's specific problems. However, as we know from Chapter 1, gifted children—different, sensitive, and very demanding of themselves—are emotionally vulnerable.

Books—and conversations about them with understanding adults—can become catalysts for helping children recognize and talk about some of the experiences, both joyful and painful, that are part of growing up different—whether that difference is due to giftedness or to unusual intellectual or artistic interests. Such discussions offer adults a low-key method of helping children become aware of the feelings they may encounter as a result of their differences. Reading and discussion can also lead to a new understanding of experiences they have already faced.

Books in which characters struggle with some of the same problems the reader has experienced can give assurance that someone else has had similar difficulty, and the reader can solve the problems vicariously with the character. If a trusted adult reads the same book and then discusses it with the child, an intimate problem can be discussed at a third-person distance. And if it is a group discussion, the child can benefit from the experiences of other children.

Individual or group discussion can lead to fresh insights that will help the child cope with difficult situations in her life. This process is especially suited to gifted children because so many of them are enthusiastic readers.

For parents and teachers, the rewards are in the reading, in the discussion, and most of all in the responses from the children. At the end of a discussion series, one student said in her evaluation, "I learned that being gifted is important." Her statement needed further clarification, but she had taken a step toward accepting her unusual talent as part of her identity.

The many gifted children who have not been formally identified have the same emotional needs as those who have been, and they too can benefit from discussions that will help them establish an identity, recognize their need for alone time, learn to get along with others, develop their full potential, and take responsibility for their drive to understand. This chapter offers theoretical and practical information on using books to enhance the emotional development of children who are different from the norm by reason of giftedness or intense interests—through the form of bibliotherapy.

Bibliotherapy

Webster's Third New International Dictionary defines bibliotherapy as "the use of selected reading materials as therapeutic adjuvants in medicine and in psychiatry; also: guidance in the solution of personal problems through directed reading." Cornett and Cornett (1980, p. 8) quote one of the classic definitions among those who use bibliotherapy: "A process of dynamic interaction between the personality of the reader and literature—interaction which may be utilized for personality assessment, adjustment, and growth."

Webster's reference to medicine has a long and honorable history. Libraries in the ancient world bore inscriptions such as "Medicine for the Mind" in Alexandria and "The Healing Place of the Soul" in Thebes. In America, the use of bibliotherapy goes back at least to Dr. Benjamin Rush, who recommended the reading of books as part of a treatment regimen for hospital patients in the early part of the 19th century.

The two definitions in Webster's refer to the two major types of bibliotherapy: clinical, for those who are coping with emotional problems, and developmental, for people who are simply facing a normal life stage or transition. [A third type, institutional, is reserved for those in mental institutions. For our purposes, we will follow Doll and Doll (1997) in distinguishing simply between clinical and developmental.] Doll and Doll recommend a cooperative effort between librarians and mental health professionals for clinical bibliotherapy, while suggesting that teachers, counselors, and parents—who have the appropriate qualifications and are motivated to do so—are quite capable of leading discussions in developmental bibliotherapy without the assistance of mental health workers.

The distinction is an important one. The type of bibliotherapy proposed in *Some of My Best Friends Are Books* is developmental, with referral to mental health professionals recommended when emotional issues are more profound. This section is designed to help readers understand the differences between the two types. They can perhaps best be described by contrasting them.

Clinical bibliotherapy occurs when people who have emotional or behavioral problems meet to discuss recommended books in a clinical setting such as a drug treatment center. With a trained mental health professional serving as facilitator, they hold a discussion or counseling session designed to address their problems, in the hope of bringing about changes in attitudes and behavior. Clinical bibliotherapy could also take place in a school, with a school psychologist working in a team approach with the librarian (Doll & Doll, 1997).

For more information on clinical bibliotherapy, see *Biblio-therapy: A Clinical Approach for Helping Children* (Pardeck & Pardeck, 1993) and *Using Literature to Help Troubled Teenagers Cope with Identity Issues* (Kaplan, 1999). The latter book is part of a series on bibliotherapy for troubled teens focused on six issues: family, identity, social concerns, abuse, health, and death and dying.

In developmental bibliotherapy (the most commonly used type), ordinary people who are facing a normal life stage or transitional period meet in community settings such as schools or libraries to discuss books related to the issues that concern them. In a school setting, groups facilitated by a teacher, librarian, school counselor, or school social worker are designed to help students resolve normal developmental issues of adjustment and growth—again, through changes in attitude and/or behavior resulting from reading and discussion. In bibliotherapy for gifted students, it is recognized that "normal developmental issues of adjustment and growth" are complicated by specific characteristics and feelings common to gifted children.

Developmental Bibliotherapy

Developmental bibliotherapy is used preventively, attempting to anticipate and meet needs before they become problems. The goal is to help people move through life's predictable stages by providing information about what to expect and examples of how other people have dealt with the same developmental challenges.

Several psychologists have created lists of developmental tasks that everyone must meet. In an article about bibliotherapy in public libraries, Lack (1985) summarizes Zaccaria's (1978, p. 29) compilation of such lists:

Life Stage	Developmental Task
Infancy	Achieving a sense of trust
Middle childhood	Achieving a sense of initiative
Late childhood	Achieving a sense of industry
Adolescence	Developing a sense of identity
Early adulthood	Achieving a sense of intimacy
Middle adulthood	Achieving a sense of generativity (a concern for others that transcends generations)
Late adulthood	Achieving a sense of ego integrity

Those who are interested in the development of gifted children will see immediately how important are the tasks for middle childhood, late childhood, and adolescence. A sense of initiative, industry, and identity are essential to enable gifted youngsters to avoid underachievement and to develop their abilities to their own full satisfaction. Yet for some gifted children, the responses of others to their giftedness make it especially difficult for them to move through these developmental stages with complete success.

Todd showed a sense of initiative when he asked his fourth grade teacher for harder math problems. Busy with 32 other students and unable to believe that Todd wanted to work harder, she brushed aside his request.

When her sixth grade class studied ancient Egypt, Sasha became so interested that she persuaded her family to travel to a nearby city one weekend to visit the museum, delaying the completion of her report. Her parents encouraged Sasha's sense of industry; the teacher, who would not accept a late report, discouraged it.

Yeung knew that he was unusually bright, but because his parents wanted their son to be "just normal, like everyone else," he had difficulty accepting his own

ability. It was a junior high teacher, patiently work-
ing with Yeung as he built a project for a science fair,
who enabled him to enjoy his talent and to develop a
sense of identity that incorporated his intelligence.

The stories of Todd, Sasha, and Yeung exemplify the impact of adults' responses to gifted children's attempts to establish a sense of initiative, industry, and identity. The reactions of other children can also either encourage or thwart the healthy growth of these children. Developmental bibliotherapy can help make the difference. Through it, teachers, librarians, counselors, and parents can help gifted youngsters recognize and articulate their feelings and can prepare them for the particular spins that being gifted puts on normal developmental tasks.

Therefore, in this book bibliotherapy is seen specifically as a way of helping gifted and talented children understand and cope with growing up different in a world that is geared to the average. It can be used to help them anticipate difficulties as well as give them a basis for self-understanding when they feel alone and misunderstood, or when they are reluctant to use their abilities because it is not popular to be smart. Through bibliotherapy, adults hope to encourage gifted children to build a strong enough self-concept that they will develop their full potential in spite of the inevitable pull toward the peer group and that they will resist pressures—both from inside and outside—toward perfection-ism. Developmental bibliotherapy can be part of a planned effort to help them meet their childhood and adolescent tasks.

Studies of Bibliotherapy

Bibliotherapy is based on the belief that our lives can be changed by what we read, particularly if there is an opportunity to discuss what we read with others. Although difficult to docu-ment, this belief persists, perhaps because of the inner certainty of those who love books; we may feel that we do not need scien-tific proof of what we so surely know. Many of us have identified so strongly with a character that we made him a part of ourselves or adopted his attitude toward a situation, and we have all been comforted by knowing that an author has perfectly described our innermost feelings. Developments in the practice of psychology have shown that group discussion can be a therapeutic process.

Research results confirming this intuitive evaluation of the effectiveness of bibliotherapy would be welcome, but studies yield ambiguous results. Bibliotherapy is an emerging discipline, and there is not yet enough research to confirm the theories behind it. As I noted in the first version of this book (*Guiding Gifted Readers*, 1988), nearly every article on bibliotherapy closes with a plea for further study. In our new century, this is still true.

In the 1970s, research in this field focused on whether reading had the power to change attitudes. Schrank and Engels (1981) and Schrank (1982) reviewed the research studies of that period and reported that while the effectiveness of bibliotherapy in some other areas was not supported, "research in this category suggests an overwhelming Yes to the question of whether bibliotherapy is effective" in changing people's attitudes (Schrank & Engels, 1981, p. 144).

It is difficult, however, to point to research findings that verify or refute the effectiveness of bibliotherapy in dealing with bright and gifted children. But the reasons for this may have more to do with the mechanics of research than with the topic under investigation.

First, inconsistencies in definition and method weaken the collective impact of findings. In an article reviewing earlier studies, Tillman (1984) reveals the difficulties of using them to make definitive statements about the effectiveness of bibliotherapy. For example, some studies have gathered information simply through a checklist that asks students how reading has affected them. In others, the effect of reading on attitudes is studied by administering a pre-test, a reading, and a post-test.

Second, in some research, there is no discussion of the book or of students' reactions to it, although other studies do include discussion as a part of bibliotherapy. If the definition of bibliotherapy includes a follow-up discussion of the reading, as it does here, then research will have to attempt to assess the entire process.

Third, most recent research studies reflect the work of counselors and other mental health practitioners who typically use bibliotherapy as an adjunct to therapy—that is, who are using it clinically. This research has concentrated on self-help books rather than on fiction, so the effectiveness of fiction remains unvalidated (Riordan & Wilson, 1989).

Fourth, research investigating the use of bibliotherapy with gifted children is rare, in part because of the failure of researchers to recognize that gifted children have unique problems that might be addressed through bibliotherapy (Hebert, 1991).

And finally, the impact of a book varies significantly from one reader to another and is determined by an overwhelming number of variables. Attempts to measure and quantify the effect of art on personality will always be thwarted to some degree by the elusiveness of the concepts involved.

Therefore, current studies can point toward but not confirm the effectiveness of using carefully selected books and well-planned discussion to help gifted students cope with giftedness. At present, only the experience of educators and children support the assertion that bibliotherapy is valuable for gifted students. Children probably say it best when they affirm, time after time, that they would want to be in a discussion group again and that it is definitely worth the time it takes from their regular schedule—typical responses when they are asked to evaluate the experience at the end of a discussion series.

Textbooks on gifted education increasingly include a section on bibliotherapy, affirming that experts in the field believe that connecting gifted children with books and giving them a chance to talk about their responses makes intuitive sense.

Since the research we do have indicates that the process has potential, continued and expanded use of developmental bibliotherapy with gifted youngsters should be encouraged. From the knowledge now available, adults who work with books and gifted youngsters can do so with the knowledge that they are using a recommended method of guiding gifted children. They must, though, proceed with caution, with respect for the infinite variability of human nature, and in the knowledge that they are practicing an art and not a science.

Qualifications for Bibliotherapists

Do parents, teachers, or librarians who lack special training have the expertise to lead a bibliotherapeutic discussion? If it is developmental bibliotherapy, the consensus is that they do. For Doll and Doll (1997), one factor that clearly differentiates developmental from clinical bibliotherapy is just this point: developmental does not require a trained mental health professional, and clinical does. Pointing out that for teachers and librarians it is very natural to listen to children talk about their feelings, they quote Bernstein (1989, p. 165), who asserts that bibliotherapy does not necessarily require training in psychotherapy, but "can be and is safely undertaken by those with less sophisticated expertise in human nature: teachers, librarians, doctors, lawyers, parents, and others."

For discussion leaders who would like additional background, *Bibliotherapy: The Interactive Process: A Handbook* (Hynes & Hynes-Berry, 1986) is highly recommended. This excellent resource offers a thorough and thoughtful explanation of the process. While it emphasizes clinical work, it also provides a good basis for developmental bibliotherapy.

Here, we take the view that many parents, teachers, and librarians are already practicing bibliotherapy to varying degrees, perhaps without knowing it and almost always without formal training. The information provided in this chapter is offered in the belief that the more these discussion leaders can learn about what they are doing, the more effective they will be.

Those who are interested in doing bibliotherapy probably already have some of the qualifications listed by Hynes and Hynes-Berry (1986):

> ➤ maturity: self-awareness, self-acceptance, tolerance of others;

> ➤ integrity: respect for self and others that enables the therapist to avoid exploitation of emotions;

➤ responsibility: an attitude of responsiveness as well as a willingness to guide group participants through potentially difficult discussions; and

➤ adaptability: the ability to adjust plans to meet the needs of the group at the moment, and to allow participants their own interpretations.

In addition to these inherent characteristics, the authors point out that the bibliotherapist must acquire and develop therapeutic attitudes, such as:

➤ empathy: the ability to understand another person's feelings without actually experiencing them;

➤ respect: the recognition of the value of another person's feelings, and of his or her inherent worth and uniqueness; and

➤ genuineness: sincerity, spontaneity, openness; awareness and acceptance of one's own inner experiences.

To use developmental bibliotherapy with gifted children, leaders should also know and enjoy children's literature, understand child development in general and that of gifted children in particular, have the trust of the children with whom they are working, and know something about counseling and discussion techniques.

The Bibliotherapeutic Process

Present theories about what happens in bibliotherapy date back to 1949, when educator Carolyn Shrodes studied the relationship between bibliotherapy and psychotherapy for her doctoral dissertation. She identified three phases of the bibliotherapeutic process, which corresponded to phases of psychotherapy. These formed the basis of subsequent concepts of bibliotherapy.

The three stages of bibliotherapy are identification, catharsis, and insight. A fourth phase, less often mentioned but especially interesting for work with gifted children, is universalization (Slavson, 1950)—the recognition that our difficulties and sense of difference are not ours alone.

Bibliotherapy depends on the dynamics set up among the reader, the literature, and the discussion. It begins with *identification*, the process by which the reader identifies with a character in the book, recognizing something of himself in, and so coming to care what happens to, that character. Mollie Hunter (1990, p. 28), author of several books listed in Chapter 8, describes identification with the understanding and skill of a fine writer:

> Even the most superficial reader will follow the incident by identifying with the character concerned in it; and so, willy-nilly, there comes a point when reader and character are involved in the same emotions....The reader...glimpse[s] a reflection of himself in another young person caught in a situation that demands the enunciation of some value, the setting of some standard. Temporarily at least, he will have had a sense of participating in the decision taken, and the process of thought set unconsciously in train may yet surface in his mind....The reader will still be essentially free to formulate his own eventual philosophy; but [he will have been shown] something of what may be implied by the choices occurring in those adolescent years.

It may sound improbable that identification with a fictional character can be such a powerful experience. But book characters are real people to most children, and children continue to see them as real people even under the close scrutiny of discussion. Coles (1989) indicates that this holds true for college students as well.

At the same time, the child's awareness of the distancing effect of literature provides a sense of safety. Lerner and Mahlendorf (1992, p. x) point out that:

> it is for the reason of emotional safety by proper distancing that literary works can do more than merely instruct us.... They...make us more sensitive to

[our] feelings and ourselves. In this way, we gain an emotional awareness that transforms us and gives us the motivation to change ourselves.

Catharsis occurs as the reader follows the character through a difficult situation to a successful resolution. Spache (1974, p. 242) defines catharsis as the:

> sharing of motivations, conflicts and emotions of a book character. Defined in psychological terms, catharsis is an active release of emotions, experienced either first-hand or vicariously. Catharsis goes beyond the simple intellectual recognition of commonalities as in identification…. It involves empathetic emotional reactions similar to those that the reader imagines were felt by the book character. Or, in another sense, the reader relives, insofar as his own emotional experiences permit, the feelings he attributes to a character in a story.

One quiet summer morning years ago, I was working contentedly in the kitchen, the children still in bed upstairs, when from Mark's room came the sudden heart-stopping sound of deep sobbing. He had been awake for some time, reading *Julie of the Wolves,* and had reached the cruel and emotionally painful climactic point in Julie's conflict between two cultures. Anyone who knows that book will recognize that Mark was experiencing catharsis. It is not a bad thing, after all, to cry over a book.

Insight is the reader's application of the character's situation to her own life. If identification and catharsis have occurred while reading the book, insight may occur during discussion or even later, as the reader reflects on the story. She may transfer her understanding of the character's personality and motivations to herself, increasing self-understanding and bringing her own options into sharper focus. Thus, insight can lead to changed attitudes, which can lead to changed behavior.

However, insight does not necessarily lead to immediate action. The discussion leader may not even always know whether it has occurred. Assumptions can be made, however. What insights might have resulted from Mark's reading of *Julie of the Wolves*? A confirmation of his sensitivity to cruelty and his tender-heartedness toward animals, a reluctant recognition that true endings are not always happy ones, and the newfound confidence that he could accept this fact, if with sadness—a growing experience for a 10-year-old.

Universalization is behind Delisle's description (1990, p. 223-224) of "John," in an article recommending bibliotherapy as one means of preventing suicide among gifted young people. Delisle affirms that John:

> probably does not realize that thousands of other persons throughout the centuries have wrestled with the same types of issues that he now confronts.... More than anything else—anyone else— what John now needs is someone to tell him that it is OK to be confused, anxious, and ambivalent. This person may be a teacher, a counselor, Holden Caulfield from *Catcher in the Rye,* or the protagonist in *Zen and the Art of Motorcycle Maintenance.* To gifted students like John, getting the *answers* to timeworn philosophical issues is less important than merely being told that his *questions* are legitimate.

This process, of course, does not take place with every reader or with every book. A discussion leader can help to bring it about, though, by asking questions that focus first on identification with one or several characters (and on the universality of the experience if that is appropriate); then on the critical situation, the way the story character handled it, and the feelings stirred in the reader in response; and finally on ways in which all of this relates to the reader's own life. A demonstration of this process will be found in the sample questions given later in this chapter.

It should also be noted that these steps do not necessarily fit neatly into a half-hour discussion session. Many readers continue to mull over books long after they have finished them. If there is not a good response to one of the deeper questions during the discussion, a seed that will lead to thought later on may nevertheless have been planted. As with parents and teachers, bibliotherapy discussion leaders will know only a small portion of the impact they have on children's lives.

Caution with Bibliotherapy

As with any helping relationship, bibliotherapists must exercise caution—always aware of the possibility that deeper problems may be present, and remembering that developmental bibliotherapy is meant to help prevent problems, not to cure them. Anyone who encourages children to discuss their feelings should know when to refer a child to a mental health professional. Children may exhibit any of several warning signals that the bibliotherapist should discuss with the child's parents or a psychologist.

There may be underlying problems if a gifted child or her parents appear to be denying giftedness. If the child shows unusual reluctance to be placed in the gifted category, or if the parents are unable or unwilling to allow the child to participate in enrichment activities, there is some cause for concern. Comments from the child may indicate prejudicial treatment at home, in the form of parental attitudes disclosed in statements such as, "If you're so smart, why can't you remember to take out the trash?"

A problem may also be indicated if a child seems unable to relate to the purpose of the book discussion group or unable to relate meaningfully to at least some of the other children in the group.

> *Jamal made it clear that he didn't want any part of a book discussion group; he slumped in his chair and glowered at the floor except when spoken to directly. He spoke as little as possible, contributing*

one comment that revealed very low self-esteem. After three sessions, he stopped attending, and after the discussion leader called his mother for a conference, the mother made arrangements for individual sessions for him—a much more appropriate arrangement in this instance than group discussion.

Responses can indicate much more than low self-esteem. There is reason to be concerned about students whose responses reveal excessive anger, aggression, anxiety, depression, fear, preoccupation with sexuality, inability to have empathy for others, little or no social life, or inordinately high or perfectionistic standards for themselves. School performance that is far below ability level, or a lack of investment in achievement in any area—even those in which the child possesses high ability, are further signals of underlying problems that might be helped by therapy.

Anna had been invited to join a bibliotherapy discussion group because her test scores indicated that she was gifted. Her academic performance had never measured up to her potential, and teachers hoped the group would bring about changes in her behavior. Although the other students in the group were her friends, Anna did not join in the discussion. It was clear by the second session that she had transferred her attitude toward schoolwork to the group; she would not read the books—not because she was too busy, but because she had decided not to participate. Recognizing that the bibliotherapy group was not appropriate for Anna, the leader referred her to the school counselor.

Of course, a leader must be concerned about a student who gives evidence of physical or psychological abuse or neglect, who shows signs of drug or alcohol abuse, or who is carrying a weapon. He or she may be alerted in discussion, for example, by a student who strongly defends the right of individuals to use drugs.

A bibliotherapist must also be aware of the possibility of serious depression or even potential suicide. Indications of depression include insomnia or other sleep disturbances, lack of interest in life or in any number of activities that formerly were motivating and exciting, emotional outbursts, noticeable weight gain or loss, and changes in clothing and dress standards. Direct mention of suicide and a strong defense of suicide as a desirable choice are clear danger signs.

These warning signals do not occur often, but a bibliotherapist should be aware of them and should realize that he or she is in a unique position to help. A discussion leader's best contribution to some children may well be a referral to a competent psychologist.

In addition to watching for signs of deep emotional problems, discussion leaders should be careful to control the depth of the discussion. It is not necessary that everything be explicitly said; participants can be trusted to take and use what they can. If a discussion at greater depth seems potentially beneficial, a teacher or librarian could ask the school guidance counselor or psychologist to serve as co-leader. In developmental bibliotherapy, without a mental health professional present, discussion leaders should not attempt to invite self-disclosures that would make participants feel exposed.

Literature for Bibliotherapy

For developmental bibliotherapy, the focus is on fiction, but nonfiction should not be overlooked.

Nonfiction

In the first two chapters, we recognized intellectual challenge as both an intellectual need and an emotional need of gifted children. For that reason, providing challenging material is a major concern for teachers and parents of gifted children, and nonfiction books are a major source of such material. In addition, nonfiction is the favored reading material for many young people.

Therefore, nonfiction is discussed in both Chapters 6 and 7, and it is included in the bibliography in Chapter 8.

However, nonfiction does not normally lend itself well to bibliotherapy, since generally it appeals to the intellect rather than to the emotions. There are of course exceptions, and it is often recommended reading for gifted students, with or without a follow-up discussion.

The most frequently recommended nonfiction is probably biography. For example, biographies of eminent women can provide role models for gifted girls (Reis & Dobyns, 1991), since girls who are not personally acquainted with women active in high-level careers may be inspired by their life stories, without need for discussion. Of course, biographies can help boys in the same way.

Fiction

Robert Coles, the psychiatrist who wrote in *Children in Crisis* with such insight of children's responses to traumatic situations, draws on his teaching experience at Harvard for a more recent book: *The Call of Stories: Teaching and the Moral Imagination* (1989). In seminars on "Literature and Medicine" and "A Literature of Social Reflection," Coles encourages medical, law, and business students to explore how a thoughtful reading of fine novels, poems, and plays can affect their lives. The stories he tells of the emotional impact of fiction on the developing values and goals of college students provide an excellent starting point for anyone considering bibliotherapy.

A child's response to fiction typically begins at the emotional level. For this reason, fiction is ideal for developmental bibliotherapy, especially when reading is accompanied by an opportunity to discuss the book with someone else who has read it. Hearing the comments of others enables the child to see that their responses are similar to his, that he is not alone in his feelings.

Using fiction for bibliotherapy, then, is not simply a matter of handing a child a book about a problem he is facing himself. A story is not a pill that will cure if administered at the proper time;

it is a starting point. To be most effective, the reading must be followed by discussion with a concerned adult who has also read the book. This statement cannot be made too strongly: *The adult must read the book too*, and must be prepared with his or her own response to the literature and with a few key questions to promote discussion.

The delightful surprise in store for adults unfamiliar with current children's literature is its high quality. There is no need to settle for the mediocre; there is plenty of the good and the excellent, and it is not boring, no matter what the age of the reader.

Nevertheless, a warning: With the rising concern over the number of social problems facing today's children, we have seen an increase in didactic fiction—stories designed to teach a lesson. At first glance, these books may seem ideal for bibliotherapy. However, fiction written for bibliotherapeutic purposes usually fails as literature—it is too earnest, and since discerning readers see through it quickly, it cannot bear the weight of serious discussion. To speak authentically to the emotions and to reflect truly the human condition, fiction chosen for bibliotherapy must exemplify literature as the art form it was meant to be.

Nonfiction and fiction are both listed in the bibliography in Chapter 8. However, the nonfiction is almost always recommended for intellectual enrichment, while for emotional growth, the emphasis is on fiction.

Logistics: Organizing Discussion Groups at School

When teachers or librarians use book discussion with high-ability students, they are most likely to do so with a group, although they may occasionally hold informal talks with individual students. This section provides detailed information on selecting children to join discussion groups, on choosing books for groups to read, and on setting a place and time for book discussion at school.

Before a leader can sit down with a group of youngsters, all of whom have read the same book and are eager to discuss it, there is much work to be done. Setting up a group means bringing appropriate children and appropriate books together, in sufficient numbers of each, at a time and place that will suit everyone's needs. The advance planning will vary considerably, depending on such factors as how the school identifies gifted students, the academic structure of the program for them (if any), the flexibility in the schedule, and how important the faculty and administration feel it is to deal with the emotional needs of gifted youngsters.

The Children

It is easier to hold effective book discussions if the children are close together in age. Students from two grade levels can meet together, but a much wider age range than that makes it difficult to choose literature that will appeal to everyone.

They should also be relatively close together in ability level. Like academic programs for the gifted, a book discussion group that combines students in the superior range with those who are highly gifted will probably fail to meet the needs of the highly gifted members; it would be better to have a separate group for them if possible.

Remembering that highly gifted people differ from one another more than do people in the superior or average ranges, the leader of this group should keep the individual characteristics of each reader in mind while selecting books. For the same reason, discussion should be specifically planned for the individual students rather than for the group in general. In addition, at least some of the books chosen for them should offer examples of highly gifted people.

With any discussion group for gifted or highly able children, the leader should know how much the children understand about their selection for the group. If the term *gifted* is used, the comfort level of the students will depend largely on how the use of the term is handled within their school. It may be a good idea in the first session to discuss how members will describe the group for children who are not included. The leader can help them avoid hurting others without downplaying their own abilities: "We're going to read books and talk about them. It's a group for good readers who like to read a lot. We're going to learn ways to think about a book after you've read it, and how to discuss the ideas in the book."

The leader should consider whether the self-concept and personal strength of each potential member is sufficient to allow participation in the group without inappropriate self-revelation or hypersensitivity. If the leader knows that a child has a specific problem that may be discussed and that it is so close to the surface that the student will be unable to think or speak about it objectively, then for the protection of the child, an individual discussion would be preferable to a group experience.

> *Tracy's parents have recently divorced, and her mother has asked Tracy's school counselor to include her in a support group for children of divorced parents. In talking with Tracy, however, the counselor has learned that she is not yet ready to discuss her experience in a group of peers. Rather than participate in a group discussion of* A Girl Called Al, *about dealing with the emotional aftermath of divorce, Tracy should be given the option of meeting individually with the counselor for a time.*

Unexpected self-revelation may well occur during group discussion, and the leader can deal with it at that time through reassurance, redirection of the topic, or by offering to talk about it after the meeting. It is better if selection of group members can minimize its occurrence. Members of a book discussion group designed to help them cope with developmental issues of giftedness should be children not currently in crisis. A group for children in crisis should be planned and led differently, with a counselor as co-leader.

A group size of six to eight is optimum. With more than eight, there may be some who will be able to remain silent because the group is large enough for them to do so. With fewer than six, the group can become ineffective if two members are absent or have not read the book.

Should group membership be optional for those eligible to join? If it is, there will be better potential for good discussion. The key is each student's interest in the topic and in participating. Those who do not wish to join now may wish to do so later.

The Books

In some contexts, bibliotherapy is practiced with little regard for the quality of the literature chosen. The only requirement is that the subject of the literature be appropriate to the goals of the discussion. For a couple of reasons, this cannot be the case in bibliotherapy with especially bright students.

First and foremost, inferior literature will not lend itself to discussions that will touch and challenge gifted students. They may not recognize the technical differences between good and bad literature, but they will certainly recognize (and mention with notable lack of grace) when a book is "bor-ing." Discussion about books perceived as boring is bound to be boring itself, for any age group.

Second, it is a disservice to skilled and enthusiastic readers to encourage them to spend their time on less than the best. Of course they will experiment with escape literature from time to time, but they can learn to recognize it, and they can learn how to find good literature when they want it. Parents and teachers who are guiding them in the larger sense of helping them develop their potential must have the courage to differentiate the inferior from the good, and must take the time to find the best for them. There is plenty of excellence in literature for children and young people as well as for adults.

To find good literature, make use of as many sources of book lists as possible. Parents and teachers should have access to *Booklist*, *School Library Journal*, and other selection aids librarians use in considering books to buy. Journals about parenting and educating gifted children often have book review sections. Even newsletters of local associations for parents of gifted children may have suggestions of good books.

Browse through the education section of bookstores; there are always books to help adults encourage children to read. For discussion purposes, however, look for publications that focus on books themselves rather than on the process of reading or on reading readiness. There is a partial list of these at the end of Chapter 6.

Develop the habit of reading reviews of children's books, keeping in mind the criteria in Chapter 6 for books that meet emotional needs while also challenging the intellectual. Good ideas can also come from other educators and even from children, too. As discussion leaders gain experience with excellent literature, they will recognize trusted authors and good writing, so they can browse effectively. Before long, by reading just a page or two, they can sense whether a book is likely to justify their time to pre-read it for use with the children they have in mind.

After gathering lists of suggested titles, leaders should preview the books and select several titles to recommend to students. It is best to suggest several titles, giving booktalks to generate interest, and have the students vote on which one the group will read. Because several copies will be needed, cost considerations may limit the choices to paperbacks.

If students must provide their books, they may wish to buy their own copies to build personal libraries, or they may borrow from local libraries. Perhaps the public library will even have multiple copies. And single copies of almost any title can be located through interlibrary loan at public libraries.

However, the most efficient way of making sure that each student has a copy of the book under discussion is for the school to provide them. Schools may have classroom sets of some titles. Multiple copies of the titles selected may fit into the library budget, or perhaps the school or gifted parent association would be willing to help with the purchase. The books can be kept in the school library for use by discussion groups in future years and can be made available to other students in the meantime.

Place and Time

Privacy is important when choosing a place for the discussion group. A special room or a corner of the school library would be best if the library is empty at the time. A corner in the classroom is not a good place to discuss feelings the participants would not want all classmates to hear.

The difficulty in scheduling a time will depend on whether children are coming to the group from more than one class and on what degree of priority the school gives to the book discussion group. It is generally not a good idea to schedule programming for gifted students at a time that requires them to miss recess, physical education, or lunch—which would take them away from social opportunities and emphasize their differences. In one school, however, these were the only options. The principal's suggestion that the students vote on the time they preferred was a happy one for all concerned.

For children in grades three to five, a series of four sessions may be adequate, spaced one week apart. Middle school students may need more time to read their books; biweekly sessions might be better for them. For high school students, book discussions could be held once a month throughout the school year. Each session should last just 15 or 20 minutes in the early elementary grades, up to a full class period for senior high students.

Book discussion groups can also be offered as part of summer enrichment programs. These sessions may be spread over a period of two to three weeks, with two or three meetings a week, since children have more time in the summer. These groups can incorporate students from different schools, granting them an anonymity that may make it easier to talk.

In planning the dates for the group to meet, remember that it may be four to six weeks after books are ordered before they arrive.

Logistics: Organizing Discussions at Home

Parents may want to discuss books with their children for a number or reasons: to supplement the reading program at school, because they are home schooling, or simply for pleasure. In addition to the suggestions offered below, consider forming a group of parents and children to read and talk together.

In an effort to continue the long, relaxed conversations she enjoyed with her children during vacations into the school year, Shireen Dodson formed a mother-daughter book club in 1995 when her daughter, Morgan, was nine years old. In *The Mother-Daughter Book Club* (Dodson, 1997) she describes their experience, offers suggestions for starting a club, and provides reading lists and discussion guides. The sub-title is enticing: *How Ten Busy Mothers and Daughters Came Together to Talk, Laugh and Learn through their Love of Reading*. What a wonderful way to make early adolescence not only survivable, but a time for bonding.

When parents discuss books with their children at home, the question of which children to involve is not an issue. Still, as with teachers and librarians planning a discussion group at school, parents must solve the problems of finding good books and finding a suitable place and time for discussion. In addition, they must consider different ways to motivate their child to participate, and they must use slightly different techniques in talking with an individual instead of a group.

Finding Good Books

The bibliography in Chapter 8 is designed to help parents as well as teachers find books that are well-written, challenging (as they must be to hold the interest of discriminating readers), and suitable as discussion starters.

In addition, parents can use the suggestions listed for teachers under "The Books" section earlier in this chapter. The children's department of the public library also carries resources such as *School Library Journal*, *Booklist*, and others. While your child browses for books, you can learn how to gain access to these materials, building a helpful relationship with the children's librarian at the same time.

Suitable Place and Time

Where and when are good opportunities for you to read and talk about books with your children? In a more leisurely era, I might have suggested firmly establishing a family book discussion at the same time every week. Some modern families may be able to manage that, and I applaud them—but I acknowledge that for most, hectic schedules require imaginative solutions.

Busy working parents can make use of snippets of time throughout the day. If books are a priority, they will be in the car, carried into the dentist's waiting room, or tucked into a backpack or purse to be pulled out while waiting for a ride or a rider. Conversations can take place in the car, over dishes, after the homework is done, or while taking a walk.

One family's tradition of "talk-talk time," available to each child after the lights go out, provides a satisfying place and time to talk about books. Another family might designate a routine chore, such as a Saturday run to the recycling center, for book talk time. For home schooling families, it can be part of the school day. Once the importance of finding time to read and talk about books is established, every member of the family can get into the act of finding time to do it—and meeting the challenge tells children how important it really is.

Motivation

With an avid reader, a parent may need do no more than mention that he or she would like to read a book the child is reading; when both have finished the book, they can talk about it over dishes or while driving home—whenever there are 15 or 20 uninterrupted minutes. Once a pattern of discussing books is established, the parent can reciprocate by recommending a book, and they will be on their way.

With a resistant reader, parents may have to be more assertive. It will help if reading time has been built into the daily schedule from the early years, and it will certainly help if the parents are readers. Some parents find that they can strike a deal with their child: they will read what the child recommends to them, and the child will read what they recommend to her—some of the time.

Discussion with an Individual Child

What a parent does in bibliotherapy will be much the same as what a teacher or librarian would do, except he or she will usually be talking with an individual instead of a group. The parent can use the same procedures for planning and leading a discussion that are outlined later in this chapter for use with a group, modifying them to suit the home situation and the child.

The discussion itself will be slightly different from one with a group. If one child is doing all of the responding, then she is more likely to become involved in the discussion than she would if she could leave some of the work to others. On the other hand, she will miss the reinforcement of ideas from peers; the parent may need to compensate for that by bringing up the points of view that other children might mention if they were there.

Just as scheduling is likely to be less structured at home than at school, so discussions at home tend to be more relaxed. Parents should capitalize on the advantages of this difference rather than worrying about following a plan too closely.

In a less structured home setting, parents may accomplish less in a given amount of time, but they have the advantage of being able to continue over a period of several years. In addition, they will bring such a wealth of family experience to the conversations that in the long run, they may well be able to accomplish much more. Imagine the following scenario:

> *The Browne family began reading to their children in the nursery, and both Marcus and Brie began reading early. When they were three and four, Dad would push back his chair from the dining table in the evening and say, "I feel a little Pooh coming on," and they would pile into his lap for a chapter or two*

of Winnie-the-Pooh. *The family read aloud on vacations and on camping trips, and it was a natural step to begin talking about the books the children were reading.*

Usually, Mother had read the books they read, and when she asked Brie what she thought of The Wolfling, *the discussion expanded to include Dad's and Jon's thoughts on why higher education is important for someone like Robbie Trent—and Marcus and Brie. Brie's excitement over* Anno's Medieval World *led to a family discussion that helped Marcus understand superstition and scientific thought in a new light, an understanding that he tucked away for further attention as he pondered budding career ideas. When Brie showed evidence of feeling uncomfortably different and out of place in her new junior high school, Mother reminded her of Jess in* A Bridge to Terabithia, *who did not fit in his family or his school, but who did have one friend and one teacher who understood. Over the years, their love of books led to productive conversations and mutual understanding for the entire family.*

Planning for Discussion

After the logistics are settled, whether working informally with a child at home or setting up a series at school, planning is necessary before discussing a book with a child. Prior to a discussion, the leader must choose a book, read it, prepare discussion questions, and motivate the children to read the book.

Choosing the Book

Chapter 6 is devoted to selecting appropriate literature for gifted students and eager readers. Briefly, we can follow the suggestions of Robinson (1989): look for situations that evoke emotions, situations that offer alternatives, and characters with whom the reader can identify.

For a good discussion to ensue, the book must deal with a wide range of human emotions, not just the fear or excitement engendered by adventure stories. When characters are faced with alternatives, readers are led to consider the options, too—a focal point for discussion. And for bibliotherapy to be effective, at least one character must be someone with whom the reader can identify.

Reading the Book

After the discussion leader chooses the book, the next step is to read it. For those not familiar with children's literature, this may at first sound like a tedious task, but good children's literature will hold adults' interest too. In fact, a book that does *not* hold the leader's interest should be reconsidered before being recommended for gifted students. One way to test for good writing is to read a passage aloud. If the tongue feels stiff and stumbles over the words, the book simply may not be well written. Look for books that glide along, flowing from word to word and from thought to thought when read aloud. But above all, read the book!

The leader must plan discussion questions related to the book; this will be easiest if she thinks about them as she is reading. She must also keep in mind the child or children with whom the book will be discussed and the purpose in discussing it with them. She can use as a bookmark a 3 x 5 slip of paper on which she can jot down page numbers and key phrases that strike her as potential discussion material. When she goes back later to write questions, she will then have an overview of the themes in the book that will be useful for discussion.

It is a good idea to allow a day or two after finishing a book to let it "settle in" before writing questions. During this incubation period, the leader will be subconsciously working on the book, and when she does sit down to write, the questions that come will be a distillation, probably of better quality and drawn more from the true heart of the book than if she had begun to write immediately. What she is doing in that dormant period is allowing the book to sift down into deeper levels of her own understanding, so that her responses will contain some measure of wisdom, as well as intellectual analysis. Some people find that certain "pump-priming" activities, such as walking, drawing, or playing a musical instrument, are helpful during this period. Students may feel that they do not have the time for an incubation period before they come to the book discussion. It can't hurt, however, to suggest it to them.

Adults may find that their immediate response to a book is that it can't possibly be used with gifted children. When they sit down with pencil and paper, they may still think that the book has nothing to offer. But if they go on with the physical act of writing, beginning with a summary of the plot, the potential of the book begins to unfold, and usually, questions will occur as quickly as one can write them down. Sometimes, of course, this does not happen; the book truly is unsuitable for this purpose. In this case, it is worth taking the time to clarify exactly why it is unsuitable. This bit of discipline helps in the ongoing definition of what the leader *is* looking for in books to use for bibliotherapy with gifted students.

Preparing the Questions

Bibliotherapy differs from intellectually-oriented book discussion in that it is based on the readers' emotional responses to the book rather than on questions of literary analysis such as plot, character development, writing quality and style. Chapter 5 focuses on discussion for intellectual understanding. Here, we will consider ways of evoking and exploring emotional responses.

For either type, the leader must know the difference between fact questions and interpretive ones and must use each intentionally. Fact questions are those to which the answers can be found in the book; the leader knows what answer he wants when he asks the question, and he will use the answer to judge how well the student has read the book. Interpretive questions are those whose answers are open to interpretation. They are "honest" questions, in that the leader does not know the answer—that is, he does not know what the student thinks. Having had time to think about it, the leader may know what his own answer is, but the student may well give an equally valid different answer. Interpretive questions are appropriate when the leader (1) assumes the youngster has read the book, and (2) is interested in the student's response.

It is best to begin a discussion with a few fact questions to ascertain the general level of understanding of and response to the book. These introductory questions also provide a warm-up period, a chance for readers to recall the impact of the book and the emotional awareness called for by the interpretive questions.

The annotations of the books listed in Chapter 8 include a few suggested interpretive questions for each book. Here is a list of general interpretive questions that can be adapted to specific books:

➤ What is the central character's biggest problem?

➤ How do you think he/she feels when…?

➤ What strengths does he/she have that help him/her cope?

➤ How has someone you know handled the same situation?

➤ What would you have done?

➤ If you were his/her best friend, what advice would you give?

➤ How would that help the situation?

➤ What effect do the people in the book have on one another?

For writing interpretive questions, the stages of bibliotherapy—identification, catharsis, and insight—are more easily understood as actions: recognizing, feeling, and thinking. In planning bibliotherapy sessions, structure the questions so that they lead students from one mental activity to the next.

For example, here are discussion questions for Constance C. Greene's *A Girl Called Al*, which can be used with gifted third or fourth graders. The questions progress from encouraging identification with Al to generating insight into the reader's own life.

Identification (Recognizing):	Describe Al; describe the narrator, who is never named in the book.
	Whom are you most like, Al or the narrator?
	Why? (Al is a leader; the narrator, a follower.)
	In what ways does Al have extra trouble because she is bright?
	How are things easier for her because she is bright?
Catharsis (Feeling):	How do you know Al is lonely, even though she never says so?
	What happens in the book to help Al overcome her loneliness?
	What effect does Mr. Richards have on Al? Do you know anyone who is as important to you or to someone else as Mr. Richards is to Al? What effect will his death have on Al? On what do you base your answer?
	How does Al feel when Mr. Richards dies? How do you know? Do you know anyone who has trouble showing feelings as Al does?
Insight (Thinking):	When do you hide your real feelings? What are the advantages of doing so? Why is it hard to show real feelings?
	Why does showing real feelings make people feel less lonely?

These questions pursue just one of the themes in the book: loneliness. An equally productive theme is Al's defiant nonconformity. To follow that theme, a discussion leader might use the same identification questions, and then continue with these:

Catharsis (Feeling):	Why has Al chosen to be a nonconformist? How do you think she feels about it?
	Think of nonconformists you know, or even of yourself, if you are one. What feelings (good or bad) do you think compel people to be nonconformists?
	How do you imagine nonconformists feel about themselves generally?
Insight (Thinking):	When do you choose not to conform? Why? What are different ways to be a nonconformist?
	When is nonconformity destructive? When is it productive?

These questions assume identification with Al more than with the narrator. If a child in the group is more likely to identify with the narrator, the leader may want to develop different questions, perhaps with the purpose of encouraging understanding of what the follower brings to a leader/follower relationship, or of developing empathy for nonconformists from the point of view of those who find it easier to conform.

For a 30-minute discussion with upper elementary children, a list of 20 questions is more than enough. Each interpretive question can carry the entire discussion, if it catches the imagination of the students. Having more questions than needed gives flexibility, preparing the leader to go in any of several directions when student interests become apparent. And for beginning discussion leaders, it builds confidence to know there is more than enough material to fill the time.

The questions listed above and in Chapter 8 are only suggestions to get started. As leaders gain experience, they will want to use their own insights and questions.

As students gain experience, they also will be able to generate their own questions. When they can do this, they are learning enough of bibliotherapy to be able to use it independently. It could become a skill they will be able to use even in adulthood—in *Reading to Heal*, Jacqueline Stanley (1999) introduces the principles of bibliotherapy for independent adult use. Although she does not use the term "developmental," her book encourages the reading of thoughtfully-selected books to help adults face typical challenges of daily living, like the developmental bibliotherapy discussed here for children.

Motivating the Children

Of course, book discussion can't proceed until the student has read the book. This may be no problem at all, or it may be a matter of some difficulty, depending on the level of interest the student already has in reading and on how the whole idea is presented.

It is clearly better to pique students' interest in the book itself, as well as in the discussion of it, than to present reading and discussing as a way of "working on gifted people's problems." (That motivation may come up later, as a natural result of conversation, and will be more authentic as a result. Or such problems may never be mentioned directly, but left unspoken, to be addressed by the child's internal processing.) The best aid in motivating children to read specific books is the leader's enthusiasm and her ability to convey it.

For the teacher or librarian planning a discussion series at school with a group of children, motivation is done according to good teaching practices. The leader gathers the group for an initial meeting and outlines her plans: duration of series, meeting time and place, how many books are to be read, how this group activity will fit into their reading program, their responsibility to read the books on time and be prepared for discussion, etc.

Agreeing to participate in the group should constitute agreement to read the books on schedule. This may be a problem in some few cases, and the leader should know ahead of time how she will deal with those who have not finished a book by discussion time. May they participate or not? One solution is to allow participation, but to try to change the parameters of the group to prevent recurrences. Allowing more time between sessions may help; so may providing more classroom reading time, as well as counting the reading done for this group toward required book reports, to provide a deadline external to the book discussion group. In practice, it is usually not a problem because students quickly learn that it is more fun—and much more appreciated by others in the group—when they participate.

When the group parameters are settled, it is time to present the first book to be read. This can be done in a brief book talk, in which the leader:

> ➤ hints at the plot or conflict in the book: "In *Jacob Have I Loved*, Louise's abilities are unrecognized, and all the family's meager resources go for voice lessons for her musically gifted twin, Caroline";

> ➤ mentions ways in which the conflict might relate to students' own experiences: "Louise grows up believing that her family loves Caroline more than they love her";

> ➤ tells enough about the characters to initiate the reader's identification with them: "Louise is hard-working and resourceful, but not much interested in schoolwork or in her own future until circumstances force her to make a decision"; and

> ➤ tells why she likes the book enough to think they would like to read it too: "I like this book especially because I liked each of the characters—even Caroline—by the end of the book."

Any difficulties in the book might be mentioned, also. The structure of Konigsburg's *Father's Arcane Daughter*, for instance, may be discouraging to some readers unless it is pointed out that the book has flashbacks that will become clearer as they read. *Across Five Aprils* will start slowly for some; the leader might pass along the judgment of one sixth grader—that the book does not get interesting until page 64!

Leading the Discussion

Whether leading a group or talking about a book with a single child, there are certain techniques that will help make the book discussion as meaningful as possible:

➤ Confidentiality is important. Group members should understand that what is said in the group should not be repeated elsewhere.

➤ Confidentiality will be difficult for some children to maintain. Therefore, it is important to help children avoid giving information that they will later regret. Children may not yet have a firm sense of how much personal revelation is appropriate. Use the "capping" technique, especially in a group: be alert to those times when a child may be saying too much, and divert attention to another question and another child, effectively "capping" the overflow of emotion and self-revelation. (The leader may speak to the child later, giving him a chance to continue the discussion individually.)

➤ Encourage children to share any ways that they have found useful for coping with common problems. Some of the more mature children may have simply adopted attitudes that enable them to transcend difficulties, at least part of the time, and it will be helpful for others to hear about these.

➤ Let the conversation flow where the group or the child wants to take it. The leader may understandably be eager to get to his prize question, the one that for him gets to the heart of the book or the problem; however, if he forces the discussion in that direction, his wonderful question may fall flat. This is not to say that he should allow the discussion to wander away from the book; rather, if the children select another theme that they are more ready and able to discuss, the leader should be prepared to follow their interest.

➤ Outline good discussion techniques with the children before beginning, and remind them of these when necessary. Some rules to establish are that everyone must have a chance to talk, that only one person may talk at a time, and that there are no right or wrong answers to many of the questions.

➤ Remember that the leader's role should not be too intrusive. He is not there to be sure they understand his interpretation of the book, but to moderate and to facilitate their own understanding.

➤ Help the children focus by highlighting the motivations of the characters, the problems in the book, and the solutions presented. Ask the children to suggest other possible solutions and discuss the likely consequences of them.

At first, it is only natural that the leader will be concerned about pacing. With experience, he can relax about time and become more involved in the discussion himself, giving real answers to the children's comments and validating their emotional responses. In a 30-minute session with upper elementary school children, it is enough if only the middle 20 minutes are spent on interpretive questions. The leader can close with a review of the major points that have been brought out, or ask the group to do this, then introduce the book to be read for the next meeting.

Goals of Bibliotherapy at Different Stages

How a child feels about being different because of giftedness or unusual intellectual curiosity is determined partly by the child's age and partly by the degree to which adults have openly discussed differences in ability. In turn, the child's level of awareness will determine the character of the book discussion.

Preschool and Early Grades

A conversation about books with preschoolers or early elementary children will be just that: a conversation, not a discussion in the sense of a series of questions and answers. Accordingly, this book does not suggest discussion questions for this age group in Chapter 8, but merely lists concepts found in the book that would be useful as the focus of a conversation.

Young children not yet able to empathize with the feelings of others or to understand the consequences of actions need adult guidance to glean as much as possible from what they read. Parents and teachers can question to learn their level of understanding and gently explain concepts they may have missed. In particular, adults cannot expect a young child to discern a subtle lesson from a book if it goes unstated. The applicability of a story to their own lives must be clearly expressed by the guiding adult.

Reasonable goals with this age are to introduce concepts, label feelings, and develop frames of reference so that when an event in the child's life recalls a story read together, the concepts can be reinforced. This process establishes the importance of books as windows into various life experiences, builds foundations for years of discussion based on books, validates the child's feelings, and assures him that talking about feelings is not only permissible, but also a positive way to release emotions.

For early elementary children, a combination of conversation and deliberate questioning can be used. Watch for signs of fatigue or restlessness, and be prepared to stop as soon as they appear. This is still a preparation time for true give-and-take discussion; the emphasis should be on the warm relationship between adult and child, with books as the catalyst for occasional conversation but not yet the focal point.

Upper Elementary

It is in the later elementary years, grades 3 – 5, that gifted programming typically begins. Many children hear the term *gifted* applied to them for the first time at this age; however, they may not know what it means or how they are expected to react.

When selected children are invited to join a gifted program, there is usually a larger group of children who are also very bright but did not meet the criteria established by the school. They, too, need to understand their potential and should be given special attention at this time.

It makes sense at this stage to discuss giftedness, talent, and appropriate aspirations with both groups. Since these are also the peak reading years, it is a particularly good time to begin book discussion groups.

A realistic goal for discussion groups with gifted children in the late elementary years is to help them become aware of the word *gifted* and gain some understanding of what it means. Looking inward, they may not yet be comfortable applying the term to themselves, but they can recognize some of the problems that gifted children in books have and how they cope. Looking outward, they can also begin to recognize the importance of empathy and respect for all people who are different, in whatever way.

On the other hand, students can talk about differences related to giftedness without using the term. In a program designed but not labeled for gifted students, fourth graders who had read *Mrs. Frisby and the Rats of NIMH* talked about why other rats edged away from the superintelligent ones who had escaped from NIMH. The students agreed that they have felt others pull away from them, and they discussed how they respond to that: by trying to be more like other people. Later, when they evaluated the series, one gain they mentioned was "learning not to edge away until you know a person better."

As children of this age gain social awareness, they become more adept at interpreting the literature they read. Still, they need the guidance of adults who are able to perceive the gaps in their understanding and tactfully expand their level of comprehension. For example, the adult can help significantly by pointing out the needs or motivations of characters in a story. With such guidance, children can begin to make connections to their own needs and motivations, and perhaps to make conscious changes in their attitudes or behavior as a result of the insight gained from reading and discussion.

Middle School

Social needs are paramount for middle school students. The major contribution of a book discussion group may lie in simply bringing bright and intellectually-oriented students together, to allow them to belong to a group of peers. They need to blend with their social group while retaining their own identity, which includes their high ability level. One goal will be to remind them from time to time of this part of their identity, so that it will be available to them to build on when they emerge from this period. Books with characters who have the same abilities or interests (whether labeled gifted or not) can help to keep them aware of their potential.

Some gifted adolescents, in middle school and senior high, become poignantly and cynically aware that adults have failed to realize the potentials that life has to offer. They may begin to question the meaning of life, and given the intensity that characterizes gifted youngsters, they may carry this questioning to the point of existential depression. Leaders should be prepared to refer any student who shows signs of depression to a psychologist or other mental health professional.

These children are becoming mature and independent enough to need less adult guidance—some of the time. Parents and teachers talking about books with them must be perceptive enough to know when to add their own insight and when to accept a child's interpretations without comment. They can also offer alternative interpretations of the literature to help students realize that the unique experience they bring to a book can lead to a valid conclusion, even if others do not agree. Adults should help students clarify personal attitudinal or behavioral goals that they develop as a result of their reading, and follow up with subsequent discussions to help them stay on track.

Senior High

During the senior high years, students become increasingly concerned about the decisions they must make for the future. High-potential students of this age are working on college and career choices, very often struggling with the issues raised by their multipotentiality and the reluctant realization that they must choose from among several abilities and interests. It is important now that they recognize that their abilities are different from the norm, become comfortable with them, and acknowledge some of the responsibilities their talent may imply.

A major goal of book discussion with senior high students is to help them consider these issues. The books chosen will be young adult and adult literature. Since these students want literature that deals in depth with the moral and ethical decisions they are making, their reading list will include some of the classics—books whose characters struggle with eternal issues, written in language that has stood the test of time. However, classics should be chosen with care to ensure that modern teenage readers can identify with the characters.

Another goal is to encourage them to continue to use bibliotherapy independently. If they analyze the process as they experience it or afterward, they can duplicate it with literature they choose to meet their individual interests and needs throughout their lives.

Young adults are eager to define what they want to read and what it means to them. Discussion leaders at this stage serve as listeners and facilitators, rather than the more directive leaders who guide discussion for younger children. Still, to enhance the possibility that bibliotherapy will have a long-range impact on attitudes and behaviors, they should find ways to follow up by staying in touch with student participants.

An Author's View

When Stephanie Tolan, the author of *A Good Courage* and other books for young adults, was asked what she would say to potential bibliotherapists, she answered that discussion leaders should realize that the purpose of writing literature is not to prescribe solutions to problems. The author is trying to create a world that is real and true, not to teach. Discussion, she said, should be open-ended, helping the child to see why things work out as they do in *this* book. The author is not saying that this is what should happen, only that this is one way it could happen. It is not the only answer.

If we look from the author's point of view, we understand that during the writing, stories are organic, developing in their own ways, and that other ways are possible. There is always the question, "What if…?" Realizing this will help derive the widest possible meanings from the story and the most flexibility in relating a book to a child's own life.

In books in which characters make life-shaping decisions, such as *Shadow of a Bull* and *Jacob Have I Loved*, the possibility of other options is especially clear. Each reader can respond to these books by making the decision for himself, adding components from his life that the author did not include in the book. Thus the book continues to live in the reader, informing his future decisions. With healthy development, children as they grow create lives that are real and true, even though they differ from the world the author creates.

Bibliotherapy: An Affirmation of Strengths

To most people, giftedness doesn't sound like a source of trouble at all. Those of us who call attention to potential difficulties for persons whose very label implies they have been blessed could be accused of making up problems where there may not be any and generally holding too gloomy a view of the lives of unusually bright children. It may appear that we have forgotten that they have strengths and joys as well as vulnerabilities and loneliness.

Not so. It is important, however, that we recognize that those whose high ability and intellectual or artistic interests distinguish them from the norm have a particular set of challenges. With that recognition accepted, we can emphasize their strengths and abilities. Bibliotherapy can be used to affirm and develop those capabilities. The fact that it is a vehicle for discussing problems should not cloud the fact that it is also a tool for calling upon the strengths of gifted children and young people. Bibliotherapy is a process uniquely designed to do just that, as Hynes and Hynes-Berry (1986, p. 58) point out:

> The emphasis on strengths plays a fundamental role in the bibliotherapeutic process. In the first place, the initiative for each step of the process lies with the participant. The facilitator can guide, but it is the individual participant who must recognize, examine, juxtapose, and integrate the feeling-responses and the understandings.... Moreover, progression from the first to the final step calls increasingly on the individual's strengths...including (1) some ability to analyze issues, (2) sufficient honesty to look at the inner self, (3) enough objectivity to view a feeling or behavior pattern from another perspective, and, finally, (4) adequate self-confidence and hope to feel that change

is possible and that one is personally capable of making such a change.

Another way of making the same point is to say again that bibliotherapy is a process of *self-actualization*. Moreover, we consider the self-actualizing process to be one that not only enhances existing strengths but also corrects discrepancies.

For gifted and talented children at home or at school, in groups or as individuals, bibliotherapy is a way of building on the strengths of their reading abilities, their analytical skills, and their heightened sensitivity. It uses and enhances their ability to see relationships, draw conclusions, synthesize, and evaluate. And it can give direction, focus, and purpose to their introspective self-awareness. It is a positive, forward thrust toward the full use of the strengths these children possess—and eventually, toward self-actualization.

References

Bernstein, J. E. (1989). Bibliotherapy: How books can help young children cope. In M. K. Rudman (Ed.), *Children's literature: Resources for the classroom* (pp. 159-173). Norwood, MA: Christopher-Gordon.

Coles, R. (1989). *The call of stories: Teaching and the moral imagination.* Boston: Houghton Mifflin.

Cornett, C. E. & Cornett, C. F. (1980). *Bibliotherapy: The right book at the right time.* Bloomington, IN: Phi Delta Kappa Educational Foundation.

Delisle, J. R. (1990). The gifted adolescent at risk: Strategies and resources for suicide prevention among gifted youth. *Journal for the Education of the Gifted, 13,* 212-226.

Dodson, S. with Baker, T. (1997). *The mother-daughter book club: How ten busy mothers and daughters came together to talk, laugh and learn through their love of reading.* New York: HarperCollins.

Doll, B. & Doll, C. (1997). *Bibliotherapy with young people: Librarians and mental health professionals working together.* Englewood, CO: Libraries Unlimited.

Hebert, T. P. (1991, June). Meeting the affective needs of bright boys through bibliotherapy. *Roeper Review, 13,* 207-212.

Hunter, M. (1990). *Talent is not enough: Mollie Hunter on writing for children.* New York: HarperCollins Children's Books.

Hynes, A. M. & Hynes-Berry, M. (1986). *Bibliotherapy: The interactive process: A handbook.* Boulder, CO: Westview Press.

Kaplan, J. S. (Ed.). (1999). *Using literature to help troubled teenagers cope with identity issues.* Westport, CT: Greenwood.

Lack, C. R. (Spring, 1985). Can bibliotherapy go public? *Collection Building, 7,* 27-32.

Lerner, A. & Mahlendorf, U. R. (1992). *Life guidance through literature.* Chicago: American Library Association.

Pardeck, J. T. & Pardeck, J. A. (1993). *Bibliotherapy: A clinical approach for helping children.* Langhorne, PA: Gordon and Breach Science Publishers.

Reis, S. M. & Dobyns, S. M. (1991, April). An annotated bibliography of non-fictional books and curricular materials to encourage gifted females. *Roeper Review, 13,* 129-130.

Riordan, R. J. & Wilson, L. S. (1989). Bibliotherapy: Does it work? *Journal of Counseling and Development, 67,* 506-508.

Robinson, D. (1989, September/October). Bibliotherapy discussions. *Ohio Libraries*, 2, 22.

Schrank, F. A. (1982, February). Bibliotherapy as an elementary school counseling tool. *Elementary School Guidance & Counseling, 16*, 218-227.

Schrank, F. A. & Engels, D. W. (1981, November). Bibliotherapy as a counseling adjunct: Research findings. *Personnel and Guidance Journal, 60*, 143-147.

Slavson, S. R. (1950). *Analytic group psychotherapy with children, adolescents, and adults.* New York: Columbia University Press.

Spache, G. D. (1974). Using books to help solve children's problems. In J. R. Rubin (Ed.), *Bibliotherapy source book.* Phoenix: Oryx Press. (Original work published 1974.)

Stanley, J. (1999). *Reading to heal: How to use bibliotherapy to improve your life.* Boston: Element Books.

Tillman, C. E. (1984, May). Bibliotherapy for adolescents: An annotated research review. *Journal of Reading, 27*, 713-719.

Zaccaria, J. S., Moses, H. A., & Hollowell, J. S. (1978). *Bibliotherapy in rehabilitation, educational and mental health services.* Champaign, IL: Stipes.

Chapter 5

Intellectual Development through Books

Since teachers are trained to teach reading and to help students become knowledgeable about books and literature, most teachers reading this book are no doubt already well versed in the information gathered here. Accordingly, this chapter is addressed primarily to parents—first to familiarize them with what is happening in schools, and secondly, to help them support and supplement that work at home.

The chapter begins by exploring how reading and discussing books, whether at school or at home, can meet the intellectual needs outlined in Chapter 2. Following that is a section on new developments in school reading programs, followed by steps for leading groups in an intellectually-oriented book discussion. Suggestions for parents who wish to supplement the school programs at home come next, and the chapter concludes with information for parents who want to be certain their students are learning how to seek information independently.

What Books Can Do for Intellectual Development

The needs listed in Chapter 2 suggest that for optimum intellectual development, highly able children should have opportunities to do the following:

➤ learn to think effectively,

➤ encounter a variety of people and ideas,

➤ benefit from individual pacing of learning experiences, and

➤ talk with intellectual peers.

Curious, eager students who read widely and well, whether identified as gifted or not, can benefit from programs designed with these goals in mind. With carefully chosen books and skilled and enthusiastic leaders, reading and book discussions accomplish all of them.

Simply reading well-chosen books challenges us to think, enables us to experience a wider range of people and ideas than we encounter in our daily lives, and permits us to move at our own pace among books of our choice.

Adding opportunities for discussion of what we have read increases the chance that we will think *effectively*, exposes us to even more people and ideas, expands our avenues of response to the reading, and provides the possibility of talking with intellectual peers.

If books are chosen for high-potential students with their age and interests in mind using the criteria for intellectually challenging books in Chapter 6, then a program of reading and book discussion—though it may lack the glamour of more expensive programs—can be remarkably effective in developing intellectual ability.

Thinking Effectively

Many bright children are able to move easily (not to say lazily) through the elementary grades without learning to make effective use of their intellectual abilities. They can listen with half an ear and pick up enough to stay up with the class. If this pattern continues for too long, they develop neither study skills nor thinking skills.

> *Daniel was a very bright child in elementary school and he shone in high school, graduating near the top of his class. No one was surprised when he was accepted at one of the most academically demanding eastern universities. However, he is not doing well there, although he is the same serious, purposeful student. He knows why: he has not learned to think analytically or to examine his assumptions. In grade school and high school, his answers were correct so often that few listened critically to what he was saying. Now, in a class of many other outstanding students, Daniel's lack of study and thinking skills is hampering his progress. His intellectual ability is not diminished, but he has not learned to use it effectively.*

Expressing ideas freely. Children who are eager to talk about their ideas are stimulated by opportunities to talk in more depth than is possible in the usual classroom discussion or casual conversation. Using their vocabularies without restraint, sharpening their thinking in talks with knowledgeable others who can spot flaws and helpfully point to discrepancies in their reasoning, they are encouraged to develop their verbal abilities.

Young people who have unusual ability to think critically, to evaluate, and to reason out unusual solutions to complicated situations should be able to voice opinions and ideas in an environment that respects divergent thinking, where their different approaches will be encouraged and heard, rather than ignored or openly rejected by others.

During the Vietnam era, a fourth-grade class discussed sending bandages and soap to the people of South Vietnam. Jeff suggested that probably the same staple commodities were needed in North Vietnam. Could the class send packages to both? This was so serious a departure from the norm that Jeff's father (not his mother, although she normally interacted with the school and would not have had to take time off work) was called in to discuss the situation—and presumably to handle it with appropriate severity. Jeff's story is an example of why a sensitive child with a global perspective needs a safe environment in which to express divergent opinions.

The sense of safety is extremely important to children whose intellectual abilities drive them to express thoughts which others may think are strange. In fact, it is essential to their further intellectual growth.

Various situations presented in books can provide safe focal points for in-depth discussions. Children can follow up on ideas a good book has generated, feeling safe enough to express even half-formed ideas without fear of ridicule. With an understanding adult or in a group with other insightful children, they can feel free to exchange views without toning down their vocabularies. These opportunities for regular dialogue with intellectual peers and bright adult friends are enriching and valuable.

Precise thinking. Too often, careless use of language and the lazy thinking it permits are accepted both in school and at home. Children must be free to speak the way their peers do, but adults can do children a great service by creating a milieu in which, some of the time, they can practice the exact expression of incisive, critical thought. In the process, they will be learning to think with improved precision. Just as they should learn the difference between "good" and "escape" literature, they should learn the difference between casual conversation and productive discussion of ideas, so they can use each when appropriate.

In individual or small group discussions, the leader has opportunities to probe for exact statements, demanding penetrating thinking that produces greater understanding. This kind of questioning can be used in any context, but books provide an especially productive opportunity for it.

> *In a discussion of Sperry's* Call It Courage, *the leader asked, "Why is someone in the book alone or lonely?" When the response was a retelling of the events of Mafatu's childhood, she said, "You are telling the whole plot. I only asked why someone in the book is alone or lonely." Nine-year-old Raul immediately answered, "Mafatu was lonely because he was afraid of the sea and everyone else was courageous," eliminating all extraneous information and zeroing in on exactly what the question asked.*

Higher levels of thinking. To develop their ability to analyze, synthesize, and evaluate (the higher levels of thinking in Bloom's Taxonomy, which is discussed in more detail later in this chapter), students should work with these processes, identifying each level of thinking as they use it. Open-ended book discussions conducted in an atmosphere that promotes respect for individual opinions can be rich training ground for higher levels of thinking.

For example, in a book discussion series with sixth graders, the leader might talk to the students about analysis, synthesis, and evaluation. As she asks about the books, she labels each question so that the students, in answering, know that they are analyzing, synthesizing, or evaluating. For the last meeting in the series, she may ask the students to bring three questions for discussion, one of each kind. The books provide the focus, and the discussion group provides the opportunity for the students to clarify the meaning of each process and learn to use those processes independently.

Encountering a Variety of People and Ideas

When trying to describe the constant need of gifted children for new information, parents and teachers often find themselves using metaphors for food. "I've never known a student so thirsty for knowledge." "She is so hungry to learn." "He is a voracious reader." These are not just clichés; they express how eager gifted students seem to observant adults. Indeed, knowledge, information, and new ideas are nourishment for their minds, and (perhaps unconsciously) they sense they are in danger of intellectual starvation without them. Book discussions can expose these receptive readers to a broad spectrum of information, to alternative ways of doing things, and to different kinds of people.

Information. Children who absorb information rapidly and well and then clamor for more should have access to many more subjects and concerns than typically are covered in the standard curriculum. The extensive range of nonfiction available through school libraries makes this need easy to meet.

However, fiction is useful in this regard, too. Literature introduces children to times and places they will never see and to lives they will not be able to live. It can expand their awareness of the variety of human concerns, styles, emotions, and ways of relating to others. And it can do this in a way that makes them care, opening doors to topics ranging from the conflict of cultures when French, English, and American Indians met in the Upper Great Lakes in the early 19th century (*The Loon Feather*), to the struggle for equality for African Americans in the post-Reconstruction era (*Words By Heart*), to the horrors of the Holocaust (*The Upstairs Room*)—subjects that might not seem real if read only in history books or newspapers.

Alternative ways of doing things. Many bright children enjoy a capacity for thought processing that includes the ability to think in alternatives, to sense consequences, and to make generalizations. To turn these abilities into skills, they must play with a variety of ideas, including some that may not be familiar to most people in their schools and neighborhoods. Opportunities to experiment with these ideas in exploratory conversations build both ability and confidence.

For example, during the reading of *The Arm of the Starfish*, a group of eighth graders might be directed to stop reading at designated points and write down whether Adam should side with Dr. O'Keefe or with Kali and her father, and to give reasons for and probable results of their decisions. They will then have the makings of a discussion that enables them to test their judgment and decision-making skills against the outcome of the book and against the ideas of their peers.

Books are laboratories for bright students—proving grounds where they can reason out solutions to complex problems, examine the consequences of their decisions, and then try something else. Good fiction reflects life truly, and as in life, the outcome of the story can depend on one small decision or a series of events beyond one's control. There are always turning points that lead to the question, "What if...?" Book discussions that consider "what if" invite the expression of divergent thought.

By suggesting books that approach an issue from several angles, adults can introduce new ways of looking at that issue, helping students toward a broader point of view. Gifted children respond readily to this expansion of vision; through their broader awareness of human potential, they will learn what is possible for themselves.

Different kinds of people. A less obvious reason why gifted children need to be exposed to a variety of people is that they can be highly critical, even intolerant, of people (including themselves) who do not measure up to their standards. They need to be aware that there are different abilities and talents, and different ways of solving problems. Exposure to a variety of people can help them develop tolerance, empathy, understanding, and acceptance of human weakness in others and perhaps also in themselves.

Literature not only provides an infinity of characters who exhibit human weaknesses and learn somehow to accept them, it introduces these characters in ways that make children care about them—and leads them to accept human weakness and to celebrate human strength.

Individual Pacing

By encouraging voluntary reading and discussion, teachers introduce flexibility into the standard classroom format, meeting individual needs by allowing for accelerated thinking, slower processing, and willingness to delay closure—all characteristics of high-potential learners.

Accelerated thinking. When a child's thinking processes are faster than normal, the pace of a typical classroom discussion can be agonizing. It is a welcome relief for pent-up frustration and boredom if, for at least part of the time, those who learn more rapidly can acquire knowledge at their own rate.

Reading is wonderful for this—it is a thoroughly self-paced activity. Skimming and rereading by turns, readers can move at whatever pace they choose. A reading program increases the amount of self-paced learning available to quicker students as soon as they become independent readers.

These youngsters should be able not only to learn at their own rate, but also to talk, at least part of the time, with others who process at an accelerated pace. Book discussions provide this opportunity. For some gifted youngsters, it may be the only such opportunity available in this period of their lives.

> *When Aaron began sixth grade at a new school, he found the pace of instruction too slow, and the other children were reluctant to accept him. He took refuge in the school library, where the librarian soon learned that he loved to read, and what is more, he was eager to listen to her suggestions. She recommended books such as* Anthem *to Aaron, and he began asking questions about the books when he returned them. Throughout the year, this give and*

take of books and talk allowed Aaron to learn at his own accelerated rate despite the repetitive pace in the classroom.

Slower processing. Though they are quick learners, gifted people are also capable of comprehensive synthesis and can benefit from a rather long incubation period to integrate new ideas. Some gifted children process information more slowly and deeply—and thoroughly—than others. Those who tend toward introversion are especially likely to be more reflective and to take extra time to reach a conclusion or decision.

Reading and book discussion, if properly arranged, can accommodate this slower processing better than the typical routine of classroom assignments. If an adult discusses the concepts of incubation and slower processing time with these students, they can gain useful knowledge about their own work patterns and learn to provide incubation time for themselves. For example, some students may realize that they will have more to offer to the discussion if they plan to finish a book a day or two before meeting to discuss it.

> *Maia is in the gifted program, but she isn't sure she belongs there. While most of her classmates are racing to be first with the right answer, she is quietly going over information in her mind, connecting new ideas with already acquired knowledge. In book discussion, however, she is ready to speak with the rest, and her well-formed opinions are respected by the group. When the teacher mentions that Maia makes good use of incubation time, she begins to understand and appreciate the advantages of her slower processing.*

Delayed closure. Earlier than most, gifted children often show the ability to delay closure—to accept a situation for which there is no immediate solution. Therefore, questions with single, final answers are not always appropriate for them. They are more likely to want to wait until all the information is in, to spend time looking at all sides of a question.

To develop this ability, they should be allowed to pursue their ideas and integrate new ones into their thinking without being forced to make final decisions or judgments immediately. They need open-ended discussion and open-ended situations to discuss.

In a book discussion, final judgments are never necessary; in fact, one result of a good book discussion will be the new insights it evokes. The discussion of a book may be only the beginning of a child's interaction with it. In fact, some children's literature intentionally provides open-ended situations; such books do not come to final conclusions, prompting the reader to consider a variety of possible endings.

Talking with Peers

We all need friends we can talk to comfortably as equals. It is hard for unusually bright children or for those with artistic or intellectual interests to find such friends—even harder than for gifted adults—and it is impossible to measure what a difference such a friend can make in their lives.

> *During the summer between seventh and eighth grades, Ben spent two weeks on a college campus at a summer program for gifted teenagers. He had never before been exposed to so many people with exciting ideas and the eagerness to talk about them. When the program ended, his parents and younger brother picked him up and took him out for dinner and then to a nearby campground to begin a family vacation. Ben was so stimulated by the campus experience that he talked about it nonstop through dinner and while they set up camp. He woke up the next morning still talking; it was late that afternoon before it was completely out of his system. Ben had discovered something momentous: There are other people like him. A new confidence began to replace Ben's long-standing sense of isolation.*

One reason the summer experience had such an impact on Ben is that it included older students. When their comprehension is advanced beyond their contemporaries', children need contact with intellectual peers, regardless of age. It is essential for them to have frequent opportunities to talk with people who challenge and stimulate them and who respect their ideas. Adults who talk about books with young people like Ben can provide intellectual challenge during the awkward years some of them experience before they attend a high school or college where they can find agemates who match their intellectual ability.

Intellectual peers offer other benefits. For one, equally-intelligent friends usually can be counted on to see through glibness and to question shaky assertions—lazy discussion techniques too easily developed by highly verbal and socially charming youngsters who benefit when their opinions are challenged in a well-managed discussion group. Also, most gifted and bright young people are socially aware, sensitive, and concerned with values and ideals at a surprisingly early age. They need to know others who can help them put these concerns into perspective so that they can develop a positive focus rather than becoming negative or cynical.

Parents, teachers, and librarians can suggest books that deal with social concerns and depict committed people taking positive action. Discussion about these books may help students see serious issues from a problem-solving point of view rather than from one of hopelessness. Such perspective-building is especially important for sensitive, concerned adolescents.

What Schools Are Doing with Books and Reading: A Primer for Parents

"Serious reading, serious teaching of reading, and inculcation of a love of reading are the proper goals of education." This is a fair summary, according to one reviewer (Alexander, 1991) of the argument presented by Jacques Barzun (1991) in his book, *Begin Here: The Forgotten Conditions of Teaching and Learning.*

Whether or not Barzun's goals are a national educational priority, methods of reading instruction continually undergo changes that alter traditional classroom reading experiences. Teachers reading this book are well aware of current trends and are possibly involved in implementing them, but parents may need a brief history. A relevant example of the pendulum used to describe educational trends in Chapter 2 is the debate labeled the "reading wars."

The century-old question continues: Should children learning to read be taught phonics, a tool for decoding words? Or should they be taught to recognize whole words without analyzing the parts? Early in the 20th century, children learned phonics, analyzing the link between letter-symbols and sounds. In the 1930s and 1940s, the phonics method was considered tedious and outdated, and the Dick and Jane readers used the whole-word, "look-say" method. In mid-century, the pendulum swung back toward phonics with the publication of *Why Johnny Can't Read* (Flesch, 1955), in which the author cited the neglect of phonics as the cause of lower literacy rates.

In the following decade, Jeanne Chall (1967) studied the relative merits of phonics and look-say and concluded that neither method, used alone, suffices. She found that presenting phonics in the early years, as children begin to read, provides a basis for later understanding of the meaning of language (Ravitch, 2000). In response to her findings, by the end of that decade, most textbooks for the early grades included phonics. However, the pendulum later swung again. Throughout the 1980s and the 1990s, the whole-word method was back in the form of the "whole language" movement.

Whole Language and Phonics

In whole language instruction, reading is taught without breaking language down into its parts (Hall & Moats, 1999). The method assumes that if children experience plenty of listening, speaking, and immersion in real literature, they will learn to read without specific instructions in discrete reading skills. A reaction to the over-use of drill, workbooks, and basal readers, whole language differs from the old look-say method in that it seeks to use real literature rather than controlled-vocabulary stories such as the Dick and Jane series, which were created specifically for the purpose of teaching students to read.

Phonics. Whole language instruction alone, however, neglects the use of phonics. Despite a 1985 report, *Becoming a Nation of Readers*, which agreed with Chall that beginning readers who learn phonics do better than those who do not, the popularity of an exclusively whole-language approach continued. However, in 1996, after years of whole language instruction (and no phonics), California students' reading scores were among the lowest in the nation. In 1997, California revised its reading curriculum to include both phonics and literature (Ravitch, 2000). Since California's huge purchasing power has significant influence over curriculum and textbooks nationwide, the pendulum was in motion again.

The "reading wars" demonstrate one disadvantage of going to the extreme with any one method of instruction. The wars are not over; in 1999 the National Council of Teachers of English officially opposed phonics instruction. Indeed, it may prove difficult in some local schools to return phonics to the curriculum; recent testing indicates that many elementary teachers lack a knowledge of phonics (Healy, 1999)—not surprising, since many grew up under whole language themselves.

Research indicates that about one-third of the children learn to read regardless of the method used, as long as they have some sort of organized instruction. These children do well with the literature-based approach of whole language. Some of the remaining children learn to read more easily if they have instruction about spelling and sounds. But one quarter of the children cannot learn to read without this instruction (Hall & Moats, 1999). These children learn differently, but they are not necessarily of lower intelligence. Some of them may even be gifted.

Given this clear example of differences in the ways people learn, it should be evident that it is important to include both phonics and whole-language approaches in a reading curriculum. Parents who monitor their children's schooling should look for a balance—exposure to phonics in the early years, and then an emphasis on real literature for advanced readers—rather than a program limited to one method or the other.

Literature. A second issue in whole language instruction which uses a literature-based curriculum is the use of books to replace stories that were artificially created for teaching purposes. In this approach, there is less use of basal readers and anthologies and more reading of whole books or story collections. This emphasis began with the desire to correct a problem: basal readers often use selections of children's books that are so simplified that they no longer resemble literature and cannot attract and hold the child's interest. Therefore, whole books are used in place of (or in addition to) the contrived selections found in reading textbooks.

In a literature-based curriculum, children read not textbooks but trade books—the children's books found in bookstores—and a classroom should have plenty of them—at least five trade books for each child in the class, according to Lynch-Brown and Tomlinson (1999). Such a program will feature daily reading aloud of good literature by the teacher, daily silent reading of books by the children, and daily oral discussion of the reading, in groups or one-to-one with the teacher.

Librarians and others interested in reading have hailed the move to real literature as a long-awaited positive step. However, it is not without its problems, and these have to do not with the idea itself, but with its implementation. The problems encountered by those attempting to implement a literature-based curriculum are mainly these: the basalization of literature, and inadequate funding.

Basalization means using whole books for reading classes, but treating them like basal textbooks by using classroom sets of a single book rather than allowing students to choose from many books available, and by following up the reading with worksheets which emphasize isolated reading skills. This practice reveals a misunderstanding of the whole language theory, and it is fed by a proliferation of commercial study guides offering prepackaged questions. Too often, these are fact questions guaranteed to deaden interest in the art of literature. "How many children never read the stories that are assigned to them, but rather simply look for the answers to the questions that are assigned simultaneously? Many do, and never have the chance to experience the power of a good book," observes Galda (1998, p. 5). An alternative approach is the use of literature circles, discussed later in this chapter.

Difficulties occur, too, if funding is inadequate to supply quantities of books, and when elementary schools do not have trained librarians who can guide teachers and students to appropriate books. Some teachers have difficulty getting books: "Even those who have money to spend and know which books they want have trouble ordering from book distributors. They assure me that it takes up to two years to get a new book into their hands. Somehow, their enthusiasm has waned by the time they get the book" (Cullinan, 1989, p. 31).

Parents and teachers evaluating a literature-based reading program can use criteria proposed by Spiegel (1990). Here are some of the questions she suggests:

➤ Is the literature of high quality?

➤ Is the language rich?

➤ Does it include a wide variety of genres, themes, and authors?

➤ Does it provide a good model for children's own writing?

➤ Do the activities focus primarily on meaning rather than on isolated decoding strategies?

➤ Do they promote a love of reading, writing, and literature?

➤ Can they be generalized beyond a particular piece of literature or a particular genre?

➤ Are enough experiences offered with the same types of activities for children to learn a particular strategy or approach?

Reading Programs for Gifted Students

According to Reis and Renzulli (1989, p. 92) in an article on reading programs for gifted students:

> the frustration faced by a precocious reader enter-ing kindergarten or first grade may be impossible for most adults to understand. When a six-year-old who loves to read and is accustomed to read-ing several books a day encounters the typical basal reading system, the beginning of the end of a love affair with reading may result. As Brown and Rogan (1983) have stated, "For primary level gifted children who have already begun to read, modification toward the mean represents a seri-ous regression."

While the authors point out that early reading and giftedness are not synonymous, they suggest that early readers need an appropriate reading program whether or not they are identified as gifted.

One model literature program for gifted students comes from the College of William and Mary's Center for Gifted Education. The Center's Language Arts Curriculum for High Ability Learners Offers Units For Grades 2 – 11. Training, Which Is Not Required But Is Highly Recommended, Is Available On The Campus At An Annual conference and at a summer institute. The Center also offers consulting, including on-site training. Teachers and home schooling parents can contact the publisher, Kendall/Hunt (www.kendallhunt.com), for materials.

In an appropriate reading program, gifted students learn to read widely, critically, and creatively, suggests Flack (2000). He asserts that a comprehensive reading program exposes gifted youngsters to a wide range of the best authors currently writing for young people, so that ultimately they recognize a passage of Katherine Paterson as easily as they recognize the distinctive style of Robert Frost. To read critically, they learn discrimination, separating the good from the bad in literature by developing and using criteria for judging the quality of what they read. In reading creatively, they integrate the new reading with what they already know, and they make use of the blend in their own way, going beyond what they read to find their own voice in writing a response.

A reading program for gifted students should include learning about authors and illustrators. Flack suggests that students can use the Internet to investigate where authors get their ideas, how authors and illustrators collaborate, and how the life experiences of creative people inform their work. "When gifted readers have access to computers and the Internet, tremendous opportunities are open to them for new learning," he says, adding, "The best general site for author and illustrator inquiries is 'The Children's Literature Web Guide' from the University of Calgary: www.acs.ucalgary.ca/~dkbrown/" (2000, p. 28).

In another treatment of the elements that distinguish a reading program specifically designed for gifted students and precocious readers, Reis and Renzulli (1983) propose a list from a study by Dole and Adams (1983):

> ➤ independent research projects,

> ➤ opportunities to pursue these projects over a long period of time,

> ➤ development of research skills,

> ➤ self-selected reading experiences,

> ➤ guided study of literary genres, and

> ➤ involvement with the Great Books Program.

To the last item I would add "or other structured book discussions," for which several models follow.

Discussing Books at School

When I was in high school, one English teacher invited six of us to form a small reading group. We met above the study hall in a loft used mostly for storage. At that time, the senior high did not even have a library; we stopped by the public library on our walks home to borrow the books we read as a group.

We met for just a few months, and I have only two specific memories: one girl said that her mother had told her that *Gone with the Wind* is not great literature (this was news to me), and we had to ask our parents' permission before we could read *Grapes of Wrath*. All the parents consented.

Despite my sparse memories, I am sure that good things happened in that group. No one called it a group for gifted students; no one identified gifted students then, just before Sputnik. It stands out in my high school experience because in that group, students truly were a part of excellence—trying to match the thinking of great authors with our own best thinking. Even under fine teachers, that did not usually happen in English class.

This group was an experiment in my high school. I don't know whether it was considered a success, or even whether it was repeated the following year. It may be that if I could listen now to one of the sessions, I would be disappointed in the quality of the discussion. But the sense of touching excellence has remained with me. Book discussion groups have the power to convey that sense, and they have that power even when they may seem not as successful as the leader would like.

Pulling a group of gifted students together for a book discussion can present logistical problems. Where ability grouping is not currently in favor, it may also present policy problems. Teachers, counselors, and librarians who attempt it, and administrators who must approve it, will want to know that it is worth the effort.

And it is, according to conclusions reached by Clark (1983). After charting intellectual characteristics of gifted children, the needs those characteristics imply, and possible related problems, she offers organizational patterns and strategies. She emphasizes that gifted students need educational programs that offer:

➤ small group discussion,

➤ flexibility,

➤ respect for ideas,

➤ time for reflection, and

➤ opportunity to compare communication and decision-making processes with academic peers.

Students discussing literature in small groups are meeting all of the above requirements. That should be good news to parents, teachers, and administrators who are concerned about the efficient use of valuable school time and about meeting the needs of all students. In schools using literature circles, a group for gifted children may fit relatively easily into the existing system.

Logistics

Arrangements for an intellectually-oriented discussion group differ only slightly from those offered in Chapter 4 for bibliotherapy groups. For a full discussion, please see "Logistics: Organizing Discussion Groups at School" in that chapter. In this section, only the differences are mentioned.

The children. Although these discussions are more cognitive than emotional, the selection of children for the group should be based on their emotional development as well as on reading ability. For younger children accelerated into older reading groups, it is especially important that their emotional level be weighed against the material to be read.

The books. The leader of intellectually-oriented discussion groups can choose from an array of books, limited only by the desire to present books of the highest quality and intellectual challenge. The usual requirements for finding appropriate books apply: knowing children's literature and what makes a book especially appealing to gifted children, examining reviews, and pre-reading all books before recommending them.

Place and time. While privacy may not seem as important here as in a bibliotherapy group, quiet is necessary. And the discussion should be in a place where students feel free to become thoroughly involved and to voice opinions with passion. Finding a time to meet presents the same challenges for both types of groups, and the same possible solutions are recommended.

The discussion can incorporate drama, art, music, guest speakers, and projects. The leader may also develop lesson plans to introduce the children to criteria for good literature so that they can move toward making their own informed judgments about books.

Discussion Techniques

In bibliotherapy, discussion is based on the reader's emotional response to the *story.* Questions, designed to clarify that response, often focus on the inner lives of the characters: Why do they act as they do? What personal characteristics lead to success or failure? What are their relationships to others in the story? What are their feelings? Their attitudes? How and why do these change?

An intellectual discussion, by contrast, aims to develop the reader's understanding of the *literature.* While the leader may ask all of the questions given above, he may also inquire into the motives of the author: Why did she decide to have this or that happen? What response did she hope to elicit from readers? How did she plan to accomplish her aims?

An example of the difference between bibliotherapy and an intellectual discussion would be these two questions from *A Bridge to Terabithia*:

> Why did Jess and Leslie spend so much time in Terabithia? (characters' motive)

> Why did Paterson have Jess and Leslie spend so much time in Terabithia? (author's motive)

In forming an answer to these two questions, we can almost feel an interior shift in focus take place. To answer the first, we try to feel our way into the minds and hearts of Jess and Leslie, while the second question moves us some distance from the story, which allows us to stand outside it and look at it analytically—to consider the author's carefully planned use of symbolism.

Another line of questioning in an intellectual discussion, evaluating the author's techniques and skill, helps to avoid limiting the discussion to the plot. Are the characters believable? How does the setting contribute to the development of the plot? To the mood? How effective is the author's use of language? In answering these questions, we gain an understanding of literature as an art form having specific methods that, if employed well, convey much more than the mere progression of words on the page can do.

Children's responses. In *The Child's Developing Sense of Theme: Responses to Literature,* Lahr (1991) outlines the stages of a child's ability to perceive theme in a story. She bases her comments on Applebee's (1978) use of Piaget's study of the gradual development of the child's ability to symbolize events.

Preschool and early elementary children—up to about the age of six—are in the pre-operational stage, characterized by egocentric and magical thinking. Visual perception is all; a child at this stage believes that a taller glass has more water in it, even if he has watched the water poured from a shorter, fatter glass. The focus on self, magical thinking, and reliance on appearances affects the child's experience of a book and his conversation about it. Very young children can understand the meaning of a story but cannot put it in their own words, while most five-year-olds can give a brief narrative.

Children from around ages seven to eleven, in the concrete operational stage, begin to use logic to explain events. A discussion leader will find these children able to summarize a story, and she can use to advantage their strong interest in understanding and analyzing experiences and relationships.

Adolescents, at the formal operational stage, are able to think more abstractly and hypothetically, and they can organize facts and events by manipulating symbols in their minds. Capable of viewing problems from several different vantage points, they can resolve conflicts through mental effort alone. Young adolescents are able to analyze the structure of a plot or the motives of the characters in a book. Older students can make generalizations as they consider the theme or author's point of view. Not everyone, even among adults, functions at the formal operational level— but apparently most gifted people do (Newman & Newman, 1983).

Thus, children see different themes in books than adults do and respond to them differently—a point for discussion leaders to remember. Furthermore, the construction of meaning is individual, based on the background and experience of the reader. This accounts for the differences in responses to a particular reading. A factually inaccurate answer, however, should be addressed. Lahr (1991) suggests doing so not with a correction but with another question—"Does that seem right?" "Are you sure?"—to encourage the child to reexamine her response.

Questions. Rather than fact questions, which have known answers, gifted children should be asked interpretive questions that require creative responses from them. Questions should be open-ended, and the teacher or leader should welcome unexpected, divergent answers or digressions that extend the topic (Baskin, 1998).

Leaders should plan questions to serve specific purposes, says VanTassel-Baska (1989). She suggests the following:

➤ factual questions to determine the students' comprehension,

➤ interpretive questions to develop a deeper understanding,

➤ divergent questions to encourage the reader to think outside the story, and

➤ evaluative questions to challenge the student to make judgments about the story.

VanTassel-Baska's question types may be easily used if the leader thinks in terms of the following opening words:

➤ factual: What happened?

➤ interpretive: Why did it happen?

➤ divergent: What if something else had happened?

➤ evaluative: What did you think about what happened? Why do you think so?

These openings provide only a skeletal framework to start the leader's thinking. A good discussion leader will build a structure based on them to suit the story at hand.

Questioning. Techniques of questioning include observing *wait time* after a question and also after a response. This pause for reflection causes anxiety for leaders but encourages more achievement for students. It also allows for the fact that while we value quick responses, we know that some gifted people process slowly. Castiglione (1987) says the average wait time is 0.2 - 0.9 seconds. If a discussion leader increases it to 3 seconds, major changes occur in the quality of the discussion. Others recommend 10 to 20 seconds after a "higher level thinking" question.

Castiglione suggests asking divergent questions to increase participation in the discussion. And if a child's answer is unclear, he suggests that the leader not say, "Your answer is unclear," but rather, "I'm not sure what you mean," so the burden of responsibility is on the adult, not the child.

Another questioning technique is "think-pair-share." After asking a question, the leader allows two minutes of individual thinking time and two minutes for students to discuss it with a partner before beginning group discussion.

Other techniques of successful discussion leaders are: asking follow-up questions, requiring students to defend their responses against other points of view, inviting one student to summarize the response of another, asking participants to describe how they arrived at an answer, and letting students develop their own questions.

What follows next is a summary of a structured approach to discussion that is well known to teachers, described here primarily for the benefit of parents.

Bloom's Taxonomy. Benjamin Bloom's *Taxonomy of Educational Objectives* (1956) lists the higher levels of thinking: analysis, synthesis, and evaluation. One way to approach book discussion with gifted children is to focus on questions that call forth these kinds of thought.

Analyzing a book involves questioning some of the author's decisions. Why did he choose that form, setting, or organization? Are there inconsistencies or inaccuracies? How does he make the characters seem like real people? Analysis questions might begin with phrases such as the following:

> What are the parts of...?
> Which steps are important in the process of...?
>   If..., then....
> The difference between...and...is....
> The solution would be to....
> What is the relationship between...and...?
> How would you have...?

Synthesis means connecting different elements of a book to each other or to knowledge the students have already acquired to create a new way of looking at the issues. Some examples of synthesis questions are:

> Can you retell this story from the point of view of...?
> How is a character from this book like...in...?
> Can you write a similar story that would...?
> Change...so that....
> Develop an original plan for....
> Good background music for a tape of the story would be....

Evaluating a book or a decision made by a character in a book requires making a judgment based on established criteria. The criteria can be developed in group discussion before the children are asked evaluative questions. Such questions could include:

Which characters are best developed?
Which character would you like to be?
Which of these stories is the most believable?
Rank these books on the basis of quality of language.
Which situation required the most courage?

Junior Great Books. A program that offers training in both forming questions and in the techniques of leading a discussion is Junior Great Books™. Although it was not originally developed for gifted students, it is often used as the first offering when a school initiates services for high-potential youngsters. Inexpensive and highly regarded, Junior Great Books™ is easily accepted as a gifted program. Furthermore, it develops a seriousness of purpose in reading and offers a structured discussion format that makes it an excellent introduction to intellectual book discussion.

For optimum use with gifted readers, a Junior Great Books™ discussion approach should be made more open, allowing opportunity for individualized responses. This requires volunteer leaders who bring to the task a lively intelligence, awareness of the characteristics of gifted children, and flexibility—but when all of that is in place, the results are rewarding. More information is available at www.greatbooks.org.

Other models. Teachers may develop their own methods of leading discussions based on preferred elements from Bloom's Taxonomy, Junior Great Books™, and other formats such as reading workshops and literature circles.

Because "the basis of instruction for gifted readers is the choosing and reading of books" (p. 15), Howe-Cousar (1990) suggests a reading program for gifted students adapted from Atwell's (1987) work with reading workshops. The program allows students to select their own books from a classroom collection, receive a few minutes of instruction, and spend much of the time in silent reading—and then asks them to record their responses in a reading journal.

She describes the discussions she leads with her middle school students, which begin with a group sharing of responses to what they have read. In these discussions, she insists that the group participants follow Probst's (1988) ground rules, which are: be receptive of each other's ideas, tentative about initial reactions, rigorous in intellectual standards, and cooperative in the search for meaning. Howe-Cousar (1990, p. 18) serves as both guide and colleague, adding her own responses to the group's (but never giving her reaction first). In her role as guide, she introduces material related to the reading. Speaking from her role as colleague, she says, "We ask each other questions."

Literature circles are a way to promote reading and discussion in small groups and may include journaling and extension projects (Noe & Johnson, 1999). They could easily be adapted for gifted children by:

➤ creating groups based on ability, especially for students with high verbal ability,

➤ selecting a wide range of appropriately challenging literature, and

➤ pacing the group at an appropriate rate.

The significance of ability grouping is discussed in Chapter 2. The selection of challenging literature will be discussed in Chapter 6. The third requirement, pacing, is especially important, since avid readers frequently read a book (or more) a day in the middle grades. Literature circles usually spend several weeks on one book and require that group members not read ahead—a swift way to kill interest for avid gifted readers who find this stipulation impossibly restrictive. When the above adaptations can be made, the early practice in discussion techniques offered in literature circles is invaluable for bright and eager readers. According to Baskin (1998), some teachers are moving forward with such changes, rather than waiting for another swing of the pendulum—good news indeed for the gifted students in their classrooms.

Authors' comments. Laudable though it may be to read books and discuss them, the sudden widespread use of this procedure has led to some concerns that books are being "used," in a negative sense, so zealously that we are overlooking the fragile nature of the art of literature. Authors, of course, are particularly sensitive to this, and some of them have written quiet protests that deserve our attention.

The poet Lee Bennett Hopkins (1991, p. xiv) raises objections to the use of discussion guides so extensive that they overwhelm the poetic experience. Describing a teaching guide for the poem "City" by Langston Hughes, he concludes, "In the time—the meaningless time—students might spend doing all this, they could relish an entire volume of poetry, coming away with so much more...!" Some poems, like some books—see Bauer's suggestions below—are best pondered over as a whole rather than analyzed.

In an open letter to teachers, Marion Dane Bauer (1991) offers several points arising from letters received from students as class assignments:

➤ Books selected for children should be appropriate for their emotional age. "There is a difference between the ability to absorb facts and the readiness to deal with issues" (p. 112).

➤ Not all books are meant for group discussion. Some need to be a private experience, "a kind of personal letter between author and reader" (p. 113).

➤ A book is more than a summary of its plot.

➤ Books should not be used to teach lessons. "Fiction is about questions, not answers" (p. 115).

Bauer's last point, especially, should be taken to heart, not only out of respect for literature, but also because it is with an openness to questions and questioning that we can offer the most benefit to sensitive, intelligent children through book discussion.

Discussing Books at Home

Although a group discussion is often not possible at home, you can meet many of the same needs through a loosely structured plan for family reading and conversation. Moreover, by providing a favorable environment at home, you can offer a haven to your children, a place where they can know they are safe to express their thoughts, ideas, and opinions without risk of censure. As parents, you can offer the psychological security that schools cannot guarantee.

Several books offer suggestions to parents who want to provide various forms of enrichment for highly able children at home (Alvino, 1985; Rimm, 1994; Saunders, 1991; Walker, 1991). Reading is surely the form of enrichment closest at hand for most families. By adding discussion to the reading, you can use books not only for the pleasure which is their primary reason for being, but also to respond to your gifted children's intellectual needs and as a focus for thoughtful family conversation.

When you encourage reading and promote book discussions at home, you are doing your part to meet the intellectual needs discussed in detail in the first section of this chapter. Your unique contribution can supplement a school reading program or compensate for your child's loss if the school does not provide an appropriate reading program.

Especially if you homeschool, you will surely want to go beyond just assigning reading to discussing it with your child as an alternative to worksheets and as preparation for your child's writing assignments. A number of specific and helpful options are offered in *Creative Home Schooling for Gifted Children: A Resource Guide* by Rivero (2002). You may also wish to view the following websites for more resources (Steindorf, 2000):

> ➤ www.home-ed-press.com—informational site on home schooling, including articles, a resource page, and an online newsletter.

➤ www.ala.org/parentspage—American Library Association listing of over 700 sites recommended especially for parents and children.

➤ www.libraryspot.com—a "reference desk" with encyclopedias, dictionaries, maps, phone books, and statistics for research.

Earlier in this chapter, the intellectual needs detailed in Chapter 2 were summarized: thinking effectively, being exposed to a variety of people and ideas, individual pacing, and being amongst intellectual peers. As a parent, you can meet these needs in ways that may not be possible at school.

Thinking Effectively

At home, your child should feel free to use the full range of her growing vocabulary, trying out new connotations as she tests the full meaning of words she has read. If she makes a mistake in pronunciation (common for children who pick up new words by reading, as well as by hearing them), you can correct her gently.

You can allow divergent thinking, recognizing that children need to try out ideas by talking about them. In this trying-out period, children may sound more convinced than they really are, and your role is to listen calmly, ask thoughtful questions, and offer your own opinions as something the child might want to consider.

You can provide enough time to consider ideas in depth. By asking follow-up questions ("What do you mean by that?") and identifying meaningless slang expressions when your child uses them, you can help your children think carefully and use language more precisely. By asking questions that require analysis, synthesis, and evaluation, you can challenge your child to think more deeply.

Encountering a Variety of People and Ideas

When you routinely take your child to the library and help him select books, you have an opportunity to expose him to new worlds of people and ideas. You can suggest books that open up new topics and new points of view. When discussing these books, you can guide your child to think of alternatives and to predict and examine the consequences.

If your child is hypercritical of others, you may make a special effort to find books that promote sympathy for people in difficult situations. Librarians are always glad to make suggestions.

Individual Pacing

Simply by helping your child find books that interest and challenge her, you are individualizing her reading. You will find suggestions and criteria for choosing books in Chapters 3, 6, and 7, and in the bibliography.

You can introduce your child to the idea of an incubation period and help him learn to recognize his own patterns of processing information. This self-knowledge will be useful in scheduling book discussions at home and can be transferred to the scheduling of school assignments and social relationships.

By allowing open-ended discussion and not expecting a conclusive answer, you can give your child experience in considering diverse approaches to problems. Your acceptance will confirm the value of different responses and encourage individuality.

Talking with Intellectual Peers

In a discussion of a book that both participants have read, the importance of the age difference between them tends to diminish. If you have a genuine desire to know what your child thinks rather than an overriding need to give your own opinion, then you and your child are starting the discussion as peers.

Parents who lack time for or interest in book discussion may find a relative or friend who can act as reading partner for their children. Although this means the loss of family interaction, it could be a mutually enriching relationship and a very satisfactory solution.

In a book discussion, whether group or individual, there is always a triad: the leader, the child(ren), and the author. As gifted children grow older, they will find authors who can play the role of intellectual peers. Thus, when you foster book discussion at home, you are setting the stage for continually introducing your child to potential peers.

If book discussions are offered at school, you can reinforce them at home with your unique knowledge of your children. If they are not offered at school, then home may be the only place where your intellectually curious children have the advantages of reading and talking about books.

Discussing Books with Your Children

The first step, if you are not sure how to begin talking about books with your children, is to read the section earlier in this chapter called "Discussion Techniques" carefully, and perhaps look into some of the references listed at the end of this chapter. Many questioning techniques, as well as the programs mentioned, can be adapted from group to individual discussion.

With this information in your background, you are ready to begin. A good starting point would be to consider the following tips from a booklet called *Communicating through Young Adult Books*, by Pat Scales:

➤ Make available as many books as your teen wants.

➤ Ask your teen to recommend books he/she would like you to read.

➤ Read the book and focus your thoughts on the adolescent main character.

➤ Discuss the book with your teenager.

➤ Encourage the exchange of ideas and opinions without being judgmental.

➤ Find a special family time to talk about books and encourage each family member (even the youngest) to join.

In addition to asking your child for book recommendations, you may wish to suggest books for him to read. You can arrange with your child to trade book recommendations so that both parents and child have an opportunity to ask the other to read a favorite book.

How do you begin a discussion? Plan ahead, thinking about your conversation as you read the book. You will probably find the plot and the characters to be the best sources of questions, although you may want to go beyond these to questions about the setting or the author's writing style.

Plot	Think about the points of *conflict* and *decision*. How did they affect the outcome of the story? What would have happened if…? Would that have been better or worse than…?
Characters	Consider their *motivation*. Why did X do as he/she did? What would you have done? How did relationships among the characters affect their choices?
Setting	In some books, the setting is enough of a factor to warrant discussion. How does the environment (social, political, natural, or family) affect the plot (decisions)? How does it affect the characters (motivation)?
Writing style	Pay attention to the author's choice of words, symbolism, and figurative language—imagery metaphors, similes. Note elements of style you relish, and mark sentences you find especially apt or beautiful.

Have two or three questions in mind as you begin talking with your child. Be certain they are real questions. Having thought about them, you may have your answers ready, but that does not make them the right answers. You must truly want to know *what your child thinks* about the question, in order to have a real discussion. The less you talk and the more you listen, the more you will learn about your child. Listen to her first, and only share your thoughts with her later.

If your child is not in a school reading program that includes the use of a reading log, you may want to encourage him to begin one at home. Different from a mere list of books that he has read, the reading log is a record of the date of the entry and the book read, followed by his responses or reactions to the book. He can write his thoughts and questions about the characters, plot, ideas, symbols, theme, or any other aspect of the story after each reading session, not waiting until he has finished the entire book. Also appropriate are comments about what he does or doesn't like or doesn't understand and personal experiences that relate to the story. What he should *not* write—because it is not really helpful—is a simple summary of the plot.

Whether he shares his journal or parts of it in discussion with you should be his choice. In any case, the thinking and analysis that have gone into the reading log should become evident in your discussions.

Using the Library

If children are to learn how to use books and other media to satisfy their craving for knowledge, they must be able to use libraries effectively. Since good school library services are not available everywhere, parents should know what resources and library staffing that students ideally would have available to them and what information-gathering skills they should acquire at each step of the way. This section is designed to help parents evaluate the school library services available to their child. If the school library program is not ideal, it may be possible to find a nearby public library with more resources and a staff willing to help an eager learner.

Resources

Just a few years ago, "library resources" referred to print (fiction, non-fiction, and reference books, as well as magazines and newspapers) and audio-visual media (such as films and tape recordings). These familiar resources are now accompanied by computers using CD-ROMs and the Internet.

Secondary school libraries are usually the first to be equipped with computers; elementary libraries usually follow, though it may take several years to do so. Therefore, many elementary students are still using print resources entirely. Your child's library books may be checked out on a computerized circulation system, but it may be the only terminal in the library, inaccessible to students. Or she may be able to use a computer to search the library's online public access catalog (OPAC). In more sophisticated libraries, she is also learning to use computers to consult online encyclopedias, to search for magazine or newspaper articles through various databases, or to search the Internet for information on a particular topic.

Parents who are evaluating library services should welcome any opportunity for their children to master computer skills, including searching for information from electronic as well as print sources. However, as schools upgrade their technological capacity, the temptation is to emphasize the purchase of computers over books. Encourage the addition of computers in your school libraries, but remember that books, too, are needed for the optimal intellectual and emotional growth of your student.

Staffing

The quality of a library program always depends on the energy, training, and commitment of the person in charge. At the secondary level, where accreditation standards apply, you will probably find professionally-trained librarians who hold a master's degree (M.A., M.S., or M.L.S.) from a graduate school of library science.

Unfortunately, elementary libraries usually lack adequate staffing. Too often, a single professional librarian oversees the libraries in several elementary schools, acting as consultant to the parent volunteers or library assistants who are there when children visit the library. These volunteers and aides are generally deeply committed to children and books, and they make children welcome in the library. Nevertheless, much is lost in schools that do not have a professional librarian who is trained to help both students and teachers use the library resources in support of the curriculum. Assistants are often called librarians; you may have to ask school officials to learn whether your child's school library is staffed by someone who holds a master's degree.

If your children attend a school without a professional librarian, learn how much they are being taught about library skills, and ask for help at the public library if necessary. Redouble your efforts to learn about children's literature, and encourage your children to read good fiction. And if possible, become a library volunteer, support the library assistant, and work for the hiring of more professional librarians in your community's schools.

For more on evaluating your school library, see the American Library Association website, www.ala.org/parentspage. Pointing out that research shows that test scores are higher for children whose school libraries have professionally-trained librarians, this site also lists questions to ask librarians and ways to support your school library staff.

Information-Gathering Skills

As electronic technology is introduced into school libraries, older research methods become obsolete. At the same time, new teaching programs blend age groupings of students for units of study, altering the traditional schedules for teaching library skills.

While these trends create a patchwork, making it difficult to say just what a student in a given grade should be expected to know about using a library, they vastly improve opportunities for students to learn. When innovative educational practices are implemented in their ideal form with a trained librarian available to plan with teachers and guide students, they offer a major advantage over traditional approaches—the opportunity to teach library and research skills *at the right time*, when the student needs the resources of the library to proceed with the study of a subject in which a skilled teacher has already sparked interest. Then the library materials are important tools and the librarian a valued resource, while the focus is on the knowledge the student wants.

The process of learning to research via print material is described below for each age level. Because children learn to use the Internet at various ages depending on accessibility, a discussion of issues related to research on the Internet follows in a separate section.

What They Need to Know and When

The ideal time to teach children to use the library is during the elementary years, when they regard the library system as both a code they can break and an exciting challenge. For middle schoolers, the system appears just easy enough to be boring, and if introduced for the first time at that age, few students pay enough attention to master it. For them, instruction in library use should be reinforcement and enhancement of skills gained earlier.

Lower elementary grades. In the early years, children should learn the basics: what resources are in the library, and how to find them.

Primary children begin by learning (if they do not already know from public library experience) that fiction books are on the shelves according to the author's last name, making the connection between the letter on the spine of the book and the label on the shelf. Soon they differentiate between fiction and nonfiction, and they learn where these sections are in the library. They also identify the parts of the book (author, title, publisher, publication date)—preparation for the bibliographies they will be asked to include with reports as they grow older.

Using the online public access catalog, they learn to locate information about a book, whether they know the author, the title, or the subject. They begin with the major classes of the Dewey Decimal system and learn how to decode the call number. Then, learning that nonfiction is in order numerically by subject, they know how to search the shelves for both nonfiction and fiction.

Beginning research, they learn how to use long encyclopedia articles effectively. They discover various reference books in addition to encyclopedias, and they learn to use the index, a key to the information in nonfiction books.

Upper elementary grades. Older students need more sophisticated techniques for gaining access to information. Whether they learn through print indexes such as the *Readers' Guide* or through an electronic program such as ProQuest or InfoTrac, they need instruction in the use of indexes to find information hidden in magazines or beyond the reach of the catalog of their local media center. Encyclopedias provide key words and phrases, as well as outlines that help organize information from several sources.

Middle school and senior high. If the basics of library use—the location of materials and the means of access to information, whether print or electronic—are taught in the elementary years, secondary school students can focus on using more sophisticated reference sources and learning correct bibliographic form.

Middle school students can learn the use of subheadings within subjects, looking up historical and geographical information in the public access catalog. If they have mastered the use of indexes to periodicals through the *Readers' Guide*, high school students can branch out to specialized references for art, biography, science and technology, education, and the humanities. They are able to recognize and use more sophisticated access points beyond the familiar author, title, and subject, and they can write correct and complete bibliographic references to books, encyclopedias, magazine articles, and Internet sites. If they have not already done so, they should begin to use the public library as well as the school library.

Helping Your Child Use the Public Library

As Internet access becomes essential to research, it is especially important for your student to establish a working relationship with the public library. Yet some public librarians report that because teens are so busy with sports and after-school work, a few parents have begun doing their research for them, coming to the library to swoop all the books on the designated topic off the shelves and take them home. These parents may have forgotten that high school teachers assign research papers to help students learn the *process* of research, so that in college it will be automatic. Over-helpful parents sabotage the learning of the process. There is a better way to help your teen use the public library. Here are some tips.

> ➤ Help your student go prepared to the library for research. Be certain she can clearly articulate the assignment for herself and to the librarian. If she cannot, have her ask the teacher or classmates to clarify the assignment before she makes the trip to the library.

> ➤ If possible, your student should take with him a written assignment sheet. Experienced public librarians have probably seen the same assignment in previous years. They can help interpret it.

> ➤ Most public libraries have converted the "card" catalog to computers. Now, to use the catalog, students must be able to type and spell accurately. Check that your student can spell any unfamiliar key words in her assignment.

> ➤ The computer catalog is not infallible. It includes mistakes and always needs to be updated, just as the old card catalogs did. Your student should be comfortable in asking for help if the catalog does not yield what he needs.

> ➤ If your student lacks library research skills, investigate what the public library offers. Many offer classes for school, Scout, or home schooling groups. Some offer classes in computer use and research. If no classes are available, a librarian can to work individually with your child.

Public libraries offer much more than print material. A librarian may direct students to videos related to the topic and to audiotapes that are available to help students who have difficulty reading. And as always, the librarians themselves are there to answer questions.

Research on the Internet

Students may know more than their classroom teachers or their parents about using the Internet. If so, they need the guidance of school or public librarians to learn to use it effectively. Parents who wish to monitor their children's education carefully should determine whether students are learning good Internet research practices, and supplement where it seems necessary. The following is intended not as a complete discussion, but only to give parents the basic information they need to judge whether their children need assistance.

In 1998, 8.6 million children under 12 went online. Within a five-year period, that number was expected to grow to 23.4 million, according to Jupiter Communications, a New York-based consulting firm. About 75 percent of these students are using the Internet to do their homework, Jupiter reports (Colhoun, 2000). So we know that by the middle school years, many students have begun using the Internet for research. There is much for them to learn in order to use it well, but one of the basics is this: beginning at this point and continuing through senior high school, parents should be certain that students know the difference between databases and search engines, and that they gain increasingly sophisticated skills in using each.

Databases. Research on the Internet should begin not by searching the web through search engines such as Yahoo! and Google, but by using electronic databases such as ProQuest, InfoTrac, and OCLC FirstSearch. The reason is simple: these databases offer information that is documented and can be verified. To be certain they are gathering valid information, today's students must learn to use electronic databases to search indexes—the *Readers' Guide* is one example—just as their parents learned to use them in print form. They can find reliable bibliographic information, magazine and newspaper indexes—and often the full text of articles—as well as cataloged websites that can be recommended for research. The indexes are those that students have relied on for years; the articles are from professional journals that provide editorial oversight. In electronic research, databases are the first step because their accuracy can be trusted, relieving the students of the responsibility for determining the value of the information they find. Still, researchers must determine whether the articles cited are current. In fast-moving fields—for example, medicine—a journal article that was accurate when it was printed may be outdated in a few months.

To access databases, which are sold by subscriptions too costly for most individuals to buy, students need the help of their school or public library. Libraries provide terminals with online access, and many provide remote access to online research materials for their patrons—that is, the students of a school library or the cardholders of a public library can enter the databases to which the library subscribes to do research from home. One mark of a good school library is the quality of instruction students receive in using databases for their school projects. If adequate instruction is not available at school, inquire at the public library.

Search engines. Students doing their homework online are probably at home, where they have easy access to search engines such as Yahoo!, Google, or Excite. Using keywords, they locate websites that offer information on a vast range of topics. They must understand that this free, unmonitored information can be entered by anyone who can put up a website, and it must be carefully evaluated by the user. Therefore, students need guidance to sort the valuable from the frivolous. Colhoun (2000) recommends that to question effectively and make sound judgments, researchers should:

> ➤ examine the qualifications of the author by looking for evidence of training or experience,

> ➤ infer any biases that may be present by noticing the suffix of the site's address (sites ending in ".com" may be selling something; those ending in ".org" may wish to influence their viewers' thinking),

➤ observe how often the site is updated. (Is the information too old for the topic?), and

➤ determine whether the information is properly documented and verifiable.

Regarding teaching students to use the Internet for research, Jacqueline Hess of the Academy of Educational Development comments: "You have to teach how to identify source bias and balance that with other sources—teach how information fits in a larger context." She goes on to say, "The art of logical reasoning— once a staple in educational training—will have to be taught again" (Colhoun, 2000, p. 8).

The Internet has forever changed the process of doing research for school projects. Using the databases and search engines they find on the Internet, today's students have at their fingertips an unimaginable wealth of information, and it will only grow. The challenge is not so much to find information as it is to know how to find and identify the most *valuable* and *trustworthy* information. As students learn to use this modern tool, they are challenged to incorporate into their work classical standards for clear thinking.

References

Alexander, D. (1991, April 21). He told us so. *New York Times Book Review*, p. 16.

Alvino, J. (1985). *Parents' guide to raising a gifted child: Recognizing and developing your child's potential*. Boston: Little, Brown.

Applebee, A. (1978). *The child's concept of story: Ages two to seventeen*. Chicago: University of Chicago Press.

Atwell, N. (1987). *In the middle: Writing, reading, and learning with adolescents*. Upper Montclair, NJ: Boynton/Cook.

Barzun, J. (1991). *Begin here: The forgotten conditions of teaching and learning*. Chicago: University of Chicago Press.

Baskin, B. (1998). Call me Ishmael: A look at gifted middle school readers. In K. Beers & B. G. Samuels, (Eds.) *Into focus: Understanding and creating middle school readers* (pp. 65-79). Norwood, MA: Christopher-Gordon.

Bauer, M. D. (1991, January/February). An author's letter to teachers. *Horn Book, 67*, 111-116.

Bloom, B., Ed. (1956). *Taxonomy of educational objectives*. New York: David McKay.

Brown, W. & Rogan, J. (1983). Reading and young gifted children. *Roeper Review, 5*, 6-9.

Castiglione, L. V. (1987). *Questioning methods for gifted students*. East Aurora, NY: DOK.

Chall, J. S. (1967). *Learning to read: The great debate*. New York: McGraw-Hill.

Clark, B. (1983). *Growing up gifted: Developing the potential of children at home and at school*. 2nd ed. Columbus, OH: Charles Merrill.

Colhoun, A. (2000, May 11-17). But—I found it on the Internet! *The Christian Science Monitor: MonitorWeek*, 1 (16), 8.

Cullinan, B. E. (1989, April). Latching on to literature: Reading initiatives take hold. *School Library Journal, 35*, 27-31.

Dole, J. A. & Adams, P. J. (1983). Reading curriculum for gifted readers: A survey. *Gifted Child Quarterly, 27*, 64-77.

Flack, J. (2000). The gifted reader in the regular classroom: Strategies for success. *Illinois Association for Gifted Children: Journal 2000*, 22-30.

Flesch, R. (1955). *Why Johnny can't read—and what you can do about it.* New York: Harper.

Galda, L. (1998). Mirrors and windows: Reading as transformation. In Raphael, T. E. & Au, K. H., *Literature-based instruction: Reshaping the curriculum.* Norwood, MA: Christopher-Gordon.

Hall, S. L. & Moats, L. C. (1999). *Straight talk about reading: How parents can make a difference in the early years.* Lincolnwood, IL: Contemporary Books.

Healy, J. M. (1999). *Endangered minds: Why children don't think—and what we can do about it.* New York: Simon & Schuster.

Hopkins, L. B. (1991). Leave me alone! Cries the poem. *Perspectives,* 7 (3), xiii-xv.

Howe-Cousar, C. (1990). *Instructing gifted middle-school readers.* Rowley, MA: New England League of Middle Schools.

Lahr, S. S. (1991). *The child's developing sense of theme: Responses to literature.* New York: Teachers College Press.

Lynch-Brown, C. & Tomlinson, C. M. (1999). *Essentials of children's reading* (3rd ed.). Boston: Allyn and Bacon.

Newman, P. R. & Newman, B. M. (1983). *Principles of psychology.* Homewood, IL: Dorsey.

Noe, K. L. S. & Johnson, N. J. (1999). *Getting started with literature circles.* Norwood, MA: Christopher-Gordon.

Probst, R. (1988). *Teaching literature in junior and senior high.* Portsmouth, NH: Heineman.

Ravitch, D. (2000). *Left back: A century of failed school reforms.* New York: Simon & Schuster.

Reis, S. M. & Renzulli, J. S. (1989, December). Providing challenging programs for gifted readers. *Roeper Review,* 12, 92-97.

Rimm, S. B. (1994). *Keys to parenting the gifted child.* Hauppauge, NY: Barron's Educational Series.

Rivero, L. (2002). *Creative home schooling for gifted children: A resource guide.* Scottsdale, AZ: Great Potential Press.

Saunders, J. (1991). *Bringing out the best: A resource guide for parents of young gifted children* (Rev. ed.). Minneapolis: Free Spirit.

Scales, P. (n.d.). *Communicating through young adult books.* New York: Bantam.

Spiegel, D. L. (1990, December). Literature resource materials revisited. *The Reading Teacher,* 44, 336-339.

Steindorf, S. (2000, May 11-17). Sites to see. *The Christian Science Monitor: MonitorWeek*, 1 (16), 9.

VanTassel-Baska, J. (1989, November/December). The fine art of discussion (Part I). *Understanding Our Gifted*, 2 (2), 5.

Walker, S. Y. & Perry, H. K. (1991). *The survival guide for parents of gifted kids: How to understand, live with, and stick up for your gifted child.* Minneapolis: Free Spirit.

Part Three:

The Books

Chapter 6

Choosing Books that Challenge

Nearly everywhere children go, they can easily pick up inexpensive books. While many of these are excellent, books of poor quality—but with enticing covers—are everywhere. How can children learn to make good choices?

Selecting books for children, and helping them select their own reading, requires thought and effort. Yet parents who carefully monitor their children's television watching may pay no attention to what the children are reading; they simply may not know what is good and what is not. (Monitoring reading, incidentally, is much more fun than monitoring television, because there are many more alternatives to bad books than there are to bad television programs.)

For teachers and librarians, too, a perennial issue is the quality of children's reading. Some say, "It doesn't matter what they read, as long as they're reading." But if we apply this attitude to children who have the potential to become serious readers acquainted with books of substance and literary value, then we do our children a disservice.

We who guide the development of children have the responsibility and the pleasure of supplying them with the most meaningful material available. Part of the pleasure is that there is a wealth of good children's literature. But what is it that makes certain books especially appropriate for *gifted* children?

Like the children themselves, the books they cherish have a special spark. This spark has been analyzed and codified so that it is possible to list the characteristics that make some books particularly good choices—not exclusively for children of high potential, but especially for them.

This chapter brings together ways to identify books that not only are good literature, but also appeal to gifted readers.

For Emotional Development

Finding literature that speaks to the emotional world of the bright or intellectually curious child requires knowledge of that world, reflected in the categories in Chapters 1 and 2 (establishing an identity, being alone, relationships with others, using one's ability, and the drive to understand) and in the longer list of categories in the index to Chapter 8, the bibliography. It also requires a wide-ranging knowledge of books that depict that world.

Meeting these two requirements takes time and sensitivity, but it can be done. Children's author Katherine Paterson (1989, p. 68-69) relates that she declined an invitation to serve on a panel on using books with troubled children, because she wants a reader to "come to a book from his own experience and take from the book what he can and will. I don't want anyone telling a child what he should get out of one of my books." But she attended the panel discussion, and was pleased to hear:

> three highly competent, obviously compassionate people tell about the healing power of the imagination. They never diagnosed a child and then prescribed a particular book. They read widely themselves and had available in their offices many books. "When I get to know a child," one of them said, "I also know four or five books that I think he might like and that might mean something to him."

To build toward that kind of intuitive response, most of us must begin with concrete criteria. Here are some components of the spark that gives a book emotional appeal for gifted readers:

1.   The characters are coping with one or more of the same problems the readers are facing, such as establishing an identity—learning how to be human in their own particular way. In *Call It Courage*, Mafatu leaves his home island in order to overcome his fear of the ocean. When he returns, he knows without being told that he has earned his place among his people.

     Characters may be in the process of accepting themselves as people who enjoy being alone, like Jamie, the quiet boy who doesn't mind being different in *Part-Time Boy*.

     They may be learning to find friends, as in *Jennifer, Hecate, Macbeth, William McKinley and Me, Elizabeth*, where Jennifer displays her own rather unusual method of making a friend when she needs one. Or they may be learning to keep friends, as are Stephanie and Rachel in *Just as Long as We're Together*, who discover that there are times when it is best to tell secrets.

     The issue may be choices about commitment to schoolwork, practice time, or to one's own talent—a theme which is especially well developed in stories set in a time when school conflicted with farm labor, as in *Across Five Aprils* and *The Wolfling*.

2.   The characters are not necessarily gifted themselves, or at least not labeled as such, but they stand alone or in a small group for their convictions. In *The Cat Ate My Gymsuit*, Marcy takes a stand against an administrative decision at school and then finds herself for the first time part of a group, when students who agree with her speak out.

3. A character may be different from his peers and may be learning to cope with this difference—which could be an interest, a family situation, a handicap, or anything that sets that person apart. For Joshua Taylor in *A Time to Fly Free*, the difference is his extreme sensitivity to his classmates' cruelty toward living creatures. Through the understanding and support of his parents, he is able to work with an older man who helps Josh learn to use his sensitivity and to temper it with realism.

4. The characters may be learning to accept someone else who is different, as in *Summer of the Swans*. This is the story of a sister's affection for a mentally handicapped younger brother, affection not always shared or understood by neighborhood children.

5. Adult characters should be present and supportive in at least some of the books. Much contemporary literature for adolescents depicts adults who are weak or absent, giving the young people more control over their own lives. They still need adult concern, however, and it is comfortingly present in books such as *Caddie Woodlawn* and Lois Lowry's books about Anastasia Krupnik and her family.

6. Some characters should be gifted adults who lead productive and enjoyable lives, and in general function well as gifted people in the adult world. The O'Keefes in Madeleine L'Engle's books are vivid examples of this.

7. Some of the child characters should clearly be gifted themselves, so that the reader can say, "He's like me. I feel that way, too. Maybe I'm not the only one who thinks this way!" Several books in the annotated bibliography meet this criterion. Young readers can see themselves in stories told as myths, too, such as Jane Yolen's *The Boy*

Who Had Wings, and they can discuss the nature of their own "wings."

8. Giftedness need not necessarily be labeled, but may be implicit—that is, it may simply be comfortably accepted—and life goes on from there. It is clear enough in stories of warm, lively, and supportive families, such as *Cheaper by the Dozen*.

9. Characters should be people to whom the reader can relate: open-minded and questioning, with a passion for learning everything, such as Nathaniel in Latham's *Carry On, Mr. Bowditch*; or idealistic and intense, with a devotion to a cause, such as Raisha in *My Name Is Not Angelica*, Scott O'Dell's novel based on a slave revolt in 1733.

10. Some books for gifted readers should depict characters struggling with issues of personal or moral courage, personal values, and moral and ethical choices. In *The Witch of Blackbird Pond*, Kit Tyler, newly arrived from Barbados, befriends an old woman who is thought by the people of her village to be a witch. Evident in the story are Kit's courage and also the greater moral struggle of her Puritan uncle.

11. Some books should have humor of a high level—spontaneously arising from a situation, springing from a character's way of looking at the world, or based on intelligent use of language. An example is *A Day No Pigs Would Die*. The character Rob's humorous use of language is unconscious, but the author Robert Newton Peck clearly knows what he is doing. Picture books, too, can provide sophisticated humor—for example, *Sir Cedric*, in which humor is based on impossible proportions in the illustrations and on elevated language of mock seriousness.

Of course, no one book can be expected to meet every item on this checklist, but a collection can. The goal is to keep the criteria in mind while gathering as many books as eager readers have time to read. With the list as a guide, and experience and exposure to a number of excellent books, it is possible for adults to develop an instinctive sense for books that will catch and hold the readers' interest and give them something to think about long after the books have been read.

For Intellectual Development

For optimal intellectual development, very bright children must learn to acknowledge and satisfy their need to know. Books that will help them achieve this goal must both satisfy and whet their curiosity, and be intellectually challenging. But just what does make a book intellectually challenging? The specific criteria for picture books are different from those for older children's books, but the underlying idea is the same: the pictures, the words, and the themes must expand the child's world, encourage further exploration, and enrich the mind and spirit with artistic integrity.

Picture Books

Writing about requirements for successful picture books, Rosemary Wells (1990, pp. 129-131) begins with feelings:

> First of all, a good picture book must ring with emotional content, so that children care about what's going on. William Steig's *Amos and Boris* and *Sylvester and the Magic Pebble* never fail to overwhelm a reader with both worry and love.... What is in them is in all of us: guilt, fear, devotion. As a writer you have little time and few pages to achieve this. The characters in a children's book must reach into the heart of the reader on page one.

Moving on to more practical criteria, Wells says picture books must be short.

> A picture book is in trouble if it's longer than eight double-spaced typewritten pages. It's also in trouble if it's bland, or if the tone is false and hysterical. It must never be cute or it will insult children. It's in trouble if it uses television characters, or if it's written by anybody with a degree in child psychology.

This last comment can be extended from child psychologists to any author whose intent is to teach or "improve" children through the writing.

Picture books are a unique blend of visual art and language. Looking for the best among them means assessing the illustrations, the text, and the fit between the two. If a book passes muster in these three ways, what further characteristics make it intellectually challenging?

Presenting a list of picture books that demand higher-level thinking skills in the pictures, the text, or both, Mockett and Welton (1990) stress the importance of books that promote creative and divergent thinking and provide humor and wordplay.

At first, these expectations may seem unrealistically high for a picture book, but the best of them have much to offer, and a rich assortment will contain all of these elements. Picture books for gifted children should have the following characteristics:

1.   Illustrations should be vibrant and original rather than stereotyped. This is what Wells means when she says a picture book is in trouble if it uses television characters—and she might have added comic book characters, as well. For example, consider a book containing Disney characters, or with pictures such as those in the reading textbooks of the past. Then see the illustrations by Marcia Brown for Cendrars' *Shadow*—artwork that evokes in

color and shape the sense of awe and mystery that is conveyed by the words of the poem.

2. Illustrations should not merely accompany the story line but complement and enhance it. Good examples are the books by Maurice Sendak, in which the expressions on the characters' faces tell the story from their own points of view. In Jeannie Baker's *Where the Forest Meets the Sea*, the illustrations show the boy's sense of the faded presence of ancient life as he explores the rainforest, adding emotional overtones that are not found in the text.

3. Details of the illustrations should be so fascinating that a child can look repeatedly and always find more: a surprise or a bit of humor, a private joke between the illustrator and the attentive child. Books by Richard Scarry and Peter Spier are prime examples. Spier's *People* invites adults to join the game, helping the child understand the variety of images on the crowded pages.

4. Some books should be provided that offer abstract illustrations that, while recognizable, still require mental exercise to be understood. Tana Hoban's *Shadows and Reflections* invite the child to study each picture to see what is really there.

5. Illustrations should not supply all of the details of information so that some imaginative effort on the part of the child is needed to complete the picture. McDermott's illustrations for the African tale *Anansi the Spider* uses geometric shapes to challenge the imagination to form images that tell the story.

6. Books should introduce new and fascinating words—satisfying to the tongue as the child learns to say them—mixed in plentiful measure amongst the familiar words. Cuteness and condescension are neither necessary nor

welcome; what is needed is respect for the child as an intelligent, learning person. Authors of good children's books about dinosaurs, for example, make the correct assumption that four-year-olds can pronounce Ichthyosaurus and Tyrannosaurus Rex.

7. Authors who obviously take delight in the use of language—whose books demonstrate a playful, joyful sense of fun with words—appeal to gifted children. Dr. Seuss books encourage children to experiment with words, making them up as necessary and bending them slightly to create a rhyme.

    Some picture books offer play with languages other than English. The text of *Abuela* includes Spanish, tantalizing an English-speaking child with the possibility of learning bits of another language. *Who's in Rabbit's House?* and other African folktales are told with the soothing repetition of sounds typical of speech.

8. Books should depict characters, whether animal or human, who display real emotions, feelings, and relationships that the child will recognize. In *Alexander and the Terrible, Horrible, No Good, Very Bad Day,* for example, Alexander displays frustration, anger, and finally resignation toward the kind of day he is having—a day in which ordinary, everyday disasters happen to him all day long, as they sometimes do to everyone.

9. Plots that are not completely predictable allow for conjecturing and discussion between adult and child as the book is read. *Free Fall* is an example—a visual presentation of a dream, leaving child and adult to interpret a story line to suit the pictures.

10. Even picture books can raise moral questions, helping young children who are already concerned about the environment, for example. These books can too easily

be cloying and "preachy," but if well done, they can offer reassurance that a child is not alone in her concerns. In *Hey! Get Off Our Train*, Burningham provides a vehicle for discussion of environmental concerns, one area that concerns gifted children earlier than most of their age-mates are aware of it.

11. Stories, pictures, and characters that are outside of the daily experience of the child can help to expand his awareness. *Anno's Journey*, the story of a journey through medieval Europe, supported by illustrations that are filled with detail and interest, presents not only other countries, but also another time.

Books for Older Children

"Language," says Barbara Baskin (1998, p. 70), "is the single most important component…in selecting engaging and stimulating material for gifted students." She argues that gifted children should have higher-level books, including books at the adult level in some cases, as well as longer and more complex books than teachers would select for most readers.

In addition, Baskin contends that theme is more important than plot, since important themes present the larger picture that intellectually able readers are eager to assimilate. She suggests that appropriate motifs for these students include philosophical, moral, and social issues, as well as studies of heroism, boundaries, and relationships.

Baskin also cites aspects of literary structure that create challenges for the reader, including time manipulations, parallel plots, ideas pulled together from several disciplines, and metaphor.

All of these criteria are considered when books for older readers are judged according to the language, style, plot, and setting. In each area, books appropriate for gifted readers are complex rather than simple, rich and varied rather than predictable, and open-ended and thought provoking rather than neatly contained.

Look for the following characteristics in books that provide intellectual stimulation for gifted readers:

Language

1. Language should be on a high level, making strong demands on the reader's vocabulary. Hermann Hesse's *Demian*, first published in 1925 in Europe, assumes an extremely well-educated reader and rewards good readers with a rich and unrestricted vocabulary.

2. As with illustrations in a picture book, language in a book for older readers should reflect and enhance the plot. In Garfield and Blishen's retelling of Greek myths, *The God Beneath the Sea*, the level of language serves to ennoble the text. In *The Phantom Tollbooth*, humorous, pun-filled language is part of the message of the book— that language itself is a source of delight and challenge. In both cases, the language accomplishes more than presenting the story; it becomes an essential part of the reading experience.

3. Books that contain pronunciation guides are helpful for gifted readers (though they are rare, and a pleasant surprise when found), since so many avid readers know words only from reading and therefore mispronounce them. One excellent teacher of gifted high school students calls this "The Calley-ope (calliope) Syndrome."

4. Look for masterfully chosen descriptive words that stimulate strong visual imagery. For example, in *A String in the Harp*, Bond's descriptions encourage the reader to picture the modern Wales that Peter knows in daily life—and later, to superimpose onto that picture the Wales of Taliesin's time, which Peter envisions.

5. As with picture books, books for gifted readers should be written by authors who delight in language and who

skillfully express nuances of thought and feeling. Joyce Carol Thomas's *Marked by Fire* is notable for the way in which language—prose and poetry—evokes place and mood, moving the story along on an emotional level.

6.   Language patterns and vocabularies from other times and places, used without apology or explanation, encourage the reader to glean the meaning from the context. Examples abound: Garfield's *Smith*, which evokes 18th century England; Mayne's *Earthfasts*, employing the language of remote corners of modern Wales; Ayn Rand's *Anthem*, with an imagined language of the future; Jean Auel's *The Clan of the Cave Bear*, which supposes a language system from the past.

Style

7.   Books for gifted readers can display the full complement of literary devices that enrich the fabric of literature and therefore the reader (whether he recognizes these devices by name or not): metaphor, simile, paradox, symbol, allusion. Poetry does this by its very nature; an example in prose is *The Bat-Poet* by the poet Randall Jarrell.

Plot

8.   In book selection as in curriculum, it is helpful to remember Maurice Freehill's (1961) insight that gifted children are "challenged by the unfinished and the misunderstood." If this is true, then at least some of the books they read should present problems that are unresolved, even at the end of the book. Such plots cause the reader to look at a situation from different perspectives, see possible conclusions, and ponder what desirable or likely options are available. At the end of *Izzy, Willy-Nilly*, for example, we know that Izzy is forever changed—but we

are left to conjecture about how the changes in her will affect her relationships with friends and family.

9.   Good readers should be developing the ability to hold different levels of meaning in their minds simultaneously, and some of the books they read should give them experience in doing this. For example, *The Village by the Sea* requires the reader to look below the storyline to understand the universal human motives that are being played out as the plot unfolds and the characters reveal themselves.

10.   The structure of a plot can put the mind to work—for instance, flashbacks, narration that shifts from one person to another, or the use of a journal format can all challenge and reward the careful reader. A good example is Konigsburg's *Father's Arcane Daughter*, in which each chapter is introduced by a dialogue between unidentified characters, adding to the mystery while simultaneously supplying clues for the surprise ending. More complex and demanding is the structure of Vonnegut's *Slaughterhouse Five*, which presents a fluid view of time through the character of Billy Pilgrim.

Setting

11.   The settings of some books allow children to experience vicariously lifestyles that are not their own; an example is the vivid description of traditional living patterns on Mafatu's Pacific island in *Call It Courage*. Children growing up in small towns or rural areas can learn something of great art museums and of life in New York City by reading *From the Mixed-up Files of Mrs. Basil E. Frankweiler*, or they can see a darker view of New York street life in *Slake's Limbo*.

Finally, to challenge intellectually, books should be written with the assumption that readers possess some background either in experience or in reading. With this in mind, one quick way of finding books that are intellectually demanding is to look for books from England or in translation from a foreign language— because authors of children's books in other countries generally assume more background and education on the part of the reader than many American children's authors do. Such books will probably contain some colloquial terms unfamiliar to American readers, but the meaning of most can be determined from the context, and they add both to the challenge of the book and to its power to expand the reader's knowledge of other cultures.

Bloom's (1956) terminology helps to form a neat statement of the characteristics of books that offer intellectual challenge to gifted students: such books invite *analysis* of characters and events, *synthesis* of ideas from the book under discussion and from anywhere else in the reader's experience, and *evaluation* of the relationships, actions, consequences, alternatives, and possibilities found in the book and in the reader's interpretation of it.

Again, it is obvious that no book will contain *all* characteristics listed for intellectually stimulating reading. However, if adults keep the characteristics in mind while they read reviews and browse the shelves of young people's literature, they will gradually be able to gather a collection that includes these criteria in abundance—a collection that will be invaluable for the gifted children and young people who have access to it.

Suggested Book Lists

In addition to the books listed in Chapter 8, several other selection guides are available for parents and teachers looking for books to recommend.

Baskin, Barbara H. and Karen H. Harris. *Books for the Gifted Child*. New York: Bowker, 1980.

Hauser, Paula and Gail A. Nelson. *Books for the Gifted Child, Volume 2*. New York: Bowker, 1988.

Hearne, Betsy Gould. *Choosing Books for Children: A Commonsense Guide*. 3rd ed. Urbana: University of Illinois Press, 1999.

Waldhorn, Arthur, Olga S. Weber, and Arthur Zeiger. *Good Reading: A Guide for Serious Readers*. 23rd ed. New York: Bowker, 1990. (For senior high and older.)

Parents looking for magazines to challenge gifted children may wish to consider *Calliope, Cobblestone,* and *Odyssey.*

References

Baskin, B. (1998). Call me Ishmael: A look at gifted middle school readers. In K. Beers & B. G. Samuels, (Eds.), *Into focus: Understanding and creating middle school readers* (pp. 65-79). Norwood, MA: Christopher-Gordon.

Bloom, B. S. (Ed.). (1956). *Taxonomy of educational objectives.* New York: David McKay.

Freehill, M. (1961). *Gifted children: Their psychology and education.* New York: Macmillan.

Mockett, S. & Welton, A. (1990, September 1). Picture books for the gifted. *Booklist, 87,* 63-66.

Paterson, K. (1989). *The spying heart: More thoughts on reading and writing books for children.* New York: Dutton.

Wells, R. (1990). The well-tempered children's book. In Zinsser, Paul (Ed.), *Worlds of childhood: The art and craft of writing for children.* Boston: Houghton Mifflin.

Chapter 7

All the Wealth:
Children's Literature

"Literature is the dominant art," says our son David, who holds a doctoral degree in comparative literature. In order to know music, sculpture, or painting, he points out, we have to know literature. Through most of history, composers have assumed listeners have read classic literature, but a writer does not normally assume his readers have heard a certain body of music. As far back as Homer, makers of literature were recognized as artists, but 2300 years later, sculptors were still considered stonecutters. In his lifetime, Michelangelo was recognized as a great craftsman, not an artist.

Historically, painters, sculptors, and musicians sought inspiration in literary themes to legitimize their work as art. Even now, the modern critic of other arts uses the history of literature as a frame of reference, while a literary critic—perhaps mistakenly—finds the history of his own field sufficient (David G. Halsted, personal communication, September 5, 1992).

If our children are to be truly educated, they must have a rich background in literature. They won't acquire all they need before the age of 18, but if we enthusiastically introduce them to all kinds of literature, they'll have a chance to become discriminating, mature readers who continue reading literature for pleasure throughout a lifetime. This chapter is designed to remind parents and teachers of the wealth of good books available to children.

The comfortable phrase, "curling up with a good book," brings to mind the prospect of spending an evening with a thick novel—a romance or a mystery, perhaps an historical novel, but certainly fiction. Although we tend to think of fiction first, the field of literature is more complex than that.

Within fiction there are several different types; there are also various categories of nonfiction. All of these are available to the child who wants to curl up with a good book—but only if she knows about them.

Here are four points to remember in using books to guide and enrich bright children:

> ➤ Some children, especially as they grow older, resist reading fiction.

> ➤ A lack of interest in this genre does not mean they must stop reading. There are many kinds of literature: *Fiction, nonfiction, biography, traditional literature, fantasy and science fiction,* and *poetry* are all discussed in this chapter.

> ➤ Gifted and talented youngsters, like other children, must be introduced to the best in literature. They will not automatically find it on their own.

> ➤ The different types of literature vary in their power to meet emotional and intellectual needs for gifted children, and their effect varies from one child to another. It is important that children be introduced to all kinds of literature, with enough exposure to each so that each child can decide which is most valuable for him or her.

Fiction will fall naturally into the hands of good readers in elementary school, but unless a planned effort is made to introduce them to other branches of literature, especially traditional literature and poetry, children may miss them altogether. Middle school and senior high students need guidance, too, to become aware of the wealth of literature as they develop into adult readers. Any kind of literature can be an important part of education—it can be a key to histories, arts, and cultures, particularly for these youngsters who are more likely to draw information from many sources and integrate it in new ways.

Guiding the reading of intellectually curious children, therefore, includes making them aware of the varieties of literature available and helping them learn which kinds have the most appeal for them. The resulting knowledge of books and of the child's own preferences is part of what makes a mature reader.

In elementary schools, the logical choice for the person to coordinate the introduction of literature through the grades is the librarian. Not every elementary school, however, boasts a professional who has time to plan and implement a program for introducing various types of literature at the appropriate grade levels. For teachers in such schools, the table below outlines a sample literature curriculum. Parents whose children have no school librarian will find that the children's staff at a nearby public library can suggest good books in each literary category.

This chapter offers background information on each literary type, criteria for excellence, and some answers to the following questions:

➤ What are the implications for work with especially bright children?

➤ How should the literature be presented developmentally, as children grow from one stage to the next?

➤ How can adults who are not yet familiar with children's literature most easily find the best?

Table 7-1. K-6 Literature Curriculum

	Picture Books	Poetry	Traditional	Nonfiction	Fiction
Kindergarten	x	x	Folktales Fairytales	x	Each genre is presented at the grade levels indicated by x or by the name of a type of literature.
First Grade	x	x	Folktales Fairytales	x	
Second Grade	x	x	Folktales Fairytales	x	Realistic Fantasy
Third Grade	x	x	Folktales Fairytales Fables	x Biography	Realistic Fantasy
Fourth Grade		x	Folktales Legends	x Biography	Realistic Fantasy High Fantasy
Fifth Grade		x	Legends Myths	x Biography	Realistic Fantasy High Fantasy Historical
Sixth Grade		x	Myths Epics	x Biography	Realistic Fantasy High Fantasy Historical Science Fiction
These are read aloud when classes come to the library.				These are introduced in the library through excerpts or booktalks.	

Fiction

Fiction (called "realistic fiction" when fantasy is considered as a separate category) is the broadest body of literature, the one found earliest by children exploring on their own, and the one most easily judged by the traits given in the previous chapter. It comprises the bulk of the titles listed in the annotated bibliography in Chapter 8.

Since authors write about what they know, and since many authors were gifted children, the characters in juvenile fiction are also often gifted. However, rarely is the giftedness pointed out; it is simply there to be recognized by child readers who see something of themselves in the story.

Types of Fiction

Realistic fiction can be divided into a number of subtypes, including adventure, animal stories, mystery, sports stories, humor, romance, and historical fiction. Most of these can be thought of as one group, although historical fiction deserves special consideration, as do series books.

How well each type suits the emotional or intellectual needs of especially talented children depends largely on the author's point of view and on how well the books are written. Each kind, but some more than others, can be treated in ways that offer intellectual challenge or provide insights into emotional development.

Recognizing Good Fiction

In order to continue to appeal to new generations of young readers, fiction must speak to their universal concerns, help them explore themselves through the characters in books, and introduce them to life in other places and times. It does this by dealing honestly with the material and with its readers.

Honesty and accuracy are the two most important criteria for children's fiction. Settings must be described so that the reader can imagine them. Plots must relate something that could plausibly happen. Above all, people must react with understandable emotions and behavior; their speech must be true to their ages and experience and to the environment established for them in the story.

Beyond that, for fiction that has enough depth to engage the imagination of sensitive readers, something should *happen* within the characters during the course of the book. Even fiction for young children offers this. *Evan's Corner*, for example, is not just a story about a boy who needs a little privacy and is allowed to turn a corner of a room into his own space. It is also about Evan's getting everything he thought he wanted, and then *realizing* (the internal event) that it is not enough. He wants to share it, too.

Especially in books for young children, watch for the comforting rhythm of language. Modern classics in literature for preschoolers provide good examples: *Good Night Moon*, *Millions of Cats*, *Blueberries for Sal*. In these books, parallel events are expressed in parallel language patterns, smooth and almost (but not quite) predictable. Literature of lower quality—such as that designed to sell in connection with a movie—lacks this polish, often written instead in short, choppy sentences that do not flow.

Historical fiction. Writers of historical fiction must walk a line between overburdening the plot with too much historical detail and using so little historical background that the book amounts to a novel placed in an historical setting. The best writers base their books on serious research and then weave realistic details into the narrative to lend authenticity to plot and characterization.

For alert and questioning readers, historical fiction should show not only the culture and daily life of the period, but it should also deal with some of the political and personal issues encountered by people of that era. An example is Esther Forbes's *Johnny Tremain*, in which Johnny, initially concerned only with his burned hand, is gradually caught up in the political and military turmoil going on around him as the Revolutionary War begins.

Series books. Depending on the subject matter and on the reading level, series books can enthrall both boys and girls, from first grade through senior high. A particular series may dominate for a few years and then change its focus or disappear. While the quality of writing varies, some series, such as the "Magic Treehouse" series for newly independent readers and the "Dear America" series for middle elementary students, are so well-written that it is not a matter of concern when a child temporarily refuses to read anything else.

Series books appeal to young children because they are confident that they can read them, and to older children because they are predictable and therefore safe. Among parents and teachers, there is some controversy over series books. Some are concerned about the stock characters and simple sentence structure, while others point out that these books smooth the way for children learning to read.

As with television, series books become a matter of concern when they are overused, blocking out more challenging reading. Ferraro (1992) quotes a mother's worry that such books can keep youngsters at the same reading level for too long. Children immersed in series books can benefit from gentle reading guidance (see Chapter 3), with a quiet acceptance of their present reading choices combined with the expectation that they will soon—or simultaneously—read books that offer more rounded characters, a greater variety of settings, and more artful use of language.

Finding Good Fiction

Young children find a "good book" mostly by watching what their friends are reading. They may also be given recommendations by the school librarian, or they may get ideas from what their teacher reads aloud. However, unless someone guides them to good books, their progress is haphazard at best.

Those who want to recommend good literature to children can follow a more systematic procedure. See the sources listed at the end of Chapter 6 and under "Books about Children's Literature" at the end of this chapter.

Another rich source of information is the librarian's own reference collection. Here are reference books and periodicals that list children's books by categories, often providing annotations or reviews for each. For most of these, inclusion equals recommendation; that is, they list only books that by some established standard merit recommendation to children. The public is usually welcome to use these references, though probably they cannot be checked out of the library. The list at the end of this chapter includes some of the most useful of these sources.

Nonfiction

It may surprise some to know that at the end of a library story hour for primary-grade children, when the children are free to find a book to check out, they are more likely to swarm to the nonfiction shelves than to picture books. No matter how attentively they have just listened to fiction or folklore, they appear to be hungry for fact as they explore on their own. It may be that as nonreaders, they feel they can gather more information from the pictures of a fact book than they can from those in a picture book whose story they do not know.

Whatever the reason, it is obvious that even at that early age, nonfiction or "information" books are important to children, and this continues to be true as they grow older. With the development of teaching methods that require students to search for information beyond their textbooks, the number and quality of nonfiction books for young people have increased dramatically over the last four decades—a bonus of the educational reforms inspired by Sputnik. Gifted students in particular benefit from exploring the views of different authors in books that offer more information at a more challenging reading level than graded textbooks can.

For readers of any age, nonfiction written for children is a good introduction to a new field. In doing research for a report on a topic with which they are only vaguely familiar—examples might be continental drift, the human brain, astronomy, or economics—older students can begin with books written for younger children to gain a quick overview of basic concepts, essential vocabulary, and an organizational framework. All of this will help them make better use of information they find later in more advanced books and articles.

Recognizing Good Nonfiction

It is not easy to write good nonfiction. Lacking a plot to maintain interest, the author must write with both a lucid style and a clear purpose. The author's attitude toward his audience and his reason for choosing to write about his topic for young people will help determine the success of his book, providing a framework that may be nearly invisible but that nevertheless gives shape to the contents.

The physical appearance of the book, the size and format, and aesthetic qualities such as the appeal of illustrations and the print type all add to the book's ability to attract and hold readers.

Beyond these essential considerations are the characteristics of good nonfiction: accuracy, readability, structure, and for especially bright readers, open-endedness and the potential for both stimulating and satisfying their curiosity.

Accuracy. Accuracy is absolutely essential in nonfiction. The copyright date should be recent, especially if the book is in a field that is changing rapidly. The dust jacket or endpapers may provide biographical material on the author, indicating his or her level of expertise. If possible, check the accuracy of a section of the text that covers an area of knowledge that is familiar to you or ask an expert to check it. Try to determine whether the author is writing from a biased point of view, keeping in mind that young children in particular are vulnerable—they are likely to believe what they read simply because it is in print.

Look for accuracy in the graphic material, also. For illustrations in science books, a clear and precise line with correct labeling is needed. Photographs may be best for some social studies books, but they should be updated when the books are revised. Graphs and charts must be clear and current.

Readability. Since the appeal in nonfiction is to the intellect rather than to an emotional response, the author must be skilled in techniques that hold the reader's interest. Readability—the way in which the material is presented—is of paramount importance. Like a good teacher introducing a new subject by referring to what the children already know, the author of a good nonfiction book will begin with an image or a setting that is familiar, then take the readers into new territory. A book for primary children on building barns, for example, might demonstrate stress factors with illustrations showing structures made of building blocks.

Nonfiction requires clear writing that is logically and sequentially presented. In addition, writing for children requires some special techniques.

Because young children cannot yet think in abstractions, abstract concepts should be supported by concrete images, either in illustrations or by giving clear examples. A description of the structure of a bridge, for instance, should be accompanied by a drawing, preferably with the parts labeled. And general statements must be followed by specific examples. Repetition is important—authors should repeat key words throughout the book and provide a summary at the end. The vocabulary should be accurate, reflecting the terms used by workers in the field discussed in the book. A glossary in books about specialized topics is always welcome. The writing style should flow comfortably, drawing the reader along.

Readability can be enhanced by the organization of the book. Maps, charts, graphs, drawings, and photographs increase readability and should be placed near the text they illustrate. An index helps readers find their way around the book. Even young readers seeking information should use some books that include bibliographies so they can learn where they can read more, and so they can become familiar with the researcher's practice of documenting sources of information.

Often, an assumed reading level is indicated either on the book or by its placement in a library or bookstore. However, gifted children with a strong interest in a topic will read beyond their grade level or even beyond their measured reading level to learn as much as they can from a book that might otherwise be considered too advanced for them. They should, of course, have the freedom to select books for older readers along with those that are at a comfortable reading level.

Structure. Nonfiction is often presented in chronological order, like a narrative. However, students are sufficiently familiar with narrative from their reading of fiction; writers of nonfiction have an opportunity to challenge with a different structure. Good nonfiction authors use various presentations: organizing their materials in lists, comparing and contrasting, using cause and effect, enumerating, providing cumulative evidence, challenging with problems to which solutions have been or must be found, offering a question/answer format, and arranging information from simple to complex. These organizational patterns require different types of thinking, more like the kinds of thinking adults do in their daily lives (Carter & Abrahamson, 1998).

Open-endedness. Finally, nonfiction for gifted readers should be open-ended. This may sound like a contradiction in terms for a fact book, but consider: Is the author clear about which statements are accepted facts and which are still unproven hypotheses? Does she use an interdisciplinary approach, indicating points at which this subject leads into other, related topics? Is there some mention of ethical questions raised by new knowledge in the field?

Much of what we memorized as children—about space, genetics, paleontology—has been modified by newer discoveries. With their ability to delay closure, gifted children are receptive to uncertainty, and they are challenged by the unknown. They should be informed of the unanswered questions and methods used in current research, and they should be stimulated to examine the field more deeply themselves. Challenging nonfiction gives satisfactory answers to some questions, but it also raises more and invites readers to continue the search for information at a new level.

Nonfiction and Gifted Readers

Intellectually curious youngsters can and should learn to select nonfiction well—to pursue their own interests through reading. It is helpful to discuss with them the characteristics of good nonfiction books so that they can make judgments for themselves.

Sometimes gifted children run into barriers as they look for new books that match their interests. Adults who can't believe that their children can read far beyond their age level may be reluctant to allow them to use advanced and expensive books. Paul, for example, discovered at the age of eight that the library in his K – 12 school had purchased a new astronomical atlas. More than anything, Reza wanted to take that atlas home, even though he could hardly carry it. In addition to the question of a third-grader's reliability with a costly new book, the librarian had to consider that it was a reference book and could circulate only overnight. However, she knew Reza and understood his passion for science; arrangements were made. For months, he came to the library every Friday afternoon and checked the book out for the weekend, always returning it early Monday morning in perfect condition in spite of the winter weather. Reza certainly gained more from the atlas than the seniors for whom it had been ordered.

When librarians are not acquainted with children such as Paul, parents or teachers may have to run interference, explaining why a child may need and merit special consideration. They may also help by coaching the child in how to respond effectively to restricting rules.

Finding Good Nonfiction

Even armed with a list of characteristics to help select the best, a reader approaching the nonfiction section of a school or public library is likely to be overwhelmed by the sheer volume of material. It is worth the time to make a list of recommended books, using reviews or booklists, before turning to the public catalog.

Reviews of nonfiction may be difficult to uncover because reviewing children's nonfiction is especially demanding—reviewers must be knowledgeable about the topic of the book as well as about good children's writing. Reviews of newly published books appear in periodicals first; it is usually at least a year before they appear in book form. The periodical *Booklist* divides reviews of books for young people into several sections, placing reviews of nonfiction books first in each case. In addition, journals for teachers often list a few new books for students among the book reviews. And newsletters for parents of children enrolled in gifted programs sometimes offer recommendations for good reading.

Finding a review of a book that sounds ideal is only the first step toward placing it in the child's hands. With so much nonfiction available, some of it highly specialized, it is unreasonable to expect bookstores and libraries to stock enough for the varied needs of curious, avid readers—underscoring the value of reviews, which prepare you to make specific requests when ordering. Once you know what you want, you can order most titles through interlibrary loan, through your local bookstore, or online.

Reference books suggested at the end of this chapter provide lists of recommended books. Some have nonfiction sections; others are entirely about nonfiction books.

Biography

Biography often becomes a favorite with young people who prefer more difficult reading. Since life stories of individuals who realized their high potential can offer intellectually and emotionally rewarding reading for gifted adults, it's important that bright children have a good introduction to this genre. Like other forms of nonfiction, biography is often assigned as part of a study unit, so most children are aware of it as a separate kind of literature by the time they are in the upper elementary grades. For gifted children in a regular classroom, biography is an excellent tool for extending the regular curriculum.

Types of Biographies

Biographies can be classified on a continuum, with nonfiction at one end and fiction at the other. At the nonfiction end, *definitive* (or *authentic*) biography relies on historical evidence, containing nothing that cannot be documented. *Fictionalized biography*, in the middle, is a blend—the author conducts extensive research and then invents dialogue or events based on the historical record. And at the other end of the continuum, *biographical fiction* is frankly fiction, with a historical person as the main character.

The characteristic that most reliably establishes where a given biography rests on the continuum is dialogue. In definitive biography, dialogue is rare and occurs only when there is a written record of the discussion. For the most part, the characters "speak" only through their letters.

In fictionalized biography, the author is free to blend fact and fiction by creating scenes in which an imagined conversation furthers or dramatizes the historical account. For a cataloging class, one of my library school professors described fictionalized biography with a memorable example: "If there is a line such as, 'After the last guest had left, Victoria dismissed the servants, retired to the royal suite, closed the door, turned to Albert, and said, "….",' then you know you have a fictionalized biography."

In biographical fiction, on the other hand, conversation flows as freely as in any other kind of fiction, even between bit players for whose very existence there is no historical record.

The type of biography children enjoy depends in large part on their age. For young children whose sense of history is not yet developed, biographies are stories that familiarize them with names such as Abraham Lincoln, Jane Addams, or Martin Luther King, Jr. Older children enjoy both biographical fiction and fictionalized biography, and talented senior high students should be encouraged to read some of the classic biographies such as Lytton Strachey's *Queen Victoria* or Eve Curie's biography of her mother, *Madame Curie*.

Recognizing Good Biography

At one time, biography was a weak link in children's literature. Much of it was didactic—written to teach a lesson—as young readers could clearly see. However, in recent years, there have been three significant changes (Flack, 1992): more biographies about women and members of minority groups have appeared, biographees are presented as real human beings rather than impossible paragons, and authors model good scholarship for their readers through the biographies they write. An excellent example of all of these developments is Albert Marrin's *Sitting Bull and His World,* one of the books recommended in Chapter 8.

Because it runs the gamut from nonfiction to fiction, biography can be judged by some of the criteria used for each. As nonfiction, it must be accurate, readable, and objective.

Historical accuracy depends on which type of biography the author has written. Even in biographical fiction, however, historical details should be authentic, as they should be in any good historical fiction.

A readable biography must bring a historical person to life, presenting characters as real people with human problems and responses. Small, intimate details make the biographee seem like a contemporary friend. Where there is dialogue, it should flow as naturally as it does in a novel.

All nonfiction writers should approach their subjects with objectivity, but it is more difficult to be objective when the subject is a person. Objectivity requires authors to maintain a balance between admiration and criticism for the biographee. Objective authors leave readers free to draw their own conclusions based on the facts; they do not suppress relevant but negative aspects of the principal character's life and place in history. Biography for children should show restraint and sensitivity in discussing character weaknesses, particularly when they are unrelated to the person's historical importance.

Finding Biographies

In libraries, biographies are usually shelved together in the nonfiction section at the point where the number 921 would occur in the Dewey Decimal system. However, the call "number" is often a B followed by the last name of the biographee, so the books appear in alphabetical order by the person whose life they tell, not by the author.

The biography section may be astonishingly large in proportion to the rest of nonfiction. How do you find the best? The sources suggested at the end of this chapter include sections on biography. Ask for the librarian's help, if necessary, to locate the biography sections in these listings.

Biography in Bibliotherapy with Gifted Students

While biography is recommended for all students, it can be used for gifted students with specific purposes in mind for them. One is to demonstrate that many trials and failures often precede success. The biographies of scientists in de Kruif's *The Microbe Hunters*, for example, provide evidence of the hours of preparation and even drudgery that must be paid for the singular moment of discovery—and it is obvious that de Kruif's scientists paid the price gladly, with lasting enthusiasm for their work. It is not difficult to imagine that this book might be informative, perhaps even inspiring for a gifted child who normally resists routine work.

Another purpose is to show the role of personal characteristics in achievement, characteristics that could be either evident or latent in the gifted child reading the book. *Carry On, Mr. Bowditch* is a good example, illustrating how Nathaniel Bowditch's inner drive, his energetic curiosity, and his thoroughness in inquiry, helped him achieve far more than usual for those with his scant opportunity for formal education.

In searching for appropriate biographies for gifted readers, look for this emphasis on the internal drives that propelled the individuals to become subjects of biographies. What is revealed about their motivation, moral imperative, intellectual curiosity, impulse to inquiry? What advantages did their high intelligence bring to them, and what problems? How did they turn their talents to their own advantage in coping with the problems? What evidence is there, if any, that they recognized their own gifts and consciously made use of them? What role did a sense of commitment, mission, or responsibility play in their achievements?

A third use of biographies with gifted adolescents is to provide them with examples of gifted people who experienced the feelings of isolation and loneliness that readers can recognize. Gifted young people, especially those with a strong sense of their own high potential, are quite likely to be able to identify with the aspirations and struggles of gifted adults such as Marie Curie, who, studying alone in her Paris apartment one night, was so cold that she piled everything she could, including a chair, on top of her bed for warmth. Some gifted teenagers can understand that to Marie, the cold and the loneliness were incidental nuisances compared to the privilege of studying science at the Sorbonne. Rather than feeling overwhelmed, they can use such people as models without necessarily expecting themselves to achieve to the same degree.

Contemplating the grandeur of the wondering, reaching, striving human spirit may be coming back into fashion. That is good news, especially for people so talented that the highest aspirations are appropriate for them. Biography can be one of the most intellectually demanding forms of literature, but it can also be among the most inspiring. On both counts, it should be part of the reading program for gifted young people.

Traditional Literature

The literatures that have been passed from generation to generation since the beginning of human culture include folk and fairy tales, fables, myths, legends, and epics. This rich heritage, once oral, is now collected in many written versions, available now to children in a greater variety and from more different cultures than ever before. It is a vital part of the background of anyone who would hope to be truly educated.

Most children will not find traditional literature on their own. When they swarm to the nonfiction shelves after the story hour, it is to science, technology, and craft books, not to the mythology or folklore sections (which are also classified as nonfiction, strange as it may seem, because they are a way to learn about the cultures from which they come). Rare is the child who spontaneously asks where to find fairy tales or King Arthur stories, although they enjoy these stories when they hear them.

Traditional literature, therefore, must be actively introduced or most children will grow up without adequate knowledge of it. Presenting it effectively requires knowledge of the ages at which children are most likely to respond to the different types.

Introducing Traditional Literature at the Best Time

Traditional literature ranges from the simplest folktale cherished by preschoolers to complex epics that form the basis of classic adult literature. Good reading guides know at which ages children are ready to respond to each type. For those who need review or are just beginning with children's literature, a brief outline follows.

Folktales. The first traditional literature a child hears, at three and four years old, is folklore—simple tales of the wisdom and foolishness of common people. Preschoolers love cumulative tales like *The Three Little Pigs, The Gingerbread Boy*, and *The Little Red Hen*.

Fairy tales such as "Cinderella," told with variations in different cultures around the world, come next, appealing to children from about five to eight years old. Although the Grimm tales are the most familiar, there are many others in collections from different countries. Any concerns adults may have about violence in fairy tales can be allayed by reviewing the wide variety available—and remembering Bettelheim's (1976) view that in their eagerness to see justice served and with their black-and-white view of the world, children are not nearly as alarmed by the violence as are adults.

Legends and Tall Tales. Fourth and fifth graders are ready for legends—stories of larger-than-life figures whose historical existence is shadowy, but whose deeds, undoubtedly exaggerated, have lived in story. The first legends most children encounter are those of England's Robin Hood and King Arthur; another example is Kate Seredy's *The White Stag*, based on Atilla and the founding of Hungary. Out of the pioneer experience in the United States came the Jack tales and stories of men like Mike Fink and

Paul Bunyan. The trademark American humor of these stories helped European newcomers cope as they struggled with the challenges that greeted them in exploring and making their homes in this land in the 18th and 19th centuries.

Mythology. By the fifth and sixth grades, as students study early cultures, they should be introduced not only to the cultures' histories, but also to their religions and mythology. In particular, a knowledge of the Greek, Roman, and Norse myths will go far toward making young people feel at home with European and American art, literature, and history.

When we say "myths" in general conversation, we mean "untruths" more often than we mean the stories human beings have used through most of history to express ultimate truths and values. The psychoanalyst Rollo May (1991, p. 9) regrets our failure in recent years to take myths seriously as givers of meaning. "Western society has all but lost its myths," he states, and "many of the problems of our society, including cults and drug addiction, can be traced to the lack of myths." Perhaps the loss is not only of our knowledge of myths, but also of our capacity to think mythologically, to use symbols to make or discover meaning in our lives.

Epics. Blending the human and the divine, as men and women interact with gods and goddesses, epics are stories of danger and heroism. Often, they form an essential part of the origins of a group's national identity. For middle school youngsters, there are excellent versions of epics, including Rosemary Sutcliff's *Dragonslayer: The Story of Beowulf* and retellings of the *Iliad* and the *Odyssey* by Sutcliff and others.

As American society continues to diversify, it becomes increasingly important to offer more than the familiar Greek and Roman myths. Folktales reveal the values and wisdom of a culture, and they appeal to children regardless of the tales' origin (Dailey, 1991). Norse mythology, Celtic legend, African tales, and Eastern European stories hold the cultural heritage of many children, some of it from so long ago that it is nearly forgotten. Books can help keep it alive. Middle Eastern and Asian traditional literatures represent the heritage of a growing number of children in American schools. A knowledge of these stories and others that appear in similar versions from different parts of the world helps children understand their common humanity. In encouraging students to think of themselves as citizens of the world rather than having a provincial outlook, traditional literature is a valuable tool.

Recognizing Good Traditional Literature

Imagine, of all that is written today, what will have survived 500 or 1,000 years from now. Even with many details lost, that distillation will provide a better picture of the essence of our time than any of us could perceive by browsing in a library today or glancing through the daily newspapers. It will have become traditional literature.

By definition, traditional literature is the best of the ancient stories—those that have survived. In many tellings over the years, folk and fairy tales have been shaped and polished. Fortunately, in the 19th and 20th centuries, scholars gathered many of them from storytellers who were still part of the oral tradition and put them into print. Myths and epics represent the highest literary achievements of the cultures that produced them. In a sense, the term "good traditional literature" is redundant.

But this does not mean that every book on the shelves is a masterpiece. How do you choose, especially for gifted children? It is best to look not for one specific story or genre over another, but for *versions* written in demanding language and which are perceptive in delving into human character—and into relationships among people and between human beings and their fate or their gods. The way to judge is to read as widely as possible.

Look first at the quality of the language. These tales, after all, represent the beginnings of our literary heritage, and the language should both respect and reflect the long history of refining that the stories have undergone. Modern versions do not always serve them well; some of the wonder they stirred in their listeners centuries ago should linger in the present telling. Rosemary Sutcliff achieves this in her version of *Beowulf;* so does Padraic Colum in his compilation of stories of the heroes who lived before the Trojan War, *The Golden Fleece.*

Illustrations, too, should convey a sense of the simple and eternal truths with which the stories are concerned. Banality and cuteness are too often found in children's books of fairy tales, but a little searching will yield books whose illustrations shine with integrity and grace. Examples of artists who illustrate traditional literature well are Kate Greenaway, Arthur Rackham, Barbara Cooney, and Adrienne Adams.

Finding Good Traditional Literature

Information about fine versions of traditional literature can be found in textbooks and reference books on children's literature. See "Textbooks in Children's Literature" and "Reference Books about Children's Literature" at the end of this chapter.

As with other "nonfiction," libraries usually carry much larger collections of traditional stories than bookstores do, and they include valuable books that are now out of print. In the nonfiction section of the children's collection, folk and fairy tales are found under sociology, Dewey Decimal number 398. Mythology may be shelved with religion in the 200s, since it was the religious literature of its culture, and epics in the 800s, with the literature of the country of origin. Each library may interpret the Dewey system slightly differently, however, and your library may be cataloged by the Library of Congress system instead of Dewey, so ask for help if necessary.

Many, many versions of the different tales are available. Here are a few examples that will appeal to good readers:

African

Bryan, Ashley, reteller. *Ashley Bryan's African Tales, Uh-Huh.* New York: Atheneum, 1998. Ages 8 – 12.

American

Caduto, Michael J. and Joseph Bruchac. *Keepers of the Earth: Native American Stories and Environmental Activities for Children.* Golden, CO: Fulcrum, 1988.

Chase, Richard. *The Jack Tales.* Boston: Houghton Mifflin, 1943. Ages 9 – 12.

Sanfield, Steve. *The Adventures of High John the Conqueror.* New York: Orchard, 1989. Ages 9 – 12.

Wood, Nancy. (Ed.). *The Serpent's Tongue: Prose, Poetry and Art of the New Mexico Pueblos.* New York: Dutton, 1997. Ages 13+.

Arabic

Alderson, Brian, reteller. *The Arabian Nights.* Illus. Michael Foreman. New York: Morrow Junior Books, 1992. Ages 9 – 12.

Celtic

McBratney, Sam. *Celtic Myths.* New York: Peter Bedrick, 1998. Ages 9 – 12.

English

Pyle, Howard. *The Merry Adventures of Robin Hood.* New York: Dover, 1968. Ages 9 – 12.

Pyle, Howard. *The Story of King Arthur and his Knights.* New York: Sharon, 1981. Ages 9 – 12.

Sutcliff, Rosemary. *Dragonslayer: The Story of Beowulf.* New York: Puffin, 1986 (1966). Ages 10 – 13.

Far East

Courlander, Harold. *The Tiger's Whisker and Other Tales and Legends from Asia and the Pacific.* New York: Harcourt, 1959. Ages 9 – 12.

Yep, Laurence. *The Rainbow People.* New York: Harper & Row, 1989. Ages 9 – 12.

Greek and Roman

Aliki, reteller. *The Gods and Goddesses of Olympus.* New York: HarperCollins, 1994. Ages 4 – 8.

Colum, Padraic. *The Golden Fleece.* New York: Macmillan, 1983. Ages 9 – 12.

Coolidge, Olivia. *Greek Myths.* Boston: Houghton Mifflin, 1949. Ages 9 – 12.

Sutcliff, Rosemary. *Black Ships before Troy: The Story of the Iliad.* New York: Delacorte, 1993. Ages 11 – 14.

Sutcliff, Rosemary. *The Wanderings of Odysseus: The Story of the Odyssey.* New York: Delacorte, 1996. Ages 10 – 13.

Norse

Philip, Neil. *Odin's Family: Myths of the Vikings.* New York: Peter Bedrick, 1998. Ages 9 – 12.

Picard, Barbara Leonie. *Tales of the Norse Gods.* Toronto: Oxford UP, 1994. Ages 9 – 12.

World

Mayo, Margaret, reteller. *Magical Tales from Many Lands.* Illus. Jane Ray. New York: Dutton, 1993. Ages 8 – 11.

McCaughrean, Geraldine. *The Golden Hoard: Myths and Legends of the World.* Illus. Bee Willey. New York: McElderry, 1996. Ages 8 – 12.

Taylor, C. J. *How We Saw the World: Nine Native Stories of the Way Things Began.* Toronto: Tundra, 1998. Ages 8 – 11.

This list is a mere beginning. There are many more collections and individual stories on the library shelves, evidence of the stature of traditional literature in the human story. For some, it is the literary form most likely to move the spirit in the same mysterious way that art and music can do. Elizabeth Cook expressed this in *The Ordinary and the Fabulous* (1969, p. 5):

> There is another door that can be opened by reading legends and fairy tales, and for some children, at the present time, there may be no other key to it. *Religio*, in one Latin sense of the word, implies a sense of the strange, the numinous, the totally Other, of what lies quite beyond human personality and cannot be found in any human relationships. This kind of "religion" is an indestructible part of the experience of many human minds, even though the temper of a secular society does not encourage it.... It may very well be in reading about a vision of the flashing-eyed Athene or the rosy-fingered Aphrodite that children first find a satisfying formulation of those queer prickings of delight, excitement and terror that they feel when they first walk by moonlight, or when it snows in May, or when, like the young Wordsworth, they have to touch a wall to make sure that it is really there. Magic is not the same as mysticism, but it may lead towards it; it is mystery "told to the children."

Fantasy and Science Fiction

For our older son's ninth birthday, I went shopping, as usual, for a book. Browsing through the juvenile shelves of a favorite bookstore, I came upon a title that was then new to me: *The Book of Three*. Something about that title, something about the very feel of the book in my hand, told me that this was the book for

David at this time and that there was something there for me, too, although just what wasn't so clear.

The book was David's introduction to fantasy, and he could not have had a better one. Later I learned that the story was based on Lloyd Alexander's extensive knowledge of Welsh legend, part of David's unknown heritage, and mine. Later still, after reading much more fantasy, mythology, and modern literature, David spent a summer studying Welsh at the University of Aberystwyth. His personal library now includes several titles in Welsh, and it will not surprise me if he returns to the study of that language in the future. All of this might have happened in any case, but it is clear that *The Book of Three* reached David at just the right moment to catch his imagination, give it focus, and send it soaring.

Fantasy and science fiction can do this for some children. They discover it—and there is much of it for them—at just the age when they are entering their own personal quests for identity and are beginning consciously to establish their personal values. The quest, and the attempt (sometimes failed) to live up to lofty ideals, are hallmarks of high fantasy. To judge from the devotion with which many young people read fantasy, it must be exactly what they need in the late elementary and junior high years.

Fantasy, Science Fiction, and Gifted Readers

Gifted readers are likely to read more fantasy and science fiction than average students; some children go through a stage lasting for several years, from the late elementary grades through junior high, during which they read fantasy and science fiction almost entirely. This observation may be what led Lynch-Brown and Tomlinson (1999, p. 120) to write, "Modern fantasy has appeal for people with nonliteral minds, for people who go beyond the letter of a story to its spirit."

The strong interest in fantasy becomes a source of concern for those parents and teachers who see it as escape literature and wonder whether the child will ever read "serious" literature again.

It is an unnecessary worry; young people do move through this stage, and if they know how to distinguish good literature from that of lower quality, they can continue later with excellent choices in other areas. And this is more likely to be the case if they are reading *good* fantasy and science fiction.

Adults sometimes have more serious concerns that gifted children can become too engrossed in science fiction and live too much in a fantasy world. If a child is able to relate to others *only* through fantasy (only through games based on fantasy, for example), then there is cause for concern. However, if this is only a part of his life and he has other ways of relating to friends, it should not be a serious worry.

The interest in fantasy should not be seen merely as a stage to be endured. Indeed, we are learning that the productive use of knowledge can be enhanced by the ability to be imaginative. Undoubtedly, creativity is a product of integrating imagination and knowledge.

Thus, it is important that children have the chance to continue to be imaginative as they progress through the grades—as they spend more and more time gaining factual knowledge in school. Fantasy and science fiction provide just such an opportunity. Perhaps this need to keep their imaginations alive is behind the voracious appetite of some gifted young people for this type of literature.

Introducing Fantasy and Science Fiction at the Best Time

For young children who have had a rich background in traditional literature in their preschool years, the introduction of fantasy may be barely noticeable. For adults who guide their reading, however, it is helpful to mark the inexact line between folklore and modern fantasy.

One way to clarify the difference is authorship. Traditional literature—true folklore—began as oral tradition and has no known author. The Grimm brothers did not write their tales; they collected them from those who were still telling them in the oral tradition. Hans Christian Andersen, on the other hand, created his stories, which incorporate many elements of folklore but are modern fantasy. Many authors since, such as MacDonald, Tolkien, Lewis, Alexander, Cooper, and LeGuin, whose works are mentioned below, have done the same, building a rich body of modern imaginative literature.

Fantasy. Elements of traditional literature linger in modern fantasy. Familiar characteristics of folklore and fairy tales blend over into fantasy in books like A. A. Milne's *Winnie-the-Pooh*, in which animals talk, and P. L. Travers' *Mary Poppins*, in which the source of magic is not fairies but Mary Poppins herself. A child can move in easy stages from these early fantasies to modern fairy tales, fantasy based on time warps, high fantasy, and science fiction. With care, she can read excellent literature every step of the way.

For early elementary school children, animal characters continue to appear in classic fantasies such as *The Wind in the Willows* and *Charlotte's Web*, echoing the talking animals of folklore. In George MacDonald's late 19th-century story, *At the Back of the North Wind*, the North Wind is a lady remarkably like a fairy godmother. Some fantasies written for this age group, such as Mary Norton's *The Borrowers*, feature characters who are miniature people, reminiscent of the elves and dwarfs of folklore.

The element of the time warp appears in Lucy M. Boston's *The Children of Green Knowe* and its sequels, and in Philippa Pearce's *Tom's Midnight Garden*. In these books, a contemporary child meets and plays or struggles with a child or children from the past.

There is much more fantasy for middle and upper elementary children than can be mentioned here. A few more titles will suggest the scope: talking animals appear in Kipling's *Jungle Books*, Lawson's *Rabbit Hill*, O'Brien's *Mrs. Frisby and The Rats of NIMH* (which might also be classified as science fiction), and in Adams' *Watership Down*, which young gifted children enjoy hearing read aloud. Children of this age read the Harry Potter series independently. These books are very different from each other and represent a wide range of reading levels, but they all appeal to children of this age, and they are all fantasies.

For older readers, another author worth knowing is Robin McKinley, whose retelling for older readers of "The Beauty and the Beast," called simply *Beauty*, is completely credible and compelling. The British authors Alan Garner (*The Owl Service*) and William Mayne (*Earthfasts*) also write fine fantasy for older readers.

High fantasy. By the fourth grade, many children have discovered C. S. Lewis' Narnia series, beginning with *The Lion, the Witch, and the Wardrobe*. There are seven books in this series, and as in most fantasy series, any one can be read independently of the others, although some children will want to read them in order. Written for middle-grade children, the Narnia series is the first experience with high fantasy for most.

It is in high fantasy that the protagonists are usually involved in a quest, drawn into it by forces beyond their control. They go willingly, but there is often some sacrifice involved and much learning—they grow up in the process of the quest. The theme is often no less than the epic and never-ending struggle between good and evil, the relationship between human beings and the gods, with ordinary human beings risking all, often alone, in their attempts to perform seemingly impossible tasks and to live up to high ideals. Authors of high fantasy typically spin out their tales in a series of books instead of a single volume because the theme is so large and the plot so involved.

High fantasy is frequently based on mythology and legend—in particular, Germanic and Norse mythology, the Welsh *Mabinogion*, and the Arthurian legends (which are also Welsh in origin). This background gives it a mythical quality that heightens the effect of the quest theme and strengthens the potential for nobility and a kind of grandeur, even when humor is also present.

Both grandeur and humor are certainly present in the second example of high fantasy children are likely to meet: Lloyd Alexander's Prydain series—five titles beginning with *The Book of Three.* Although Alexander tells his stories with a light touch, his purposes are serious. To achieve them, he departs from Lady Charlotte Guest's edition of the *Mabinogion*, which is the basis for his fantasy series. When Eilonwy declares her independence in favor of Taran, she breaks from the Celtic legend, and Alexander's story becomes an American fantasy, protesting the monarchy (May, 1991).

Children may also discover in the late elementary grades Ursula LeGuin's Earthsea Trilogy (*A Wizard of Earthsea*, *The Tombs of Atuan*, and *The Farthest Shore*), and the Dragon books of Anne McCaffrey.

Middle school readers enjoy Susan Cooper's series, which begins with *Over Sea, Under Stone.* They have probably already found Tolkien's *The Hobbit*, and some may attempt the trilogy that follows, *The Lord of the Rings*, although it is more difficult. McKinley's *The Blue Sword* and its prequel, *The Hero and the Crown*, for readers of middle school age and older, are also in the tradition of high fantasy.

Science fiction. At some time during the middle school years, students may shift from fantasy to science fiction. Or they may read science fiction without ever having read much fantasy. The line between the two is blurred.

One way to distinguish them is to remember that fantasy could not happen in the future because it includes imaginary creatures (and often magic), while science fiction tells what could conceivably happen based on current scientific knowledge. A further distinction may also be that fantasy is concerned with the development of the internal, intrapersonal world, while science fiction is more concerned with that of the external, interpersonal world.

Science fiction includes an emphasis on technological expertise, and it comments on what future societies might be like based on present predictions regarding the environment, population density, and the likelihood of catastrophic war. Or as Rosenberg (1986, p. 182) puts it, science fiction is "speculative about the potential uses of science and speculative about the potential future of mankind on this world and within the universe."

Rosenberg goes on to identify several types of themes in science fiction. Here are some of her types, with examples:

➤ Hard science — Isaac Asimov, *I, Robot*
➤ New wave — Anthony Burgess, *A Clockwork Orange*
➤ Dystopia/Utopia — Ray Bradbury, *Fahrenheit 451*
➤ Religious — Frank Herbert, *Dune*
➤ Ecology — Piers Anthony, *Omnivore*

Interestingly, children's science fiction often differs from that written for adults (Nodelman, 1992). In many science fiction novels for children, the view of technology is strongly negative, and the path to a better future lies in returning to a pre-technological age.

Science fiction is not often written for very young children because the content is so complex. It is in the upper elementary grades that students may begin reading William Sleator's *House of Stairs*; John Christopher's trilogy, *The White Mountains*; and Madeleine L'Engle's *A Wrinkle in Time* and its sequels.

By middle school, students are reading books like Natalie Babbitt's *Tuck Everlasting* and are also beginning to read adult science fiction. Frank Herbert's *Dune* series, Michael Crichton's *Andromeda Strain* and *Jurassic Park*, Ray Bradbury's *Fahrenheit 451*, and many of Madeleine L'Engle's books are some of the titles middle and senior high students enjoy.

Intensified concern for the quality of life often prompts senior high gifted students more than others to become interested in reading utopian literature and also dystopian books, which are not about ideal societies but about society gone wrong. Aldous Huxley's *Brave New World* and George Orwell's *Animal Farm* and *1984* are examples of good literature in this category.

Recognizing Good Fantasy and Science Fiction

Good fantasy and science fiction are judged much like good fiction of other types. Plot, setting, literary style, and convincing characters are just as important here as elsewhere. The criteria for literature that meets emotional and intellectual needs listed in Chapter 6 apply here, too.

Science fiction lends itself to one particular flaw: it often relies too much on adventure and provides too little in the way of characterization or plot complexity. Plenty of action is an initial draw, but good science fiction also has characters who are real enough to grow—that is, something changes within the characters—and a plot that retains interest. Action alone quickly becomes boring to discriminating older readers.

One additional criterion, which may sound paradoxical, is that good fantasy and science fiction must be believable. The reader must be drawn into whatever world the author has created and must believe in it; the created world must be consistent within itself. And the theme—the underlying thread that reveals the author's attitude toward the intrapersonal or the interpersonal world, must be based in truth.

Finding Good Fantasy and Science Fiction

There are excellent, prolific authors in both fields, and one way to find good fantasy or science fiction is to look for these and other books by the authors named above. But we have certainly not mentioned all of the authors worth knowing. To learn more, consult the booklists suggested at the end of this chapter. Not all of these references list fantasy and science fiction separately, so you may need to search in the fiction section of the reference book.

Usually, fantasy and science fiction are shelved with fiction on library shelves, but some libraries either shelve them in a special section or place stickers on the book spines with symbols identifying specific types of fiction.

Mythology, Fantasy, and Gifted Children

If I have overemphasized traditional literature and fantasy in this chapter, it is because I believe that the one is neglected and the other unfairly maligned, and that together they offer a vital mixture for the balanced development of gifted children.

Mythology and high fantasy in particular validate the inner drive to cherish high ideals, to make commitments that cannot be justified on rational grounds, to find meaning outside of oneself. In our contemporary world, it may be only in literature that some adolescents can find such affirmation. For especially bright and talented children with their emerging sense of the potential in themselves and the accompanying confusion about how or whether to reveal it and use it, every possible source of affirmation must be recognized and encouraged.

Poetry

It is not difficult to introduce poetry to children, and the rewards are great—but it does require a special approach. No matter how effectively parents and teachers encourage children to explore other forms of literature, many lose their enthusiasm when they consider introducing poetry. The result is that children also may grow up feeling vaguely uneasy with poetry, not understanding it and not knowing how to approach it.

This is a regrettable loss. For the very young child who is experimenting with sound and language, the rhythm and non-sense syllables of nursery rhymes provide invaluable enrichment. Nursery rhymes may sound light and frivolous to adults, but they appeal to young children at a critical point as they master one of the most important tasks of early childhood: the acquisition of language.

The elastic mind of a child of four or five shows an agility for learning foreign languages that the more rigid mind of the adult has lost. Parents who grow impatient with the repetition of Mother Goose rhymes need to understand that their child's language ability is greater than their own and that his fascination with the sounds reflects his intelligence as he works at learning language.

In addition, poetry is one way to encourage intuition and imagery while the child is learning also to think more scientifically and literally. Music is another way, but children will be exposed to music in at least some forms whether or not adults make a conscious effort to introduce it. Unless someone deliberately shares poetry throughout the elementary years, most children will be left with a nursery school level of awareness of poetry—as serious a handicap, in its way, as it would be to enter middle school with "Three Blind Mice" as their highest musical attainment.

Many children are offered nursery rhymes when they are preschoolers. From then on, however, their exposure to poetry may be limited to a few poems in elementary school reading texts or taught as part of secondary school literature courses. They need more guidance than this if they are to learn to love poetry—more guidance than other forms of literature require. They will surely discover books by Beverly Cleary, for example, in the second or third grade simply because Cleary is part of the culture of children of that age, but they are not likely to discover each new step in poetry for themselves.

Preparing to Introduce Poetry

For poetry more than for any other form of literature, adults must love it themselves—or learn to love it—in order to give it to children. Teachers know that they have to make an effort to find time in the day for poetry if it is important to them. It may be up to parents to keep poetry alive in their children if teachers cannot.

How can you as a teacher or parent achieve this if poetry has not previously been part of your own life? You can go to the public or school library for books of poetry for children and books about children's literature. If children's poetry has never held much appeal for you, it is a good idea to begin with the poetry sections in the children's literature books, which are probably in the reference section.

More background reading may help. *Climb into the Bell Tower* (1990) by the poet Myra Cohn Livingston is a collection of writings and speeches spanning her career, from 1967 to 1986. Admittedly based on her personal point of view, this book nevertheless offers helpful touchstones for evaluating children's poetry.

For example, Livingston summarizes the contributions of several well-known poets: William Blake leading the way from the older didactic poetry (verses designed to teach moral lessons) by insisting on the need for "joy, dreaming, and play," Lewis Carroll and Edward Lear adding nonsense and wordplay, Robert Louis Stevenson focusing on a child's everyday experiences, Shel Silverstein reviving didactic poetry but using humor so skillfully that readers may not realize that he is teaching as well as providing entertainment.

Livingston makes a distinction between comprehending and apprehending poetry. Comprehension, she says, is complete understanding, while apprehension is "the almost unconscious awareness of what is rumbling beneath the words, the intuitive understanding.... I tend to view literature and art in terms of apprehension, and I suspect children do too" (p. 208).

Livingston also speaks of image and symbol. Image is necessary, but it is not enough. "To pretend that poetry is sugar-coated rhythm and rhyme and image is to rob [children] of the ability to deal with more serious aspects of life that they will surely meet, in ways we do not even suspect" (p. 131). To convey adequately the more serious, darker side of life, poetry must transcend image and offer symbol; it must lead from a picture to a universal response that the reader can remember and adapt when in need. Symbol offers:

> the opportunity to respond beyond stereotype, beyond despair, with new insights and meaningful action. Symbol helps us learn that change is possible, that action is possible, and that each of us has the creativity to effect that change and action in a unique way....Symbols...sustain and strengthen us when times are out of joint (p. 132).

After reading and reflecting on such background material, you can examine poetry anthologies, both traditional and modern. Begin a pattern of reading a poem or two aloud, along with prose, at story time. You could begin with just two collections: Untermeyer's *The Golden Books Family Treasure of Poetry* and Harrison and Stuart-Clark's *The New Oxford Treasury of Children's Poems.* Inevitably you will develop favorites, and so will the children. When you find yourself or the children reciting lines spontaneously at appropriate moments, you will know that poetry is alive in your home or classroom.

Introducing Poetry

Poetry requires a unique approach. With other kinds of literature, teachers introduce examples to children as soon as they can read well enough to decode the language, and the children generally continue independently to find other examples if they are interested. However, until early adolescence, poetry is more accessible to children if they can hear it rather than read it silently, and they will need adult suggestions of poetry that will appeal to them. The different approach is to be more active in finding poetry to present and to plan for time to read it aloud.

The teaching of poetry should begin with plenty of reading aloud until children have effortlessly learned a few poems "by heart." Gradually, discussion can then begin about the power of poetry. Rhythm, for instance, can be felt by the children when they are encouraged to sway with the lines of Stevenson's "The Swing," and they can hear how the words of David McCord's "The Pickety Fence" reproduce the staccato sound of a stick being pulled along the top of a picket fence.

Generally it is thought that the best way to teach poetry to young students is to draw on their imaginations, reading a poem aloud and then inviting them to respond to it through another medium, such as movement or drawing. Analysis—discussing elements of poetry like meter and imagery—is usually considered best left for secondary students. Textbooks in children's literature often suggest creative ways to introduce poetry.

Parents may have more fun simply reading poetry aloud rather than teaching it, and teachers as well may wish to introduce poetry by reading a poem each day. To choose well, parents and teachers need to know what kinds of poetry will hold the interest of children of different ages.

From Mother Goose rhymes in the preschool years, children in the primary grades grow to love humor and nonsense verses that play on words. Middle elementary children begin to enjoy ballads and other narrative poetry, and they prefer modern children's poems with ordinary, everyday language and content to traditional poetry. At all ages, humorous poetry is a great favorite—Shel Silverstein is always welcome. In order to explore the potential for emotional depth in poetry, some lyric poetry should be presented as well to older students. Senior high students should take literature courses that introduce them to a variety of poets and types of poetry, including modern poets such as Maya Angelou and John Updike—poets whose allusions are more familiar to contemporary readers than are the references found in the poems of historical writers.

Recognizing Good Poetry

As the title of one book of children's poetry tells us, "It doesn't always have to rhyme." Poetry is not necessarily about rhyme; it *is* about rhythm, though, and words, and the concise, even startling expression of thoughts and feelings.

Poetry's *rhythm* appeals to young children: they clap their hands or bend their bodies to the beat of the lines. They should experience a variety of poetic meters, and poetry with lines of varying length.

Words used in good poetry are vivid, evoking strong, clear images, like the opening line of Irene Rutherford McLeod's "Lone Dog":

I'm a lean dog, a keen dog, a wild dog, and lone.

They are also imaginative, perhaps made up for the occasion or used in a new context, like e. e. cummings' words "Just-spring" and "mud-luscious" for his poem, "In Just-." For young children, Dr. Seuss books offer imaginative and creative uses of words.

Children, especially highly verbal children, respond well to poetry with unfamiliar words. There is no need to worry about a controlled vocabulary—the rhythm and the content of the poem carry the listener along.

The *expression of thoughts and feelings*—the humor, the narrative, the moods expressed in lyric poetry—should use subject matter of interest to children: animals, friends, heroes, the stuff of their lives.

Children prefer poetry that rhymes; limericks are a favorite. They respond to a strong rhythmic beat, and they love humor. Two favorite poets are Shel Silverstein and Jack Prelutsky, both of whom rely on humor, but children should learn to go beyond these two to other poets and other types of poetic expression.

There is a difference between poetry and verse. Verse usually rhymes, as does some poetry, and both typically have meter. But poetry incorporates other, more sophisticated poetic elements as well, such as onomatopoeia, word play, alliteration, and literary techniques used in prose: imagery, metaphor, symbolism. Verse, like poorly written prose, *tells* too much ("John was sad."). Poetry, like good fiction, *shows* an image ("John walked slowly, his hands in his pockets and his head down") and leaves the reader to interpret as he will. Verse explains all; poetry leaves something out for the reader to add—to apprehend, in Myra Cohn Livingston's word.

What is considered acceptable content for children's poetry, especially for adolescents, has undergone a change in recent years, along with the change in fiction for young people. Contemporary poets write about the harsh realities of modern life— hence modern poetry provides a vehicle of expression for the outraged idealism that is one characteristic of gifted children and adolescents. Such poetry assures gifted students that others share their moral concerns, and it can prompt discussions that allow them to voice their own feelings.

Finding Good Poetry

In the library, poetry is shelved in the Dewey Decimal 800s, the literature section; the 800s are subdivided by country, so that American poetry is 811, British poetry is 821, and so on. As with other types of literature, recommended books of poetry are listed in the booklists mentioned at the end of this chapter.

Many excellent anthologies and books by individual poets are available for children. Only a few are listed here:

Adoff, Arnold. *Slow Dance Heart Break Blues.* New York: Lothrop, Lee & Shepard, 1995. Ages 13+.

Gordon, Ruth, compiler. *Pierced by a Ray of Sun: Poems about the Times We Feel Alone.* New York: HarperCollins, 1995. Ages 13+.

Harrison, Michael and Christopher Stuart-Clark, compilers. *The New Oxford Treasury of Children's Poems.* Toronto: Oxford University Press, 1997. Ages 4 – 8.

Janeczko, Paul B., compiler. *The Place My Words Are Looking For: What Poets Say About and Through Their Work.* New York: Bradbury, 1990. Ages 9 – 12.

Livingston, Myra Cohn, compiler. *If the Owl Calls Again: A Collection of Owl Poems.* New York: Macmillan, 1990. Ages 9 – 12.

Myers, Walter Dean. *Harlem.* New York: Scholastic, 1997. Ages 4 – 8.

Nye, Naomi Shihab, compiler. *The Space between our Footsteps.* New York: Simon & Schuster Books for Young Readers, 1998. Ages 13+.

Untermeyer, Louis, compiler. *The Golden Books Family Treasury of Poetry.* Sturtevant, WI: Golden Books, 1998 (1975). Ages 4 – 8.

Willard, Nancy. (Ed.). *Step Lightly: Poems for the Journey.* New York: Harcourt Brace, 1998. Ages 9 – 12.

Books about Children's Literature

The preceding is only the briefest introduction to the wealth of literature for children. As with the literature itself, there is plenty to read *about* children's literature.

Essays on Children's Literature

Purely for inspirational reading, books written about children's literature are a delight. They give insight into the work of writing for children, heighten appreciation of the literature, and leave no doubt that creating literature for children is much more than child's play. Following are just a few titles:

Egoff, Sheila, G. T. Stubbs, and L. F. Ashley. *Only Connect: Readings in Children's Literature.* 3rd ed. Toronto: Oxford University Press, 1996.

Paterson, Katherine. *Gates of Excellence.* New York: Lodestar, 1988 (1981).

Paterson, Katherine. *The Spying Heart: More Thoughts on Reading and Writing Books for Children.* New York: Lodestar, 1989.

Textbooks in Children's Literature

For teachers who wish to refresh memories of their children's literature course, for parents who homeschool or who have never studied children's literature, and for the many people who assist children in school libraries without the benefit of professional training, textbooks written for college courses in children's literature provide excellent background reading.

Textbooks offer much more information than is given here on the various kinds of literature, including plot summaries of hundreds of books, as well as critical commentary. Many of them suggest activities for introducing literature to children in the classroom. Creative parents can adapt the ideas to home use.

Look for texts in the school or public library, or in the library of a college or university that trains teachers. Parents may wish to select a favorite for purchase, since these are really reference books, containing too much to absorb in one reading. The following texts provide a good introduction:

Lynch-Brown, Carol and Carl M. Tomlinson. *Essentials of Children's Literature.* 3rd ed. Boston: Allyn & Bacon, 1999.

Nilsen, Alleen P. and Kenneth L. Donelson. *Literature for Today's Young Adults.* 6th ed. New York: Longman, 2000.

>As the title implies, this book focuses on literature for young people between the ages of 12 and 20.

Norton, Donna E. *Through the Eyes of a Child: An Introduction to Children's Literature.* 5th ed. New York: Prentice-Hall, 1998.

>Including criteria for evaluating and selecting books using the principles of child development, this text provides strategies for involving children in literature, as well as comprehensive lists of books for children.

Sutherland, Zena and May Hill Arbuthnot. *Children and Books.* 9th ed. New York: Harper-Collins, 1996.

>This title has long been a classic in the field of children's literature.

Reference Books about Children's Literature

Here, at last, is the promised list of reference books about children's literature. In these books, you will find titles and annotations for books recommended for specific reading levels and on specific topics. Librarians use these reference sources to select books for library purchase, so you may have to ask for access to them and will probably have to use them in the library. But if you want to find a recommended book on coin collecting for your eight-year-old, a biography on Beethoven for your one-year-old, or appropriate science fiction for your 13-year-old, here is the place to look.

Preschool through Middle School

Cianciolo, Patricia Jean. *Picture Books for Children.* 4th ed. Chicago: American Library Association, 1997.

> Covering nursery school through junior high, this annotated list includes fiction, nonfiction, and poetry. There is also an essay on illustrations in children's books.

Cianciolo, Patricia Jean. *Informational Picture Books for Children.* Chicago: American Library Association, 2000.

> For 250 picture books for preschool through middle school children, evaluated for both aesthetic and literary merit, this list covers a variety of subjects including biographies, numbers and arithmetic, and arts and crafts.

Gillespie, John T., ed. *Best Books for Children: Preschool through Grade 6.* 6th ed. New Providence: Bowker, 1998.

> This listing of books that have been recommended in at least two respected sources of reviews of children's literature covers fiction and nonfiction for elementary students. Biographies are especially easy to find here, with a separate section and an index.

Gillespie, John T., ed. *Best Books for Junior High Readers.* New York: Bowker, 1991.

> This addition to Gillespie's "best books" series includes books that may be of interest to advanced fifth and sixth graders, as well as to students in grades 7 through 9. Both subject and grade-level indexes are provided.

Kobrin, Beverly. *Eyeopeners! How to Choose and Use Children's Books about Real People, Places, and Things.* New York: Penguin, 1988.

Kobrin, Beverly. *Eyeopeners II: Children's Books to Answer Children's Questions about the World around Them.* New York: Scholastic, 1995.

> Kobrin's books are enthusiastically and entirely devoted to nonfiction.

Pierce, Kathryn Mitchell. *Adventuring with Books: A Booklist for Pre-K – Grade 6.* 12th ed. Urbana, IL: National Council of Teachers of English, 2000.

A list of both fiction and nonfiction, this book gives annotations without reviews. Although it is published by the NCTE, it covers more than English or the humanities, with sections on social studies, biographies, the sciences, the arts, and recreational activities.

Elementary through Senior High

Carter, Betty. *Best Books for Young Adults: The History, the Selections, the Romance.* 2nd ed. Chicago: American Library Association, 2000.

This compilation of the lists of "Best Books for Young Adults" provides annotations of all books chosen for the annual lists.

Estell, Doug, Michele L. Satchwell, and Patricia S. Wright. *Reading Lists for College-Bound Students.* 3rd ed. Lawrenceville, NJ: Peterson's, 2000.

For over 110 colleges, *Reading Lists* provides suggested reading compiled from faculty members, websites, and catalogs—not (in most cases) required reading, but books the faculty would like new students to have read by the time they arrive on campus. There are also reading lists related to subject areas, such as business, political science, and history. These lists make very interesting reading for college-bound high school students who want an idea of what's ahead for them.

Lynn, R. N. *Fantasy Literature for Children and Young Adults: An Annotated Bibliography.* (4th ed.) New York: Bowker, 1994.

With an easy-to-use index, this resource annotates thousands of fantasy novels and story collections for readers in grades 3 through 12 and provides information on the genre of fantasy.

Outstanding Books for the College Bound Chicago: American
    Library Association.

Pamphlets listing categories that include fiction,
nonfiction, biography, and other topics are sold in sets of
50. A 1996 book by the same title lists the books, adds
annotations, and costs less than the set of pamphlets.
Both are available from the American Library Association at www.ala.org, or 800/545-2433.

References

Bettelheim, B. (1976). *The uses of enchantment: The meaning and importance of fairy tales.* New York: Knopf.

Carter, B. & Abrahamson, R. F. (1998). Castles to Colin Powell: The truth about nonfiction. In K. Beers & B. G. Samuels (Eds.), *Into focus: Understanding and creating middle school readers* (pp. 313-332). Norwood, MA: Christopher-Gordon.

Cook, E. (1969). *The ordinary and the fabulous.* London: Cambridge University Press.

Dailey, S. (1991). Folktales—The rainbow bridge between cultures. *Media Spectrum,* 18 (4), 3-5.

Ferraro, S. (1992, December 6). Girl talk. *New York Times Magazine,* pp. 62, 63, 86, 98.

Flack, J. (1992). Biography (Part I). *Understanding Our Gifted,* 4 (4), 17-18.

Livingston, M. C. (1990). *Climb into the bell tower: Essays on poetry.* New York: Harper & Row.

May, J. P. (1991). *Lloyd Alexander.* Boston: Twayne.

May, R. (1991). *The cry for myth.* New York: Norton.

Nodelman, P. (1992). *The pleasures of children's literature.* New York: Longman.

Rosenberg, B. (1986). *Genreflecting: A guide to reading interests in genre fiction.* 2nd ed. Littleton, CO: Libraries Unlimited.

Chapter 8

Annotated Bibliography

This bibliography is arranged according to grade level:

➤ Preschool: For the Very Young
   Two and Three Years Old
   Four Years Old

➤ Early Elementary: Kindergarten through Grade Two

➤ Upper Elementary: Grades Three through Five

➤ Middle School: Grades Six through Eight

➤ Senior High: Grades Nine through Twelve

Under each grade level grouping, books are arranged in alphabetical order by the authors' last names. Each listing is followed by an annotation that includes a brief plot summary, a few comments about the potential value of the book—including mention of Caldecott awards for picture books and Newbery awards for books of fiction for young people—and in most cases, discussion aids. For preschoolers and for children in the early grades, discussion aids are often merely suggested themes that an adult will want to have in mind when talking casually about the book. For older children, specific questions are suggested to stimulate the thinking of discussion leaders.

These questions are offered only as a starting point. Each leader will learn to develop questions based on her interpretation of the book and on her knowledge of the children who will be discussing it.

The questions suggested are the core or interpretive questions to be asked after children have warmed to the discussion with some introductory questions. In planning a discussion, the leader can choose core questions that look promising and then plan appropriate introductory questions.

Categories

Suggestions for discussion of each book are based on the *characteristics* of intellectually and artistically talented children and on the *issues* they face—which were presented in the first two chapters. Because they are related to the emotional and intellectual development of highly able children, these characteristics and issues mark ways in which books and book discussion can be most useful, and each is considered in this volume to define a "category" of discussion topics and questions. Following are brief explanations of how books were chosen to represent each of these categories.

Achievement	plots that question whether or not a bright child will achieve.
Aloneness	books that can help bright youngsters explore feelings of isolation. These books offer opportunities to assure them that requirements for time alone vary from one person to another and that time alone can be both necessary and productive.
Arrogance	characters who display arrogance to cope with the feeling that they do not fit in.
Creativity	characters whose creative impulses set them apart.

Developing imagination	books that will stimulate thinking, observing, and questioning—keeping children in touch with the joy and power of using their imaginations.
Differentness	stories dealing with people who are different because of characteristics such as ability, insight, and sensitivity.
Drive to understand	the most wide-ranging category, listing books that will challenge children intellectually and present them with ideas they may not otherwise encounter. The goal has been to suggest books that will both satisfy and whet the heightened curiosity that these children experience. In some cases, no questions are suggested for discussion of these books, since topics for discussion should suit the child's interest. Questions may also be curriculum-driven.
Identity	books that can help highly able children work toward a strong self-concept, accepting talent as a positive attribute. Remembering that such children often feel different and somehow "wrong," adults can discuss these books to help them be comfortable with their differentness. In these books, giftedness is not necessarily explicit or even represented in one of the characters.
Intensity	characters who are unusually focused on an interest, ability, or cause, with a single-mindedness not shared by most children their age.
Introversion	people who prefer to spend much of their time alone and who use that time creatively.

Moral concerns	personal or community issues that require difficult decisions.
Perfectionism	examples of what happens when a character puts too much emphasis on a perfect product.
Relationships with others	books that facilitate discussion of interdependence, empathy, and respect for others with different or lesser abilities. In addition, some of these books promote an understanding of friendships and how they are formed.
Sensitivity	characters who are intensely aware, introspective, unusually alert to the hurts of others, or particularly susceptible to being hurt themselves.
Using ability	books that raise questions about decision-making, about the responsibility gifted people have for their own talents, and about the rewards that can follow the best use of those talents.

Using the above headings, the *Index of Categories*, which follows the bibliography, is a guide to the books that are annotated in this chapter. Characteristics and issues change with age, and each category will be found only in the appropriate grade level groups. Most index entries are matched by questions in the bibliography, but in some cases, the index entry acts as a reference to a related category. For example, questions suggested for Aloneness may be easily adapted to a discussion of Introversion, so while a book may be listed in the Index under both headings, questions might be found in the annotation under only one of the two. Again, this bibliography is intended only to indicate possibilities, with parents and teachers developing their own approaches based on suggestions given here.

In the booklists that follow, nearly all of the books for pre-schoolers through second graders are picture books. Illustrators are named only when they are different from the author.

This bibliography includes many books published in the last five years, as well as a number of older titles—because children's books don't have to be new to be considered better. The reading life of an adult may span decades, so most adult books enjoy a period of popularity and then fade as interest turns elsewhere. But a new generation of young readers comes along about every four years, keeping much-loved older books in print as long as children find them meaningful. And older books often provide challenging reading, with longer, complex sentences, wide-ranging vocabulary, and a glimpse of values and patterns of thought from an earlier time.

Still, even excellent children's books do go out of print occasionally and then later are reprinted. Nearly all of the books listed here were in print in 2001; I have retained a very few currently out-of-print titles because they are used as illustrations in earlier chapters. If a book you seek is out of print, I hope you will be able to find it at your library, through interlibrary loan, or with the help of a book search service.

Finally, the decision regarding whether a book is fit for eight-year-olds or ten-year-olds is always somewhat arbitrary. Many of these books can be enjoyed by children older and younger than the ages and grade levels given. I have assigned books to grade level categories with the level of discussion, as well as the reading level, in mind; this may mean, for example, that a book labeled elsewhere for lower elementary children is listed here for upper elementary students, because the discussion the book can generate is more suitable for older students. In some cases, picture books provide a quick introduction to a personal or moral issue, useful as discussion starters with middle school or even senior high students. The *Index for All Ages* identifies books suggested for this purpose.

Preschool

The preschool years, those of greatest intellectual growth in human development, cover a wide age span. Consequently, books for infants are decidedly different from books for four-year-olds. Accordingly, this preschool bibliography is divided into three sections: For the Very Young, Two and Three Years Old, and Four Years Old.

Books are listed at the age when they first appeal to children who have been read to enough that they relate easily to books. A title recommended here for three-year-olds might be better held until later for a child who does not have this experience. Likewise, a book suggested for twos and threes may continue to hold interest for years and may still be appropriate for fours and fives. The best measure of a book's appropriateness for any child is that child's response to it.

For the Very Young

Books for infants and toddlers come in specialized sizes and shapes. Some are chunky, roughly three inches square and an inch thick. Most are "board books," with pages made of thick cardboard; others are made of fabric. The board books are so popular that classic titles are now being re-issued in this baby-proof format. Since most children are about two years old before they can reliably turn paper pages one at a time, the new materials are a boon to parents who want to read to their children in the first two years. Illustrations are often photographs, since their realism helps children relate the picture to three-dimensional objects in their surroundings.

Reading aloud to the very young child is best done by parents who are highly attuned to their child—sensitive to and accepting of her unique responses—and so do not approach reading with preconceived ideas of how she "should" react to a book. The child may be fascinated for the first three pages, and then lose interest. A book that is a favorite one week may be supplanted by another the next. One particular picture may hold the child's interest, while the rest of the book is ignored. All of this signals the child's readiness to learn according to her own schedule. Parents who enjoy *observing* the child's interest without trying to manipulate it will be the most successful at reading to the very young.

For those who wonder how much a child grasps from books before he or she can talk, consider this true story:

> *When 18-month-old Chris had an upset stomach, his mother was directed to feed him only fluids for one day. The toddler grew hungry, and as usual, he communicated this fact to his mother by standing in the kitchen and pointing up to the spot on the counter where he knew bananas were kept, although he could not see them from his position on the floor. Always before, this had produced at least part of a banana, but today, inexplicably, his mother said no. He tried pointing and chattering repeatedly; she was kind but adamant. Surely, he reasoned, she must not understand, but he knew how to explain. He strode purposefully into the living room, searched through his books until he found the right one, turned the pages to the picture of a banana, and marched back into the kitchen, pointing repeatedly to the banana in the book and then to the counter.*

Here is a small sample of books for children like Chris. Parents are urged to browse in the preschool section of a good bookstore for a better idea of all that is available to them.

Bridwell, Norman. *Clifford's Bathtime.* Cartwheel, 1991.

Clifford the puppy does not want a bath, but he enjoys it when he gets one anyway. He climbs onto the floating soap, and when he falls off, the rubber duck rescues him. The humor is not missed by one-year-olds, as parents can tell by the giggling when Clifford falls off the soap.

There are many other Clifford books, some for older children.

Brown, Deni. *What Can You Find Around the House?* Dorling
Kindersley, 1993.

In board book format, photographs present some of the
items—toys, food, pets, tools—that a child sees daily around the
house, inviting him to find and name familiar objects. Others in
the "What Can You Find?" series are *On the Farm, On the Beach,*
and *In the Yard.*

Brown, Margaret Wise. *Goodnight, Moon.* Illustrated by Clement
Hurd. Harperfestival, 1991.

This is a wonderful sleepytime book, with illustrations growing softer and dimmer as the little rabbit, tucked into bed, says
goodnight to the beloved objects in his room. A favorite for generations, it is now available as a board book.

Carle, Eric. *The Very Busy Spider.* Philomel, 1995.

For the older child in this age group who can listen to narrative, Eric Carle's books are delightful. In *The Very Busy Spider,* he
describes a spider spinning her web. She is interrupted by a horse
who invites her for a ride, followed by many other animals, all
encouraging her to join them in their daily rounds. Always, the
response is the same: the spider does not answer. She is very busy
spinning her web. At last, when a rooster asks if she wants to catch
a fly, her web is complete, and she promptly does exactly what the
rooster suggests. When the owl asks who built the beautiful web,
the spider does not answer. It has been a very busy day, and she
has fallen asleep.

As we watch the silver strand develop into a web, the child can
feel it, raised on the page. The growing web and the comforting
repetition of the refrain, along with illustrations that capture the
essence of each animal, make this book a favorite.

Eastman, P. D. *Are You My Mother?* Random House, 1998.

A young bird who has lost track of its mother asks various
unlikely creatures if they are his mother until his mother predict-
ably returns.

The mother of a curious and active one-year-old says that this is the first "plot" book her son sat through, and that it is a good bedtime book at this age.

Hill, Eric. *Spot in the Garden.* Putnam, 1991.
This board book features the well-loved puppy, Spot, as he enjoys a morning in the garden. After greeting the birds and helping his father work among the plants, Spot picks some flowers for his mom and returns to the house, where he waters the plants in his own window box.
Many other Little Spot board books are available.

Hill, Eric. *Where's Spot?* Puffin, 1994.
Spot's mother looks for her puppy all over the house—in the grandfather clock, in the piano, in the closet. She finds an unexpected creature in each location, but no Spot, until the turtle under the rug suggests she try the basket.
Not a board book, this flap book has moveable tabs the child lifts to discover the hidden animals, something some children enjoy doing by the age of eight or nine months.

Hoban, Tana. *Black on White.* Greenwillow, 1993.
This board book offers pictures of various shapes—a fork, a spoon, an elephant, glasses, keys—in stark black outlined against a white background. A companion book is *White on Black.* Both books are designed for infants, who are thought to see the high contrast of black and white before they discern colors.

Hoban, Tana. *Colors Everywhere.* Greenwillow, 1995.
Not for infants, but for one-year-olds who are ready to distinguish objects and colors, this book is a feast of both. On each page, a clear and brilliant photograph is accompanied by a side panel showing a rainbow of the colors in the picture, banded in sizes to show their proportion in the photograph. There are animals, birds, fish, flowers, and people, as well as familiar objects such as plastic dishes, and some that may be new to the child,

, such as a ride at an amusement park. The end pages gather all of the photographs together in a collage for more discussion. Suitable for many ages, *Colors Everywhere* can be used with very young children to label objects, identify colors, and match pictures from the body of the book with those on the end pages.

Hoban, Tana. *Red Blue Yellow Shoe*. Greenwillow, 1986.

These clear color photographs display objects in the baby's world—shoes, a block, a ball, a stuffed bear—in bright colors, introducing the child to names for the colors as well as labels for the objects.

Ross, Katharine. *The Little Quiet Book*. Illustrated by Jean Hirashima. Random House, 1989.

This small board book with pleasing illustrations tells us that "quiet" is a spider, the fireplace, and a chipmunk, among other examples. In the companion, *The Little Noisy Book*, "noisy" is a hammer, a brook, wet sneakers, and so on. Each book presents both familiar and new sources of quiet or sound.

Seuss, Dr. *The Foot Book*. Random House, 1988.

A good beginning Seuss book, this one shows one foot and then two feet in various positions, with the rhyming text so typical of Dr. Seuss.

Shaw, Charles G. *It Looked Like Spilt Milk*. Harper, 1993.

In white silhouettes on a blue background, we see shapes that look like a tree, a squirrel, or spilt milk. They turn out to be—a cloud.

A good stimulus for imaginative looking, this is now available as a board book.

Stone, Erika. *Baby Talk*. Grossett and Dunlap, 1992.

Here are pictures of babies being tickled, cuddling with a dog, playing peek-a-boo—with a text of universal phrases we say repetitively to children. Flaps for the child to open add to the interest.

Two and Three Years Old

Children of two and three, with their rapidly growing skills of comprehension, are attentive read-aloud companions. They are ready to follow a simple plot, and they enjoy humor in text and illustrations. After hearing a story outlined while viewing a word-less picture book, they can tell it themselves. They enjoy the rhythms of more complex language, and they linger over pictures as they strive for understanding. By now, reading aloud and trips to the library should be an established part of family life, and the child's home library should be growing.

Barton, Byron. *Bones, Bones, Dinosaur Bones.* HarperCollins, 1990.

With simple text, bold colors, and clean lines, Barton presents an introduction to the work of paleontologists, showing the youngest dinosaur buffs that after bones are found, they are dug up, packed in trucks, transported to a museum, and reassembled. Demonstrating serious respect for the intelligence of his readers, the author includes illustrations of eight dinosaurs, labeling them and (adults reading the book aloud will be glad to know) providing a pronunciation guide. This book may well clear up a mystery for beginning dinosaur fans, bringing science and a level of credibility to a subject that has been overwhelmed by cartoons in recent years.

Brett, Jan. *The Hat.* Putnam, 1997.

The Scandinavian winter is coming, so Lisa hangs her woolen clothes on the line to air. When a sock falls from the line and a curious hedgehog pokes its nose inside, the "hat" sticks to his prickles. Other animals laugh at Hedgie, but he answers by listing every advantage he can think of in wearing clothes. Taking this to heart, the other animals don Lisa's other clothes as the wind blows them off the line. Meanwhile, in border pictures, we see Lisa in the house, engaged in her daily activities until she realizes she has lost a sock—then she must go in search of her hats, scarves and mittens as well. The illustrations of Lisa's farm home and the winter landscape are lovely and full of conversation starters—a good introduction to another country.

Brown, Margaret Wise. *The Runaway Bunny.* Illustrated by Clement Hurd. HarperFestival, 1991.

In this conversation between a bunny and his mother, the bunny suggests that he might run away, and his mother gently tells him what she would do to find him if he did. Clearly, no action of this little bunny will separate him from his mother and her love for him.

Charlip, Remy and Lilian Moore. *Hooray for Me!* Illustrated by Vera B. Williams. Tricycle, 1996.

Here is a joyful picture book celebrating the individual. The section on relationships with others can lead to conversation about how the child fits into her family and into her neighborhood. The section on identifying with things the child does ("I'm my dog's walker") is good for expanding from the book into the child's own life. Wise use of this book can enhance the child's self-concept. Personalize the book, talking about your own family, your own neighborhood, and your child's place in them.

Crews, Donald. *Carousel.* Greenwillow, 1987.

With pictures of a carousel and a calliope created as collages and then photographed by a moving camera, Crews gives the impression of the movement and sound of a carousel in this brief but memorable book.

The book invites children to relate their memories of riding or seeing a carousel to the feelings triggered by pictures—a synthesis of visual imagery and physical experience.

Crews, Donald. *Freight Train.* Mulberry, 1993.

The only words in this book identify the kinds of cars in a freight train and their colors, and then where the train goes. The impact is produced visually by means of the illustrations, and the effect is amazingly emotional for such an austere format. The illustrations give the sense of a train slowly gathering speed and then racing through tunnels, past cities, and over trestles until it is gone.

Reading it aloud, an adult will hear speed and volume increasing in her voice, and then will almost hear the whistle. The child will have an experience in visual and sensory imagery.

Fleming, Denise. *In the Small, Small Pond.* Holt, 1998.

Colorful images made by pouring colored cotton pulp through handcut stencils illustrate the variety of life even in a small pond. The few words on each page are rhymed, fascinating, and memorable, telling of the activities of each of the creatures: "Sweep, swoop, swallows scoop." The changing colors tell us that the seasons are passing, until the tadpoles we met at the outset are frogs burrowing into the mud for the winter.

Developing imagination.

Fleming, Denise. *Time to Sleep.* Holt, 1997.

When Bear decides it is time to find a spot to hibernate, she first tells Snail that winter is coming. Snail tells Skunk, and so on, until the news has spread full circle back to Bear, who by now is sound asleep in her den. From frost on the grass to bright leaves to shorter days, each animal recognizes another sign of fall as they all trundle off to sleep. The text has the comfort of a repetitive pattern, and the illustrations are vibrant and imaginative.

Developing imagination.

Gag, Wanda. *Millions of Cats.* Paper Star, 1996.

The very old man sets off to find a cat for the very old woman, and when he cannot choose among the millions of cats, he takes them all home. The very old woman protests that so many cats will eat them out of house and home, so the very old man asks the cats to decide which is the prettiest. After the ensuing struggle, only one homely kitten is left; under the tender loving care of the old couple, it grows healthy and plump—the prettiest cat of all.

Parents should be aware that when the cats quarrel and disappear, the very old woman concludes, "I think they must have eaten each other all up"; adults may or may not wish to create their own explanation of what happened to the cats as they read aloud. This old and well-loved story is still recommended for the comforting repetition and the refrain, "Hundreds of cats, thousands of cats, millions and billions and trillions of cats."

Gibbons, Gail. *Farming.* Holiday House, 1988.

The illustrations take us through a year on a farm, outlining the seasonal changes and the outdoor and indoor chores for everyone. This traditional family farm supports both livestock— chickens, pigs, sheep, horses, cows, and even a beehive—and crops, including a garden, an orchard, a cornfield, hay to mow and store in the hayloft, and a sugar bush.

Parents will probably read the book through once and then abandon the text, using the illustrations as a springboard for conversation—adding all they know, as well as asking and answering questions based on the pictures. Attentive three-year-olds will want to stay with each page until it is thoroughly understood before moving on. Gibbons' books inspire questions that will drive even parents of three-year-olds to reference books for the answers.

Giganti, Paul. *How Many Snails? A Counting Book.* Illustrated by Donald Crews. Mulberry Books, 1994.

This is a counting book with a difference. In addition to counting Crews' colorful pictures of snails and fish and flowers, the child is asked to notice, for example, how many fish are red, and then how many red fish have their mouths open, and so on.

Following this pattern, a parent can easily ask other questions about other sets in each picture, making this a book for creative interaction—new each time it is read.

Hest, Amy. *In the Rain with Baby Duck*. Illustrated by Jill Barton. Candlewick, 1999.

Baby Duck does *not* like rainy days, so today she is in a bad mood. Mr. and Mrs. Duck lead the way through the rain for Pancake Sunday at Grampa's, waddling and shimmying along, enjoying the rain as ducks should. Baby Duck pouts and dawdles, grumbling the whole time: "Wet face," "Mud, mud, mud." But while her parents cannot understand a duck who doesn't like rain, her Grampa can. In the attic, he finds a beautiful umbrella and matching boots, and he explains to Baby Duck that a long time ago, her mother had been a baby duck that did not like rain. Then Grampa takes Baby Duck, with boots and umbrella, for a walk in the rain. They waddle, they shimmy, they hop in puddles—and Baby Duck sings a happy song.

Sensitivity. Although Baby Duck acts exactly like a two-year-old, older children, too, will ask for this book again and again. They will recognize the mood swing from pouty and grumpy to happy and singing, and perhaps acknowledge that a little understanding and a new attitude can change a day from miserable to happy. The story is one that can be recalled in similar situations long after it's read, and the appealing illustrations will draw the reader into Baby Duck's affection-filled world.

Hutchins, Pat. *Rosie's Walk*. Aladdin, 1983.

"Rosie the hen went for a walk...and got back in time for dinner." The text is deliberately commonplace; the real story is told in the illustrations. The child watches in suspense as the fox nearly catches Rosie over and over again, landing in positions of ever greater indignity as the story goes on. The fact that Rosie is blissfully unaware of the fox also gives the child the delightful opportunity to be in on a secret.

Although this is not a wordless book, it offers the advantages of one by encouraging children to "read" the pictures and tell the story in their own words, and to laugh at the understated humor of it all.

Krauss, Ruth. *The Carrot Seed.* Illustrated by Crockett Johnson. Harper, 1993.

A little boy plants a carrot seed, and despite everyone's warnings that the seed won't grow, he weeds and waters faithfully. The reward for his labors is one very large carrot.

Kuskin, Karla. *James and the Rain.* Illustrated by Reg Cartwright. Simon & Schuster, 1995.

It's going to rain all day, but James is undaunted. Gathering his yellow raincoat, rubber boots, and a large umbrella, he sets out. On his journey, he meets a succession of animals: one cow, two ducks, and so on to ten cats. At each encounter, he asks the words of Kuskin's poem:

> "What do you do in the rain?" said James.
> "Do you have any excellent rainy day games?"

As it turns out, all of the animals love the rain, and they demonstrate the various ways in which they embrace a rainy day. Then, the growing entourage strolls on to the next meeting. In the end, the cats reveal that they enjoy the rain best from in front of a roaring fire. In the final picture, James and all of the animals are gathered in a cozy room, asleep in front of the fire.

Developing imagination. The dramatic illustrations and bold colors, as well as the rhythm of Kuskin's poetry, carry the story for a young listener. Meanwhile, the child is absorbing Kuskin's imaginative language—including several words made up to fit the occasion, with meanings either readily plain to the child or given Kuskin's definition in the poem. Both verbally and artistically, this book will enrich the child's world.

Lowrey, Janette Sebring. *The Poky Little Puppy.* Illustrated by Gustaf Tenggren. Golden, 2001.

Five puppies dig a hole under the fence and go exploring the wide, wide world beyond it. Only four arrive at the top of the hill, and when they look for the poky puppy, they discover that he is sniffing the rice pudding their mother is making for dessert.

Home they tumble, but their mother, who is displeased about the hole under the fence, sends them to bed without supper. But the poky little puppy, when he arrives home late, gets rice pudding. The theme repeats twice more, but the third time the poky puppy misses his dessert. The next morning, the sign over the hole under the fence seems convincing enough to provide a satisfying end to the story.

A favorite among the Golden Books, this classic offers more challenge than some newer books for twos and threes. The repetitive pattern is longer than is now typical, and each time through there are subtle changes that move the story line along. The poky little puppy and his siblings offer a satisfying reading experience for the child who is ready to point to objects as he counts.

McCloskey, Robert. *Blueberries for Sal*. Viking, 1987.

Little Sal and her mother go to Blueberry Hill to pick blueberries to can for the winter on the same afternoon that Little Bear and his mother come to the other side of the hill to eat blueberries to grow fat for the winter. Each intent on finding berries, mother and child, and bear and cub become separated, confused, and then reunited.

The charm in this favorite book is in the parallel situations, underscored by repetitious phrasing and in the child's ability to see what is about to happen before the inevitable unfolds.

Miller, Margaret. *Guess Who?* Greenwillow, 1994.

Who goes to school? Seagulls? Puppies? Umpires? No-o-o— (turn the page) CHILDREN! Miller illustrates a series of questions with improbable answers, followed by the one the child guesses all along, with vivid photographs. *Guess Who?* is an intensely interactive book combining the ridiculous with the predictable, told with a delicious suspense. Parent and child who share this book will inevitably end up laughing with the child's delight at getting the right answer yet again.

Drive to understand. All the while the child is guessing the right answer, she is also learning to identify the photographs of the wrong answers: juggler, potter, crab, hot-air balloon, veterinarian, parrot, violinist—so this happy book is also a picture dictionary for young children.

Opie, Iona. *My Very First Mother Goose*. Illustrated by Rosemary Wells. Candlewick, 1996.

In choosing some 68 rhymes for this new collection, Opie, a co-editor of *The Oxford Dictionary of Nursery Rhymes*, seems to have intentionally sought the most comforting of the genre, leaving those depicting violence and mayhem for the scholars. Rosemary Wells apparently agreed: her illustrations feature rabbits, cats, mice, pigs, and bears whose droll expressions add warmth, humor, and original insight into the well-known plots. For example, is it possible that Humpty Dumpty's fall was in fact caused by a small rabbit who did not want to eat his coddled egg?

This is a happy book, an ideal marriage of text and illustrations. It will entertain readers of all ages, as another generation of parents teach their children to love language—beginning with the polished rhythms of Mother Goose.

Piper, Watty. *The Little Engine that Could*. Illustrated by George and Doris Hauman. Grosset and Dunlap, 1978.

On her way over a mountain with good things for girls and boys on the other side, a little engine stops, unable to go farther. Several large, proud engines refuse to help, but finally the Little Blue Engine says she is willing to try, although she has never been over the mountain. With the classic line, "I think I can, I think I can, I think I can.... I thought I could, I thought I could, I thought I could," she succeeds.

Some children carry with them into adulthood the lesson about perseverance so gently taught in this book.

Scarry, Richard. *Richard Scarry's Best First Book Ever.* Random, 1979.

Each page of Scarry's book is filled with pictures for discussion with labels to promote vocabulary building. A very slight story line carries the Cat family through a day that allows Scarry to touch on colors, counting, letters, and shapes, as well as everyday events such as housework, school, shopping, trips to the doctor's office and to a farm, and more. The book presents a wide range of information for discussion and plenty of detail for sharp eyes to search out, with an adult asking questions to guide the search. Children can then spend time alone with the book, looking for more.

Waddell, Martin. *Owl Babies.* Illustrated by Patrick Benson. Candlewick, 2000.

Sarah and Percy and Bill respond differently when they wake up in their nest and find their Owl Mother gone. As they wait for her return, Sarah is reassuring and Percy is reassured. But Bill, the littlest, repeats the refrain, so basic to a child's experience: "I want my Mommy." When she returns and says, "You knew I'd be back," Sarah and Percy agree: they knew it. Bill says simply, "I love my Mommy."

Identity; Relationships with others. With its simple message that Mommy will come back, *Owl Babies* can be a very important book for children entering daycare. Young children identify with Bill, even speaking his line with him each time, and jumping up and down when the little owls bounce up and down on their branch at Mother Owl's return. This book offers a way to remind children that Mommies sometimes have to leave—Mother Owl is searching for food for her babies—and provides comfort to a growing young mind.

Four Years Old

The eager, expansive four-year-old of high ability probably already experiences some sense of being different from his playmates. Books can increase his understanding that he is an individual with differences to be enjoyed and celebrated, help him gain skills in getting along with other children, encourage his lively imagination, and add to his rapidly growing knowledge base. Such books can build his confidence and pleasure as he begins to learn about himself. Because he is ready to conceptualize some self-understanding and social skills, the following annotations include pointers—and in some cases, suggested questions—for casual conversations about issues that may concern the bright four-year-old.

Albert, Burton. *Where Does the Trail Lead?* Illustrated by Brian Pinkney. Simon & Schuster, 1991.

A book to ponder through the winter, remembering the warmth and scents of summer, this is a gentle story of an inquisitive boy who has the self-confidence to be off on his own, exploring the trail from his family's summer cabin to the sea. He encounters tide-pools, blueberries, an abandoned railroad track, a ghost-town of shanties, and much else, all depicted in scratchboard illustrations with sweeping lines, just right for sand and sea. At the end of the day, he is welcomed by his family, cooking fresh-caught fish around the campfire in the twilight, at the edge of the sea.

Aloneness; Developing imagination. A quiet, introspective book, *Where Does the Trail Lead?* encourages daydreaming and exploration, as well as more careful observation on hikes along real trails.

Alexander, Lloyd. *The Fortune Tellers.* Illustrated by Trina Schart Hyman. Puffin, 1997.

Alexander has created an original folktale, marked by gentle humor and just enough complexity to challenge perceptive four-year-olds. A disgruntled carpenter, hearing his fortune told, concentrates only on the promises and not on the very large "ifs" the fortune-teller adds in warning. Nevertheless, things turn out exactly as he hopes when the fortune-teller disappears and the carpenter accidentally replaces him, hedging his bets by adding conditions to his predictions as the original seer had done.

The tale is set in Cameroon, home of the illustrator's son-in-law. The Caldecott Medallist's illustrations of the landscape, the marketplaces, the people, and the interiors of homes and shops are truly fine. Colorful, descriptive, and whimsical, they reflect the wit and humor of the text.

Drive to understand. Much can be learned from the illustrations alone. Ask the child to notice and identify details in the pictures. Follow the ubiquitous monkey through the book. Discuss the story line and help the child understand the paradoxes in the fortune-teller's answers. For more mature children, find Cameroon on a globe or atlas.

Anno, Mitsumasa. *Anno's Counting Book.* HarperTrophy, 1986.

This wordless book begins with a snowy landscape for zero. The "one" page shows one adult, one child, one tree, and one building; then, on subsequent pages, two of each, and so on, progressing to 12. In the meantime the seasons change, the clock tower shows the time for each number, a tower of blocks increases by tens, and the trees, buildings, and people offer enough variety for many discussions with much observing, identifying, and counting to be done along the way.

Drive to understand. There is always something more to see in Anno's illustrations, and the child will enjoy looking with an adult and then alone.

Base, Graeme. *My Grandma Lived in Gooligulch.* Abrams, 1990.

When Grandma lived in Gooligulch, she made a practice of taming wild animals—Australian animals with strong rhythmical names that carry Base's rollicking verse along. A wombat pulled Grandma's gig (cart), while a bandicoot rode beside her. The night the emus came to dine, a great fuss ensued when a frill-necked lizard appeared. Finally Grandma sailed off to sea (by then it seemed to be her only option), but the author suggests that Grandma is probably back in Gooligulch now.

Base depicts 21 animals and Grandma on the fly leaf, with a chart to help the child identify each. Interspersed throughout the text pages are gorgeously colored double spreads to give us a better view of the animals. Enticing as the pictures are, the text is equally memorable and challenging, full of names of Australian birds, animals, and plants, and laced with an occasional Australian term (gig, two-up, petrol) for the child to add to his vocabulary.

Developing imagination. A child who hears Grandma's story read by one who has a sense for the rhythm will soon be reciting sections on her own. This book could easily lead to others, fiction and nonfiction, about Australia.

Bryan, Ashley. *Turtle Knows Your Name.* Aladdin, 1993.

The little boy has a very long name, Upsilimana Tumpalerado. Eventually, he can remember all of it, and on that day, his delighted Granny takes him to the beach, where they dance his name dance. As always when there is a name dance, Turtle swims to the surface to hear the name and then dives to the bottom to spell it out in shells on the ocean floor. But though Upsilimana Tumpalerado knows his name, it is too long for his friends, and they still call him Long Name. One day, Granny challenges Upsilimana Tumpalerado to tell her *her* name, and he goes searching to find one who knows it—Turtle, of course.

Both the colorful illustrations and the story are full of joy in this retelling of a West Indian tale. Upsilimana Tumpalerado must have a firm sense of his place in the world, with his name written on the bottom of the sea, a Granny who patiently teaches him to remember it, and villagers who respond to his questions by circling around him, dancing and singing.

Identity. Remind the child of the various traditions that her family has developed to impart the same sense of place and foundation.

Burningham, John. *Hey! Get Off Our Train*. Crown, 1999.

A boy and his stuffed dog go to sleep after a day of playing with a toy train. In a dream sequence, they go for a train ride through the night, stopping for such diversions as playing ghosts in the fog and going for a swim. Each time they return to the train, a new animal has climbed aboard. The boy challenges each with "Hey! Get off our train," but each pleads for sanctuary—the elephants are being killed for their tusks, the seals find less food in polluted waters, etc. Each ends the plea with "and soon there will be none of us left"—so of course, all are allowed to join the group on the train. When the boy's mother wakes him for school, she tells him that the house is full of animals—all have come home with him.

Drive to understand; Moral concerns. Burningham's book is included in this list because environmental issues are among the moral concerns that gifted youngsters may worry about more deeply and earlier than most children. The train metaphor may help children conceptualize the problem. No solutions are offered here, but discussion about what the child and his family can do to help the environment is a logical follow-up and will reassure the child that there is something he can do.

de Gerez, Toni. *Louhi, Witch of North Farm*. Illustrations by Barbara Cooney. Viking Kestrel, 1986.

Feeling restless one day, Louhi makes trouble by stealing the sun and the moon and hiding them "behind nine great locks, behind nine great doors in her storeroom in Copper Mountain." Darkness covers the earth, and the people are very worried. Even Vainamoinen, the Great Knower, lacks the power to make Louhi give up the sun and the moon. But Louhi learns that Seppo, the smith, is forging an iron collar and nine iron chains to capture her. She opens the door to her storeroom and restores the sun and the moon to their rightful places. Under the warmth and glow of their light, spring returns to the earth.

Developing imagination; Drive to understand. This story from the *Kalevala*, the epic poem of Finland, is retold with poetic skill, and the pictures faithfully create the atmosphere of the northern sky and landscape. Together, de Gerez and Cooney make the story not only accessible, but irresistible to four-year-olds.

Demi. *The Empty Pot.* Holt, 1996.

Ping lives in China, and even in a land where everyone loves flowers, he is known for his skill in growing things. One day, to choose a successor, the Emperor gives every child, including Ping, a seed. In a year, the children are to return with the plants from their seeds, and the new Emperor will be chosen based on the results. Ping plants his seed hopefully and cares for it tenderly, watering and transplanting and providing the best soil, but he fails—nothing grows. He must return to the Emperor with an empty pot. The Emperor is delighted with Ping's honesty, and the story finishes with a surprise ending.

Demi's delicate illustrations evoke old China and suit the folkloric quality of the story—a memorable introduction to another time and place for a discerning child.

Identity; Moral concerns; Perfectionism. In talking about the book, mention that Ping is not only honest but also courageous, willing to admit failure. In this, he is encouraged by his father, who assures him that he has done his best. Our best is enough, if honestly done, even when we seem to fail.

Gerrard, Roy. *Sir Cedric.* Farrar, Straus and Giroux, 1984.

Finding life at the castle a little boring, Sir Cedric heads off in search of adventure. In the middle of the forest he meets Black Ned, who challenges Cedric to a duel. Cedric wins, rescuing the maiden Matilda. At the feast announcing their wedding, Black Ned appears with an army. Cedric meets the challenge, and his army wins the battle—in time for tea.

Developing imagination. All of this is told in verse, accompanied by illustrations at once rich and charming. Both text and illustrations incorporate a subtle, droll humor that will be appreciated by sophisticated young readers.

Gilman, Phoebe. *Something from Nothing.* Scholastic, 1993.

Joseph's grandfather is a creative, thrifty tailor who makes a wonderful blanket for his new grandson. As Joseph grows, the blanket becomes worn, and Mother suggests throwing it out. "Grandpa can fix it," says Joseph, and Grandpa finds "just enough material" to make something smaller from the good cloth that remains. This pattern is repeated until the last fragment of blanket is only large enough to cover a button. When the button is lost, Joseph, now a schoolboy, finds just enough material to make—a wonderful story!

Basing her story on a traditional Jewish folktale, Gilman offers three parallel stories. Each double-page spread shows, on the left, a cutaway view of a two-story building in the Jewish quarter of a city somewhere in Eastern Europe. On the top floor lives Joseph's family, with his father's cobbler shop curtained off from the living space. On the ground floor, his grandparents live and work. Below the floor, a family of mice carry on busy lives that reflect the activities of the people above them. The right-hand pages are filled with active street scenes, with horse-drawn wagons and vendors displaying their wares. Each page offers much to discuss.

The love in the faces of all of Joseph's family adds immensely to the appeal of this book. The text is repetitive and reassuring, with the well-worn polish of a traditional tale.

Developing imagination; Drive to understand. The illustrations offer so much to see that an attentive three-year-old becomes completely engrossed, even following the shift from physical to intellectual object when there is just enough material left to make a story.

Handford, Martin. *Where's Waldo?* Candlewick, 1997.

Waldo hikes to a variety of interesting places—a museum, a fair, the seashore, a railway station—each place illustrated in a double spread, teeming with people and miniature stories. The reader is invited to find Waldo at each location, and Waldo's post-cards invite us to find other people and events on each page, too. At the end, however triumphant we may feel about our success in finding Waldo, we face one last challenge: Waldo says that on his travels he has lost his camping gear, one item at a time. Can we find it?

Developing imagination. Like books illustrated by Peter Spier, Richard Scarry, and Mitsumasa Anno, this one is filled with detail, encouraging careful observation and story telling. Adult and child will find new interest with each viewing.

Heine, Helme. *Friends.* Aladdin, 1997.

First published in Germany, this picture book shows three friends—a mouse, a rooster, and a pig—as they spend a day together, defining friendship as they share their adventures. "Good friends always stick together," "Good friends always decide things together,"—even, at the end of the day, "Sometimes good friends can't be together."

There is humor in the illustrations, and a touch of European landscape.

Relationships with others. Each of the friends' definitions of friendship can be explored, with examples from the child's experience as a test of validity.

Hutchins, Pat. *Shrinking Mouse.* Greenwillow, 1997.

Four friends—Fox, Rabbit, Squirrel, and Mouse—watch with concern as Owl flies off to a distant forest, shrinking as he goes. Will he disappear? One after another, they follow to bring him back, each one shrinking in turn while those remaining watch in growing distress and then follow. Yet when they reach the forest, all are the proper size! They turn to see that the wood they had left is now too small, and hesitantly they return, only to find that when they arrive, it is just the right size. Some of them begin to understand the principle of spatial perspective that is at work here, and the child will chuckle with understanding too.

Drive to understand. Looking at the pictures and hearing the friends talk about what they see, the child can learn what perspective is and transfer that awareness to other books and landscapes.

Relationships with others. Each of the friends is concerned about the others, and each tries to help regardless of their worry. Mouse, who suddenly understands what is happening, gladly comforts the others, and we can guess that he will explain in a friendly way.

Hutchins, Pat. *Titch*. Aladdin, 1993.

Titch has an older sister and brother, and they have larger bicycles, noisier musical instruments, and higher-flying kites than Titch does. But more exciting than Pete's large spade and Mary's fat flowerpot is Titch's tiny seed, which "grew and grew and grew."

The lesson is clear: potential counts for more than size, and young children who are constantly trying to keep up will be reminded of their own potential by this simple story.

Identity. What else grows besides seeds? What will *you* be like when you get bigger?

Relationships with others. How can big children help little children? Is there anyone smaller than you whom you can help by being kind?

Lionni, Leo. *Frederick*. Knopf, 1990.

Frederick is a field mouse who sits alone while the other mice store food for the winter. When they chide him for not working, Frederick responds that he *does* work: while they gather food, he is gathering sun rays, colors, and words. The others are reproachful, but in the winter when they are cold and their food supply is dwindling, Frederick is able to warm and nourish them with his words evoking the sun and the colorful flowers. Frederick is a poet, and the mice know that he offers more than food.

The torn-paper illustrations and the simple wisdom in the story make this book a favorite. Some children will empathize with Frederick's day-dreaming and his avoidance of tasks, but they may also learn to value "alone time," which may very well be a new concept for them, and one that needs reinforcement from an adult. Frederick's quiet acceptance of himself as he is, even though it sets him apart from the others, is a quality some gifted children have even at this age. For them, it is good to see the other mice learn to value Frederick's special contributions to the group.

Creativity; Developing imagination; Differentness; Identity; Introversion; Using ability. What makes it all right for Frederick not to work with the others? Can the child tell you when she feels like Frederick, thereby identifying her own need for time to reflect?

MacDonald, Golden. *The Little Island.* Illustrated by Leonard Weisgard. Picture Yearling, 1993.

Life on this little island in the ocean includes spiders and chuckleberries, lobsters and seals, kingfishers and gulls—and a kitten who comes to the island one day and learns the secret of how an island is really a part of the land.

The lyrical prose and award-winning illustrations make this book a delightful way for children to learn what an island is.

Drive to understand. The kitten reflects the child's sense of wonder, imagining what she cannot see—that is, the island's connection to all the land underneath the water.

Marzollo, Jean. *Sun Song.* Illustrated by Laura Regan. Harper-Trophy, 1997.

Cued by Marzollo's gentle poem, Regan has created illustrations that follow the sun's light through a single day, shining on the spots of a newborn fawn, warming the rocks at the water hole, calling the sheep, waking a boy and his puppy, gloriously illuminating tulips and lilacs, painting the evening sky, and slipping away toward night. The poem offers new words to stretch a child's listening vocabulary, and the illustrations are luminous and evocative.

Developing imagination. These illustrations can be a spring-board to help the child see, for example, the colors in a sunset.

Drive to understand. After reading *Sun Song,* a teacher or parent can follow up by pointing out differences in light and shadow at different times of day, recalling the book while watching where the sun is in the sky as the light changes.

McCloskey, Robert. *Time of Wonder.* Viking, 1989.

McCloskey's book evokes in words and pictures a child's experience of late summer in Maine. Weather is a factor to be reckoned with, and the children in the story pick up the adults' apprehension about the approaching hurricane, but they also observe their parents' knowledgeable preparation for it and their sturdy survival of the storm. Coziness and family security are the themes. Awareness and enjoyment of nature pervade the book, along with a respect for its power and wonder at its mysteries. Where *do* hummingbirds go in a hurricane?

Although it is full of action, the book is also quiet and thoughtful, acknowledging the moods of children whether at play in the sunshine, singing to cover fear in a storm, or experiencing a bittersweet farewell as they leave for another school year.

Developing imagination. What places are special for you, as the coast of Maine is for the children in this book? How does it feel to know you are standing where other children stood hundreds of years ago? Or to wonder over the age of a fossil? What other places or events or objects have caused you to wonder? What do you find to wonder about on a simple walk near your house?

Micklethwaite, Lucy. *I Spy: An Alphabet in Art.* Mulberry, 1996.

This most original alphabet book is a collection of well-known paintings by artists such as Jan van Eyck, Jan Vermeer, Georges Seurat, and others less familiar now in private collections or in museums in the United States and Europe. In each, Micklethwaite has selected a detail to represent a letter of the alphabet, inviting the child to scrutinize the painting carefully to find, for example, a Nest in a floral still life, or challenging the child to recognize an Orange in a painting by Matisse.

Developing imagination; Drive to understand. This beautiful art book, whose only text is "I spy with my little eye…" provides a brilliant way to introduce fine art to young people. Using paintings to play "I spy" with her own children, Micklethwaite found that they frequently found details she had not noticed before. She says: "By making these paintings accessible, I was enabling my children to build up a store of images in their own minds which must inevitably lead to some interest in fine art." By using this book, even parents who know little of art can do the same for their children.

Milne, A. A. *The Complete Tales of Winnie-the-Pooh.* Illustrated by E. H. Shepard. Penguin, 1996.

This is a fine gift for the fourth birthday of a child who already has plenty of experience with books—but do not begin at the beginning when you read it to a child of this age. The dialogues in the introductory material and in the first chapter do not label the speakers, causing difficulty for young listeners trying to follow without benefit of punctuation. Rather, plunge right into one of the stories—each chapter can stand alone. Your child will learn them all and develop favorites, and the characters will become part of his imaginary menagerie.

Identity; Relationships with others. This is a wonderful bedtime reader, full of wisdom, humor, and acceptance of self and others.

Sharmat, Marjorie Weinman. *I'm Terrific.* Illustrated by Kay Charao. Holiday House, 1992.

Jason Everett Bear tells himself and others how terrific he is, but this gains him no friends. So he changes his approach—instead of doing everything right, he does everything wrong, annoying others in the process. Finally, he decides that he is neither terrific nor terrible; he can be just Jason Everett Bear. His friends welcome Jason Everett Bear just as he is.

Arrogance; Identity. This is one of those books that provide catch-words that parent and child can use to identify different moods and behaviors long after the book is read. Develop the idea of being "terrific" (showing off) or "terrible," and how anyone can change from one to the other depending on what kind of day she is having. Be sure to talk about being just Jason Everett Bear—just yourself—and help the child identify when she is doing that so she can begin to recognize how it feels.

Relationships with others. Can your child recognize when other children are being "terrific" (showing off) or "terrible" (behaving badly because they feel bad about themselves) or just being themselves? If he can begin to watch for this, it will be a big step toward understanding and empathizing with others.

Steptoe, John. *Stevie.* HarperTrophy, 1986.

Robert's mother takes care of a little boy, Stevie, while the boy's mother is at work. While Robert is in school, Stevie plays with Robert's toys. After school, Stevie trails along after Robert like a little brother and disrupts his play with his friends. Robert resents Stevie, but when Stevie's family suddenly moves away, Robert remembers the good times he had with Stevie.

Relationships with others. Discussion should bring out the fact that we all have strong and weak points, and it's best to look for the good in others—while we can still be friends with them.

Tresselt, Alvin. *Hide and Seek Fog.* Illustrated by Roger Duvoisin. William and Morrow, 1988.

The fog approaches from the ocean and stays for three days, keeping the lobstermen and sailors off the water and the children inside by the driftwood fire.

The text and the illustrations by Roger Duvoisin blend beautifully to evoke the calmed, quiet, introspective mood induced by a heavy fog. If the book is read slowly, thoughtfully, liltingly, both child and adult will pick up the mood of cozy settledness.

Conversation about this book can focus on the warm inside feel of a rainy or foggy day, the quiet pleasure of working alone on a favorite project, or the contentment of playing alone while knowing that there are people in the next room or coming home soon. The child who can appreciate such experiences is on the way to becoming a self-reliant person, capable of being at peace with himself.

Van Leeuwen, Jean. *Amanda Pig on Her Own.* Illustrated by Ann Schweninger. Puffin, 1994.

This book contains four stories about Amanda, whose older brother Oliver has just begun school. Amanda misses him but then learns that she is never *all* alone, and so she learns to be happy entertaining herself. She also learns how to feel better when sick in bed, the disadvantages of a messy room, and what a Bad, Sad, Mad Day is like. Young readers will recognize the feeling of frustration when nothing goes right.

Aloneness. Beginning readers can read this on their own, and it is a good book to remember when a child feels alone, or a room is a mess, or a day seems to go all wrong.

Identity. While Amanda learns to entertain herself and what it is like to have a bad day, she is also learning that she can handle daily difficulties—she is more capable than she thought. So is every child, but this is often not pointed out to them in so many words. Use this book to clarify your child's awareness of her own growth, connecting recent specific examples from events at home or preschool to Amanda's experiences.

Early Elementary (K–Grade Two)

Alderson, Sue Ann and Ann Blades. *Ida and the Wool Smugglers.* Groundwood Books, 1999.

Ida and her family are new settlers on an island off the west coast of Canada, raising sheep and farming. But there is a problem—smugglers from the mainland occasionally steal the farmers' sheep. One day, Ida's mother asks her to take bread to their nearest neighbors, the Springmans, who have a new baby. Although brother John thinks Ida is too young, she is the only one free to go, and so she sets off on her way, choosing a route that takes her through the meadow so she can see her pet ewe and the twin lambs along the way. When she hears the whistles of smugglers signaling to each other, Ida has to find a way to save the ewe and her twins.

Identity. Using this simple story of bravery and responsibility, with lovely illustrations evocative of the past, parents can talk about the roles children used to play in helping families and neighbors, and they can ask a variety of questions: What do children do now to help? What do you do in your family to make things go more easily for everyone? What are you old enough to do that makes you proud—as proud as Ida was to hold the Springmans' new baby?

Aliki. *Feelings.* Greenwillow, 1986.

This is not a story, but a book showing on each page a different familiar childhood event—a birthday party, a space capsule created of wood blocks and then destroyed, getting lost in a store, being bored—with the characters commenting on their positive and negative feelings.

Aloneness. Identify lonely or alone situations in the book (such as boredom). What do you do when you feel like that? What else could you do?

Identity. A calm, objective discussion of both good and bad feelings based on the book can help a child recognize and accept her own feelings later, when emotions may run so strong that rational discussion is not possible: How would you feel if this happened? Why? What would you do? Are there other times when you feel the same way? How do you act when you feel that way? Is it all right to feel that way? Do other people ever feel the same way that you do?

Relationships with others. This book can be used to help children focus on how other people feel as well as on how they themselves feel. How can you tell what these people are feeling? How can you tell when your friends feel angry, lonely, or happy? What do you do in those situations?

Anno, Mitsumasa. *Anno's Journey.* Paper Star, 1997.

This wordless book shows a man journeying on horseback through a medieval European landscape. The reader who looks carefully will be able to identify a fair, a duel, a foot race, a ping-pong game, and many visual jokes—the book is full of details to observe and discuss.

Drive to understand. A child can pore over this book for hours, continually finding something new. An adult can enrich the experience by questioning: What are they doing? Tell me a story about this. What do you think this is?

Baker, Jeannie. *Where the Forest Meets the Sea.* William Morrow, 1988.

A boy and his father spend a day on the beach between an Australian rainforest and the Great Barrier Reef. The boy ventures into the rainforest, which his father says has been there for one hundred million years. He wonders about the age of the forest and the creatures that have lived there, and the collage illustrations reveal outlines of animals and people from the past, superimposed on the present-day forest. Back on the beach, the boy wonders about the future: Will the forest remain? Will it be there when he returns? Again the illustrations display shadow outlines, this time of tourists, cars, and hotels obliterating the view of sea and sky.

The illustrations provide a photographically realistic view of a rainforest, while including the element of imagination. The ecological concern, of course, is very real, as a final note confirms.

Developing imagination; Drive to understand; Moral concerns. Adults working with gifted children can use the book for information (about rainforests), to stimulate imaginative thinking (What animals and people lived right *here* in the past? Will live here in the future?), and to focus on environmental concerns.

Bang, Molly. *Dawn.* Morrow, 1983.

Dawn's father tells her the story of how, shortly after he found and rescued a wounded Canada goose, a young woman magically appeared and began to weave light, strong sails for the ships he built. He married her and they had a child, Dawn. The sails the woman made for their family boat were especially fine. A wealthy client demanded sails like them; she protested that it would take too much out of her to make more such sails, but when her husband insisted, she relented. Just as the sails were nearly finished, he impatiently opened the door of the room where she worked— and saw the Canada goose, pulling out its breast feathers and weaving them into sailcloth. At his appearance, a flock of geese flew into the room and carried her off. At the end of her father's story, promising to find her mother and bring her back in the spring, Dawn sets off in the small boat her father had made for the three of them.

Developing imagination; Drive to understand. Ask the child to imagine a sequel to Dawn's story. Or point out that *Dawn* is based on the Japanese tale of the Crane Wife, and suggest comparing the two stories.

Bang, Molly Garrett. *Tye May and the Magic Brush.* (Adapted from the Chinese.) Mulberry, 1992.

Tye May is a poor orphan who longs to paint. One night in a dream, she receives a magic brush from a woman who tells her to use it carefully. With her brush, Tye May paints birds and animals that come to life. Soon, she paints for the poor: a loom for a weaver, an ox cart for a farmer. A greedy landlord and then the Emperor want Tye May to paint for them. She pretends to cooperate with the Emperor, but his greed causes disaster for him and his court.

Some say that Tye May still goes from village to village, painting for the poor.

Using ability. This is a read-alone book about the wise use of gifts. Why does the brush work well for Tye May and cause such trouble for the Emperor? What *is* the wise use of gifts—what does the woman mean when she says, "Use it carefully"?

Base, Graeme. *The Eleventh Hour.* Puffin, 1997

For his eleventh birthday, Horace the Elephant plans a party. He invites eleven guests, whips up a feast of eleven treats, and plans eleven games. The guests arrive early and play games until the hour appointed for the feast: 11:00. Then—surprise and mystery!

But there have been clues. Each luscious illustration contains clues—and red herrings—in the form of anagrams, clocks, riddles, hidden creatures, mirror writing, and jumbled messages. In a sealed section at the end of the book, Base reveals the clues, all the while encouraging the reader to deduce the answer through careful observation.

Drive to understand. The appeal of this book is not limited to just one age group. The verse, illustrations, and story line will have great appeal to older preschoolers, and early elementary students must read to figure out the clues. Children of middle elementary age are fascinated by codes of any kind and will certainly enjoy the intricacy of Base's concoctions. Some clues—Egyptian cartouches and Latin inscriptions, for example—are probably beyond most readers of any age without explanation. Every reader will find plenty of challenge here.

Base, Graeme. *The Sign of the Seahorse: A Tale of Greed and High Adventure in Two Acts.* Puffin, 1998.

In this tongue-in-cheek undersea environmental drama, a gang of Groupers forces Pearl's and Finny's father, "a fine, upstanding Trout," to sell the Seahorse Café, while the Soldiercrabs, led by Pearl's truelove, Bert, leave to find the source of pollution that has killed a nearby reef. With the end of the Café, Pearl leads the local fish to a new reef, while Finny and his Catfish Gang stay behind to punish the Groupers. Overhearing that an open spigot on an oil barrel is causing the harm, Finny tries to close it and fails. But Bert succeeds, and then the Soldiercrabs return to capture the Groupers. Finally, all follow Pearl's secret Sign-of-the-Seahorse trail to the new reef, where Pearl and Bert are reunited and the miscreant Grouper Gang members are put to menial tasks at the new Seahorse Café.

The plot is complex, and much of the vocabulary would be considered beyond them by any formal measure, but the lush illustrations and the flawlessly rocking rhythm of the verse carry young listeners along, holding their interest for reading after reading. For very bright children, in fact, the allure of all those fascinating words may be part of what holds their interest; another draw is the map of the ocean floor with a key for the trails followed by various members of the cast. Certainly the plot and level of language keep the adult reader alert. And the quietly pervasive humor is appreciated by readers of any age. This is recommended as a read-aloud for children in the early elementary years.

Drive to understand. Because of the complexity of both plot and language, this book, like other Base offerings, presents a delightful intellectual challenge.

Moral concerns. Underneath the fun, Base presents a serious message about environmental pollution. How did those reeking barrels get there in the first place?

Relationships with others. Finny and his Catfish Gang present themselves as punk adolescents, yet they prove that their hearts are in the right place. While *The Sign of the Seahorse* can be appreciated simply for its artistry and humor, it would also be possible to use Finny as an example of the importance of judging people by what they do rather than by how they look.

Brown, Ruth. *If at First You Do Not See.* Henry Holt, 1989.

A caterpillar goes off in search of food, but each time he thinks he has found a meal, he discovers that he has stumbled onto one creature or another who does not want to be eaten. At last, a scarecrow puts the caterpillar in his pocket where he can rest. When he awakes, the caterpillar has become a butterfly.

The illustrations carry the story. On each page, the text continues around the margins so the book must be turned. When it is upside down (if the reader looks carefully), the creature who is reluctant to become dinner appears. Imbedded in the right-side-up picture of the grass or flowers that looked so good to the hungry caterpillar is an upside-down picture of a man or a witch, but we must work a bit to find it.

Developing imagination. In Brown's book, the child's imagination is called into play to make sense of both story and pictures.

Bulla, Clyde Robert. *Daniel's Duck.* Illustrated by Joan Sandin. HarperTrophy, 1982.

Growing up in a Tennessee mountain cabin, Daniel wants to learn to carve like his brother Jeff, who carves so well that his proud parents say that someday he may carve as well as Henry Pettigrew, a man widely known as the best wood-carver in Tennessee. Daniel's father gives him wood and a knife, and Daniel thinks for some time before he finally carves a duck looking backward. At the spring fair, at which the family hopes to sell the handiwork they have made all winter, people stand in silence before Henry Pettigrew's carved deer, but they laugh when they see Daniel's duck. Mortified, Daniel seizes the duck and runs to throw it in the river. He is stopped by an old man who quietly explains that there are different kinds of laughter. People laughed at Daniel's duck because it made them happy. The duck is good, says the man—who is no other than Henry Pettigrew.

Creativity; Differentness; Using ability. Daniel's differentness is represented by his interest in carving animals merely for the sake of their beauty while his practical brother carves useful dishes. It is Daniel's divergence that leads him to carve the duck looking backward. It would be worthwhile also to mention Henry Pettigrew's understanding. Daniel's work is better understood by older people than by children, indicating that he will "fit in" better when he and his peers are adults.

Intensity; Perfectionism. For a child who already shows signs of being dissatisfied with work that is not perfect, Daniel's story offers a chance to talk about how one product is seen differently by different people. There is no one standard of perfection; the key is to do one's best and enjoy the result.

Sensitivity. Daniel displays two kinds of sensitivity—one through his period of thoughtfulness before beginning to carve, and the other through his assumption that the laughter was derisive. The first can be positive and productive; the second type of sensitivity can be damaging if not understood and counteracted.

Bunting, Eve. *Dandelions.* Illustrated by Greg Shed. Voyager, 2001.

Mama and Papa, with Zoe and her younger sister Rebecca, travel to the Nebraska Territory in a covered wagon to claim the land Papa had found when he came here the summer before their journey. Papa is joyous, excited about beginning a new life, but Mama looks backward to the home they left in Illinois. There are almost no trees here, and the horizon stretches as far as they can see. Even the soddie, the sod house Papa builds, seems to blend in with the waving grasses. Mama fears that Zoe and Rebecca will get lost if they stray too far; Mama worries about everything.

Eventually Zoe realizes that Papa worries, too—about Mama and about the baby that is coming in the fall. Then, on the way home from her first trip to town with Papa, Zoe finds dandelions growing along the trail. They stop and dig up a clump to plant on top of the soddie as a gift to Mama—the gold of the dandelions will make their home stand out against the sameness of the prairie. The next morning, as the family gathers in hope that the newly transplanted dandelions will take hold, put down roots, and thrive in their new home, Mama realizes that they, too, are transplants who must be strong enough to thrive.

Drive to understand. Some children will understand the metaphor of the dandelions, and some will read this book simply as a story of pioneers traveling to a new life. Either way, the sensitively told story and the earth-tone illustrations, so appropriate for the story, convey a sense of what it is to leave home and go to a strange land—an experience still common to Americans from many places.

Bunting, Eve. *The Man Who Could Call Down Owls.* Macmillan, 1984.

The man calls down owls by waving his willow wand toward the moon, and the boy Con is always among those who watch. The owls sail down silently, settling on nearby branches and even on the man's hat and cloak. Then one night a stranger watches, and the next night he appears again, this time in the old man's cloak. Con sees the large, beautiful white snowy owl for the first time that night, and he knows that the old man will not return. Eager for the power to command the birds of the air, the stranger has killed the old man and taken his hat, cloak, and willow wand, but these do not instill the old man's power. The owls come to him only to scratch and claw until he flees. Finally the owls settle on Con's shoulders and hover around him, filling the night with love.

The death of the old man is off-stage, understood implicitly by older readers, and not frightening. The language conveys the mystery and quiet awe surrounding communication between humans and other life forms—clearly the man's power is in love and respect, not coercion, though the stranger fails to see this. In fact, owls are called down by imitations of their call, not by wands, but Bunting captures the wonder felt by the watchers, and the silence of the want adds to the mythical quality of her story. This book could be discussed with older youngsters as well, making the point that the appearance of power is not equal to the real thing.

Identity. What power enables the man to call down owls? Why does the stranger not have that power? What does power—or "personal power," or authenticity—mean? Why did the owls settle on Con's shoulders?

Carrick, Carol. *Stay Away from Simon!* Illustrated by Donald Carrick. Clarion, 1989.

Living on Martha's Vineyard in the 1830s, Lucy fears Simon, an older boy who does not come to school because he cannot learn. One day in a snowstorm, Simon starts to follow Lucy and her younger brother, Josiah, home, so Lucy takes a shortcut through the woods to avoid him. After she realizes she is lost, Simon suddenly appears in the storm, takes Josiah on his back, and walks on. Not knowing what else to do and swallowing her fear, Lucy follows. Just when she is at the point of exhaustion, her father appears on horseback through the snow. Simon, who knows the woods, has been taking them home. From her parents' understanding and kindness toward Simon, Lucy learns some sympathy, and when she takes hot cider to the barn where Simon has insisted on sleeping, she learns why he was following: he had learned from Lucy's song "One, two, buckle my shoe" how to count to 10, and he wanted to show her.

Carrick wrote this book to help children overcome fear and misunderstanding of the mentally disabled, who would be in school these days, but were shunned and outcast back then. By highlighting that contrast, she also illumines the continuing tendency, especially among children, to draw back from those who are different. Some adults may object that this book teaches children not to avoid strangers. But Simon is not a stranger; he is well known in Lucy's community. He is only different in a way that she does not understand.

Drive to understand. How did her parents' comments change Lucy's attitude toward Simon? (Information helps to reduce fear.) In what other ways are people different, causing distrust? What information would help?

Relationships with others. Should Lucy have feared Simon? Why or why not? Can you suggest better ways for her to handle the situation?

Carrick, Carol. *What Happened to Patrick's Dinosaurs?* Illustrated by Donald Carrick. Clarion, 1988.

While Patrick and his older brother Hank rake leaves, Patrick tells his story of how dinosaurs disappeared. Dinosaurs, he tells Hank, used to do everything for people—build their houses and roads, even put on shows to entertain them. They wanted to teach people, but the people were interested only in lunch and recess— so the dinosaurs built a space ship and left.

Developing imagination; Creativity. For children at the dinosaur stage who probably know something of scientific theories about the dinosaurs' disappearance, this book is a counterpoint in fantasy. How satisfying it is to make up a story to explain a mystery, especially a happy story to explain a sad mystery! Patrick's story, used in conjunction with nonfiction about dinosaurs, can help children separate fact from fiction and see that each has its place. What other mysteries can we explain by making up stories?

Using ability. Some young readers—eager learners frustrated by classmates who are interested only in lunch and recess—may be interested in following up on the point of Patrick's theory. If you have a child who relates to this aspect of the book, ask him to describe where Patrick's dinosaurs went, what they are doing there, and how the people received them in a place where they wanted to stay. You may hear a version of what the child would like to find at school.

Cendrars, Blaise. *Shadow.* Translated and illustrated by Marcia Brown. Aladdin, 1995.

The French poet Blaise Cendrar's poem, "La Feticheuse," evokes an image that goes far beyond that cast by an object between the earth and the sun. It incorporates the idea of spirit, both haunting and enchanting, and the mystery of the African jungle. Brown's illustrations capture the mood of the text, conveying an eerie—but not at all frightening—sense of awe of the unknown that Shadow represents.

Developing imagination. The text, translated as it is from poetry, offers a challenge to young listeners and readers to comprehend it both intellectually and emotionally. The illustrations are original and abstract, enhancing the text to add to the total experience of the book.

Cleary, Beverly. *Ramona the Brave.* Illustrated by Alan Tiegreen. Avon, 1995.

Trying hard to grow up, Ramona enters first grade, where calm, task-oriented Mrs. Griggs is not as exciting or as understanding of Ramona's idiosyncrasies as Miss Binney was last year. Ramona struggles with the consequences of crumpling the art work of a student who copied her owl, with moving into a new bedroom at home and finding it scary to be alone, and with the need to create a slipper from a paper towel after she throws her shoe at a German shepherd that chased her as she walked to school. Throughout the book, she experiences the fears and triumphs of a first-grader in a loving family with supportive teachers.

Creativity; Differentness; Relationships with others. This book is just an introductory example of the work of Cleary, who is enormously popular because she knows exactly how to capture the vulnerabilities of children such as Ramona—gifted, creative, spunky, independent, always feeling different. Ramona's predicaments and solutions delight children who are always getting into scrapes and feeling misunderstood themselves. Cleary's books have been loved for 30 years, and even as adults, her readers remember how comforting it was to find someone like them.

Clifton, Lucille. *Everett Anderson's Friend.* Illustrated by Ann Grifalconi. Holt, 1992.

This is the story of how Everett Anderson finally admits that new neighbors can be a pleasant surprise, even if the family does have all girls, including Maria, who can beat him at races. Eventually, Maria is even welcome to play with Everett and Joe and Kirk.

Told in verse, the story has gaps that the child can fill with his own inferences.

Relationships with others. Maria provides clear evidence that the way to find a friend is to be one. Preschoolers can understand her natural friendliness toward Everett in spite of his rejection of her—and the happy result of this friendliness.

Cooney, Barbara. *Island Boy.* Puffin, 1991.

A simple story of the life of Matthais Tibbetts, born the first of 12 children in the first family on Tibbetts Island (a fictional island off the coast of Maine) around the turn of the century. The family flourishes on the island, but eventually all return to the mainland; even Matthais leaves the island to serve as cabin boy and then master on a sailing vessel. After 15 years, though, Matthais returns to the empty house, bringing his bride, Hannah, with him. Their three daughters leave when they are grown, but after Hannah's death, Annie and her son, also named Matthais, return. Life continues on the island as the grandfather, daughter, and grandson sell vegetables and milk to vacationers on nearby islands. In good time, Old Matthais, the "Island Boy," dies during a trip to the mainland on rough seas. Young Matthais may stay on the island—we do not know. We do know, though, that Old Matthais has lived a complete, fulfilled, and successful life.

Cooney's illustrations set the mood for this description of a life of hard work whose rewards are the simple enjoyment of family and the pleasures of making good use of the abundance provided by land and sea. Without preaching, Cooney speaks of these basic values and of the satisfaction they bring. Her story is a strong statement of the richness to be found in a sense of family and place.

Drive to understand; Identity. For children who have no experience with living on an island or with the northeast coast of our country, *Island Boy* provides a narrative of a way of life similar enough to their own to facilitate understanding, but different in time and place.

de Paola, Tomie. *Tomie de Paola's Book of Poems.* Putnam, 1988.

Gathering poems for young children from classic to modern, Tomie de Paola has collected works by Lewis Carroll, Langston Hughes, Jack Prelutsky, Eve Merriam, X. J. Kennedy, and many others, and then has added his own artistic talents to produce this book. It is recommended here as an example of many fine books of poetry—an important ally in any effort to enhance and encourage the imaginations of young children.

Developing imagination. Especially for younger children, poetry is better enjoyed than analyzed.

Dorros, Arthur. *Abuela.* Illustrated by Elisa Kleven. Puffin, 1997.

Rosalba tells of a day in the park with her *abuela* (grandmother). Rosalba imagines flying over New York City with her *abuela*, seeing the harbor, the airport, the streets and office buildings, the Statue of Liberty. Rosalba's narrative is sprinkled with terms in Spanish, her *abuela's* language, offering just enough challenge to invite an English-speaking child to become fascinated with the words. The illustrations are joyous, colorful, and rich in details to explore.

Developing imagination. Invite the child to imagine with you what you would see if you flew together over a familiar place. For a young child, begin with a small space, such as her own block; enlarge the area for older children.

Drive to understand. This is a delightful book to introduce a child to New York City and to another language. A glossary of Spanish terms is included.

Ehlert, Lois. *Red Leaf, Yellow Leaf.* Harcourt Brace Jovanovich, 1991.

In this excellent example of a nonfiction book for early readers, Ehlert describes planting and caring for a sugar maple tree. She tells how it grew in the woods before it was transplanted to a nursery, then to a garden center, and then to the hole already dug for it in the backyard, and how it changes through the seasons. The book is visually rich, with realistic and meticulously accurate details of maple flowers and roots; yet the illustrations are presented in close-up views so that the reader must supply the context mentally. Notes at the end of the book give information about the parts of the sugar maple, as well as instructions for selecting and planting a tree.

Drive to understand. This book answers questions children at this age may never have considered. Discussion could raise more questions: How is planting a tree like planting a bean seed? How is it different? Why?

Relationships with others. For some children, discussion of pets or animals as friends may be a good introduction to the skills of friendship. Certainly, Ehlert considers trees her friends. Caring for a living thing, even a tree, is much like caring for a friend, requiring being aware of what the friend needs to thrive, and supplying these things as much as possible.

Ferris, Jeri. *What Are You Figuring Now? A Story about Benjamin Banneker.* Illustrated by Amy Johnson. First Avenue, 1990.

Benjamin Banneker (1731-1806) was a freed black man, a Maryland farmer who studied astronomy, clocks, and mathematics—matters of great interest at the time he lived, when ships sailed by the stars and there were only two books in many homes: an almanac and the Bible. His formal schooling lasted only four winters before he had to work full time on the farm. But when he was 20, he borrowed a watch, took it apart to analyze how it worked, and reassembled it. Then he used his drawings to build a clock out of wood, and he became famous as the man who built his own clock.

With his study of astronomy and his skill at math, he became a surveyor—so well known that he was appointed by President George Washington and Secretary of State Thomas Jefferson to assist Pierre L'Enfant in laying out the streets of Washington, D.C. He decided to write an almanac, which required hundreds of mathematical calculations to predict the phases of the moon and eclipses; his almanac was known for its accuracy. Only after age

60 did he stop farming his 100 acres to devote himself to math and astronomy, still living in his cabin with his wooden clock.

Banneker constantly hungered for conversation concerning ideas about books, math problems, and what was happening elsewhere in the world. The emphasis on this, plus the fresh writing style and the ability of the author to compel us to truly care for Banneker, recommends it for intellectually curious readers.

Drive to understand; Intensity; Using ability. What quality kept Banneker going when he had no one to talk to? How was his family important to him? With whom do you talk about books or math or other favorite subjects? Why is it important to have someone to talk to about these things?

Gilks, Helen. *Bears.* Illustrated by Andrew Bale. Ticknor & Fields, 1993.

With life-like illustrations; clear, brief notes; and a map showing where in the world each species is found, this nonfiction book provides basic information on the eight kinds of bears in the world. The reader learns what the bears eat, what dangers they face, how they rear their young, and how they interact with humans. The conditions bears need for survival are included, raising awareness of human responsibility without sentimentality.

Drive to understand. This book could serve as a model for introducing young readers to wild animals. The use of scientific nomenclature is explained briefly, and a chart shows the shape, color, relative size, and scientific name for each bear. The text is varied for interest but provides parallel information, demonstrating what is pertinent to an understanding of animals living in the wild. The bear is an especially happy choice for a book such as this, since many children have loved bears from babyhood.

Goble, Paul. *Iktomi and the Berries: A Plains Indian Story.* Orchard, 1992.

Iktomi is the Lakota (Sioux) name for the trickster character in much of native folklore. In this story, retold and illustrated by Paul Goble, Iktomi dresses in his finest clothes to go hunting, thinking of how his relatives will praise him for the meat he will bring back to them. Instead of returning in triumph, however, he misses seeing the prairie ducks, scares the ducks away when he falls into the river, and nearly drowns through foolishness when he tries to gather berries reflected in the water.

The humor is in the contrast between his fine regalia and his ineptitude—between show and substance. Goble points this out by showing in italics the comments listeners are expected to make as the narrator tells the story, indicating that they know Iktomi well and can see through his pomposity. Thus, the children learn to look through the surface of a character to the quality that lies below, and they learn also how foolish it is to boast.

The story can be used for discussion if we don't strain too hard for parallels. Iktomi, a stereotypical folkloric character, will not change, but children will—a fundamental difference. Ask a few leading questions and let children draw their own conclusions.

Relationships with others. Where does Iktomi place blame when things go wrong? What foolish things does he do? Why, despite his foolishness, do people like him enough to continue telling stories about him?

Goble, Paul. *The Legend of the White Buffalo Woman.* National Geographic Society, 1998.

In this beautiful book, the author of many beautiful books about the Plains Indians tells their most important sacred legend: the story of how the Great Spirit, in a time of trouble, sent a white buffalo calf in the form of the White Buffalo Woman to give the tribes the pipe (often called the peace pipe) and a new way to pray. Goble begins with a creation story, then tells of the visit of the White Buffalo Woman, and concludes with a description of how the tribes found the red clay from which to make their pipes.

The illustrations are majestic and compelling, well suited to the subject. An "Author's Note" sets the legend in historic context. At the end are precise drawings of several pipes, with an explanation of the meanings of some of the symbols used in making one.

There is also a map showing the location of the Pipestone Quarry, now a national monument, in Minnesota.

Drive to understand. Some children will approach this book intellectually, showing curiosity about the pipe and the history, and perhaps wanting to visit the Pipestone Quarry. Others may respond simply to the beauty and mystery of the story and the illustrations. Adults should be sensitive to these individual responses and should use them as a guide for further discussion.

Godden, Rumer. *The Story of Holly and Ivy.* Illustrated by Barbara Cooney. Puffin, 1987.

Ivy is an orphan who goes looking for an imaginary grandmother at Christmas. Holly is a doll in a toyshop who wishes for a girl to own her. Mrs. Jones wants to celebrate Christmas so much that she decorates a Christmas tree for the first time, and Mr. Jones is the policeman to whom Peter, who works at the toyshop, turns when he discovers that he has lost his key to the shop. Holly, Ivy, and Mrs. Jones are united, thanks to Peter, on Christmas Day, and each wish is granted.

This story is told from three alternating points of view—Holly's, Ivy's, and Mrs. Jones'—so the reader must hold three separate stories in mind until they merge.

Drive to understand. In addition to this intellectual challenge, this is a heartwarming story with an implied appreciation for home and family.

Hall, Donald. *The Man Who Lived Alone.* Illustrated by Mary Azarian. David R. Godine, 1998.

The man who lived alone builds himself a camp near the farm of relatives, where he had lived and worked as a boy. He is very much an individual, growing and canning his own vegetables, hunting for meat, and working in town for a few days each year to earn the cash he needs to pay his taxes. He makes friends with an owl and takes pride in his mule. He can do anything with his hands: solder, build a house or a shotgun, shoe a horse or a mule. He likes to keep his own hours, and he sometimes works all night.

His aunt and uncle, and then his cousin and her husband and daughter, are close enough for company when he wants it, and he often helps them out.

The man who lived alone is alone but not lonely; rather, he is resourceful, affectionate, and generous. His life is not typical, but it is self-sufficient and he is content. This book's unusual theme provides assurance that spending time alone is not necessarily negative, and in its non-judgmental reporting, it exemplifies tolerance for a different way of life.

Aloneness; Creativity; Differentness; Introversion. A reading of this book can lead to a conversation about people we know who live alone or who spend a great deal of time alone and are happy doing so. The idea is simply to indicate to the child that being alone can be done well and is potentially a positive experience.

Hall, Donald. *Ox-Cart Man.* Illustrated by Barbara Cooney Porter. Viking, 1979.

The ox-cart man lives in New England at a time when embroidery needles still come on ships from England. In October, he and his family load all of the produce from their farm that they can sell onto the ox cart, and he walks 10 days to Portsmouth. There, he sells everything, even the cart and the ox. He buys a few necessities and walks back home, where he and his family begin preparing for next October's trip. While the ox-cart man carves a new yoke and builds a new cart, his wife spins flax into linen, his daughter embroiders the linens, and his son makes brooms.

The story is about the self-sufficiency of the farm family, with everyone sharing in the work that sustains them. The illustrations carry much of the story, providing details for discussion as well as evoking the New England seasons and the well-regulated, productive life that results from the family's work.

Drive to understand. The family makes use of everything available to them, some of which will be new to contemporary readers. For example, what does the farmer actually do when he splits shingles to sell? What does the child know about spinning flax into linen, making maple syrup, or shearing sheep?

The book can also be enjoyed simply by examining the pictures and discussing the many details of the hardworking family's life.

Heller, Linda. *The Castle on Hester Street.* The Jewish Publication Society of America, 1990.

Julie is visiting her grandparents and listening to her grandfather tell stories about his journey from Russia to America. Grandfather's stories are fanciful, full of magic and wealth and fame. Grandmother counters with her stories of the realities: crowded ships, Ellis Island, and hard work as they raised their family.

Drive to understand. Together, they give Julie—and the reader—a taste of Jewish immigration and the undaunted spirit that sustained the newcomers as they made their places in their new home. As a result, Julie receives the gift of her own heritage; for non-Jewish children, the book is a telling of history that incorporates painful fact, unquenchable humor, and the spirit of a people.

Hill, Elizabeth Starr. *Evan's Corner.* Illustrated by Sandra Speidel. Penguin Putnam, 1993.

Living in a two-room apartment with a family of eight, Evan wants a space of his own. His mother suggests that he choose a corner for his own place, and after doing so, Evan adds to it a picture, a plant, and a turtle. When his brother Adam asks why he wants a corner of his own, Evan says, "I want a chance to be lonely," and when Adam asks if he can come into Evan's corner, Evan helps him choose a corner for himself. But Evan is not entirely happy in his corner, and his mother understands why: "Maybe you need to step out now, and help somebody else."

Evan's story illustrates simply and beautifully the need to balance time alone and time with others, a lesson that gifted people must learn over and over. This book introduces the concept in terms a preschooler can understand.

Aloneness; Introversion. Why does Evan want to have a chance to be lonely? What is good about being alone? How does he know when he has had enough time alone? What do you do when you need time alone? What do you do when you have had enough?

Drive to understand. Especially for children not familiar with cities, the illustrations in this book reveal the profusion of inner city life in details of home, streets, shops, and playgrounds. Evan finds a way to cope with it, and he is part of a stable, loving family.

Relationships with others. Why is Evan not completely happy in his corner? Will he want to go back there after he helps Adam decorate his corner? Why is it important to step out and help somebody else? How can someone who enjoys being alone also be a friend?

Hoban, Tana. *Shadows and Reflections.* Greenwillow Books, 1990.

This wordless, plotless book is simply a collection of photographs of buildings, animals, and people, showing them in shadow and reflection. Discuss this visual treat first with book in hand—what do we see in the picture, what do we see that is *not* in the picture?—and then again on a walk, looking for the beauty in the shadows and reflections all around us.

Developing imagination.

Hoff, Syd. *Who Will Be My Friends?* HarperCollins, 1987.

Looking for friends in his new neighborhood, Freddy finds that the adults are friendly but busy, and the children ignore him. Undiscouraged, Freddy plays alone, throwing and catching a ball in full view of the other children. When they notice how well he handles the ball, they ask him to join them.

The obvious messages in this book are that it is easier to be accepted if we have something to offer to others, and that it is sometimes necessary to take the initiative in order to find friends. There are more subtle messages, however: Freddy does not force himself into the children's game; rather, he quietly lets them see what his skills are. He seems to understand their reluctance to accept him immediately without being hurt by it.

Relationships with others. For a young gifted child who feels rebuffed, this book can demonstrate that if we offer ourselves and our skills to others without being presumptuous, it is easier for them to accept us. Conversation about this will require a light approach—just a suggestion by the adult and then listening for a response from the child, which will then guide the duration and direction of any further dialogue.

Isadora, Rachel. *Ben's Trumpet.* Mulberry, 1991.
Ben plays an imaginary trumpet as he listens to the musicians from the Zig Zag Jazz Club. He plays for his family and himself until other boys tease him for having no trumpet. The trumpeter for the Jazz Club sees that Ben has stopped imagining himself playing and invites Ben to the Club, where he begins teaching him how to play. Stunning black and white illustrations capture the art-deco style of the '20s, and the pages seem to vibrate with the music.
The intensity of his desire to be a musician sets Ben apart. Alone and different, he is vulnerable to the taunts of other children, especially when he allows his imagination to take over. But it is just this that catches the attention of a potential mentor—something that, in real life, may make all the difference.
Creativity; Differentness; Intensity. Does your child know people like Ben (adults or children) who have interests so strong that they seem different from most people? If not, can you help the child meet such people? Point out that those who succeed in difficult fields such as music are often as dedicated to their pursuits as Ben is to his. The difference is positive, although it is not always viewed that way by children.

Johnson, D. B. *Henry Hikes to Fitchburg.* Houghton Mifflin, 2000.
Henry and his friend decide one summer day to go to Fitchburg to see the country, each in his own way. Henry will walk the 30 miles, and his friend will work until he earns enough money for the train ride. While Henry wades a river, gathers flowers to press in his old music book, and finds a bird's nest, his

friend moves the bookcases in Mr. Emerson's study, sweeps out the post office, and cleans Mrs. Thoreau's chicken coop. At last he has earned enough, and he rushes for the train, the requisite 90 cents in hand, to arrive in Fitchburg in time for sunset. Henry arrives by moonlight, acknowledging with a smile that the train was faster and explaining that he stopped for blackberries, which he offers to his friend.

This gentle introduction to Henry David Thoreau and his ideas is based on *Walden,* in which Henry imagines a conversation outlining two ways to go to Fitchburg and explaining why he prefers his own. In vibrant illustrations, we see the friend enjoying his plan and Henry savoring his, with the reader left to make a choice— but it is clear that Henry has had the more adventurous day.

Differentness. The real-life Henry was different all his life, apparently contentedly so. In this story, his friend follows the more usual method of travel, while Henry's choice is consistent with his wish to spend as much time as possible doing things that interest him. This lovely book may help a parent or teacher affirm a child who is concerned about having ideas that are different from the norm.

Relationships with others. Although Henry and his friend have very different approaches to life, they respect each other's choices and remain friends. In particular, it is helpful to note that Henry, the different one, is comfortable both with his own unusual path and with that of his conventional friend.

Kellogg, Steven. *Best Friends.* NAL, 1992.

Kathy and Louise are best friends. They share everything— until Louise's aunt and uncle take her to a mountain resort for the summer. Kathy misses Louise, but when Louise's card sounds as though she is having too much fun to miss Kathy, jealousy and anger are added to Kathy's loneliness as she waits for Louise to return. Kathy is cheered by anticipation of the arrival of puppies, due after Louise returns. The new neighbor has promised Kathy the first spotted puppy—but the first pup is brown, so it goes to Louise. When it is clear that there will be no more pups in this litter, Kathy's hurt is magnified—but Louise offers to share the brown puppy.

Louise displays the generosity of friendship on two occasions: returning with gifts for Kathy, and sharing the puppy. Kathy experiences a turmoil of negative feelings related to friendship—jealousy, anger, alienation—but she also shows fairness and maturity in recognizing that Louise would take good care of a puppy, and in not alienating Louise by expressing her hurt and anger. The friendship is saved through Louise's warm generosity and Kathy's patient forbearance. The illustrations are worthy of comment, too: they are humorous, telling stories in detail and facial expressions that illuminate the text.

Relationships with others. Discuss the element of chance: Louise has an aunt and uncle who invite her to the summer resort; the only pup happens to be brown. This summer, Louise is lucky, but sometimes chance runs the other way. Is it fair to be angry or jealous when someone is simply lucky right now? How can we learn to rejoice with the other in her happiness while we wait for our own luck?

Larry, Charles. *Peboan and Seegwun.* Farrar, Straus and Giroux, 1993.

In the far northern part of what is now Michigan, Wisconsin, and Minnesota, home of the Anishinabe (Ojibwa), the transition from winter to spring is sometimes violent, sometimes gentle. One of several Anishinabe stories about the change in the seasons, this story is a gentle version. An old man, Peboan, sits alone in his lodge at the end of winter when a young man, Seegwun, arrives. Peboan greets the newcomer and offers him a pipe. Peboan and Seegwun talk all night, describing how each affects the Earth: When the old man tosses his hair, leaves fall from the trees; and when the young man shakes his head, rain falls, plants grow, and birds sing. In the dawn light, Seegwun sees that Peboan's icy face is melting, melting until the old man melts completely away. What is left is a spring beauty, one of the first flowers of the northern spring.

The language of this story is formal and dignified. The illustrations are both imaginative and meticulous, some suited to myth and others full of authentic details of the plants and animals of the northern forest. Most interesting are the pictures of the Anishinabe people as they pursue their daily lives before European contact: fall, winter, and spring scenes of ice fishing, bear hunting, canoe building, and rice gathering.

Developing imagination. With this purpose in mind, focus on the story, the meaning of the old man and the young one, and the metaphors each uses in describing his season. Enjoy the beauty of the illustrations, the colors and the mood evoked by each.

Drive to understand. After reading the story aloud, read or paraphrase the author's note, helping the child understand the pictures and the way of life they illustrate. Look for details in each picture: Can you find the otters sliding down their icy chute into the water? Try to identify the steps in gathering and storing wild rice. With children who live in the north, each spring wildflower can be identified and labeled, as can the birds.

Lobel, Arnold. *On Market Street.* Illustrated by Anita Lobel. Mulberry, 1989.

Like the Anno books, this one is to be pored over for the detail in the illustrations. In content, it is simply an alphabet book with such commodities as apples, books, clocks, and doughnuts for sale on Market Street, but each page presents a picture of a person made up of gloves, hats, ice cream, and so on.

Developing imagination. The drawings and the rich colors may prove inspirational. Give the child some time with this book, and then ask what he could draw for Market Street.

Lyon, George Ella. *Who Came Down that Road?* Illustrated by Peter Catalanotto. Orchard, 1996.

A boy and his mother go for a walk along what his mother says is an "old, old, old, old road"—just a trace, really, a path that has been traveled for thousands of years. "Who came down that road?" he asks, and she answers that her great-grandparents came down that road soon after they were married. He asks again, and she goes back farther, to when soldiers came down the road during the Civil War. Again he asks, and she tells him of pioneers before the soldiers, and Indians before the pioneers, and then back to the buffalo who came to the salt lick, and the mastodons, and then to the fish in the sea that covered this place and left the salt lick. Still the boy questions, until finally she speaks of "the mystery of the making place." As the text retreats in time, the illustrations become more dreamlike, with superimposed figures. On the last pages, as mother and son walk on, wondering, their footprints emerge from the crowded tracks of all who have gone before.

Developing imagination. George Ella Lyon lives near the buffalo trace that inspired this book. Other places, too, can inspire discussions like the one she imagines. Who lived by this lake? Who floated down this river? Who stood here, where we are, and looked up at the same stars?

Drive to understand. For older children in this age group, this book evokes a sense of history and of our connectedness to it. It could easily lead to a timeline and to more books about any one of the travelers who came down this road.

Martin, Bill and John Archambault. *Knots on a Counting Rope.* Illustrated by Ted Rand. Owlet, 1997.

Sitting with his grandfather in the glow of a campfire, a blind Indian boy asks the old man to tell him the story again, to "Tell me who I am." Grandfather wants Boy to learn to tell the story by himself, and speaking in turns, they trace the history of Boy's birth and his learning to "cross the dark mountains"—a metaphor for when we feel afraid to do what we have to do. Boy learns to ride a horse, even to race his horse by counting the gallops and feeling the turns. As they finish the story, Grandfather ties another knot in the counting rope, marking Boy's growing confidence as he faces both the challenge of blindness and his Grandfather's aging. By the time his Grandfather dies, Boy will know with certainty who he is, what he can do, and that he will not be alone in crossing the dark mountains.

Differentness. His blindness makes Boy different, but with his Grandfather's encouragement, he faces the challenge without bitterness. He does not win the race, but his family is so proud of him for riding "like the wind" that winning does not matter. What is important is how well he handles his difference.

Identity. While few children have a story as dramatic as Boy's, this book can remind parents that every child needs to know that he is special, nurtured, and growing strong, just as Boy learns from his Grandfather's story. Parents can create a personal story of and for their own child, to build his sense of identity. "Crossing the dark mountains" can become a useful metaphor in family communication.

McDermott, Gerald. *Anansi the Spider: A Tale from the Ashanti.* Holt, 1988.

Anansi the Spider is a folk hero to the Ashanti people, a rogue who escapes trouble through his wits, rather like Br'er Rabbit. In this colorfully illustrated tale, Anansi's sons, each with a special talent, come to his rescue when Anansi is lost and swallowed by a fish. An argument ensues over which son should receive the reward, a shining white ball. Since the spiders cannot reach a decision, Nyame, the God of All Things, takes the ball into the sky where it shines forever as the moon.

The illustrations are characteristic of McDermott's work—brilliantly colored geometric shapes creating distinctive images. Children love this story and will ask for it again and again.

Drive to understand. Anansi is a good introduction to non-European folklore for preschoolers.

Mora, Pat. *Tomas and the Library Lady.* Illustrated by Raul Colon. Dragonfly, 2000.

Not a full biography, but a true and significant incident in the life of a real person, this is a story from the childhood of Tomas Rivera, who was born in Texas to a migrant family in 1935 and died in 1984, the chancellor of the University of California at Riverside. It begins with the family's annual drive through the summer heat from Texas to Iowa to pick corn. In Iowa, Tomas listens to his grandfather tell stories, and with Papa Grande's encouragement, he walks downtown to the library to find more stories. Noticing his reluctance to enter, a librarian kindly offers him a drink and brings him books. Tomas spends all day reading, and when the library closes, the library lady lets him take books home, checked out on her own card. All summer, Tomas goes to the library whenever he can, reading his library books to his family in English and teaching the library lady a few words of Spanish. At the end of the summer, Tomas teaches her a sad word: *Adios.* He gives her a loaf of *pan dulce,* sweet bread, from his mother. And in the car on the way back to Texas, he reads his new book, a gift from the library lady.

Developing imagination. Imaginative readers can identify with Tomas's ability to see a dinosaur and to feel the warm neck as he holds on for a ride, and to lose himself in books until the library lady lets him know that the library is closing.

Drive to understand. Although it skims over the difficulty and poverty of migrant living, this book introduces the concept to young readers, while offering an example of a real boy who had a very strong drive to learn and understand. For children who take easy access to plentiful books for granted, Tomas's story adds a new and valuable perspective.

Rappaport, Doreen. *The Boston Coffee Party.* Illustrated by Emily Arnold McCully. HarperTrophy, 1990.

Based on a Revolutionary War incident related by Abigail Adams in a letter to her husband, John, this is a story of Sarah

Homans and her mother, who led a group of women in protest against a merchant who hoarded coffee in order to sell it at high prices.

This "I Can Read" book shows young readers how people who care about injustice can make a difference. The children may need some background, however. In discussion, be sure that the child knows that this is a true story, and that she understands the issues. Explain why items such as coffee would be scarce in wartime, and how hoarding drives up demand and thus prices. Define any new words such as "patriots" and "merchant," if necessary. Point out that the women were patriots who cared enough about winning the war to spend time sewing shirts, that the merchant only wanted to make money on the war shortages, and that this difference was the source of the animosity between the women and Merchant Thomas. In fact, not all colonists agreed that they should be fighting for freedom from England; the merchant may have been one of those who disagreed.

Drive to understand; Moral concerns. Why were the women so angry? Did they have a right to be angry? Was this a good way to express it? War brings out strong feelings and causes people to do things they would not ordinarily do. What evidence do we see of that now?

Rohmann, Eric. *The Cinder-Eyed Cats.* Crown, 1997.

This story, told in rhyme, is of a boy who sails through the sky to a tropical island where five sleek cats greet him. Boy and cats are joined in a dream-like sequence by ocean creatures, dancing underwater in the moonlight and around a campfire. With the dawn, boy and cats are alone on the beach; the boy sails off and the cats slumber, waiting for the moon to come around again. While the poem provides the framework, it is overwhelmed by clear and detailed illustrations of benevolent cats—tigers, really—and colorful sea creatures of all kinds, a visual feast swirling through the tropical day and mysterious night.

Creativity. For the imaginative child, this book offers much to ponder and to enhance with movement or music.

Developing imagination. For the more literal-minded child, the story issues an invitation to fantasy, while the elegant cinder-eyed cats and the brilliant and varied creatures of the deep offer an opportunity to enjoy beauty for its own sake.

Sendak, Maurice. *Outside Over There.* HarperTrophy, 1989.

A fantasy told with pictures as much as with words, this is the story of Ida, who rescues her baby sister from the goblins, who turn out to be babies, too.

Ida is intuitive, resolute, and brave, a girl of about six who knows her own mind and does what needs to be done. The illustrations are full of details to be pored over and discussed.

Identity. The impact of this book is emotional rather than intellectual. The strengths in Ida's character may speak for themselves, but adults might wish to reinforce the child's awareness by mentioning what is admirable about Ida, how her baby sister and father feel about her, and why. Perhaps a time can be recalled when the child showed some of Ida's qualities.

Developing imagination. With its fairy-tale quality, this book is recommended for its potential to stir the child's imagination, both visually and verbally.

Steig, William. *Sylvester and the Magic Pebble.* Weston Woods, 1990.

This is the much-loved story of how Sylvester the donkey finds a magic pebble and then, frightened by a lion, wishes in panic to be a rock. And he is. His parents and all of the creatures of Oatsdale search long and hard for Sylvester, but no one recognizes that the rock is the object of their search. Winter comes and Sylvester falls into a long, hopeless sleep, while at home his parents grieve. In the spring, determined to cheer themselves up, they picnic at the very spot where the magic pebble lies on the ground next to the rock that is Sylvester. His father admires the pebble and places it on the rock. Sylvester wishes to be himself again—and instantly, he is.

Told with simple dignity and moving dialogue, the story is memorable for the purity of the emotional experience of parents who lose a beloved child—softened by the fact that we know that Sylvester is alive and unharmed. We are deeply concerned about how he will become a donkey again, but not frightened. Young children can find security in seeing how much parents love their children, without being asked to deal directly with the concept of death. And should anyone miss it, the ending states the moral. Sylvester's family may want to use the magic pebble for a wish someday, but not now. Reunited in their home, the three hug each other—"What more could they wish for? They all had all that they wanted."

Identity. A child who understands that his parents, too, would search diligently for him and would grieve as Sylvester's parents did if he were Sylvester will gain awareness of his own importance as a valued member of his family.

Sensitivity. Readers will be touched and moved by the worry and love that shine through this story. An overly-intellectual child may gain a measure of softness and awareness of emotions through a story such as this one, while a sensitive child may find it a vehicle for feelings that otherwise remain felt but unexpressed.

Swift, Hildegarde H. and Lynd Ward. *The Little Red Lighthouse and the Great Gray Bridge.* Harcourt Brace, 1988.

Every night, the little red lighthouse on the Hudson River sends out a beam of light to warn boats about the rocks, and when there is fog, the man who turns on the light every night also sets a bell to ring a warning. The lighthouse keeps boats safe, and it is very, very proud of its work—until a huge bridge is built, making the lighthouse feel very small indeed. When a great light first shines from the top of the bridge, the lighthouse sadly believes that it is no longer needed.

One foggy night, the man does not come, and without the bell from the lighthouse, a tugboat crashes on the rocks. The bridge calls down, saying that its light shines for airplanes; the little red lighthouse is still needed for the ships on the river. But the lighthouse cannot turn on its light or its bell alone. Finally the man appears—some boys had stolen his keys. The lighthouse knows now that it is still needed, and while it knows it is small, it is still very, very proud.

There really is a little red lighthouse on the Hudson River, which closed when the George Washington Bridge opened in 1932. In part because of this book, first published in 1942, it was restored as part of a park. Beyond the history, however, the story is a gem for its spare, memorable phrasing, its personification of the lighthouse in a way that invites small children to identify with it, and the gentle statement of the universal need to be needed.

Identity. Children enjoy books about small things—animals, machines, lighthouses—that nevertheless have the authenticity they crave. The lighthouse's lesson that it is still important, even after it learns that it is small in comparison to the bridge, can reinforce the same lesson for a young reader.

Using ability. It is important to the lighthouse to be needed. What do you do that helps others? How do these things let you know that you are needed?

Viorst, Judith. *Alexander and the Terrible, Horrible, No Good, Very Bad Day.* Illustrated by Ray Cruz. Aladdin, 1987.

The youngest of three brothers, Alexander goes through a day that includes finding nothing in his cereal box (his brothers find treasures in theirs), having the only cavity when they go to the dentist, and learning that the store has sold the last sneakers of the color he wants. The day goes from bad to worse, and the only solution seems to be to move to Australia. But, says his mother, some days are like that—even in Australia.

Despite Alexander's undeniably awful day, when he rolls over to go to sleep, the reader knows that tomorrow will be better. Some days are indeed like that, and even young children can learn that when they have a day like Alexander's, it does not mean that something is wrong with them.

Relationships with others. Parents can talk about their own bad days. Recognizing the phenomenon and learning that tomorrow probably *will* be better is a step toward maturity.

Viorst, Judith. *Rosie and Michael.* Illustrated by Lorna Tomei. Aladdin, 1988.

Michael tells why Rosie is his friend, and Rosie, in parallel terms, tells why Michael is hers. There is no plot here, but a lot of understanding of what friendship is: tolerating imperfection, plotting (and accepting) friendly pranks, sharing fears and sorrows, keeping secrets, forgiving mistakes, and tolerating idiosyncrasies.

For a gifted child who feels rebuffed and is puzzled about how to be a friend, discussion could grow out of each page of this book. What exactly are Rosie and Michael doing for each other here? The analytical power of the intellectually gifted youngster should help her to generalize, or to follow adult generalizations, from the situations Viorst presents.

Relationships with others. Do you know any friends who treat each other this way? Does anyone do this for you? When did you last do this for someone else? Can you plan to do this for someone tomorrow? Tell me how it turns out.

Ward, Lynd. *The Silver Pony.* Houghton Mifflin, 1992.

In 80 pictures, this wordless book tells the story of a lonely Midwestern farm boy who escapes to the wider world via his imagination. A winged pony takes him on flying rides, and on each trip, they find some other lonely child living his or her particular life: fishing through the ice, struck by a devastating flood, keeping pigeons on a city rooftop, shepherding in the West. Each child originates from a different ethnic group. The bond that the farm boy has with them is loneliness and his ability to give something to them on his imaginary flights.

Aloneness; Creativity; Introversion. This book would best be used by a child looking through it alone first and then telling an adult the story portrayed by the pictures. The adult can bring out themes of the common experience of loneliness, the similarities between the children, and the fact that the lonely farm boy has something to give. Each child will tell a slightly different story, revealing his or her own feelings, and discussion can arise from that story rather than from a preconceived list of questions.

It is important to take time with this book. If the reader yields to the temptation to go through it once quickly, much will be lost.

The Silver Pony is listed also in the Upper Elementary section. Your knowledge of the children who will enjoy the book will help you decide when the book should be presented.

Whelan, Gloria. *Hannah.* Illustrated by Leslie Bowman. Random, 1993.

Hannah is nine in 1887 and is very excited when the new teacher comes to board at her family's farmhouse in northern Michigan. Hannah has never gone to school—she is blind, and her mother has kept her at home, saying there is no point in sending "poor Hannah" to school. Miss Robbin is the first person to show Hannah around the farm, encouraging her to touch, feel, and smell the farmyard animals and the flowers growing in the northern woods. When Miss Robbin asks if Hannah can go to school, her mother reluctantly assents.

The first day does not go well: Carl, the oldest boy in school, teases her and trips her, and she gets lost trying to find her way home alone. Hannah is ready to give up, but Miss Robbin and her father encourage her. The teacher creates an abacus so Hannah can learn arithmetic, and she tells Hannah's parents about the new Braille system that enables the blind to read and write. Hannah is eager, but the Braille device costs five dollars—too much for her parents to spend. Then comes the potato harvest, with a prize for the person who gathers the most potatoes. The contrite Carl, who won the prize the previous two years, has an idea that surprises Hannah: while she has gathered potatoes, enjoying for the first time the pleasure of doing what everyone else is doing, others have helped fill her basket over and over. Hannah wins the prize; soon she will be able to write about it.

With an accurate historical sense for her northern Michigan setting, Whelan has written a moving story that young readers can enjoy independently. Hannah's keen observation of life around her through careful listening enhances the reader's perception of the mental life of a person who does not see.

Differentness. How is Hannah made to feel different from others? How is she made to feel that she is like others? In what ways have you helped someone who is different in some way feel comfortable in a group? In what other ways could you do so?

Relationships with others. Sometimes people do not say exactly what they mean. Hannah's mother is an example of this. What are all of the reasons you can think of that Hannah's mother does not want her to go to school? Do you know of someone who sounds gruffer than he or she actually is? Why did Carl act as he did, both on Hannah's first day of school and at the potato harvest? What does Hannah do that helps people like her?

Sensitivity. What exactly happens at school that causes Hannah to try to go home alone? How could she have reacted differently?

Wiesner, David. *Free Fall.* Mulberry, 1991.

The plot line is scant in this wordless picture book. A boy merely sleeps and dreams, waking in the morning to his familiar room. The strength is in the surreal illustrations, which for adults call up a wealth of associations: Alice in Wonderland, Gulliver's Travels, the art of Dali.

The jacket carries a brief poem describing a dream—an optional text that can be used to follow the pictures, which do progress from one to another in a dreamlike way. It is a journey of strange but familiar images, with a safe return. *Free Fall* is a Caldecott Honor Book for 1989.

Developing imagination. A child can follow the poem or choose to make more (or less) of the pictures, according to his or her experience and imagination.

Wisniewski, David. *Elfwyn's Saga.* Lothrop, Lee and Shepard, 1990.

Elfwyn (beloved of elves) is born blind because of a curse that a rival Viking, Gorm the Grim, has called down upon her father, Anlaf. The Hidden Folk deplore the curse and care for her, and she grows up seemingly with second sight. When Gorm brings a large crystal into Anlaf's hall to sow discontent, only Elfwyn recognizes the danger it presents to her people. Her ensuing actions result in her blindness—the curse—being lifted.

Telling an original story that is based on Icelandic history and legend, this book, with its cut-paper illustrations, is a visual and conceptual delight and a challenge to young readers and listeners.

Drive to understand. Themes for discussion are both factual (Viking history, Icelandic history, the aurora borealis) and legendary, including the ancient theme of good and evil.

Wood, Douglas. *Old Turtle.* Illustrated by Cheng-Khee Chee. Pfeifer-Hamilton, 1992.

In the early days, when animals and fish and stones and mountains and stars could all speak and understand one another, an argument began as each of the beings of the world described God in terms familiar to themselves but foreign to the others: "'God is gentle,' chirped the robin. 'He is powerful,' growled the bear." The argument grew louder until Old Turtle, who seldom spoke, called for silence. Old Turtle said that God is all that the others had said and more. And, said Old Turtle, a new creature is coming, who will be a reminder of all that God is. But when the people came, they too began to argue. They hurt one another, and they hurt the earth. Then one day, another voice called for silence, and the mountain, the ocean, the stone, all spoke of seeing God not only in themselves, but in one another as well. Finally, the people heard, and they, too, learned to see God in the beauty of the earth and in each other.

Drive to understand; Sensitivity. On one level, *Old Turtle* is about views of God drawn from nature—a good choice for parents who want their children to have a sense of the sacred without doctrinal overtones. But on another level, it is not about God so much as it is about the fact that people have, and regrettably argue about, differing views of God. Full of metaphors for God, the story is a metaphor in itself. The story line is told simply enough for a kindergarten child to follow, yet the concepts will challenge older children as well. The illustrations are lush watercolors with an abstraction that well suits the subject.

One of the characteristics of gifted children is an early interest in God, with questions that go beyond the stories introduced in religious training. Regardless of a family's religious perspective, this is a beautiful book to develop an understanding of the differences and potential similarities in expression of religious insight.

Yolen, Jane. *Bird Watch: A Book of Poetry.* Illustrated by Ted Lewin. Paper Star, 1999.

Yolen's poems about birds reflect varying moods, including humor, thoughts on her preference for winter birds over Christmas lights, and acceptance of the death of a bird that flew into a window. Yolen's poetry, like her prose, gives a child new ways to think.

Drive to understand. A final page identifies each bird in the poems and illustrations, with habits and habitats.

Yolen, Jane. *Owl Moon.* Illustrated by John Schoenherr. Philomel, 1987.

On a cold, moonlit, winter night, a little girl and her father go owling. Leaving the warmth of the farmhouse, they cross snowy fields and enter the dark woods—silently, for when you go owling, you must be quiet. In a clearing, they stop, and Pa calls to the owl. At last the owl answers, swooping overhead through the tall trees. Pa's flashlight beam catches the owl as it settles onto a tree branch above them, and for long minutes they look into its eyes. Then it rises and glides away.

Developing imagination. Yolen's prose is very close to poetry, and Schoenherr's illustrations give us moonlight on the snowy fields and woods of his own farm. Both words and pictures reflect the sense of awe that is part of the unique experience of quiet and respectful eye contact with a wild creature. A three-year-old who has learned quiet gentleness can feel this, but *Owl Moon* is appropriate for older children, too.

Upper Elementary (Grades Three – Five)

Adderholdt, Miriam and Jan Goldberg. *Perfectionism: What's Bad about Being Too Good?* Illustrated by Caroline Price Schwert. Free Spirit, 1999.

Some youngsters are perfectionists, wanting so much to do everything perfectly that they consider second place a failure. Eventually, some try to avoid risking failure by refusing to accept new challenges. *Perfectionism* is written not for but to perfectionistic teens, but parents and teachers can use it with younger students by absorbing the concepts in the book and presenting them to elementary children in modified form. The insights that the book offers are as important for adults working with gifted youngsters as it is for the students themselves.

Perfectionism; Using ability.

Alexander, Lloyd. *The First Two Lives of Lukas-Kasha.* Puffin, 1998.

Lukas is a vagabond and a scamp in an unspecified town in 15th-century Persia. A wandering magician's trick transports him to Abadan, where he is immediately greeted as king. It soon becomes obvious that he is only a puppet king, and Lukas finds himself caught up in palace politics and then in the imminent war with the neighboring country of Bishangar. Refusing to use bloodshed to solve problems, Lukas manages to bring peace, growing up considerably in the process.

This is a light and lively story, with the gradual maturing of Lukas handled so deftly that it is quite natural and believable that a vagabond could act like a king. Nur-Johan, the Bishangar captive who turns out to be Queen, presents a contrast to Lukas in her youthful purpose and determination, yet Lukas can teach her how to recognize when using one's wits is more effective than her direct and literal approach might be.

Identity. Point out places in the story at which you knew Lukas was growing up. Describe Lukas and Nur-Johan and how their backgrounds determine their character and behavior. How did each change? Lukas says of his having been sent to Abadan, "I'll have to make my own sense" of the situation. That's a profound statement. Are there situations in your life that are hard for you to explain or understand? Have you "made your own sense" of them? Could you? How does Lukas do it?

Moral concerns. What decisions did Lukas make that showed maturity?

Alexander, Lloyd. *The Iron Ring.* Puffin, 1999.

Tamar, the young king of Sundari, loses a game of dice to Jaya, king of Mahapura. The result is that Tamar, a member of the warrior caste to whom honor is everything, leaves Sundari to journey to Mahapura as Jaya demands. At the beginning, Tamar travels alone except for Rajaswami, his old tutor, but his retinue grows. In India's golden age, animals speak, and soon Tamar and Rajaswami are joined by a monkey king, an eagle, and by Mirra, a *gopi* (village milkmaid), whose cleverness and spirit contribute much in the struggle to reach Mahapura. The little group is drawn into a great battle, as several kings vie for leadership in the region. Tamar has reason to ask again and again what honor requires of him as he tries to be true to his *dharma*.

Alexander's fascination with Celtic mythology led to the Prydain series, set in Wales. Now he turns to the ancient mythologies of India and explores as well the nature of *dharma,* the meaning of honor, and the limitations of caste systems. *The Iron*

Ring is a quest story, with forces for good pitched against evil, requiring Tamar to seek his own interpretations as we all must in the process of growing up. A brief exploration of the old caste system in India would be useful before reading the book.

Drive to understand. In considering the questions under *Moral concerns,* look at them first from the Indian point of view, and then from the American point of view. How do the answers change? How would you explain what Tamar learns from the chandalah?

Identity. How does one know what one's *dharma* is?

Moral concerns. How can Tamar justify leaving his subjects in Sundari to follow his idea of honor? Was Ashwara right to refuse to fight anyone except Nahusha? In what ways does Rajaswami change his ideas of right and wrong?

Perfectionism. What would be your advice to Tamar when he finds it difficult to follow his *dharma* exactly as he thinks he should?

Blos, Joan W. *Brothers of the Heart: A Story of the Old Northwest 1837-1838.* Aladdin, 1993.

Shem Perkins's family moves to Michigan in 1837, when statehood opens up the land. He is 14 and is called "the fiddler's crippled son" because he had been born with a malformed leg and foot. That summer, he leaves home and finds work in Detroit, then is sent on a winter expedition to Mackinac Island and the wild western shore of Michigan. Left alone in a cabin, he expects to die. But Mary Goodhue, an old Indian woman known for healing, finds him. Nearing the end of her life, she stays with Shem and teaches him, and eventually shows him how to return home.

As in her earlier book, *A Gathering of Days,* Blos captures the rhythms of the language of the time in this well-researched novel. She also tells the story of Shem's inner growth during a few short but difficult months as he transcends his disability. When he returns to southeastern Michigan, Blos says, "his stride was unashamed"— the limp not vanished by any means, but so outshone by Shem's personal strength, courage, and purpose as to be unnoticed.

Drive to understand. This book can be read for understanding the lives of early settlers in a new state, for appreciation of American Indian values, and for its tale of wilderness survival.

Identity. Why was Mary Goodhue able to help Shem overcome his difference when his parents could not? What traits do Mary's husband and Shem have in common? What traits do you have that enable you to compensate for other, less desirable traits?

Brink, Carol Ryrie. *Caddie Woodlawn.* Illustrated by Trina Schart Hyman. Aladdin, 1990.

Caddie is 11 in 1865, growing up in a pioneer family in Wisconsin. A tomboy, she fords the river and runs through the fields with her brothers, while her older sister, the sedate Clara, learns more lady-like ways. From her father, Caddie learns to repair clocks and to respect the Indians who still live near the Woodlawn farm, and she risks her father's anger in a sudden decision to ride to the Indian camp to warn them of danger. From her father she also learns to value the wisdom of strong women and to aspire to become one.

Brink's novel is a compilation of stories that the real Caddie Woodhouse told to her granddaughter, the young Carol Ryrie. Caddie is remembered and her story is loved by many grown women who saw themselves in the active, assertive Caddie when they were young readers.

Differentness; Identity; Intensity. How has Caddie's unusual childhood helped her become a strong and good woman? What people do you know who are like Father, Mother, Cousin Annabelle, Tom, and Caddie's teacher? What are you learning from other people in your life?

Moral concerns. Caddie faces some choices in the course of this book that could lead to discussion of decision-making. Ask what those decisions are and why Caddie chose as she did.

Bunting, Eve. *Train to Somewhere*. Illustrated by Ronald Himler. Clarion, 1996.

A relatively unknown part of our country's history is that between the 1850s and the 1920s, "Orphan Trains" carried homeless children from the crowded cities of the East to the farms of the West. Many parents just arriving in the United States could not find work that would support a family, and some gave up their children in desperation in the hope that the children would find a better life. Some children found loving homes, and some found endless work as field hands or housemaids in return for their room and board.

Train to Somewhere is set in 1888, when Marianne rides an Orphan Train with Miss Randolph and a group of children who need homes. West of Chicago, the train makes several stops at small towns where people gather to choose a child to take home. At every stop, Marianne searches for her mother, who had promised to come get her. Neither pretty nor old enough to be strong, Marianne is the only child left at the last stop in Somewhere, Illinois. The people waiting there are not what she wanted, and she is not the boy they wanted, but they warm to each other immediately. Despite the heartbreak of Orphan Trains, we know that Marianne has found a loving home.

Aloneness. The children on the Orphan Train must have felt very alone. How did they help each other feel less lonely? Even though she is alone, how does Marianne know that her mother loves her?

Drive to understand. How does the need for Orphan Trains fit into American life at the time? What was life like in the cities? On the farms?

Moral concerns. How were the Orphan Trains a good solution for children whose parents could not take care of them? How were they not? Do you have ideas for a better solution? Or for how the Orphan Train solution might have worked better?

Relationships with others. Even though the children on the Orphan Train are in a difficult situation, there are many examples of kindness in the book. What are they? How do they help? What kindness have you shown recently? How do you think it helped? Do you know someone in a difficult situation whom you could help with kindness?

Byars, Betsy Cromer. *Summer of the Swans.* Illustrated by Constantinos CoConis. Viking, 1996.

Since their parents' divorce, Sara and her older sister Wanda and younger brother Charlie have lived with Aunt Willie. Charlie has been mentally disabled since he was ill at age three, and Sara is fiercely protective of him. At 14, she is also concerned about her moods, her appearance, the size of her feet, and Joe Melby, who seems to have taken Charlie's watch. Then Charlie gets lost, and in the search for him, which Joe joins, Sara develops a new perspective.

The characters are especially well drawn in this book, and Sara and Joe in particular will stand as models of empathic and caring behavior in situations where impatience might be expected. Byars' descriptions of Charlie's thinking can help children who have been ignorant or afraid of the mentally disabled to develop a sympathetic understanding. This understanding can be generalized, with sensitive guidance, to a tolerance and valuing of all others who are not so quick as a gifted child.

Arrogance; Drive to understand; Relationships with others. How do the different characters treat Charlie (include negative treatment)? How did you feel about the different ways he was treated? How can we understand those who tease? How and why does Sara help Charlie? Why is she able to understand so well how he feels? Is there someone you know who needs your help? Are you the kind of person who offers help when it is needed? Why or why not?

Conly, Jane Leslie. *Racso and the Rats of NIMH.* Illustrated by Leonard Lubin. HarperTrophy, 1991.

In this sequel to her father's popular book, *Mrs. Frisby and the Rats of NIMH,* Conly continues the story of Jenner, one of the dissenting rats from the earlier book. Jenner has left the rats to return to the city, and from there his restless son Racso sets out to join the colony that the rats of NIMH have founded at Thom Valley. Insecure about how he will be accepted and endowed with a false sophistication from life in the city, Racso resorts to lies and boasting to win a place in the colony. The quiet competence, humility, tolerance of hard work, and cooperative spirit of the other rats gradually have an effect on Racso. As they work together to prevent a dam from flooding their valley, Racso learns how to contribute to the group effort, and eventually he becomes the hero he has wanted to be.

Racso displays the bravado many uncertain children exhibit. Both those who are like Racso and those who are annoyed by children like him will understand how Racso feels about his own behavior. Discussion can emphasize how important the patience and understanding of others is in changing Racso.

Arrogance; Identity. Why does Racso lie, steal, and boast? What kind of behavior is more effective when joining a new group? Why is it hard to do? What qualities in Nicodemus help Racso? Do you know someone who has those qualities? What is that person's effect on you?

Relationships with others. What situations can make anyone feel as Racso does about himself? How does this affect how people get along with others? What can help?

Dahl, Roald. *Danny the Champion of the World.* Illustrated by Quentin Blake. Puffin, 1998.

Danny's whole purpose in telling his story is to let us know that his father, without a doubt, is the most marvelous father a boy has ever had. He is very convincing. Danny's mother died when he was a baby, and his father is raising him alone. They live in a gypsy wagon next to the gas station his father owns somewhere in rural England. Danny's early years are filled with engines and car repair, and by the age of five he is a fine mechanic. His father tells fascinating stories and walks Danny to school every day.

All of this is wonderful, but the real excitement begins when Danny is nine and wakes one night to find his father gone. He soon returns, and Danny learns that for the first time since Danny's mother died, his father has gone to Mr. Hazell's wood to pursue an old passion: poaching pheasants. Danny is appalled, but as he learns more about the tradition, the reasons for it, and the many others who share his father's passion for it, Danny and the reader see this activity in a different light. Danny becomes Champion of the World by contributing a new and creative idea that eventually involves the entire community. But first, he uses his precocious skill and ingenuity in a courageous nighttime rescue when his father is in trouble.

Danny is exactly the sort of character that children of this age love to read about. He is living a life of freedom that many would envy, his father respects his ability to learn and teaches him grown-up, real-world skills, and his considerable creativity is appreciated by all. In addition, Dahl uses English terms that present a mild challenge for good readers, and Danny's father explains to Danny—and to the attentive reader—a number of very interesting things about engines, the natural world, and the political issues surrounding pheasant hunting. Above all, Dahl writes with an intelligent humor that will have children laughing aloud as they get the jokes embedded in the narrative.

Drive to understand. Discuss the new things you learned from this book: about life in England, gypsy wagons, hunting and fishing, etc.

Moral concerns. How do you feel about poaching pheasants from Mr. Hazell's wood? How would the same arguments for or against it apply (or not apply) to poaching deer in the United States?

DeClements, Barthe. *Nothing's Fair in Fifth Grade.* Puffin, 1990.

When Elsie Edwards joins their class, the fifth graders groan. Elsie is not just fat; she is gross. She scrounges food at lunchtime because her lunchbox contains only broth, a carrot, and a pear. Then lunch money begins disappearing from desktops, and they realize that Elsie steals money to buy candy. But as Jenifer and her friends gradually get to know Elsie better and learn that her need to eat stems from problems at home, they see past her appearance, to a real person with feelings they can relate to. Jenifer resents Elsie's A's in math, until Elsie helps her understand fractions, and Jenifer realizes that Elsie is an excellent teacher. A scary hitchhiking incident brings all of the friends together, and finally they join in an effort to help Elsie get through the rest of the school year without getting into trouble so she can come back next year.

A former school counselor who has now published several books for children and young adults, DeClements has a firm knowledge of upper elementary children and creates believable characters of all ages. This book was originally published in 1981; some of the references—for example, to records and television shows—are outdated, but the theme is timeless.

Differentness. In what ways is Elsie different from others in the class? In what ways is each of the students different from his or her friends? What things do all of the students have in common?

Identity. Sometimes it is easy to discount the value of a person who is overweight. What good qualities does Elsie have that Jenifer and her friends would not know about if they had not made the effort to get to know Elsie better? How might this change your assumptions about anyone you know?

Relationships with others. Jenifer and her friends would be called "mean" from the point of view of a new child in their class. What causes them to behave this way at first? What causes them to change their minds about Elsie?

Dragonwagon, Crescent. *Home Place.* Illustrated by Jerry Pinkney. Macmillan, 1990.

Hiking in the woods, a family comes upon remnants of a vanished homestead—daffodils, a chimney, a stone foundation. Digging just a little, the girl discovers a marble and part of a china doll. A family has lived here, and the hikers imagine how they lived, trying to reconstruct the ordinary daily events in the lives of unknown people long gone.

Drive to Understand. The book stretches our awareness of our own lives by imagining lives much like ours lived generations ago. The book evokes wonder about how things both change and remain the same, and it adds depth and meaning to our daily concerns, such as those about the weather and about a family meal—concerns that do not change over the centuries.

Erdrich, Louise. *The Birchbark House.* Hyperion, 1999.

This novel, Erdrich's first for young people, opens with a vignette: a group of voyageurs find a baby girl, the sole survivor of the smallpox epidemic that has killed her Ojibwa family, alone on an island in Lake Superior. Fearing that she, too, is sick, the men paddle away, but one of them tells his wife of their discovery. The woman, the fearless Tallow, rescues the infant and brings her back to her home island, where she nurses the baby to health and gives her to a family to raise. The story follows Omakayas (Oh-MAH-kay-ahs) and her new family through her seventh year. Omakayas admires her older sister, is annoyed by her younger brother, and deeply loves her baby brother, Neewo. Helping her mother and grandmother with the gardening, rice gathering, food preservation, and making of clothes from animal skins, she also realizes that she has a special relationship with wild creatures, especially with Andeg, her pet crow. Her adoptive grandmother watches for further signs that Omakayas will be a healer. This one eventful year includes the winter of 1847, when another smallpox epidemic changes their lives. Omakayas learns much about death as well as life, and especially after she learns from Tallow the truth about her origins, she begins to understand her unique powers.

A member of the Turtle Mountain Band of Ojibwa, Erdrich researched the history of her own family and found ancestors who lived on Madeline Island in Lake Superior, the island in the story. Her descriptions of daily life—the tasks and the stories—are woven into the story line, and Ojibwa words are seamlessly included, with a glossary for more detail. Her illustrations enliven and expand the story—those who have gathered stones on the shores of the largest Great Lake will immediately see that the six small stones in one illustration are not generic; they are clearly Lake Superior beach stones. But beyond the authenticity, Erdrich has created in Omakayas a compelling character—a strong, loving, intuitive girl with an intensity and love of life. We want to know more about her, and we look forward to following Omakayas and her family in subsequent books in this projected series. For young readers who love Laura Ingalls Wilder's stories of American pioneer life, Erdrich's series promises to illuminate the same period in history through the eyes of an Ojibwa girl.

Drive to understand. There is so much information embedded in the story that this book can easily be used to enhance curricula. Questions might be based on contrasting life on this Lake Superior island with life in Boston in 1847, or on learning more about the mission schools, the treaties Fish Tail wants to be able to read, and methods of cooking—parents and teachers can generate many ideas to help children learn more about American Indian life in the 19th century. See also Marrin's *Sitting Bull and His World*, in the Middle School listing.

Identity. How does the combination of what Omakayas learns from her grandmother and what she learns from Tallow help her understand herself? How does this strengthen her sense of who she is, her identity? She is only seven at the time of this story— why does she seem so mature?

Intensity. Consider all the ways in which Omakayas shows her determination and love for what is important to her—for example, holding Neewo for so long when he is sick. What in your life do you care so much about? How do you know?

Relationships with others. Think about the ways in which Old Tallow is both tough and tender. How is it hard for her to live with her toughness, and how does it help others? Who do you know who appears to be tough, but might have some tenderness, too?

Evans, Cheryl and Anne Millard. *Usborne Illustrated Guide to Norse Myths and Legends*. Illustrated by Rodney Matthews. EDC Publishing Co., 1986.

With brief introductory sections on the history of the Norse people and on myths and religion, this informative book establishes a context that helps an analytical reader develop an understanding of how myth impacted the lives of these people. The body of the book features two-page retellings of Norse myths, reinforced by a wealth of colorful illustrations. A map of Europe sets the myths in geographical context; a Who's Who and a listing of names and places provides a very useful glossary.

This book is a fine introduction to a body of mythology that has lent more to our culture than we normally recognize. It can be used as a basis for role-playing, as a beginning point for more reading of Norse myths and of other mythologies, and as a starter for discussion.

Drive to understand. How and why are Norse myths different from Greek and Roman or African or any other mythology? What does the Norse mythology tell us about the beliefs of the people? About the warrior image of the Vikings?

Fitzhugh, Louise. *Harriet the Spy*. HarperTrophy, 1990.

Harriet spends her after-school time spying on neighbors. She keeps a notebook filled with comments—not all of them flattering—on them and on her classmates. Shortly after Harriet's nurse, Ole Golly, leaves the family to get married, the other sixth graders discover Harriet's notebook and form a plan to get revenge. Harriet responds to the loss of Ole Golly and of her two best friends with the sturdy independence that got her into trouble in the first place. Her parents and teachers, though, eventually help her use her keen powers of observation and her writing ability in positive ways. Gradually, Harriet softens enough to apologize, and her friends return.

Harriet is a prickly person who comes to realize at the end of the book that she is intelligent. She has never known what to do with her precocious insights, and she has used her ability in negative ways. The problem is really only pointed out, not solved, in this book.

Arrogance; Relationships with others. Why is Harriet's notebook so important to her? Why does she write so many stinging comments? How does her intelligence get her into trouble? How can it help her get out of it? If you were writing a sequel to this book, what would you have Harriet do to make and keep friends, but still be herself? When is it all right not to be popular?

Difference; Identity; Using ability. Harriet has been using her special ability in ways that have given other people good reason to dislike her. Do you know anyone who does this? Why do people behave in this way? What are the disadvantages of doing so? What do people who act like this need from others to help them change? What can they do for themselves to change? What will enable Harriet to use her ability more positively?

Fleischman, Paul. *The Half-a-Moon Inn.* Illustrated by Kathy Jacobi. HarperTrophy, 1991.

Aaron Patrick's mother leaves him at home alone for the first time when he is 12—he was born mute, and until now has never been away from her. She has taught him how to read and write, but she worries because he cannot call for help. A blizzard keeps her away too long, and Aaron sets out over roads he has never seen to search for her. Lost, he finds that his writing is of no use— no one he meets (in what is apparently 18th-century England) can read. He is turned into a servant boy by the pickpocket proprietress of Half-a-Moon Inn, and later escapes only through his wits.

This is part fantasy, part mystery, and much suspense, heightened by the drawings—all elements that children of this age love to find in fiction.

Drive to understand. The setting and Aaron's muteness add interest and information to this challenging adventure story.

Fleischman, Paul. *Seedfolks*. Illustrated by Judy Pedersen. Harper-Collins, 1999.

In a decayed section of Cleveland, a young girl from Vietnam plants six lima beans in a sheltered spot in a vacant lot in memory of her father. An elderly Rumanian woman sees her return to care for them and alerts her neighbor, the school janitor, who waters the beans when the weather turns too hot. An old man who speaks no English begins a garden, building on his knowledge of farming in Mexico. A lonely Korean widow finds a community among the gardeners. A young black man tries to win back an old girlfriend by planting her favorite—tomatoes. An English nurse brings her patient, a stroke victim, in his wheelchair, and he chooses to plant only flowers.

Fleischman tells the story in the words of 13 people—gardeners and observers—whose lives are affected by the neighborhood garden they all cherish, a garden that creates a community not without problems. *Seedfolks* speaks of individuals overcoming fear, prejudice, and emotional shells as they work in their separate garden plots. At first they work alone, but eventually they begin surmounting language barriers to help each other and share their harvest.

Drive to understand. Advanced readers may enjoy Fleischman's ability to write in different voices, as he speaks through people with very different backgrounds. For example, compare the vocabulary and styles in the stories of Curtis, Nora, and Amir. What can you guess of their personalities from their choice of words?

Moral concerns. What does Sam mean when he says, "I smiled back. That's my occupation"? What is Sam's role in this book? Think of someone who plays the same role in your community. What can you learn from Sam and people like him?

Relationships with others. Tell an experience you have had like that of the woman who tells Amir, "Back then, I didn't know it was *you*...."

Fritz, Jean. *Where Do You Think You're Going, Christopher Columbus?* Illustrated by Margot Tomes. Paper Star, 2000.

This lively biography tells much more than that Columbus sailed to what was to become known as America in 1492. Fritz follows Columbus on all four of his voyages, describing his bravado and his stubbornness, his successes and his failures, and providing along the way glimpses of the late 15th-century European view of the world.

The contrasts are instructive. Columbus was a good seaman but a poor governor. He returned to Spain from his first voyage to a royal welcome, but from 1493 to the end of his life, he faced one disappointment after another. Although he was clearly intelligent, the qualities that carried him through these difficulties were persistence and faith in what he was doing. This book offers a way of demonstrating the importance of these characteristics to gifted students who may be trying to rely too much on native intelligence alone.

Drive to understand; Using ability. What words would you use to describe Columbus's character? What qualities made him a good explorer? A poor governor? Why do we hear only of his successes? Do you know of other famous people who failed as well as succeeded? What characteristic was most important to Columbus's success? Do you share any of his traits? What are the advantages of having these traits? What are some disadvantages? How can you enhance the advantages and overcome the disadvantages?

Galbraith, Judy. *The Gifted Kids Survival Guide for Ages 10 and Under.* Illustrated by Albert Molnar. Free Spirit, 1998.

Written to help students understand what the label "gifted" means, this book explains what giftedness is and how it relates to some of the frustrations that gifted children experience in school, with peers, and at home. It includes reassuring information and practical help for making friends and for fighting boredom.

The book is written *to* children in a comfortable, conversational tone. The format makes extensive use of graphics to add impact, and the writing style is informal. Children respond well to both, so they are able to make use of the information and suggestions; however, the dominant value of the book may well be the assurance it offers to gifted children that they are not alone.

Identity. Five sections of the book cover various issues of identity for gifted children. Adults may wish to select sections of the book that seem especially pertinent. It may also be wise to give some thought to whether group or individual discussion would be best.

Relationships with others. Getting along with others is discussed in sections on friends, coping with teasing, and "gifted grief at home."

Goble, Paul. *Death of the Iron Horse.* Aladdin, 1993.

On August 7, 1867, a group of Cheyenne derailed a Union Pacific freight train in Nebraska to protest the railroads' incursions into their territory. After the derailment, the Cheyenne plundered the freight cars, taking not money but all they could carry of goods their people could use. Goble's telling gives the story a mythic quality.

Simple but beautiful illustrations recall the destruction caused by conflict, with the majestic expanse of the West as a backdrop. The story is told from the perspective of an old Cheyenne man who, remembering years later, might have told it to his grandchildren.

Drive to understand. Since this story is based on fact, discussion can lead to further exploration of the disruption of the various American Indian cultures.

Moral concerns. The book can be used as a springboard for discussion that examines both sides. Were the Cheyenne wrong? How can we determine whether they were or not? Consider the story from the point of view of the men on the freight train. Were they wrong? In what way? Who was stealing what, and why, and with what justification?

Greene, Bette. *Philip Hall Likes Me. I Reckon Maybe.* Illustrated by Charles Lilly. Puffin, 1999.

Eleven-year-old Beth Lambert is the second best student in her class, but she sometimes suspects it is only because she lets Philip Hall be first. In fact, when some of the men in town offer to pay for part of her college education, Beth rises to first place. The friendly—and sometimes argumentative—rivalry between Beth and Philip continues throughout the book, against a background of rural and small town Arkansas.

Each chapter is a story unto itself in this book, a typical pattern in books for young children. Together, they provide a greater understanding of the lives of black children in the rural south, of typical elementary-school boy-girl rivalries, and of some of the dilemmas posed by giftedness. Beth is an assertive, saucy girl whose impetuosity sometimes gets her into trouble—and she is appealing in her recognition that this is so.

Relationships with others. In what ways does Beth grow up a little in the year that the book records? What does she learn about getting along with others? What do you do to be a good winner? A good loser? How could you do better?

Using ability. What does Beth learn about being first? Philip, about being second? What is wrong with "letting" someone else win—for you, for the other person, and for the relationship?

Greene, Constance C. *A Girl Called Al.* Illustrated by Byron Barton. Puffin, 1994.

Al(exandra) has an extraordinary IQ, but she doesn't work to capacity and is a nonconformist. She explains all this when she meets the narrator (a girl of Al's age who is never named) shortly after Al moves into the same apartment building. Al is also lonely and is defensive about her weight and her parents' neglect. The narrator introduces her to Mr. Richards, the building janitor, and he very gently works to help Al lose weight and to relieve her loneliness.

Achievement. Giftedness is mentioned just once, but that Al is gifted is clear from her conversation and her insights. The emphasis of the book is three-fold: on the gradual development of sensitivity to the feelings of others, on the common courage of people facing loneliness, and on the way in which friendship can compensate for lost family ties. This book is better used with third and fourth graders than with older gifted children.

Aloneness. What sets Al apart and contributes to her loneliness? What does she offer to the narrator and her family, and to Mr. Richards? What does the narrator offer Al? How will Al become less lonely over time?

Differentness; Identity. Why is it important to Al to think of herself as a nonconformist? How does her nonconformity increase her problems? How does it help her with them? How does her intelligence help her cope? How do you know she is lonely, even though she never says so?

Relationships with others. Al is a very strong character, clearly the leader in the girls' relationship. Discussion can begin with this relationship: What do the two girls have to offer each other despite their differences? What does Al need from other people? Would you be willing to give it to her? What would make it difficult for you to do so?

Henkes, Kevin. *The Zebra Wall.* William Morrow, 1999.

At 10, Adine is the oldest of the five Vorlob girls, followed by Bernice, Carla, Dot, and Effie. The new baby's name will begin with F, and the wall in the nursery is ready, newly painted with a mural featuring flowers, frogs, ferns, fish, and a fairy. But this time it is different: Aunt Irene comes for a visit and gives every evidence of staying—in Adine's room. The baby's arrival brings surprises and a change in plans, but the Vorlob family is flexible and up to the challenge.

Unhappy as Adine and her sisters are with Aunt Irene's presence, they manage to hold their tongues and to accept their parents' decision to welcome her. Very gradually, Adine learns to see the situation from Aunt Irene's point of view and moves toward her own acceptance.

Relationships with others. What makes Aunt Irene's visit difficult for Adine? How does Adine warm up to her aunt? What surprised you about Aunt Irene? Think of someone with whom you are not comfortable. What surprises might they have for you if only you knew them better?

Hermes, Patricia. *Heads, I Win.* Illustrated by Carol Newsom. Minstrel, 1989.

The fifth grade is going to elect a class president, and Bailey enlists her best friend, Kevin, to help her campaign against Janie, the leader of a group of girls. Winning is especially important to Bailey because she believes it will persuade the social worker to let her stay in her present foster home—if Ms. Henderson wants her. Long ago, Bailey heard a social worker say that no one wanted her, and she is wary of assuming too much. Events prove, however, that Bailey is wanted and that she has earned both respect and affection.

In her toughness and savvy, Bailey is reminiscent of Gilly Hopkins. She and Kevin begin campaigning by superficial means—counting and buying votes—but Bailey comes to realize, through Janie's taunting, that she must *earn* votes. From Kevin, she learns that she can do so—already has, in fact—through her own character.

Identity. Why does Bailey believe she'll be a better president than Janie? Do you agree? Why or why not?

Relationships with others. Name all of the lessons Bailey learned that you can. What is the hardest to learn? Why?

Hest, Amy. *Love You, Soldier.* Illustrated by Sonya Lamut. Candlewick, 2000.

Katie is seven when the war comes and her father leaves in an olive green uniform. She and her mother stay in their New York City apartment—her mother working in the hospital and Katie spending hours in the public library. Her mother's friend Louise comes to live with them, since her husband Jack is in the army, too, and soon Louise gives birth to a baby girl. Katie loves Rosie—but then the worst possible news comes. Katie's father has been killed in the war. Katie and her mother stay on in the apartment with Louise and Rosie until the war ends and Jack and Louise's brother, Sam, come home. Then there are more changes, which Katie is reluctant to accept. But their elderly neighbor, Mrs. Leitstein, encourages her, saying, "Love is risky, but it's worth it."

The challenges of developing an identity are intensified for Katie, who must learn to adjust, accept, and risk more than most growing children. She is helped in doing so by the love around her—from and for her parents, Louise, Rosie, Mrs. Leitstein, and finally Sam, the cause of the greatest risk. We are confident that despite the loss of her father and the unknown future, Katie will be fine.

Identity. In what ways does Katie grow up from age seven to the end of the book? What and who help her grow in a healthy way?

Honeycutt, Natalie. *The Best-laid Plans of Jonah Twist.* Simon & Schuster, 1988.

Fourth-grader Jonah is not good at making plans, but for his friend Granville, planning is a strength. Granville's plan to get Jonah's mother to let Jonah keep one of Granville's kittens seems to be working. However, his plan to avoid having to work on a project with Juliet Fisher fails, so the three must cooperate on a report on elephant seals. Juliet is the fourth-grade busybody and has no friends, as Mrs. Lacey points out when she asks Jonah and Granville to give her a chance. Meanwhile, Woz the hamster disappears, and Todd, Jonah's older brother, is sure that the kitten has killed it. And Mr. Rosetti, an elderly neighbor, is also missing, but no one is concerned about that except Jonah.

There are no dramatic changes here, only a slight shift in Jonah's and Granville's attitudes toward Juliet, who displays negative characteristics typical of gifted children, especially girls. (She is a good student whose bossiness, blunt honesty and focus on ideas outrank her interest in interpersonal relationships.) The two boys develop tolerance for Juliet and respect for her ability, despite her direct and somewhat prickly manner.

Relationships with others. How did you feel toward Juliet at the beginning of the book? At the end? Explain the change, if any. Will Jonah and Granville and Juliet be friends from now on? Why or why not? If so, what changed? If you know someone like Juliet, how do you act toward her? Were you surprised to hear that she had been crying? Did it change your feelings about her? What makes her bossy? Will that change? What could make it change?

Hunter, Mollie. *The Mermaid Summer.* HarperTrophy, 1990.

Eric Anderson is a Scottish fisherman who does not believe in mermaids until he sees one and, along with his crew, is nearly drowned. Knowing that the incident is a punishment for having scoffed at mermaids and fearing more trouble, Eric decides to leave his fishing village and find work on an ocean-going vessel. From far-away places, he sends gifts back to his family. When grandson Jon blows the conch shell sent by Eric, the call summons the mermaid. Soon, Jon's sister Anna, who especially longs for her grandfather's return, is drawn into a struggle with the mermaid, first for one of her grandfather's gifts, and eventually for the lives of the village fishermen. But Anna and Jon prevail, with a little help from their mother, their grandmother, the Oldest Fisherman, and the Howdy, the seer of the village. They outwit the mermaid, and soon thereafter Eric returns.

This is a satisfying fantasy based on the traditional literature of Scotland. A model of the criteria Hunter has listed elsewhere for good fantasy, it is a story based in long-ago forgotten truth and is a happy blend of the unknown and the feared with the real world and the manageable. Many readers can identify with Anna's loyalty and stubbornness, and with Jon's frustration and courage as he follows his younger sister's lead.

Drive to understand. It may be better to avoid emotional questions about folklore and fantasy. Such questioning requires the child to make verbal what is understood at a preverbal level and might better be left there. Question then for intellectual understanding: Compare Hunter's story to other mermaid stories. Why are mermaids seen as enemies? What would you like or dislike about life in a fishing village?

Juster, Norton. *The Phantom Tollbooth*. Illustrated by Jules Feiffer. Random, 2000.

Milo, who is so bored with life that he never knows what to do with himself, drags home from school one day to find a large package in the living room. Opening it, he finds One Genuine Turnpike Tollbooth. Milo assembles it, drives his small electric car up to the booth, and pays the toll. The road beyond takes him to the Kingdom of Wisdom and the two rival cities, Dictionopolis and Digitopolis, founded by the king's quarrelling sons. Two daughters, Sweet Rhyme and Pure Reason, had kept the peace until they were banished. Milo sets off to find the sisters, accompanied by the Watchdog, Tock, and the Humbug. They drive through the Forest of Sight (where the city of Reality has disappeared because people were too busy to look) and the Valley of Sound (which is silent because people became too busy to listen). Beyond the Mountains of Ignorance they find Rhyme and Reason in the Castle in the Air, and they return them to the Kingdom of Wisdom. When Milo returns home, he finds that his adventures have made him aware of how much there is to see and do in the world—he will not be bored again.

New thinking is called for not only by the symbolism in the plot, but also by the language, which is full of puns (which are a favorite language game for children of this age) and literal interpretations of verbal expressions—as when Milo and his companions inadvertently "jump to (the Island of) Conclusions." Frivolous as it all sounds, Milo does change during the course of the book. The refreshing use of language, the symbolism, and Milo's struggle with boredom should all appeal to gifted readers.

Drive to understand; Using ability. Describe Milo at the beginning and end of the story. How did he change? What changed him? How did the trip help him know what to do with himself? Is this book silly or serious? How is it silly? How is it serious? Why did the author write it? What messages lie behind the story? Did it make you think of words, numbers, and spending time on unimportant tasks in a new light? How?

Kaufman, Gershen, Lev Raphael, and Pam Espeland. *Stick Up for Yourself! Every Kid's Guide to Personal Power and Positive Self-Esteem.* Free Spirit, 1999.

Adapted from materials written for a college-level psychology course so that children from eight to 12 years old can use it on their own, this book is also accompanied by a teacher's guide. Discussion of general issues of self-esteem, labeling feelings, naming future dreams (and how to get there), and developing interpersonal relationships are especially useful. The difference between role power and personal power, for example, can be a helpful concept as hypercritical youngsters learn how to be effective in their criticism of authority figures.

Identity. Information on self-esteem could be adapted to the particular needs of highly able children learning to come to terms with exceptional talent.

Relationships with others. This book includes useful information on building good relationships with others as a necessary step toward developing self-esteem.

Using ability. The section on naming dreams and how to get there offers suggestions that can be helpful in making good use of an outstanding ability.

Kendall, Carol. *The Gammage Cup: A Novel of the Minnipins.* Illustrated by Erik Blegvad. Odyssey, 2000.

For 880 years, the fictitious Minnipins have lived in their valley in the Land Between the Mountains, isolated from the world and remembering the story of Gammage, who led them there, and Fooley, who floated away over the mountains in a balloon 440 years ago and returned with a few little-understood but well-revered artifacts. The Minnipins live tidy, well-regulated lives, with only a few exceptions: Gummy, who scribbles poetry; Mingy the Money Keeper; Curley Green, who likes to paint; Walter the Earl, the only Minnipin who studies history from the few written records rather than relying on legend; and Muggles, who timidly at first but then more boldly thinks for herself rather than following the traditional ways without question. The story starts slowly but builds to an exciting climax as the five outcasts lead the other Minnipins in a brave and successful effort to save their valley from invasion.

Differentness. The theme of nonconformity can lead to discussion about rules—spoken or unspoken—that are difficult for some to follow. What conformities do we expect, like the green doors on (almost) every house in Slipper-on-the-Water? When is it appropriate not to conform to expectations? When is it inappropriate?

Identity. Why does Muggles change from being like everyone else in Slipper-on-the-Water to just being herself? How does she do it?

Relationships with others. How do we treat people who do not conform? What happens to Muggles when she stops following others' expectations and begins saying what she thinks? How does she avoid offending others when she speaks out?

Kendall, Carol. *The Whisper of Glocken: A Novel of the Minnipins.* Illustrated by Imero Gobbato. Odyssey, 2000.

In this sequel to *The Gammage Cup,* the Watercress River floods, forcing the Minnipins in Water Gap to flee upstream. Reaching Slipper-on-the-Water, Glocken, bell-ringer of Water Gap, realizes his dream of meeting the Old Heroes of the Gammage Cup. Glocken finds them living quite ordinary, settled lives—but the Old Heroes hail Glocken and the four Water Gapians who have fled with him as the New Heroes who will find and repair the source of the flooding. So five very ordinary Minnipins from Water Gap set out on their own adventure, discovering their latent heroism as events require.

The writing is more subtle and demanding than in *The Gammage Cup*, with vocabulary, metaphor, and proverbs to challenge the middle elementary reader. Imagination is called into play as the reader creates the Minnipin world from vivid description. Each of the five New Heroes, despite insecurities, peculiarities, and weaknesses, manifests true, self-sacrificing heroism at one time or another, and they offer tolerance and support to each other as they work to free the Watercress and save their Land Between the Mountains.

Drive to understand. For good readers who love to read, this is an excellent introduction to fantasy.

Knowlton, Jack. *Maps and Globes.* Illustrated by Harriett Barton. HarperTrophy, 1986.

Beginning with ancient maps drawn on clay or silk cloth and Polynesian stick chart maps, the author moves quickly on to Magellan's voyage and the advent of more accurate globes. In the section on geographical terminology, he introduces and defines words such as *latitude* and *longitude, elevation* and *depth.* Then he demonstrates various kinds of maps: physical, political, and specialized maps that show features such as metal deposits and stagecoach lines. He concludes by suggesting a visit to the library to explore atlases.

Barton's illustrations are clear and closely tied to the text, which goes directly to the point, providing much information cleanly and efficiently. Providing satisfying initial information while at the same time opening the door for future learning, *Maps and Globes* is a model nonfiction book.

Drive to understand. Many concepts are introduced that the child may wish to explore further, and the invitation to the library makes it clear that there is more to learn.

Koch, Kenneth and Kate Farrell. *Talking to the Sun: An Illustrated Anthology of Poems for Young People.* Metropolitan Museum of Art, and Holt, Rinehart and Winston, 1985.

This is a gorgeous book. To give children a sense of the beauty of poetry, Koch and Farrell have assembled English poems from the 15th century to the present, and poems translated from 11 ancient and modern languages. Their poets include Shakespeare, Blake, Rimbaud, Rilke, Lorca, and Li Po. They have sought not children's poetry, but poetry children will enjoy at different times in different ways.

To illustrate this range of poetry, they have selected paintings and other objects from the collection of the Metropolitan Museum of Art. Where the connection between a poem and a work of art may not be clear, a brief comment illuminates.

Drive to understand. In her introduction, Farrell refers to "the mood [a poem] puts you in." Visual art also suggests moods, and here the children can experience the effect of both poetry and art and the different moods resulting from each. In an appendix on helping young people appreciate poetry, she recalls an image from the conductor Leopold Stokowski, in which the world of art is seen as an oak tree whose branches are the different art forms—music, poetry, painting, and dance—all expressions of the human need to create art. This book brings two branches of the oak/art tree together so well that we long to add others. It is a very rich book indeed for the imagination of a growing child, one to keep and reread for all the years of growing up.

Konigsburg, E. L. *From the Mixed-up Files of Mrs. Basil E. Frankweiler.* Aladdin, 1987.

Claudia Kincaid persuades her brother Jamie, who has enough money to finance the project, to join her in running away. Following Claudia's careful plans, they hide in New York's Metropolitan Museum of Art for a week. At first, Claudia's reasons for running away are unclear even to her, but as she becomes fascinated by the mystery of a statue that the museum has just purchased, she realizes what she wants to accomplish before she returns home.

Drive to understand. Written with a light touch, this is nevertheless not a frivolous book. It gives children who do not live in New York much incidental information about the city, the Metropolitan Museum, and art. In addition, it portrays inquisitive children who have had superb educational opportunities and who are appealing models for lively, intellectually curious young people.

Identity. Why did Claudia want to run away at first? What is her reason by the end of the book? Why does she want to be different? What are some advantages of being different? How could someone like Claudia accomplish the same thing without running away? What does Mrs. Frankweiler mean when she talks about having some days when, rather than learning new facts, it's good to "allow what is already in you to swell up until it touches everything"?

Konigsburg, E. L. *Jennifer, Hecate, Macbeth, William McKinley, and Me, Elizabeth.* Yearling, 1985.

Jennifer and Elizabeth become friends on Halloween of Elizabeth's first year at William McKinley School. Jennifer says she is a witch, and she does some mysterious things that make it seem possible that she is. Elizabeth becomes an apprentice witch, and all winter the girls meet at the library on Saturdays to study witchcraft, planning to make a magic potion that will enable them to fly.

Elizabeth is lonely at first in the new school. Jennifer, being gifted and black, is different and is not included in the school's social life, but she seems unconcerned about it. A subtheme is Elizabeth's gradual separation from Jennifer's influence, with Jennifer's help, so that the friendship becomes more equal than the original follower/leader relationship.

Aloneness. Do you think Jennifer is lonely? Why or why not?

Differentness; Identity. Why does it not seem to bother Jennifer that she is not popular at school? Do you think she is happy just as she is? Why or why not? How do you know when Elizabeth begins to do more thinking for herself? Why does this happen?

Relationships with others. Why is Elizabeth uncomfortable at the birthday party? Do you agree with her behavior? Why is she more comfortable with Jennifer? Why does Elizabeth finally pull away from Jennifer? How does this affect their friendship? What does each girl offer to the other?

L'Engle, Madeleine. *A Wrinkle in Time.* Farrar, Straus and Giroux, 1990.

Fourteen-year-old Meg Murry, her younger brother, Charles Wallace, and Calvin O'Keefe travel through time and space in search of Mr. Murry, a scientist who disappeared while experimenting with a tesseract, a wrinkle in time. When they find him, they must use all their strength to free him and themselves from the force of evil.

Almost all of the characters in this story are very intelligent, and the three children respond in different ways to the difficulties this causes them in relating to others. L'Engle creates a world in which it is psychologically safe to be gifted and in which the characters care for and challenge one another.

Differentness; Identity. How are the children different from their schoolmates? How does each feel about being different? How do we show that we do or do not value differences among people?

Drive to understand. Like many of L'Engle's books, *A Wrinkle in Time* features an entire cast of gifted characters. For one thing, they each exhibit the drive to understand, a trait that an intellectually curious reader will easily recognize. What is more, they show that such a drive adds meaning and purpose to living. The book is intellectually satisfying to gifted children also because of frequent references to math, science, literature, and music. Challenging discussions based on the book could begin with the question, "What do you think about life on Camazotz?"

Levine, Gail Carson. *Ella Enchanted*. HarperTrophy, 1998.

When Ella was born, Lucinda, the sentimental and impulsive fairy, bestowed a gift upon her without sufficient thought as usual: obedience. Ella would always be obedient. Growing up in the home of a wealthy merchant, Ella was protected from her gift by the watchful caring of her mother and Mandy, the cook. But the Lady Eleanor dies when Ella is 15, and Sir Peter sends Ella to finishing school. There, the envious Hattie learns that Ella is compelled to obey every order, and she uses this knowledge to make Ella's life miserable. When Ella flees to find Lucinda and beg her to take back her gift, she survives a near-fatal encounter with ogres and meets kind elves and friendly giants, but fails to gain freedom from the fairy's gift. The adventure forces her to realize how dangerous the gift is, both to her and to those she loves—even to the prince.

Ella is intelligent and high-spirited, and her struggle to be herself and to make her own decisions is the story of this book. Gradually, the reader realizes that it is also a modern retelling of the Cinderella story. *Ella Enchanted* is a delightful book to read simply for the pleasure of it, but it also offers ideas for discussion. The climactic inner battle in which Ella finally wins freedom from Lucinda's influence is especially worth attention if leader and children can articulate it as a metaphor for growing up—a struggle which in real life must happen more than once.

Identity. Why is it important that Ella learn how not to be always obedient, but to make her own decisions? Why is it important for Ella, as well as for Char and Kyrria? Why is it important for anyone? How is Ella finally able to overcome the effects of Lucinda's gift?

Moral concerns. What are the advantages of being obedient? What are the disadvantages? What guidelines can help you decide when it is best to be obedient and when not?

Relationships with others. What qualities in Ella make her a good friend for Char? What role does Ella's friendship with Arieda play? Hattie and Olive are caricatures, as is often the case in fairy tales—what kind of "friendship" do they represent?

Lindgren, Astrid. *Pippi Longstocking.* Translated by Florence Lamborn. Illustrated by Louis S. Glanzman. Puffin, 1997.

A series of vignettes tells about Pippi, who has come home to Villa Villekulla after sailing with her father. She lives alone in the family home and is wonderfully free. Very strong, with no parental restrictions and the freedom to do just as she likes, Pippi goes from one adventure to another, following her own unique logic, to the amusement of neighborhood children and to the huge enjoyment of the reader.

Using ability. Pippi provides fantasy material and plenty of independence and divergent thinking for beginning readers, girls and boys alike. Adults who met Pippi decades ago still light up when they talk about her, putting Pippi Longstocking in the same category as Caddie Woodlawn—a timeless heroine.

Lindgren, Astrid. *Ronia, the Robber's Daughter.* Peter Smith, 1994.

On the night Ronia is born, a fierce storm brings lightning that cracks Matt's Fort, her father's castle, in two. Matt, his wife Lovis, and his band of robbers, rejoicing over the birth of this dark-haired daughter, are not concerned. They simply abandon the north half of the castle and continue to live in the south fort. The high-spirited Ronia grows into a fearless explorer of the forest and the mountains around Matt's Fort.

One day, exploring Hell's Gap—the fissure between the two parts of the old castle—she meets Birk, son of Borka, the other robber chieftain in the area. Soldiers have come too close to Borka's territory, so he and his band have taken up residence in the north fort without the formality of asking permission. From then on, Ronia and Birk explore the forest together, coming to depend on each other for company and for safety among the forest folk such as the gray dwarfs and harpies. As their affection for each other grows, the inevitable conflict between their fathers builds. When it reaches its climax, the independent Ronia chooses Birk, leaping Hell's Gap as evidence of her decision. Soon, Ronia and Birk leave their families, unable to accept the hatred between their fathers and unwilling to pursue the robber's life. Sweet reconciliation comes eventually, after they have spent an idyllic summer in the Bear's Cave. The two bands of robbers join forces, but the soldiers make the robbing life ever more difficult. When they grow up, we know, Ronia and Birk will lead the band toward a more lawful life.

Ronia is as strong-minded as Pippi is, but her story is a strong narrative rather than a collection of loosely linked incidents. Ronia is a memorable heroine, and Birk, too, is an independent thinker. The deep friendship between them is a very moving love, but it is the love of children. There are only a few vague hints from the adults that it could be more, and there is the simple certainty on their part that they will always be together. Swedish author Lindgren displays her love for the atmosphere of the northern forest in every season, and this, along with the presence of the folkloric forest creatures, adds a uniqueness to the setting that suits Ronia's character completely. With its distinctive writing style and unusual names, this book may need more introduction than most, but once students have an understanding of the setting and characters, they will be eager for more. This is a book that parents as well as teachers may want to read aloud, for their own pleasure as well as for that of their children.

Arrogance. Why do Matt and Borka talk to each other the way they do? What purpose does it serve? When they change, toward the end of the book, what has brought about the change? Why are they no longer arrogant?

Moral concerns. Why are Matt and Borka robbers? Why will Ronia and Birk not be? What are the reasons for the change?

Relationships with others. Describe Ronia's personality, and Birk's. What personal traits do they have that enable them to become friends, even though their families are enemies? What traits do you have that help you make friends?

Lowry, Lois. *Anastasia Krupnik*. Bantam, 1998.

In her green notebook, 10-year-old Anastasia records her favorite words, important private information, and a list of "Things I Love!" and "Things I Hate!" When she learns that her mother will have a baby boy in March, she adds "my parents" and "babies" to the Hate list, but stops short of running away when her father suggests that she give the new baby whatever name she chooses. Anastasia writes a horrible name in the green notebook. Over the next few months, she considers becoming a Catholic and changing her name, learns how to listen to her 92-year-old grandmother, falls in and out of love, decides she likes her name—and records all of this in the green notebook, occasionally moving an item from the Hate list to the Love list. Eventually, even "babies" appears on the love side of the ledger.

Anastasia is a bright, inquisitive, sensitive girl who is doing her best to make sense of both the world and the process of growing up. She vaguely dislikes her teacher without knowing the reason. The reason is clear to the reader when the teacher rejects a poem that Anastasia has written because it does not rhyme. Later, her teacher makes a special effort to be kind, and Anastasia moves her name to the Love list. Anastasia's parents are models of support and understanding for a gifted child. There are no major issues here, only Anastasia becoming more aware of herself through her own efforts and with her parents' help.

Identity. How do *people* get moved from the Hate list to the Love list? What do they all have in common? Describe the difference between the college students' and Anastasia's attitude toward Wordsworth. Do you know people who have the students' attitude? What are the consequences? (If it seems appropriate, discussion leaders may want to add questions related to Anastasia's knowledge of and attitude toward her own giftedness.)

Macauley, David. *Cathedral: The Story of Its Construction.* Houghton Mifflin, 1981.

By giving specific dates and names, Macauley adds authenticity to this book of fiction—a story of how the people of a French town worked together for 86 years to build "the longest, widest, highest, and most beautiful cathedral in all of France." The illustrations show in exquisite detail how the land was cleared and foundations built; how the buttresses, piers, stairways, vaults, windows, and even bells were constructed; and how the village grew around the cathedral over the years. Correct architectural terminology is used, and a glossary provides definitions.

Drive to understand. Cathedral is used here to represent others of Macauley's books (*Castle, Underground*, etc.), which answer questions most curious children have asked, if only to themselves. Macauley writes with respect not only for the object constructed, but for the people who do the work, and he never writes down to his audience. His books are a good introduction to serious work in the adult world.

MacLachlan, Patricia. *Arthur, for the Very First Time.* Illustrated by Lloyd Bloom, HarperTrophy, 1989.

When he is 10, Arthur goes to stay with Great-Aunt Elda and Great-Uncle Wrisby for the summer because his parents are fighting. In addition, Arthur believes that his mother is going to have a baby, which he does *not* want. Life is very different with Uncle Wrisby and Aunt Elda—they live on a farm, so they teach Arthur about nature and about farm life. Their pet chicken, Pauline, sleeps in the kitchen, and their pig, Bernadette, will give birth to piglets soon. They also have neighbors, including Moira and her grandfather Moreover, the veterinarian. Moira calls Arthur "Mouse" as they become friends, and Arthur learns that her family problems are more troubling than his are. Nevertheless, Moira is a positive person who urges the timid "Mouse" to do something—and Arthur does.

This is a story of friendship and of Arthur's growing sense of purpose, his nascent self-understanding, and eventually the shift in his attitude toward a baby, which is directly due to his experience with Bernadette's piglets. The book includes Aunt Elda's story, which will remind readers of MacLachlan's later and better-known *Sarah, Plain and Tall.*

Identity. What did Arthur do? Why? How has he changed? So much is unresolved at the end of this book that some discussion can center on what the reader thinks will happen next. How will Arthur be different when he returns to his parents? How will his family be different?

Montgomery, L. M. *Anne of Green Gables.* New American Library, 1991.

As an 11-year-old orphan, Anne is adopted by a 60-year-old Prince Edward Island farmer, Matthew Cuthbert, and his sister, Marilla. Anne is red-haired, bright, and eager to please, but above all, she is impetuous and imaginative. Despite her best efforts, she is forever getting into trouble. The story follows her for the next five years, through friendships, problems at school, and misunderstandings. The reader watches as Anne learns to tame her romantic nature, Anne growing more mature and thoughtful in the process.

First published in 1904, this book is refreshingly old-fashioned and idealistic in comparison to today's "problem novels." (Some will say too idealistic—how could anyone who has lived through Anne's childhood have survived so well?) However today's readers may view Anne's efforts to "be good" and Marilla's efforts to avoid spoiling her, the underlying desire to make something good of one's life is a needed example, and well done here. Perhaps it is just the distance in time that allows this book to make the point without preaching.

Identity; Using ability. Anne has no problems with recognizing and using her intelligence, so she can be a positive example. In what ways are you like Anne? In what ways could you be like her if you had lived in her time? Who are kindred spirits for you? Might Anne be one? Why or why not?

Moser, Adolph. *Don't Feed the Monster on Tuesdays!* Illustrated by David Melton. Landmark Editions, 1991.

Subtitled *The Children's Self-Esteem Book*, this non-fiction book is designed to be read by parents and children together. Psychologist Moser explains how children can replace negative feelings about themselves with positive ones. Imagining a monster inside our heads that makes us feel bad about ourselves—others call it "bad self-talk"—he suggests that on Tuesdays, children avoid feeding the monster by saying only nice things to themselves and others. This will become easier on Wednesday, and then every day—and the rewards, in the responses sure to come from other people, are great. Moser touches on perfectionism, making the point that to feel good about oneself, it is not necessary to win every time; it is only important to do one's best.

This is one of a series of books by the same author for children from ages nine through twelve, each addressing a different issue in healthy psychological development. Besides self-esteem, the series covers stress, anger, grief, and lying. In each book, he describes and defines the problem in terms familiar to children, making it clear that others experience it too. Then he shows the way to solutions. Because the books are written in simple language with cartoon-like illustrations, they look like children's books, but my local bookseller shelves them with books on parenting, highlighting the importance of parent involvement in reading the books and helping the child deal with these issues. Parents will want to read them first and may be surprised to learn how serious these concerns are to their children.

Drive to understand; Identity; Perfectionism; Relationships with others.

Naylor, Phyllis Reynolds. *Shiloh.* Yearling, 1992.

Eleven-year-old Marty Preston is walking through his beloved West Virginia countryside one Sunday when he comes upon a dog—a frightened beagle who clearly yearns to befriend Marty and who follows him home. But Marty's family can't afford to feed a pet, and his father returns the dog to its owner, Judd Travers, whose reputation for meanness is based in part on his mistreatment of his hunting dogs. When the beagle (whom Marty has named Shiloh) escapes and returns to the Prestons, Marty hides him, even from the rest of his family, while he tries to find a way to earn enough money to buy the dog. The crisis comes when Shiloh is attacked in his hiding place by a neighboring German shepherd, and Marty's parents—and Judd—discover Marty's secret.

Marty is caught in a dilemma in this Newbery winner because both the law and the weight of local custom conflict with his passionate desire to protect Shiloh from a cruel owner. Although his parents are supportive, they insist that Marty must work the problem out on his own. His manner of doing so shows uncommon courage, maturity, and wisdom, along with a recognition of the need for compromise.

Identity. What is it in Marty that causes him to question rules that others around him follow easily? Imagine Marty in 15 years—what might he do then to protect a dog like Shiloh? How and why might Marty be different from his parents when he is grown?

Moral concerns. Did Marty make any decisions that you would not have made? Was his parents' position a good one? Why or why not?

O'Brien, Robert C. *Mrs. Frisby and the Rats of NIMH*. Illustrated by Zena Bernstein. Aladdin, 1999.

Worried about the illness of her son Timothy, Mrs. Frisby goes to Mr. Ages, a wise older mouse, for medicine. Later, when it is clear that Timothy is too weak to be moved from their garden home before it will be destroyed in spring plowing, Mr. Ages sends her to the rats for help. Thus, she learns how the rats had been captured and groomed in a laboratory at NIMH, their intelligence enhanced until they learned to read. They finally escaped, and they set up their own civilization under a large rosebush on the Fitzgerald farm. Now they are planning to move again, this time to a remote valley where they can be self-sufficient, no longer dependent on Mr. Fitzgerald's grain. Mrs. Frisby learns also that her husband Jonathan, who had died the previous summer, had been a laboratory mouse who escaped with the rats. He died during an attempt to help them. The rats are therefore eager to help Mrs. Frisby, although they, too, are in danger.

The super-intelligent rats of NIMH are so different from other rats that they want to live differently, according to their own ideas and values, even though they do not entirely agree among themselves on those values. One question the book raises is how much separateness is called for by a high intelligence, and why.

Differentness; Identity. After escaping from NIMH, the rats are uncomfortable with other rats, who edge away from them. If you have experienced this, how do you respond? What are advantages of the rats' separate civilization? What are the disadvantages? This story is an extreme: What examples of the same impulse to separateness do we see among people? What are the advantages and disadvantages of separateness? What compromises are possible? What is your preference?

Moral concerns. Nicodemus and others argue that a life made easy by machinery is too easy, causing the rats to lose a sense of purpose in meaningful work. What do you think? What would be the result if they used their leisure time to learn more? What if people did the same?

Paterson, Katherine. *Bridge to Terabithia.* Illustrated by Donna Diamond. HarperTrophy, 1987.

Sensitive and interested in art, Jess is a misfit in his family and in his school. When Leslie moves to Jess's rural area of Virginia and joins his class, she frees him to play and learn in the country of their imaginations, Terabithia. After Leslie is killed in a flooded stream, Jess must face her death and his aloneness. Although he is still different from others, he realizes that he has gained strength from his friendship with Leslie and is comfortable being himself now.

Katherine Paterson wrote this book after the death of a special friend of her own son, and it rings with the truth of the relationship between two sensitive people who find strength and validation in their friendship. Many children can respond to that truth whether or not they themselves have such a relationship, and this book is highly recommended for bright and sensitive upper elementary readers.

Aloneness; Introversion. Why do Jess and Leslie enjoy Terabithia so much? What other places could serve the same purpose? Do you have such a place? Would you like to have one? How would you find it? When would you go there? What would you do there? Would you go alone or with someone else?

Differentness; Identity; Sensitivity. How is Leslie different from the other students at Jess's school? How is Jess different? How does each one feel about being different? What would happen if they tried to change in order to fit in better? If you could meet them, would you like them better as they are, or if they changed in some way? Do you know anyone who seems different from the group, but who is pretty good at being who he or she is?

Drive to understand. Describe the difference in background between Jess and Leslie. Why is the trip to Washington, D.C. so important to Jess? Have you had any such experience?

Relationships with others. How do Jess and Leslie recognize each other as potential friends? What does Leslie offer to Jess? What does Jess offer to Leslie that leads to their building a friendship? What do you offer to and gain from special friends?

Using ability. Why has it been so difficult for Jess to develop his artistic talent? What will he have to do to be able to use his talent? What traits will help him? What traits do you have that would help you if you were in his situation? What talent do you have that you can develop? Is it harder or easier for you than for Jess? Why?

Phelps, Ethel Johnston. *The Maid of the North: Feminist Folk Tales from around the World.* Illustrated by Lloyd Bloom. Holt, 1987.

Phelps has gathered folktales from Europe, Africa, the Far East, Asia, and North America, the common thread being that the main character in each is a woman who is spirited, clever, or brave—a heroine instead of a hero.

Drive to understand. The feminism is not belabored. These are simply good tales, little-known and therefore fresh and spritely, in the authentic folklore form. They are good reading for both boys and girls.

Rodgers, Mary. *Freaky Friday.* HarperCollins, 1991.

Annabel Andrews and her mother trade places, so Annabel goes through the day in her mother's body and sees herself as others speak to her "mother" about her. She learns that her brother loves her despite her impatience with him, that the housekeeper will not clean her room because it is so messy, that the boy she admires thinks she is ugly and awful, and that her teachers are frustrated with her underachievement.

The book is sometimes hilarious as the reader follows Annabel's thoughts and reactions. The high point is her mother's interview with her teachers, in which Annabel learns that she has a high IQ and that her teachers are concerned about her lack of achievement. When she and her mother resume their own bodies, she finds that her mother has had her braces removed and her hair cut and has bought Annabel a new wardrobe. Instant transformation from an ugly duckling to a budding beauty—what every adolescent girl would love to have!

Achievement; Using ability. How will Annabel's behavior change as a result of the inner changes that take place within her in this story?

Identity. What is it about the interview with her teachers that makes Annabel want to change? How would Annabel describe herself at the beginning of the book? How would you describe her at the end? What inner changes take place? Why? Do you know anyone like Annabel? What do you think he or she is like inside?

Smith, Janice Lee. *The Kid Next Door and Other Headaches: Stories about Adam Joshua*. Illustrated by Dick Gackenbach. Harper-Collins, 1987.

The kid next door is Nelson, and in these five stories, Adam Joshua and Nelson learn how to overcome significant personality differences in order to be friends—beginning with "The Kid Next Door," in which they share their treehouse despite Adam Joshua's messiness and Nelson's neatness. In "A Dog Named George," Adam Joshua learns that a dog is worse than a baby sister and is not as good as a friend, either, but he loves George anyway. Nelson, however, does not. When Adam Joshua learns that Nelson has outgrown Superman in "The Superman Kid," he thinks that this is another difference between them—but then he looks from his house into Nelson's room and sees Nelson playing Superman in solitary dignity. The boys join forces in "A Visit from Cynthia" to fight back when Nelson's cousin turns out to be tough and mean. And when Nelson stays for the night in "Nelson at Night," Adam Joshua learns to cope with personal habits very different from his own.

Adam Joshua and Nelson provide a primer in how to be friends with someone even when they are different, as Adam Joshua learns to appreciate the good and accept the difficulty in having Nelson as his best friend. Nelson isn't perfect, but then Nelson wouldn't think Adam Joshua is perfect, either. And "if you needed a friend who made you happy sometimes, and sometimes made you mad, and kept you trying hard to be a friend yourself, Nelson worked out fine."

Relationships with others. Why do Adam Joshua and Nelson keep trying to be friends? What do they gain besides their friendship?

Speare, Elizabeth George. *The Sign of the Beaver*. Yearling, 1994.

When Matt and his father come from Massachusetts to Maine to claim land that the father has purchased, they are the first white family to settle in the area. They build a log cabin and plant corn, and then Matt's father goes back to Massachusetts for his mother, sister, and the new baby, leaving Matt alone to tend the corn. When he is caught in a bee swarm, Matt is rescued by an Indian and his grandson, Attean. The old man asks Matt to teach Attean to read in return for food. Attean is not receptive to reading; his parents have been killed by whites and he has no liking for their culture. But gradually he teaches Matt survival skills, and they become friends and then brothers. When the tribe moves on, Matt is invited to join them. His family has been so long in coming that it seems they might not come at all, so the decision is not easy. Although Matt faces the winter alone, he decides he must stay. Just before Christmas, his family arrives, delayed by typhus.

In this good introduction to historical fiction, Matt is introduced to another culture and must recognize that in some ways, it is superior to his own. The book can lead to discussion of ways in which all people adapt to their unique environments and develop patterns of living that make sense—because those ways are effective in the situations the people regularly face.

Drive to understand. What besides survival skills does Matt learn from Attean and his family? What does he teach them?

Sperry, Armstrong. *Call It Courage.* Aladdin, 1990.

When Mafatu was three, his mother was killed at sea. Mafatu survived, but his childhood experience left him afraid of the sea, a coward in the Polynesian world where courage is everything. Rejected by all, Mafatu finally leaves Hikueru, his home island, and sails to a deserted island where he must depend only on himself for survival. While providing food and shelter and building a new canoe, he also kills a shark, a wild boar, and an octopus. Finally he must flee the island, pursued by a band of men from a nearby island. Having so abundantly proven his courage to himself, Mafatu returns home to the welcome of his people.

This fast-paced adventure will hold children's attention and give them a vivid picture of life in another part of the world. Mafatu's journey is the classic quest story, and he sets for himself tasks that correspond to the rites of passage marking the beginning of manhood in many societies. Although younger gifted children can read *Call It Courage* with enjoyment, those in the upper elementary grades are at a more appropriate age to respond to the story of Mafatu's search for identity.

Identity. Why did Mafatu leave Hikueru? Why did he explore the island he found, even though he suspected it might be one of the dark islands? Why did he go to the plateau instead of leaving the island when he heard the drums? Describe Mafatu's character. What traits helped him survive psychologically (survive the teasing and rejection of his people)? Physically (survive the dangers of the sea and the island)? Do young people in the United States face challenges in growing up that these traits will answer? How can you use the traits that Mafatu had or developed?

Stolz, Mary. *A Dog on Barkham Street.* Illustrated by Leonard Shortall. HarperTrophy, 1985.

Edward is in the fifth grade, and his mother still says that before he can have a dog, he must prove that he is responsible enough to take care of it. Edward tries—and so does his friend, Rod, whose mother has the same rule—but so far, neither one has been able to stay responsible long enough. Meanwhile, Edward tries various ways of coping with living next door to Martin, a bully two years older and 20 pounds heavier than Edward.

Then, Edward's Uncle Josh comes for one of his rare visits. Uncle Josh is a "traveler"—he left home at the age of 16 and has been traveling ever since, finding manual work whenever he needs a little money. At first, Edward and Rod are in awe of Uncle Josh and his carefree, responsibility-free way of life. But then Edward notices that Uncle Josh is a bit lazy, avoids committing to anything, and has a disconcerting way of looking off into the distance, seeming to be far away much of the time. Uncle Josh has successfully avoided responsibility all his life, and Edward can see that it is not entirely a pretty picture. On the other hand, Uncle Josh has brought something with him: a collie-mix dog named

Argess. As long as Uncle Josh stays, Edward has a dog. Argess even defends Edward against Martin.

Things are going very well until the morning Edward wakes up to find that Uncle Josh has gone on his way, taking Argess with him and leaving only a note. That is also the day Edward learns that Martin will be waiting for him after school with a group of sixth-grade boys, and that Rod has had an argument with his family. The two friends decide not to go to school that Friday, and together they find adventure that becomes truly frightening for a time and puts all of the trouble at home in a new perspective.

It is always good to have a book available to help discuss the bully problem. In this book, Edward's father has some insights, which Edward begins to comprehend, into why bullies behave as they do. Stolz has also written *The Bully of Barkham Street*, with more on Edward's relationship with Martin and the understanding required to deal well with bullies in the neighborhood.

Relationships with others. Would you have any advice to offer Edward about how to deal with Martin? What would you add to Edward's father's explanation of why some people become bullies? How is Uncle Josh's way of life hard on the people around him? Why do you think Uncle Josh seems to be "far away" much of the time? Do you know anyone who has the same characteristic? If so, is it for the same reason you gave for Uncle Josh, or for some other reason? Do you ever seem that way to others? How does it affect them?

Using ability. Why is responsibility important? Why is it so hard for Edward and Rod to prove that they are responsible? Can one be too responsible? Are you responsible enough, or too responsible? How does it affect your ability to make the best use of the intellectual, artistic, or athletic talent you have?

Stolz, Mary. *Go Fish.* Illustrated by Pat Cummings. Harper-Trophy, 1993.

Eight-year-old Thomas lives in Florida with his grandfather. On this long summer day, observing Thomas' restlessness, Grandfather puts a marker in his book and suggests that they go fishing.

Later, Grandpa cooks dinner, and then they sit on the porch and watch the sun set while Grandpa tells another story of their African heritage.

The action is simple—deceptively so—but Thomas' mind is always moving, remembering what Grandpa has taught him, questioning, stretching to understand how old Grandpa's fossil fish is, how long ago his ancestors lived in Benen, and so on. Grandpa is a patient teacher, and the bond between these two family members is strong.

Drive to understand; Using ability. This book is recommended for the quality of the conversations between Thomas and his grandfather, both remembered and current, and for the sense of wonder, both described in the story and evoked in the reader. How can we comprehend a time span of millions of years and recognize what a small part of history is represented by the time span we know? Even as adults, we return to the effort to comprehend this—an effort that never fails to stretch our minds and spirits. Children can benefit from being introduced to this practice of wondering by an adult who shares his or her own such practice with them.

Thomas, Joyce Carol. *Brown Honey in Broomwheat Tea.* Illustrated by Floyd Cooper. HarperTrophy, 1996.

In this collection of a dozen lyrical poems, National Book Award winner Thomas writes of home and loving family, as well as of family trees broken by the journey from Africa. Mostly she speaks of the beauty and strength of African-American identity in lilting, thoughtful poetry, reinforced by earth-toned illustrations that celebrate strong and loving family relationships.

Drive to understand. Children who do not share Thomas's African-American heritage may derive new understanding from poems that address it, even obliquely, such as "Brown Honey in Broomwheat Tea" and "Family Tree."

Identity. Children of this age can enjoy poems that speak of self-worth and self-confidence, such as "Cherish Me," "I Am a Root," and "Becoming the Tea."

Using ability. The beginnings of a decision to use ability may be found in "Magic Landscape."

Tolan, Stephanie. *A Time to Fly Free.* Scribner, 1983.

By the time he is in fifth grade, Joshua Taylor has developed a defensive wall to keep from being hurt by the cruelty of other students to animals, to weaker students, and to himself. But this year, the wall no longer protects him. His teacher is unimaginative and humorless, and school is unbearably boring. One day, Josh simply walks out. His parents agree to a temporary leave of absence while his mother looks for a new school, and Josh begins to work with Rafferty, a retired man who cares for injured birds. Even here, Josh cannot escape the fact of cruelty, and he begins to face his own responsibility to accept it and to go on in spite of it.

Tolan writes with perception of the feelings of a highly gifted child who does not fit in, describing both his stress and the reactions and concern of the adults around him. This book will invite discussion of both sensitivity in people and sensitivity to the environment. It will give parents and teachers insight into the feelings of children like Josh that may surprise them.

Aloneness; Introversion. Why does Josh leave school? Do you understand how he felt? Have you ever known anyone else who you think might have felt that way? What clues do you have that make you think so? If such a person cannot leave school, how else can he or she deal with the situation? Is it all right that Josh does not have close friends his own age? Describe Josh as you think he will be when he is an adult.

Differentness; Identity; Intensity. Why is Josh so comfortable with Rafferty and his parents, but not with his own classmates? Does this bother him? What will he be like when he is grown up?

Using ability. What effect will dropping out of school have on Josh's ability to make good use of his intelligence? What responsibility (if any) does a bright person have to use his or her intelligence? Who determines what is a "good" use of intelligence? In making that decision for yourself, what factors would you consider?

Ward, Lynd. *The Silver Pony.* Houghton Mifflin, 1992.

Fully annotated in the Early Elementary section, this book can be used with older elementary children, too. The stories they tell about the pictures should be more detailed than those of younger children.

Creativity; Introversion. Discussion can focus on the loneliness of each child that the boy visits and on what compensations they may have. Children of this age can develop an appreciation of the fact that there are other people like them in the world, even though they may not live nearby. As they grow older, they will have opportunities to meet more people like them.

Whelan, Gloria. *Miranda's Last Stand.* Harpercollins, 1999.

After Miranda's father is killed in the Battle of Bull Run, she and her mother stay at Fort Lincoln, where her father had been stationed, and Mama supports them as a laundress for the soldiers. Growing up at the fort, Miranda is taught to hate Indians, especially Sitting Bull, who led the Sioux at the Battle of Bull Run. When Miranda is 10, Mama receives a letter saying that Miranda has inherited her grandparents' farm. They long to move, but first they must save enough money to last until the first crops come in. Then Buffalo Bill Cody hears of Mama's skill as a painter, and he asks her to travel with his Wild West Show and paint backdrops of the West. In Buffalo Bill's Wild West Show there is an entire Indian village, including three children who become Miranda's friends, and later, Sitting Bull himself. When Miranda hears Sitting Bull tell the story of Bull Run from his point of view, she realizes that she must give up her hate, even though she knows Mama cannot.

Miranda's story is set first in the Dakota Territory in 1886 and then moves from Chicago to Washington, D.C. and the northeastern states. The description of life in Buffalo Bill's Wild West

Show and of the people—including Mr. Cody, Annie Oakley, and Sitting Bull—is a wonderful example of historical fiction for this age group. The beautiful descriptions of the land give evidence that Whelan has traveled the routes she describes. She raises a complex question and handles it smoothly in a fashion well-suited for children of Miranda's age, making this book an excellent introduction to a balanced picture of one of the most dramatic and misunderstood events of late 19th-century United States history.

Drive to understand. The Battle of Bull Run was such an emotional event that only recently have children's books begun to appear with a balanced view. For older students in this age group, this book can be used along with Marrin's *Sitting Bull and His World*, described in the Middle School section.

Identity. Miranda finally realizes that she is a person who can "climb out of herself." What does she mean? Can you do that? If you have not done it yet, can you learn how to?

Moral concerns. Was Miranda right or wrong to hide her mother's money? To give Sitting Bull's medicine to her mother? How do you reach your answers to these questions—what factors do you consider?

Relationships with others. It seems unlikely that Miranda and Quick Fox could become friends, but they do. What do they have in common? What does each one of them do to overcome the barrier between them? What personal qualities did it take for each of them to be able to do this? Which of these qualities do you have, and when have you used them in this way?

Willard, Nancy. *A Visit to William Blake's Inn: Poems for Innocent and Experienced Travelers.* Illustrated by Alice and Martin Provenson. Harcourt Brace, 1987.

This collection of poems about a visit to an inn hosted by poet William Blake is enhanced by pictures of the inn's interior, with one wall cut away like a dollhouse so readers can see everything inside. Each poem creates an imaginative world of its own, but all are tied together by the mystical spirit of William Blake and the poetry he wrote 200 years ago.

Drive to understand; Using ability. Willard's poems should be read aloud and enjoyed. Some lines could be memorized for the sheer pleasure of knowing them by heart. The illustrations can be examined for the unexpected surprises on every page. A few poems written by Blake could be read aloud, too. Willard has used some of Blake's rhythms, and children will enjoy comparing them.

Wisniewski, David. *Golem*. Clarion, 1996.

Over 400 years ago, the Blood Lie, a rumor that Jews used the blood of Christian children to make Passover bread, swept over the city of Prague. Christians who believed this story threatened the lives of the Jews of Prague. According to legend, in seeking a way to avoid violence, Rabbi Loew created a Golem, shaping a man out of clay and bringing the clay figure to life with words from the Cabala. Rabbi Loew explained to Golem that it had been created to protect the Jews by night and to serve in the synagogue by day. When the Jews were no longer in danger, Golem would return to the earth. Eventually, the enemies of the Jews rioted at the gates of the Jewish ghetto. In protecting the Jews inside, Golem grew to enormous size and strength, raging out of control and causing too much destruction. After this, the emperor guaranteed the safety of the Jews, and Rabbi Loew caused Golem to return to clay. This was a poignant moment, for Golem had learned to love life. The legend concludes with the possibility that, when needed, the Golem could come to life again.

The Golem legend raises questions of good, evil, and the gray area between the two, in which humans sometimes lose control over forces too strong for them. Wisniewski illustrates his version of the Golem legend with forceful cut-paper collages so compelling that this book earned the Caldecott Medal in 1997. A long author's note at the end summarizes the history of the Golem, the Cabala, Rabbi Loew's historical connection to the story, and a brief history of persecution of the Jews. It compares the Golem story to the Frankenstein story and ends with the suggestion that the impetus for the Golem, the need of the Jews for protection, lives on in the nation of Israel.

Drive to understand. Why were rumors like the Blood Lie started?

Moral concerns. What characters in this story represent evil? In what way? Who represents good? In what way? Which does the Golem represent, and how? Name characters in other stories who represent both good and evil. How is this true of people?

Relationships with others. Relationships between two groups of people, the Jews and the Christians, in this story were very bad indeed. How did individuals in the story work to bring peace? When two individuals reach the point of telling untrue stories and threatening each other, what can be done to improve the situation? What have you done to improve such relationships?

Yep, Laurence. *Hiroshima.* Scholastic, 1995.

This short novella is the story of Sachi, a composite of several survivors who were children in Hiroshima at the time of the bombing and who later came to the United States. On the morning of the bombing, Sachi and her sister Riko are walking together to their jobs that support the war effort—Sachi to join her classmates in tearing down houses to form a fire lane, and Riko to answer telephones at army headquarters in an old castle. Meanwhile, the *Enola Gay* is flying toward Hiroshima with one 8900-pound atom bomb, its American crew hoping this bomb will end a terrible war begun four years earlier, when Japanese pilots attacked American ships at Pearl Harbor on a quiet morning like this one.

In spare prose, Yep reviews the attack and its aftermath, including statistics—which, he tells us in an Afterword, were difficult to verify. No one really knows how many people were living in Hiroshima, how many were killed that day, or how many died later from radiation. Sachi survives by jumping into a river with many others, but her face is terribly disfigured, and 10 years later she is one of 25 "Hiroshima Maidens" brought to the United States for 18 months of plastic surgery performed by volunteer American doctors. Now every year on August 6th, she is among the Japanese who place candles in boxes on the river in memory of those who died on that date in 1945. Every year new names are added to the list, as survivors continue to die from radiation poisoning.

Drive to understand; Moral concerns. This book is easy to read but may be difficult to discuss. The story is told without sentimentality, so it can be used simply as an informational piece. But Yep includes a chapter on efforts made toward world peace since the bombing, and his book can also be a point of departure for discussion of current efforts to curtail nuclear weapons.

Yep, Laurence. *Later, Gator.* Hyperion, 1995.

Teddy is the unsentimental but imaginative older brother who gives the considerate and thoughtful Bobby practical gifts, such as socks, partly out of his resentment at how much everyone likes Bobby. This time, he outdoes his own reputation for causing trouble: he gives Bobby a pet alligator. To his astonishment, Bobby is thrilled, their mother falls in line, and the relatives are impressed. But their father, whose chicken dinner was fed to the alligator before he got home, announces that henceforth Oscar will eat garbage. Suddenly, Teddy is helping Bobby find food for the alligator. Their search through Chinatown's restaurant garbage cans alarms the members of their father's club, who immediately assume that his business is failing and rally to help the boys find food. As the story plays itself out, Teddy realizes that Bobby is more perceptive than he thought, and he begins to feel protective and brotherly toward Bobby.

Basing his story on a childhood experience with an alligator named Oscar and a brother with whom he grew up in San Francisco, Yep closes with an Afterword, stating that now that alligators have been declared endangered, he knows it was wrong to buy one. But he has written a warm and funny story that will keep young readers laughing, and give them something to think about regarding sibling relationships. At the same time, he gently reminds us that there is more to the lives of Chinese people in San Francisco than tourists see in restaurants.

Relationships with others. Bobby says, kindly, that it takes someone like him to handle their friends and someone like Teddy to handle their enemies. What does he mean by this? Which role would you play? What are Bobby's strengths? What are Teddy's strengths? What can they offer each other? What can they learn from each other?

Sensitivity. What examples of Bobby's sensitivity can you identify? Can you follow them? What examples can you give of sensitivity in your own recent experience?

Yolen, Jane. *The Boy Who Had Wings.* Illustrated by Helga Aichinger. Crowell, 1974.

In ancient Thessaly, Actos is born with wings. His father is ashamed of so different a child, and his mother makes a cape to hide the wings. Actos grows up isolated from other children, never attempting to fly or to let others know that he has wings. Then, his father is trapped in a snowstorm, and Actos, using his wings at last, is the only one who can find and rescue him. Still, his family ignores him until finally his wings shrivel and drop away—but Actos remembers always the soaring freedom of flight.

The author writes that the inspiration for this story is both mythological and autobiographical. "It might also serve as biography for anyone who has ever been blessed with a gift—whether of writing, painting, or the like. For to be different…is not an easy thing when, as a child, you are longing to be like everyone else. I think I have been much luckier than Actos. Though there were times when I would have loved to be average, not a writer, I neither lost my wings nor gave them away. And now that I know that my writing can bring pleasure to others…I am grateful and proud of my wings."

Differentness; Identity. This picture book is recommended here for older children who can discuss symbolism. What different kinds of wings are people born with? How do parents and others avoid or hide a child's wings? What are your wings?

Using ability. What happens to a person who never uses his wings? How can people grow up without losing their wings or giving them away? What adults do you know who only learned to use and enjoy their wings in adulthood—like the author? What are you doing to keep your wings?

Middle School (Grades Six – Eight)

Abeel, Samantha. *Reach for the Moon: What Once Was White.* Illustrated by Charles R. Murphy. Pfeiffer-Hamilton, 1994.

Inspired by the works of an established artist, 13-year-old Samantha Abeel has responded with moving, insightful poetry and prose. Charles Murphy's watercolors are realistic but often have mystical overtones; Abeel's writings tell the story or reflect the emotion she perceives in each painting.

The story of how this book came to be is as inspirational as the book itself. Samantha Abeel is not only gifted but also learning-disabled. For the first years of schooling, her inability to comprehend numbers, tell time, or make change overshadowed her insight and her verbal gifts. Recognizing Samantha's writing talent, her seventh-grade English teacher, Roberta Williams, chose to encourage her strength and to overlook difficulties with spelling, verb tenses, and due dates. At the request of Elizabeth Abeel, Samantha's mother (herself an artist), Williams arranged a summer writing program for Samantha based on the art of family friend Charles Murphy. The result is not only this book; it is also a success story for Samantha and a demonstration of what can happen when schools, parents, and mentors work together on behalf of a child who does not fit the mold.

Differentness; Using ability.

Adderholdt, Miriam and Jan Goldberg. *Perfectionism: What's Bad about Being Too Good?* Illustrated by Caroline Price Schwert. Free Spirit, 1999.

Many gifted teenagers are victims of perfectionism, harboring so strong a desire to do everything perfectly that they consider second place or a grade of "B" a failure. Some go so far as to avoid risking that failure by refusing to accept new challenges or to take advanced courses.

Perfectionism speaks to these students, describing its effects on the mind, body, and relationships and then prescribing practical steps toward becoming more realistic about expectations. Counselors, teachers, and librarians will find the book a useful tool for school-based discussions of giftedness, and parents can use it effectively in the home. The insights it offers are as important for adults working with gifted youngsters as they are for the students themselves.

This book can be used independently by students in the middle grades or in senior high. For younger students, parents can gather ideas from the book and present them to their children in whatever way seems appropriate.

Perfectionism; Using ability.

Alexander, Lloyd. *Westmark.* Laurel Leaf, 1982. (A trilogy including *The Kestrel*, 1982 [out of print] and *The Beggar Queen*, 1985.)

A printer's apprentice who flees when his master's press is destroyed in a time of political upheaval, Theo meets a rich assortment of characters in quick succession: a street urchin; two "river rats"; a charlatan and his sidekick, a dwarf; revolutionary students, including a cartoonist and a thief; courtiers; and royalty—all of whom reappear as the trilogy unfolds. Ruled by a weak king who is controlled by a power-hungry chief minister, Westmark falls into war with a neighboring kingdom as civil unrest builds. The street urchin, Mickle, learns that she is Westmark's princess, and Theo grows to love Mickle while he also joins the revolutionary students who help Mickle's army defend

Westmark from the neighboring Regian army. Far from staying in the safety of the palace, Mickle proves to be a fine general. When the war against the Regians is won, however, she and Theo must address the civil unrest within Westmark and a further threat from the exiled chief minister.

This trilogy traces Theo's growth from a young and naive printer's devil to a thoughtful, complex young man who recognizes and regrets his own potential for violence. His loyalties are divided first between the monarch and the rebels who struggle for a republic, then between his natural pacifism and the raging desire for vengeance that rises when a friend is killed. At the same time, he tries to understand his motivations—to please one of the revolution's leaders, Justin, or to follow his own inner commands.

The writing is deceptively simple, and the plot perhaps too dependent on coincidences, but the ideas are demanding and require a thoughtful response. Intellectual challenge is also provided by frequent shifts in locale as different facets of the story come into play.

Drive to understand. Discussion related to intellectual curiosity will view the story from a socio-political level, looking, for example, at the causes of political unrest. Alexander has based his story on the history of the French Revolution. What are the similarities between pre-revolutionary France and Westmark? Why is Westmark ripe for rebellion?

Identity; Intensity. Readers can interpret the story at a personal level, exploring the development of Theo's character as he grows. What results does his need to prove himself lead to for himself? For others?

Moral concerns. What does Theo learn as he struggles with the pacifist and the warrior within his character? What contradictory values or impulses do you recognize within yourself? What can you learn from Theo's experience?

Using ability. How can Florian so steadfastly oppose his background, giving up his birthright? What motivates him?

Arkin, Alan. *The Lemming Condition*. Illustrated by Joan Sandin. HarperTrade, 1989.

On the day of the great leap into the sea, a lemming named Bubber talks to his friend Crow, who raises questions Bubber can't answer: *Why* would they jump into the water? Can they swim? In his confusion, Bubber turns to Arnold, a lemming he has always admired, and finds Arnold uninterested in the questions. His Uncle Claude assures him that there is no problem; it's just something lemmings do. Seeing that he will not learn more from a fellow lemming, Bubber returns to Crow, who flies him to a pond so he can test how water feels. When he realizes he cannot swim, a sense of doom overtakes Bubber. An eccentric old lemming reassures him, saying the race to the sea won't happen because lemmings can't agree on anything: "You couldn't get an agreement on what time to have lunch, never mind a mass suicide."

When the run begins, Bubber joins it, more afraid of isolation than of the consequences of the run to the sea and feeling close to other lemmings for the first time in his life. But when the ocean looms ahead, Bubber stops and hides among rocks so the tide of lemmings will not carry him with it. The next morning, he returns to the burrows where he finds a few surviving baby lemmings who have slept through the run. Foreseeing that the whole process will begin anew with them, Bubber passes by, heading east away from the ocean and telling the young ones he is not a lemming anymore. "What are you then?" they ask. "I'll let you know when I find out," Bubber answers.

Aloneness; Differentness. The Lemming Condition is a good starting point for discussion of the importance of standing alone and doing your own thinking. Explore the role of each character and what they represent: Arnold, the blindly-followed leader; the old lemming, an ineffective rebel; Crow, the questioner; Bubber, the young seeker. Who are their counterparts in a real-life scenario of following the crowd without thinking? What makes Bubber stop running? Did he make the right decision? Why?

Identity. Could you play the role of the Crow—the questioner—for yourself? If not, who plays it for you? Consider how difficult life will be for Bubber alone. How hard would life be if you made Bubber's choice? Would it be worth it? Where would you find help?

Avi. *The Fighting Ground.* HarperTrophy, 1987.

Jonathan is 13, tilling the fields with his father near Trenton, New Jersey, when the bell from the tavern a mile and a half distant sounds an alarm. It's April 3, 1778; his father is recovering from a war wound, and Jonathan is sent to learn the news, and then—both parents order—he is to return home immediately. Learning that 15 Hessians are marching from Pennington, and eager to fight, Jonathan disregards his parents' directive and joins the hastily-gathered band of colonists under command of a zealous and not entirely trusted corporal. All is confusion when they meet the enemy on the road; Jonathan flees and is captured by three Hessians. Neither Jonathan nor they know who won the battle, and although they speak only German (translated in the back of the book), making verbal communication impossible, Jonathan begins to feel a degree of comfort with them. They find an abandoned farmhouse for shelter, and when Jonathan enters a shed for a bucket with which to milk the cow, he discovers a young child, a boy who will not speak to Jonathan but who, when Jonathan asks "Mama?," points to where his parents lie shot. In the night, as the Hessians sleep, Jonathan escapes with the boy and runs through darkness, stumbling upon the remnants of the colonial band. A Frenchman in the group speaks to the child, who in a torrent of French tells of his parents' deaths and shrinks from the Corporal, who wants to return to the house to kill the Hessians. The Corporal insists that Jonathan lead the way, but it becomes clear that the Corporal has been there before. It was he who had killed the boy's parents, because they were informers. In an agony of indecision, Jonathan switches loyalties from the Corporal to the Hessians and back, but he is finally forced at gunpoint to aid in the killing of the Hessians. He returns home just 24 hours after he left, changed forever.

Chapters are titled by the time, highlighting the brevity of this period that changes Jonathan's life. There is a complete lack of the glory that Jonathan had expected; he experiences only fear and confusion and uncertainty as to what the colonists are doing and why. Germans, Americans, and French are all good and bad by turns—human, sympathetic characters with flaws. Avi has written a story of how war takes over, ignoring human values.

Drive to understand. Discuss the differences between what Jonathan expected and what he found. How does the reality of Jonathan's experience square with what we see of war—or any kind of violence—on television? Analyze how representatives of each nationality are admirable and despicable. What is Avi saying by depicting them in this way?

Moral concerns. How did Jonathan's view of his father change? Did any of your views change as a result of reading this book? Should the Revolutionary War have been fought? Were there other ways of settling the issues? Are there now?

Avi. *Nothing but the Truth.* Avon, 1991.

Philip Malloy is a high-spirited ninth grader, passionate about track and less interested in English. His English teacher, Miss Narwin, is passionate about literature and less understanding of the extra-curricular interests of ninth-grade boys. Unable to take Jack London and *Call of the Wild* seriously, Philip earns a "D" in English and is stunned to learn that he cannot try out for the track team with a "D" on his record. Things deteriorate from there. Encouraged by a homeroom teacher who is casual about rules, Philip hums along with *The Star-Spangled Banner* after he is transferred to the homeroom of Miss Narwin, who takes literally the rule that students must "stand at respectful, silent attention" for the playing of the national anthem. She sends him to the office, and due to another rule that cannot be bent, Philip is suspended. Not listening to Philip carefully enough to understand all the nuances of the situation, his parents encourage him to stand up for his rights. Because of similar partial understanding on the part of school authorities, each with his or her own agenda, the incident explodes into a national scandal. With one miscommunication after another, the situation spins entirely out of control; in the end, no one wins.

Written as a documentary, this book is entertaining as a satire on high school rules, but it is more than that. A sympathetic reading yields insight into the motives of each character. The ease with which a number of small, subtle shadings of the story build inexorably into a major misunderstanding is instructive. Philip is not unlike many students who would score well on a test of intellectual ability but who lack the interpersonal ability to see from someone else's point of view.

Differentness; Identity; Relationships with others. Realistically, what could Philip have done to get along better with Miss Narwin? What in his background or personality prevented him from doing this? When could Philip have asked for advice, and from whom? Why did he not do this? If you could advise Philip, what would you say? What have you learned from his experience that might be useful to you?

Moral concerns; Using ability. Choose a member of the school faculty or administration in the story and consider whether he or she did anything wrong, and if so, why. Ask the same questions regarding Philip, Philip's parents, one of the other students, and the media. What were the consequences for each?

Avi. *The True Confessions of Charlotte Doyle.* Illustrated by Ruth Murray. Avon, 1992.

In the summer of 1832, 13-year-old Charlotte Doyle boards the *Seahawk* in Liverpool to rejoin her family in Providence. Though her father had planned carefully so that she would be accompanied, the other passengers do not arrive. Charlotte, a young lady taught to obey her elders and to avoid informal contact with servants, sails with only Captain Jaggery and his rough, rebellious crew for company. She soon realizes that she is in grave danger and must decide where her loyalties lie. Because she has to, she learns to be a sailor, doing so well that she earns the crew's respect. The Charlotte Doyle who disembarks in Providence in August is very different from the girl who had left the Barrington School for Better Girls in June.

Appealing to both boys and girls, Charlotte's story is much more than just good mystery and adventure, although it is certainly that. Charlotte must change internally, without guidance or model, in order to survive. When she joins her family, she is expected to change again, a challenge she will not accept.

Arrogance. Charlotte would not have called herself arrogant, but readers of her story might. What role does arrogance play in her decisions?

Drive to understand. Avi's story offers readers a compelling picture of life in the early 19th century, providing plenty of opportunity for comparisons and further exploration.

Identity. Discussion can center around Charlotte's decisions. Why would she adapt to the sailors' life, yet be unwilling to re-adapt to her family's? Which is more truly Charlotte, and why? In 10 years, will Charlotte have one life or the other, or a blend? If a blend, describe what you think it will be.

Relationships with others. What can you learn from Charlotte's ability to get along with the sailors?

Using ability. How would the social rules of her time affect Charlotte's future? Are there situations now that cause people to straddle two lives, two expressions of themselves? How is it done? Is it healthy for them?

Billingsley, Franny. *The Folk Keeper.* Atheneum, 1999.

On the Mainland and in the northern isles, Folk Keepers are those whose duty it is to feed and pacify the Folk—vicious cave creatures, mostly teeth and wet mouth, who eat only flesh—to keep them from harming animals and crops. To gain the power of a Folk Keeper, a post awarded only to boys, Corinna has disguised herself as "Corin." Lacking the opportunity for an apprenticeship, she learns the trade by native ability, wit, and a toughness that places the highest priority on personal survival, with a quickness to seek vengeance when she is threatened and a determination to retain the independence she has won. When she is summoned by Lord Merton to go to his Manor house at Cliffsend, far to the north, she refuses his first offer—that she will be raised as a lady (for she knows that ladies can be powerless)—and only later agrees to go on the condition that she be appointed Folk Keeper for the estate. At Cliffsend, she is treated as part of the family and is befriended by Finian, heir to the Manor House and the estate. To protect herself from these northern Folk, stronger and fiercer by far than those she has known on the Mainland, she must learn who the Lady Rona was, and why there is a tiny grave near the chapel. She finds that she must also protect herself and Finian from Sir Edward, who had hoped to inherit from Lord Merton. As she does so, facing darkness and danger, she also learns who she is, the source of the strange powers she has always had, and how to regain one she has lost: the power of The Last Word.

Drawn from the selkie legends of the Scottish islands, *The Folk Keeper* is told through Corinna's journal, marked by saints' days and solstice rhythms. It can be enjoyed simply as a good story, or perhaps as an introduction to fantasy or to the folklore of the northern British Isles—but Corinna's story also serves as a metaphor for finding ourselves. Corinna gains control over her own life only when she gives up the power she has known as Corin. Determined to follow her lonely path independently, she finds at the last minute that there is more promise and growth in sharing her destiny.

Arrogance; Using ability. Early in the story, Corinna is proud of her position: "I control the Folk. Here I'm queen of the world." With her statement in mind, explain this: Arrogance is often the other face of fear. Give examples from your own experience. What happens to Corinna's arrogance as she learns more about her abilities?

Differentness. Corinna is different in many ways. How is this a problem for her? When is it not a problem? When it's not a problem, what factors make it unimportant that she is different?

Identity. "There is a price you pay for power," Corinna writes. What price has she paid? What does she gain when she gives up the power? Name others you know, in public or private life, who have traded something of their identity for power. For what asset besides power might one pay with a loss of personal identity? If you are doing this, what would you change? What would you gain if changed?

Relationships with others. Corinna has a strong need to take vengeance when she feels wronged; Finian does not understand this. What is the reason for the different response of each? What does Corinna learn from this, and how does she change?

Bond, Nancy. *A String in the Harp.* Aladdin, 1996.

Unhappily spending a year in Wales while his father teaches at the University of Aberystwyth, Peter Morgan finds on the seacoast a strange silver object—a tuning key for a harp. The key sings to him, enabling him to see events that happened hundreds of years ago—scenes which eventually Peter realizes are from the life of the 6th-century Welsh bard, Taliesin, to whom the key belonged. As Peter concentrates on Taliesin's story, he becomes more distant from his family. His father and his sisters, Becky and Jen, become more concerned about him. At last, with his sisters' support, Peter realizes what he must do about the key, and the family is reunited.

The fantasy story of Peter's visions of Taliesin is convincingly counterbalanced by the reality of the area of Wales in which the Morgans live and the Welsh people who become their friends. Bond's sense for the setting—both geographical and psychological—is sure, and readers will feel that they have gained some important knowledge about the essence of Wales.

Aloneness. Jen thinks that perhaps Gwilym isn't "solitary from choice." Why then is he solitary? Is his aloneness something to worry about? If so, what should Gwilym do to improve his situation? What should others do to help him?

Drive to understand. This book is part realism, part fantasy. How can you balance the rational and irrational aspects of the story?

Identity. What differences are there in Jen's and Becky's responses to Peter's behavior? How do they correspond to the reactions of Dr. Owen and Dr. Rhys? Why do these people respond so differently?

Conford, Ellen. *And This Is Laura.* Pocket Books, 1987.

Everyone in Laura's family has a special talent except Laura. Even when she learns that she is psychic and gives a credible performance as the second lead in a school play on short notice, her feelings of being ordinary and therefore unworthy persist. When she finally expresses her sense of inadequacy to her parents, they point out that she is an "A" student. They both explain that she is valuable to them as a person, not for her gifts. Her gifts are for her to enjoy, not for them to use as a basis for loving her.

Laura is an example of a sibling unsure of where she fits in within a gifted family. Not recognizing or appreciating her own talents until circumstances or other people point them out, she is like many gifted girls who minimize the quality and importance of their abilities, limiting what they accomplish because of a low self-concept.

Identity. In what different ways does Laura recognize each of her gifts?

Relationships with others. If you were Laura, would you be convinced by her parents' reasons for loving her? Why or why not? Why is it especially difficult for people who have a lot of talent to know why other people like them?

Using ability. What difference will it make to Laura to have learned about her ability? What difference will it make to others?

Cooper, Susan. *The Dark Is Rising.* Aladdin, 1999.

On his eleventh birthday Will Stanton learns that he is one of the Old Ones, called to struggle through the ages against the Dark. The Dark is rising this Christmas season in one of a series of attempts to dominate the world. Will's task is to search for the six Signs that the Old Ones will need in the final battle against the Dark. His search takes him to distant places and to bygone centuries, while he learns, under the tutelage of Merriman Lyon, to use the powers of the Old Ones. Throughout, he remains an 11-year-old boy, living in the warmth of a large family.

This is the second book of Cooper's *Dark Is Rising* sequence. The first is *Over Sea, Under Stone,* and following *The Dark Is Rising* are *Greenwitch, The Grey King,* and *Silver on the Tree.* All are good adventure stories, but they also hold much to ponder for those who continue to think about a book long after they have finished reading.

Drive to understand. A Newbery Honor Book, this well-written fantasy is excellent for good readers—challenging in its structure, as Will travels from one century to another and meets some of the same characters in each. The sequence of five books is steeped in the folklore of old Britain; some readers will want to know more about the body of lore that is so basic to much of our present heritage.

Cooper, Susan. *Dawn of Fear.* Illustrated by Margery Gill. Aladdin, 1989.

Living near London during World War II, Derek and his friends, Peter and Geoffrey, are thrilled by the excitement of bomb raids that interrupt their school days. Wishing they could stay outside and watch the planes flying overhead, they obey the air raid drills reluctantly. Nighttime raids, when they and their families must leave their warm beds and go to their shelters, are a nuisance but not really disturbing to the boys. Their main interest is the camp they are building in a field near their homes, where they stow precious gear in case of an imagined attack, unconsciously imitating the family shelters. They are pleased when

Tom, a 16-year-old who will soon join the Merchant Navy, offers to help. When a neighboring gang destroys the camp, Tom leads them in retaliation in the form of a mud-ball raid. But the mud-ball slinging ends in a serious standoff between Tom and the leader of the other gang, a boy older than Tom who is shirking his military duty. As the younger boys watch, they are overwhelmed by the reality of the anger they see, which goes far beyond their games. They recognize the potential for real danger, and for the first time, all of them fear the power of violence. That night, before Derek has had time to come to terms both with the strength of the adult anger he has just witnessed and with his own fear, another raid brings the real war much too close to home.

Since most readers think of Susan Cooper as an author of fantasy (see above), it may be surprising to find this earlier novel—a work of historical fiction written with clear insight into the psychology of very real adolescent boys. It is valuable because it is definitely a "boy's book" (although girls will be moved by it, too), and because it offers a view of another society in another time and provides some vocabulary challenges. But it is also valuable because it so skillfully contrasts the glamour of the face of war with the truly frightening realities behind it. It can be used with early adolescents in discussing the strength of human emotions and the danger inherent in romanticizing them without respecting their dark side.

Drive to understand. How is the fight between Tom and Johnny connected to the war? Why do the younger boys feel fear as they watch the older boys fight, although they have not feared the bombs? Is it good or bad to feel fear? Why?

Identity. How does Derek change during the time frame of this story? What more does he learn about himself? How will he be different in the future? What events in your life (including events less serious than Derek's experience) have caused you to know yourself better and to grow?

Relationships with others. What is the difference between Derek's friendship with Peter and his friendship with Geoffrey?

When does it first appear that Geoffrey may be more "real" than Derek had thought? What will help them become closer friends in the future?

Creech, Sharon. *Chasing Redbird.* HarperTrophy, 1997.

Zinny (for Zinnia) Taylor is somewhere in the middle of seven children, growing up on a farm near Bybank, Kentucky. Although—or because—she is part of a large and loving family, at 12, Zinny feels lost. Since her parents are always busy with the others, Zinny spends as much time as possible with Aunt Jessie and Uncle Nate, whose house "fits snug up against" Zinny's. Things are quieter on their side of the house—their daughter Rose, who was just Zinny's age, died of whooping cough caught from Zinny when the girls were four, and since then they have loved to have Zinny there. Just recently, though, Aunt Jessie died suddenly, and Zinny is sure it was her fault. And now Jake Boone has returned to Bybanks. When Jake brings gifts to Zinny, she believes that he is trying to reach her older sister May through her. In the past, boys who have liked Zinny at first have always later switched to May—perhaps because Zinny has a prickly exterior. In any case, Zinny has no idea why Jake would like her. In short, Zinny feels guilty and unlikable, and she does not talk much. Then she discovers the slate stones that mark the beginning of an old, long-overgrown trail which leads from Bybanks right through their farm. Zinny determines to clear the whole trail. As she does, working through the summer, she also uncovers her own tangled feelings, learns parts of her own story she had forgotten, and even comes to believe that Jake might like her after all.

This is a story for the better readers in this age group—for those who are able to interpret metaphor and who will enjoy the figurative language Zinny and her family use. Creech brings characters from one of her books into another—in *Chasing Redbird*, we hear about Zinny's best friend Sal, who has moved to Ohio—another loss for Zinny. Sal's story is told in *Walk Two Moons*, described next.

Identity. How does Zinny's compulsion to clear the trail relate to her search for her own identity, separate from the other Taylors? How aware does she become of her strengths, as well her weaknesses? How aware are you of your origins? Your strengths and weaknesses?

Introversion. Zinny clearly needs time alone. What other evidence is there that she tends toward introversion? If she saw herself in that light, what would she do to accommodate that after she finishes the trail?

Relationships with others. Why does Zinny treat others as roughly as she does? Why does she not believe that Jake could like her? How would she treat him if she believed otherwise? What does this say about relationships, in general?

Sensitivity. How do Zinny's parents show their awareness of her grieving for Aunt Jessie? For what else is Zinny grieving? Would you call Zinny a sensitive person? Why or why not? How aware are you of when others may be more sensitive to events than they show?

Creech, Sharon. *Walk Two Moons.* HarperTrophy, 1996.

A little more than a year after her mother left Sal and her father on their farm in Kentucky, Sal and her grandparents set out to trace her mother's journey to Idaho. On the week-long road trip, Sal tells Gram and Gramps the story of Phoebe, a girl Sal met when she and her father moved to Euclid, Ohio, shortly after her mother's departure. Sal and Phoebe became good friends, despite their differences—Phoebe's family is stiff and "respectable" in contrast to the simple warmth of Sal's father and Gram and Gramps. But Phoebe's mother disappeared too, giving the girls something in common and helping Sal put her own loss in perspective.

Although it is simply told, this winner of the 1995 Newbery Medal is a complex story—or rather, two stories, of Phoebe and of the trip to Idaho—many-layered and offering opportunities for serious discussion. Both girls are surrounded by loving adults, including their mothers; this is a book in which the characters search for understanding rather than laying blame. As Sal tells Phoebe's story, her own is blended with it, and the reader watches Sal glean snatches of insight from her own words.

A striking feature of the plot is how strong the characters are in their impacts on each other. Because the book is for younger readers, character analysis of each individual is sketchy, but the interrelationships among the people in the story are compelling. *Walk Two Moons* invites immediate re-reading. In fact, that might be a good idea with these questions in mind:

Identity. In what ways does Sal grow up in the year this story covers?

Relationships with others. What does Sal learn about her own situation from watching Phoebe's family? How does her experience help her be a friend when Phoebe's mother leaves? What does she see that Phoebe cannot see? Why? Why is Ben potentially a good friend for Sal? How do your feelings about Margaret change as you gain more information? How do your feelings about Ben change? Your feelings about Mrs. Winterbottom? Mr. Winterbottom? Sal's mother? How does learning more about people affect our relationships with them?

Curtis, Christopher Paul. *The Watsons Go to Birmingham—1963.* Laurel Leaf, 2000.

Kenny Watson is nine and his brother Byron is 13, "officially a teenage juvenile delinquent," according to Kenny. Their father has a terrific sense of humor; their mother is the kind of person who knows how to patch up a misunderstanding between Kenny and his best friend; and their little sister, Joetta, is so soft-hearted that she defends Byron no matter what he does. Against the background of this nurturing home life, both boys struggle with the dangers at school. Kenny has two major vulnerabilities—he is smart and likes to read, and he has a lazy eye—so he concentrates on defending himself against teasing and bullies. Byron is sometimes one of the bullies, and sometimes not; but always he is into more and more trouble.

Finally, their parents decide to take Byron to Momma's hometown in Alabama, where he will spend the summer with Grandma Sands, who has a reputation for toughness. Daddy readies the Brown Bomber, the 15-year-old family car, for the long drive from Michigan, and Momma carefully plans the trip for maximum economy, safety, and educational value. Byron turns sullen, and Kenny watches to see whether it will be Grandma Sands or Byron, the two meanest people he knows, who will win the epic battle he foresees. However, Grandma Sands turns out to be not big and mean, but old, tiny, quick, and so insightful and loving—but always in charge—that Kenny knows immediately that Byron will lose the battle. But in the few days of the Watsons' visit, they experience first-hand the racial tension growing all over the South; they no longer think Byron will be safer in Birmingham than in Flint. When they return home, Byron has a new perspective on himself and his family; he has grown up enough to be a proper big brother to Kenny and to begin to mold his own future.

The story is told through Kenny's eyes, a true and consistent view of the world as seen by a fourth-grade boy. This first novel is both a Newbery Honor Book and a Coretta Scott King Honor Book for 1996 and holds a long list of other honors. Although entirely fictional, it is based on the bombing of the 16th Avenue Baptist Church in Birmingham on September 15, 1963, in which four teenage girls were killed. Curtis has brought the impact of that bombing to life for the reader by making the Watson family real and then sending Joetta to church on the Sunday a bombing occurs. In an Epilogue, he outlines the story of the civil rights movement, placing the Watsons' trip to Birmingham in the center of history.

Aloneness. How does Kenny realize that he has been alone? What is his part in changing that? Is this an idea you can use?

Differentness. Kenny accepts the reality that he will be teased for being smart. Would this happen in your school? What is the best way to respond?

Drive to understand. This book can introduce children to the civil rights movement and to the need for it. Why does Momma plan so carefully for the trip? Why are she and the children frightened when they stop in Tennessee?

Identity. Kenny knows that he is smart and that he likes to read, but he often calls himself stupid. In what situations does he do this?

Moral concerns. The Watson children have apparently known little about racial tensions before they go to Alabama. What do you think will be their long-term response to what they learned there? What is your response?

Relationships with others. What is it about Kenny and Rufus that makes them good friends? What makes Byron change his behavior toward Kenny?

Sensitivity. Would you agree that Kenny and Bryon are sensitive people, but in different ways? Describe the differences.

Cushman, Karen. *The Midwife's Apprentice.* HarperTrophy, 1996.

When the story begins, the only name she knows is Brat. About 13 years old, she lives in medieval England without home or family and fends entirely for herself. Then the village midwife discovers Brat sleeping in a dung pile for the warmth. She calls her "Beetle" and agrees to provide food and shelter in exchange for work. The food and shelter are meager, and the midwife is stingy with her knowledge, too, but Beetle watches and learns as much as she can. As her confidence grows and she finds a place in the life of the village, Beetle changes her name again to one more fitting: Alyce. But she fails in her work one day and runs away, finding work in an inn. There, she learns that the one fault the midwife found in her was that she gave up. Alyce returns to the village, overcoming her timidity, and takes her place as the midwife's apprentice.

Winner of the Newbery Medal, this small book offers a vivid and unforgettable picture of medieval life. At the same time, it is a truly and simply told story of a complex process: the coming-of-age of a girl who at first has only her own resources for support. Alyce is plucky. She accepts help when it is offered, grasps at every opportunity to learn, adds a natural compassion to her increasing knowledge, and is willing to learn from her mistakes. Her story provides a good example for students who may be reluctant to do these things for themselves.

Achievement. What personal qualities does Alyce need in order to grow from being a homeless beggar to a midwife's apprentice? Which of these are also needed by young people growing up in the 21st century?

Drive to understand. What other books have you read that are set in medieval England or Europe? Imagine a conversation between Alyce and a character in one of those books. How would their stories be alike? How would they be different?

Perfectionism. What was it in her background that caused Alyce to decide to run away? When someone you know has given up, how was that person thinking as Alyce did?

Using ability. What factors does Alyce consider as she makes the decision to return to the village and pursue midwifery?

Danziger, Paula. *The Cat Ate My Gymsuit.* Paper Star, 1998.

Shy, overweight Marcy Lewis is propelled into the small group of student leaders when a favorite teacher is dismissed and Marcy proves her ability and willingness to speak out in the effort to have the teacher reinstated. To her amazement, Marcy finds that Joel, the smartest, most self-assured boy in the class, likes her— and that Joel's family life, like hers, is not entirely happy. As the students work together, they come into conflict with some members of the adult community, including Marcy's father, but Marcy's self-confidence grows.

It may be necessary to point out that this book was first published nearly 30 years ago, at the beginning of the women's movement, and to give some background on Marcy's mother's discomfort with speaking her own mind, since she may not seem credible to some readers. But that will not be a major problem for most students. The characters line up so clearly on one side or other of the issue of firing the teacher that it is easy to discuss the real theme of the book: standing up for one's own beliefs against following the majority—a good theme for middle school students to consider.

Aloneness. How does one decide when to be part of the majority and when to be different? Is it worthwhile for Marcy to be different? Is it worthwhile for you? Under what circumstances?

Identity. What makes shy Marcy speak up when Mr. Stone announces Ms. Finney's leaving? Why is Joel so self-confident? What does he mean when he says that when he grows up, he wants to be Joel Anderson?

Relationships with others. Marcy finds herself in a situation that gives her a chance to know other students better and gives them a chance to know her, too. How does that happen? What role does Marcy play in making it happen? In your own situation, what could you do to make it happen if you needed to? What might be the rewards of doing so?

de Kruif, Paul. *Microbe Hunters.* Harcourt Brace, 1996.

This exuberant book is a collection of biographies of the scientists (Pasteur, Koch, Bruce, Reed, Ehrlich, etc.) who worked to discover causes and cures of diseases such as anthrax, malaria, diphtheria, hydrophobia, yellow fever, and syphilis. Written in 1926, it is recommended with reservations because of stereotypical comments about women and various ethnic groups, and a more casual attitude toward experimenting with animals and human beings than we expect now.

Despite these drawbacks, the book can be useful. If adults discuss these characteristics with students in light of the time in which de Kruif wrote, they can then focus on what he intended to convey: a contagious enthusiasm for scientific search and the role of patient, persistent, routine, dull work—and luck—in bringing about exciting discoveries. These men were gifted, courageous, fallible, devoted, and above all, hard-working. The stories of their searching are still inspirational for young scientists.

Drive to understand. What questions does the book raise about medical ethics?

Using ability. What made these people work so hard? What causes would be likely to call forth such devotion in you?

Fenner, Carol. *Yolonda's Genius.* Illustrated by Raul Colon. Aladdin, 1997.

After one of her classmates is shot and some bigger boys introduce her six-year-old brother, Andrew, to drugs, Yolonda's mother moves her family from their Chicago neighborhood to Grand River, Michigan. Momma finds a good job and settles happily into a house with trees in the lawn, but Yolonda has more trouble adjusting to the slower pace of Grand River. It feels safe, and she misses the constant need to be alert to danger. Tall and heavy, smart and sharp-tongued, 11-year-old Yolonda has never been adept at the jump-rope games the other girls played—or at making friends. In Chicago, where most of the kids in her school were black, the social order had been clear. In integrated Grand River, it is murkier.

For Andrew, there are other problems. He has trouble reading and does not speak unless he must, but he expresses thoughts, feelings, and his considerable insight through the music he makes on the harmonica his father had given him when he was still in his crib. When Shirley Piper befriends Yolonda and asks if she is a genius, Yolonda looks up the word in the library. None of the definitions fits Yolonda, but when she reads a quotation from John Hersey—"True genius rearranges old material in a way never seen before"—Yolonda suddenly knows that Andrew is the genius in the family. When the safety of Grand River proves to be illusory and Andrew and his music are in danger, Yolonda makes it her business to prove Andrew's genius to the world. A visit to Aunt Tiny in Chicago and to the blues concerts in Grant Park gives her the opportunity she needs.

This Newbery Honor Book offers hints of many themes for discussion.

Achievement. Why does her mother object to Yolonda's dream of becoming a police officer? What do you think she should do? What do you think she will do?

Creativity. How does Andrew's musical talent help him? How might it be a problem for him?

Identity. Now that she has taken care of Andrew, what does Yolonda need to learn about herself?

Intensity. Why is Andrew so single-minded about his music? What are the advantages and disadvantages of that?

Relationships with others. Why is it hard for Yolonda to make friends? What does she need to learn?

Ferris, Jeri. *Native American Doctor: The Story of Susan LaFlesche Picotte.* Carolrhoda Books, 1991.

Susan LaFlesche (1865-1915), daughter of Omaha Chief Iron Eye, was sent to the Elizabeth Institute for Young Ladies in Elizabeth, New Jersey; to the Hampton Institute in Virginia; and to Women's Medical College in Philadelphia. She returned to the Omaha reservation in Nebraska to work as doctor, interpreter, and political leader for her people. In telling Susan's story, Ferris includes much information about American Indians' difficult transition from traditional to European ways, and she gives an unflinching portrayal of white domination, including the illegal purchase of native land (making farming impossible for American Indians) and the greed-motivated sale of alcohol.

Not fictionalized, this is a biography, with historical records used as sources for quotations. The illustrations are photographs taken during Susan's lifetime.

Using ability. Susan had many advantages, but she also faced many obstacles. What personal qualities helped her overcome those obstacles in order to make good use of her abilities and her opportunities? What elements in her environment, family, and background were helpful to her? If you had been Susan, what would have been most difficult for you? How would you have handled it?

Fox, Paula. *The Village by the Sea.* Yearling, 1990.

While her father has heart surgery, 10-year-old Emma is sent to stay with his sister, Aunt Bea, and her husband, Uncle Crispin. They live on Long Island in a house on the shore, a childless house where Emma is lonely until she meets Bertie, the girl next door. Emma and Bertie spend days building a village from shells, twigs, and other natural objects they find on the beach. Emma's stay remains difficult because of Aunt Bea, who is cold and unpredictable—not at all like Emma's father, Bea's much younger half-brother. Emma gradually pieces the family story together in conversations with family members and with Bertie, and she is finally able to forgive even Aunt Bea's most incomprehensible act.

The challenge in this book is the psychological study of Aunt Bea—and the requirement that the reader, too, piece together the family story from clues dropped in conversation. The tension and suspense are psychological—this is an introspective mystery, not an action book; it is about getting along with others by developing a sophisticated understanding of human behavior.

Relationships with others. Why is Aunt Bea hard to get along with? Could you have forgiven Aunt Bea as Emma does? If so, what kind of thinking and understanding would lead you to forgive her? What examples of understanding and forgiveness do you see in the people around you? In the adults? In the children? Can you remember a time when understanding a destructive act helped you withhold your anger?

Galbraith, Judy and Jim Delisle. *The Gifted Kids Survival Guide: A Teen Handbook.* Ed. by Pamela Espeland. Illustrated by Harry Pulver, Jr. Free Spirit, 1996.

This is the "revised, expanded, and updated edition" of a title that has been popular since 1983, written to and for teens and providing information about every aspect of giftedness that can be useful to them as they grow up gifted. After taking plenty of time to explain definitions of giftedness, intelligence, and testing, the authors discuss ways students can take charge of their own education. The final chapter, "On Being a Teenager," discusses adolescence in general, drugs and sex, and suicide among gifted teens, with suggestions for prevention.

The authors are veterans in the field of gifted education, and the conversational tone of the book attests to their knowledge and comfort with gifted adolescents.

Arrogance. In discussing how students can ask for appropriate educational programs, sample conversational ploys are presented that can be generalized to help young people understand how they can avoid sounding arrogant.

Identity; Relationships with others. A chapter devoted to relationships includes helpful information on finding friends, handling teasing, developing conversational strategies, and getting along with parents.

Perfectionism; Using ability. A segment offers suggestions for mastering this potentially destructive characteristic.

Garfield, Leon. *Smith.* Illustrated by Antony Maitland. Sunburst, 2000.

A street urchin and pickpocket in 18th-century London, Smith steals a document from a man who is then murdered by men seeking the document Smith has pilfered, but which he cannot read. The murderers then pursue Smith. In his flight, he meets and guides home a blind judge who takes Smith into his home. The suitor of the judge's daughter accuses Smith of the murder, and Smith goes to Newgate Prison. With the suitor's help, Smith escapes, but he has been led into a trap. As Smith tries to protect his friend the judge, he discovers that he is being betrayed by a highwayman that he has always admired. Eventually, the tangle of shifting friends and enemies is straightened out, with the suspense lasting until the very end.

Drive to understand. This exciting murder mystery, like all of Garfield's work, is well-written, challenging fare for good readers. Garfield provides a far better picture of the dangerous realities of the streets and highways in 18th-century England than any nonfiction description could. Most of the characters are rascals or worse, presented sympathetically but with no excuses offered for their behavior—good background for discussion of the social implications of poverty and the diversity of human character.

Greene, Bette. *Summer of My German Soldier.* Puffin, 1999.

Patty Bergen's parents are cold and distant; her father, in fact, is physically abusive to her. Living in a small Arkansas town during World War II, this 12-year-old experiences the loneliness that results both from such an emotionally barren home and from the lack of friends who can match her own highly verbal, quick-thinking nature. Only when visiting her maternal grandparents in Memphis, where the family's Jewish traditions are honored, does Patty feel at home.

When Anton Reiker, a German soldier, escapes from a nearby prisoner of war camp, Patty hides him in the apartment above the Bergen garage. The son of a history professor at the University of Goettingen, Anton had been a medical student in Germany before the war. He sees both beauty and value in Patty, and he is the first person she has met whose wide-ranging interests and good educational background provide companionship for her. Anton risks his safety in a bid to protect Patty from her father's beating, but then he must leave to avoid detection and bringing danger to Patty and Ruth, the family housekeeper who also protects Patty.

This book offers many themes for discussion: physical abuse, low self-esteem in both Patty and her father, the importance to Patty of Anton's caring for her and seeing good in her, and the distinction that must be made between "German" and "Nazi." And of course, there's prejudice—against Germans, African-Americans, and Jews. Of all the characters in the book, Anton—the German soldier, the enemy, the POW—and Ruth, the African American housekeeper, are the most prejudice-free and sympathetic.

Aloneness; Differentness. What qualities set Patty apart from others in the story? Why do some people see good in her? Why do others not? How do the reactions of others determine Patty's behavior? In what ways is she independent of their reactions? What is the basis of the courage that enables her to hide a POW?

Drive to understand. Explore the story of Anton's father's choice to be quiet and live—the evidence that there was opposition in Germany to Hitler's military policies.

Moral concerns. Consider the prejudice in the story against Germans, Jews, and Negroes. Who is prejudiced against whom? Explain why.

Hahn, Mary Downing. *Daphne's Book.* Camelot, 1995.

Jessica is dismayed when her seventh-grade English teacher pairs her with Daphne in a book writing and illustrating contest, but Mr. O'Brien will not change his mind. Daphne is the best artist and Jessica the best writer in the class, and together he expects that they will produce something really good. Jessica is losing her friendship with Tracey, and she is convinced that working with the silent and unpopular Daphne will accelerate that loss. As she gets to know Daphne, however, Jessica finds herself more comfortable with her than she was with Tracey. The two girls allow their imaginations to work, creating a fantasy world out of which comes their book.

As their friendship grows, Jessica visits Daphne at the home she shares with her younger sister Hope and their aging grandmother. The grandmother's health and mental state are rapidly deteriorating, but Daphne fears that she and Hope will be sent to an orphanage if anyone knows this. Finally the situation becomes so bad that Jessica tells her mother, breaking her promise to Daphne. Daphne's grandmother is sent to a hospital, where she dies, and Daphne and Hope go to a children's home. Daphne and Jessica are reconciled when Jessica visits to tell Daphne that their book has won the contest, and when she learns that Daphne and Hope will go to live with relatives of their mother whom the social worker has located.

The behavior of Daphne's grandmother and the old house in which Daphne lives are in disturbing contrast to Jessica's family, which is comfortable and stable even though her parents are divorced and her mother is about to remarry. Despite the differences, Jessica and Daphne come together because they find they can talk to each other better than to anyone else. They are alone but for this one friendship, and for the moment, it is enough.

Aloneness. What reasons might Mr. O'Brien have for pairing Jessica and Daphne, other than their talent? Why are they not popular? What qualities do they have that compensate for their lack of popularity? Predict their futures.

Relationships with others. Why are Jessica and Tracey moving apart? Why does Jessica want to hide her growing friendship with Daphne? What qualities in Jessica enable her to learn from this situation? In Jessica and Daphne's friendship, what does each girl learn about herself? Who benefits most from the relationship?

Hamilton, Virginia. *The Planet of Junior Brown.* Aladdin, 1993.

Junior Brown is obese, and he is an artist and a musician. The adults in his life are his mother (who wants Junior to be cultured but is not able to understand his art or listen to his music), his piano teacher (who is demented, but Junior cannot afford to recognize that), his absent father, and Mr. Pool, the school janitor. There is also Buddy, a fellow student who has no family and who is part of an underground network that helps homeless boys survive in New York City. Buddy and Mr. Pool watch Junior slip toward insanity, but they are eventually able to begin helping him back to reality.

Best for older students in this middle-school group, this well-written book offers challenging reading and at least two themes that would be useful for gifted students to discuss: the frustration of Junior's talent, symbolized by the silent pianos; and the challenge of getting along with others, exemplified by Buddy, a leader who progresses from teaching his boys to live for themselves to teaching them to live for others. In spite of his strength, it is clear that Buddy also needs help—a reminder that we are all interdependent, none of us completely self-sufficient.

Relationships with others. Why does Junior need Buddy? What does he offer to Buddy? How do Nightman and Franklin help each other? Identify a leader whom you follow. What do you offer to that person?

Using ability. What does Junior need in order to use his artistic and musical talents? What does Buddy need?

Hunt, Irene. *Across Five Aprils.* Illustrated by Albert John Pucci. Berkley, 1991.

Telling the story of a southern Illinois family through the five years of the American Civil War, this book depicts the pain of families and communities divided by loyalties to both North and South. Jethro Creighton is nine when the war begins, and within a year, he has the responsibility of managing the farm that feeds those family members still at home. Through letters, the family follows the sons who are at war, and they face danger and hatred because one son has joined the Confederate Army.

A minor theme is the growth of Jethro, whom his unlettered mother recognizes as having special talent. Encouraged by the schoolteacher before he goes off to war and by the newspaper editor in a nearby town, Jeth follows the war through newspapers and atlases and works to improve his crude country speech. He will be the first of the family to go to college.

Drive to understand. The book presents many ideas for discussion. In talking about giftedness, include the distinction between intelligence and education, the need to look behind poor speech patterns for a good mind, and the value of an education to those who cannot take it for granted.

Relationships with others. For what reasons do some people in this book criticize others? What is your own response to the criticisms, at the beginning of the book and at the end? In real life, what are your reasons for sometimes looking down on other people? What can you do to develop your own tolerance for people who are different from you? Is it worth the effort? Why or why not?

Using ability. What does Matt mean when he says the replacement teacher has a "mean and pinched-in mind"? How does Shad encourage Jethro to learn without school? Give examples of people who have expansive minds. How can you cultivate that for yourself?

Jarrell, Randall. *The Bat-Poet.* Illustrated by Maurice Sendak. HarperTrophy, 1996.

The bat stays awake during the daytime and wants the other bats to do so, too, to see all of the wonders that he sees. They will not, so he makes up poems to tell them about the day. They do not understand. He tells his poem to the mockingbird, who comments on the rhyme scheme and the meter, but misses the feeling altogether. Only the chipmunk will listen. The bat makes more poems, including, eventually, one about bats that he wants to share with the other bats. But when he goes to the barn to find them, they have all gone to sleep for the winter.

Older elementary children will appreciate the story line, which parallels Plato's story of the man who left the security of the cave, and when he returned could not make the others understand his descriptions of the wider world. Both stories can be used to help gifted children understand the uniqueness of their perceptions and why those perceptions are not always shared by others.

Creativity; Differentness; Intensity; Sensitivity. The bat-poet never found another bat who would listen. How did he feel about that? What did he do about it? Have you ever felt that you wanted to say something that no one else could understand? How did you find someone to listen? If you couldn't find anyone, what did you do instead?

Kaufman, Gershen, Lev Raphael, and Pam Espeland. *Stick Up for Yourself! Every Kid's Guide to Personal Power and Positive Self-Esteem.* Free Spirit, 1999.

Adapted from materials written for a college-level psychology course so that children from eight to 12 years old can use it on their own, this book is also accompanied by a teacher's guide.

Discussion of general issues of self-esteem, labeling feelings, naming future dreams (and how to get there), and developing interpersonal relationships are especially useful. The difference between role power and personal power, for example, can be a helpful concept as hypercritical youngsters learn how to be effective in their criticism of authority figures.

Identity. Information on self-esteem could be adapted to the particular needs of highly able children learning to come to terms with exceptional talent.

Relationships with others. This book includes useful information on building good relationships with others as a necessary step toward developing self-esteem.

Using ability. The section on naming dreams and how to get there offers suggestions that can be helpful in making good use of an outstanding ability.

Kelly, Eric P. *The Trumpeter of Krakow.* Illustrated by Janina Domanska. Aladdin, 1999.

Joseph Charnetski is 15 in 1461 when his father's house and fields are destroyed; he flees with his parents to the busy medieval city of Krakow. There, they meet the alchemist and scholar, Kreutz, and his niece, Elzbietka. Kreutz finds lodging for the family and work for Joseph's father as a trumpeter in the church tower. But those who destroyed the Charnetskis' home have followed them to Krakow, seeking the Tarnov Crystal, the safe-keeping of which has been the responsibility of the Charnetski family for generations. Kreutz, too, is in danger. One of his students is systematically hypnotizing him to gain the secret of turning base metals into gold.

The setting of this book is one of its strengths, giving a picture of Krakow as a medieval center and of the 15th century as a time of transition from superstition to science. The story is suspenseful, and the subplot raises questions about the moral uses of knowledge. Written in 1928, it provides the intellectual challenge often found in older books.

Drive to understand. What situations can you name in which scientists are now asked to work for gain rather than for knowledge?

Moral concerns. What is the responsibility to society of anyone with unusual knowledge, ability, or intelligence?

Using ability. How valid are the arguments Tring uses to persuade Kreutz to do the experiments Tring wants him to do? In Kreutz's position, what would have been your attitude toward the general interest in making gold from base metals?

Konigsburg, E. L. *Father's Arcane Daughter.* Aladdin, 1999.

Winston Carmichael has grown up taking care of his younger handicapped sister, Heidi, but now Caroline has returned. Their father's daughter from a previous marriage, Caroline had been kidnapped and was presumed dead. Through her efforts, both Winston and Heidi develop in ways that would not have been possible without her, but the question always remains: Is this really Caroline?

This is a sophisticated mystery with a challenging structure of flashbacks featuring unidentified speakers. Caroline's role as change agent can lead to discussion of ways in which we are all potential change agents for others.

Identity; Relationships with others. Why was it important for Heidi to know that she was gifted? What was even more important to Heidi's and Winston's adult success than their intelligence?

Using ability. Why was Caroline so important to both children? Winston says that Heidi has the makings of a brave soul but lacks the focus. What does he mean? What happens when people are unable to fulfill their potential? What characters in the book had special gifts? What were those gifts? What else did these people need if they were to be able to use their gifts?

Konigsburg, E. L. *The View from Saturday.* Aladdin, 1998.

The Souls are a group of four students in Mrs. Olinski's sixth-grade homeroom, but only they know their name. They are also a winning Academic Bowl team. As they move through the finals and beat first the seventh-grade team and then the eighth-grade team, Mrs. Olinski develops several answers to the repeated question, "How did you choose them for the team?" In truth, she is not sure herself. Readers understand gradually why these four belong together as they follow the story of each one, interlaced with Mrs. Olinski's story and with episodes from the Bowl contests.

By accident, Noah Gershom is the best man at the wedding of Ethan Potter's grandmother and Nadia Diamondstein's grandfather. By coincidence, Julian Singh sits next to Ethan on the bus on his first day at their school. While maintaining a socially safe distance from the new boy, Ethan surreptitiously supports Julian—who, in addition to being new, speaks politely, quietly, and with a British accent—as he faces classmates' teasing. Soon Julian invites Ethan, Nadia, and Noah to tea, served on Saturday afternoons at the bed-and-breakfast his father is establishing. From then on, the four are drawn together through compatible interests, shared values, and complementary abilities. As they become more comfortable with each other, they decide they need a project, and Julian suggests that they help Mrs. Olinski, who has recently returned to teaching after an accident that left her a paraplegic. Julian proposes that they help her gain confidence in coping with the students who might take advantage of her—the same students who teased Julian. The Souls find ways to do this so subtly that it is only after Mrs. Olinski has chosen them and they have won the final contest that she realizes that they have also chosen her.

This book is not for everyone, but there are those who will cherish it. As the narrators take turns telling their stories, interspersed with vignettes from the Academic Bowl contests, the location shifts from Florida to New York, and we meet the same secondary characters in different stories and settings. The structure in itself would make a challenging book, but these four sixth graders have much to offer, each in his or her unique way. The level of their language will be very comfortable for verbally gifted children who too often monitor and tone down their language. The Bowl questions, too, are challenging, and the author thoughtfully provides the answers at the end. Finally, the main characters are insightful, thoughtful, clever, and motivated. The Souls are young people who do not fit the mold and might well have been lonely if Julian had not invited them to tea. Together, they are unbeatable in more ways than one.

Aloneness. Consider all the ways in which Mrs. Olinski feels alone. Why was Julian the first to mention helping her? Which of the others also feel alone? How do their feelings change during the book, and why?

Arrogance. Is any one of the Souls arrogant? If so, how do the others make allowances? Why do they do so? Do you see this happening in the people around you?

Creativity. Describe ways in which the main characters are creative. Are you creative in any of the same ways? In what other ways?

Differentness. Julian is different; Ethan knows instantly that he will be teased. If this happens to newcomers in your school, who tries to change it? What qualities does it take to change it?

Identity. Each of the Souls is comfortable with who he/she is, even though they are all different from most sixth graders. How did they achieve this level of comfort?

Introversion. What role does Ethan play? How does his quiet, observant manner help? What other positives are there in being somewhat introverted? The first time they have tea, Ethan says he has gained something and lost something. What does he mean? Consider the same questions for the other Souls.

Perfectionism. Mrs. Olinski does not want to choose honor roll students for her team because they don't want to risk making mistakes. What is the problem with not wanting to take risks?

Relationships with others. Consider what Nadia and her father mean about giving a "lift" and "switches." What does Ethan mean when he comments, "Sometimes silence is a habit that hurts"? How are the four Souls an example of this statement: "Friends are people who are different but who complement—fill in for—each other"?

Sensitivity. What examples are there in the story of people being sensitive to the feelings of others? What examples are there of people who are more easily hurt than most of their peers expect them to be? What examples can you give from your experience of each of these kinds of sensitivity?

Using ability. Why is Mrs. Olinski looking for team members who say "Now what?" instead of "So what?" Which do you say? What difference does it make in your use of the special abilities you have?

Latham, Jean Lee. *Carry On, Mr. Bowditch.* Illustrated by John O'Hara Cosgrave. Houghton Mifflin, 1973.

Nathaniel Bowditch grew up in Salem in the age of sailing ships. He had a quick mind, especially in math, and it was clear that he should go to Harvard. But there was no money, so instead, he was indentured for nine years. People who recognized his brilliance offered the use of their libraries, and Nat never stopped learning. He taught himself languages, mathematics, and astronomy, and when he went to sea, he learned navigation. Soon he was teaching others, and before he was 30, he had written a book on navigation that is still a standard text.

This biography is a story of both physical and intellectual adventure. In addition, it includes several themes related to giftedness: Nat's thirst for learning and the necessity of persistence; the eagerness of uneducated sailors to learn and Nat's commitment to teaching them; and his commitment to accuracy and the importance of risking a new approach, trusting new knowledge rather than traditional methods. Nat's zest for learning and his disregard for obstacles shine throughout the book.

Drive to understand. This story could be read simply for the pleasure of learning how Nat navigated through days of fog, finding the harbor through the sheer power of mathematics.

Identity. People think of Nat as a "brain." What is your response to that?

Using ability. Have you ever felt as though you are "stumbling on other people's dumbness. And—you want to kick something"? What traits does Nat have that enable him to overcome that while continuing to use his brain? What can you learn from Nat?

L'Engle, Madeleine. *The Arm of the Starfish.* Laurel Leaf, 1980.

Adam Eddington has been hired to work in the island laboratory of Dr. O'Keefe the summer after he finishes high school, and he finds himself caught in an international struggle for the information generated by Dr. O'Keefe's experiments. Each side in the contest seeks to enlist Adam, and he must decide for himself which group to support.

In this, another of her warm and loving large-family settings, L'Engle raises the issue of the moral use of one's information and intelligence. The plot is tightly written and suspenseful, and it will lead to discussions of good and bad uses of intelligence and knowledge, the need to learn to trust one's own instincts, and the awareness that intelligence alone is not enough.

Moral concerns. What guides Adam in deciding which side deserves his allegiance?

Using ability. What qualities does Adam have besides intelligence? What qualities must he develop in order to play his role effectively? In what ways does he succeed in developing these qualities? In what ways does he fail?

Lewis, Barbara A. *The Kid's Guide to Social Action.* Free Spirit, 1998.

In the hands of an encouraging adult, this very practical guide can provide an answer to the anguish some bright and sensitive children feel as they become aware of all of the wrongs in the world. Written by a teacher who has successfully guided her students to make a difference (their efforts have resulted in the cleanup of a hazardous waste site and in the passage of two new laws in Utah), *The Kid's Guide to Social Action* gives concrete suggestions that *kids* can use to bring about change. Lewis includes tips on "power skills," including interviewing, speaking, surveying, petitioning, fundraising, and campaigning. There is a long list of some of the resources available to the budding activist, as well as a section on changing or initiating legislation.

Moral concerns; Using ability. Throughout are stories of kids who have taken action, individually or in groups, and who have been heard. Although there have been failures, which are freely acknowledged, the book is upbeat and the message is clear: there is something we can do. This would be a good book for a religious education program, as well as for homes and schools.

Relationships with others. The guidelines given here for effective advocacy can be generalized as tips for getting along with authority figures.

Marrin, Albert. *Sitting Bull and His World.* Dutton Children's Books, 2000.

The Lakota Sioux chief Sitting Bull was born in 1831 and died in 1890. During his lifetime, the traditional way of life of the Plains Indians virtually disappeared. He led his people as the U. S. Army, the railroads, and gold prospectors moved into the Plains, and as the buffalo, mainstay of the Indians' existence, was driven close to extinction. After he participated in the defeat of George Armstrong Custer at the Battle of the Little Big Horn in 1876, Sitting Bull was portrayed as a savage warmonger in the popular press; yet he was a charismatic leader of his people, a warrior who defended tribal lands with courage and vision, and was called the greatest Indian of his time by a former adversary. Rather than enter a reservation in the United States, he led his band to Canada after Little Big Horn, but had to return because as the buffalo diminished, the people began to starve. Ultimately, the book relates not only the eradication of the Indians' hunting grounds and villages, but also the elimination of their religious ceremonies, their heritage, and their way of life—in Marrin's term, ethnocide.

Marrin's biography is a balanced story, alternating the American Indians' view of events with that of the whites. Complementing the history of Sitting Bull's life, the author describes the American West in the 19th century, especially the profound differences between the white and Indian cultures. Neither white nor Indian is seen as blameless, but the reader does come to understand how economic and political pressures both in Washington and in the Army resulted in the killing of the buffalo and in the destruction of the way of life of a whole people. Sitting Bull stands out unforgettably as a man of courage, character, and integrity.

Drive to understand. How does reading a book like this change your understanding of the American Indians, or the whites, or any other people with a culture different from your own?

Identity. By the time Sitting Bull was 38, the Lakota people said that he "owned himself." What does this phrase mean to you? Whom do you know who owns himself or herself in this sense? What qualities do these people have that may have helped them own themselves? What steps would you have to take to own yourself? What would be the advantages of this to you?

Moral concerns. Given the vast differences in the cultures of the whites and the American Indians, how could the advance of the whites across the continent have been better managed? Have the changes in ways of thinking in the last 150 years made it easier to understand and handle a situation like this? In what ways do the same mistakes continue, here and elsewhere?

McCaffrey, Anne. *Dragonsong.* Bantam, 1977.

Menolly is growing up on the island of Pern during a time of threadfall, of spores periodically falling from the sky and consuming all living matter not under shelter. Her father is the head of a fishing village that is protected from threadfall by tradition and by the dragons that live on the island. However, the main theme is not the conflict between dragons and threadfall, but that between Menolly's unusual musical gifts and the tradition, strongly held in her own village, that says women cannot become Harpers. Forbidden her music, Menolly flees the safety of the village to live alone, escaping threadfall as she can. When she is caught without shelter in a threadfall, she is rescued by a dragon and its rider and taken to a weyr, a protected place where the dragons help her recover. There she finds shelter, friends, and finally recognition of her talents and encouragement to use them.

This is not the high fantasy of Cooper or LeGuin, a mighty struggle between good and evil, but rather a tale of a more insidious struggle much closer to our daily reality. Menolly's gentle enemy is the tradition-bound closed-mindedness of Yanus, her father, who is a good man, a solid and reliable leader, and a hard worker—but not a man of vision, not one who accepts change easily. Her mother, Mavi, accepts and reinforces Yanus's rule; only Menolly's brother, Alemi, understands her, but he has no power to help. The Harper Elgion, who serves the role of village pastor, is a force toward enlightenment, but change will be too slow for Menolly and her passion for music.

Creativity; Intensity; Using ability. What experience in your own life helps you understand the strength of Menolly's desire to use her music? Was she right to leave the Sea Hold? What else could she have done?

Drive to understand; Moral concerns. Where do we see too close a following of tradition, superstition, and slowness to change affecting our world? In what ways does it prevent people from growing? What balancing forces (like Alemi, Elgion, and the weyr) do you see?

Moser, Adolph. *Don't Feed the Monster on Tuesdays!* Illustrated by David Melton. Landmark Editions, 1991.

Subtitled *The Children's Self-Esteem Book*, this non-fiction book is designed to be read by parents and children together. Psychologist Moser explains what children can do to replace negative feelings about themselves with positive ones. Imagining a monster inside our heads that makes us feel bad about ourselves—others have called it "bad self-talk"—he suggests that on Tuesdays, children avoid feeding the monster by saying only nice things to themselves and others. This will become easier on Wednesday, and then every day—and the rewards, in the responses sure to come from other people, are great. Moser touches on perfectionism, making the point that to feel good about oneself, it is not necessary to win every time; it is only important to do one's best.

This is one of a series of books by the same author for children from ages nine through 12, each addressing a different issue in healthy psychological development. Besides self-esteem, the series covers stress, anger, grief, and lying. In each book, he describes and defines the problem in terms familiar to children, making it clear that others experience it too. Then he shows the way to solutions. Because the books are written in simple language with cartoon-like illustrations, they look like children's books, but my local bookseller shelves them with books on parenting, highlighting the importance of parent involvement in reading the books and helping the child deal with these issues. Parents will want to read them first, and they may be surprised to learn how serious these concerns are to their children.

Drive to understand; Identity; Perfectionism; Relationships with others.

North, Sterling. *The Wolfling.* Illustrated by John Schoenherr. Puffin, 1992.

Growing up in rural Wisconsin in the 1870s, Robbie Trent leads a rigorous life, lightened by the companionship of his pet, a wolf pup, and by the friendships of his teacher, Hannah Hitchcock, and his neighbor, the Swedish-American naturalist Thure Kumlien. His hard-working and demanding father expects Robbie to end his education at the eighth grade and work for him until he is 21. Robbie must buy his time from his father if he hopes to continue his education, and he is encouraged by others to do so. He needs this encouragement, because it is difficult for him to see a way out of the obligation imposed by his father.

Robbie's story is based on the life of the author's father, with the historical accuracy documented in a separate section. The story is particularly useful for discussing the differences in values between parents and children, and the need for children to be encouraged by other caring adults. Robbie's father is not uncaring, and he is sympathetically depicted as careworn, with the shortsightedness that often comes with the daily struggle for a livelihood.

Drive to understand. How does Robbie feel about his father? What causes his father to feel as he does about Robbie's education?

Using ability. Why is it important for Robbie to continue his education? What traits does Robbie need to develop in order to do so? Do you think he will succeed? What traits does he already have that will help him? If you were in Robbie's situation, what person do you know who would help you as Thure Kumlien and Hannah Hitchcock helped Robbie?

O'Dell, Scott. *My Name Is Not Angelica.* Yearling, 1990.

When she is 15, Raisha and others from her African village are captured by another tribe and sent to the Caribbean island of St. John to be sold as slaves. Raisha, renamed Angelica, becomes a house slave, but the others, including Konjo, who is Raisha's betrothed and their village leader, endure much harsher conditions working in the fields. Konjo soon escapes to head a group of runaways in planning a revolt. Joining the escapees, Raisha witnesses the climax of this small band's role in a general slave revolt.

Based on the slave revolt of 1733-34, this book meets the high standards that we expect in O'Dell's work. Raisha is strong, independent, and self-sufficient, like the young women in other books by O'Dell. The book is well researched, and the reader feels both the justice and the hopelessness of the cause. The oppressing whites are shown with some sympathy, too, enmeshed in a system that inevitably enslaves the masters. This is a fine historical novel for the upper elementary grades, clarifying the issues and telling the story on a very human level.

Aloneness. What examples do we have here of people standing alone for something they believe is right? What gives them the inner strength that enables them to be so brave?

Drive to understand. How is Raisha like Karana in O'Dell's *Island of the Blue Dolphins* and like Bright Morning in his *Sing*

Down the Moon? What common threads do you see in O'Dell's books about conquered and oppressed people? How can you tie these themes to current events?

Moral concerns. Why did some whites respond to slavery like Governor Gardelin did and some like Preacher Gronnewold? What justifies the disobedience of authority that culminates in rebellion? When is rebellion *not* justified?

Paterson, Katherine. *Come Sing, Jimmy Jo*. Puffin, 1995.

Eleven-year-old James Johnson belongs to a family of professional country music singers. Their new agent, upon hearing the child sing, urges him to join the family on stage. James's feeling for the music helps him overcome his initial fear, but he finds that it is not as easy to become comfortable with the new identity that comes with performing. He does not want to become "Jimmy Jo" instead of James, he does not want school friends to know that he appears on television each Friday night, and he is not happy about the rivalry his popularity sets up between him and other members of his family.

The stability in James's life comes from his grandmother and his father. Family relationships and tolerance of difficult personalities are well portrayed. Grandma encourages James to sing, saying "You got the gift.... It ain't fittin' to run from it.... The Lord don't give private presents." James's challenge is to use his gift while at the same time remaining himself.

Identity. Why is it so important for James to remain *James*? Why does it not bother his mother to change herself for the sake of publicity? How would you feel if you were James? Why? Why does James feel that he betrayed his Grandma? Do you agree that he did? What could you say to help him feel better about that?

Using ability. How is James's gift a "burden" to him? ("Sometimes the gift seems more like a burden.") What are the rewards he gets from singing? Are they worth the sacrifices? Identify a gift or talent of yours. What would be the sacrifices and rewards of developing it fully? Do you want to? How would you? Discuss

Grandma's statement that "The Lord don't give private presents." To what extent do gifted people have a responsibility to use their gifts? If you think there is no responsibility, what other reasons are there to use gifts?

Paterson, Katherine. *Jacob Have I Loved*. HarperTrophy, 1990.

Growing up on an island in Chesapeake Bay, Louise is convinced that everyone despises her and loves Caroline, her beautiful, musically talented younger sister. Not until she is 17 does Louise recognize that she is gifted intellectually and capable of doing anything she chooses. Others are willing to help, but she must make the choice.

A Newbery winner, this complex book has several themes other than giftedness, and a thoughtful teenager will find much here to think about, including: sibling rivalry, responsibility for one's own decisions, tradition-breaking and respect for tradition, and going one's own way despite feeling uncomfortable about being different.

Differentness. How could Louise have responded more helpfully to her feelings of being different?

Identity. How do Caroline's and Louise's pictures of themselves affect their behavior? their decisions? How accurate are their pictures of themselves? How does being gifted affect each girl's childhood? What difference does it make (in personal happiness, in career choices, in the way you treat other people) to know that you have a special ability?

Relationships with others. Louise has what might be called a prickly personality. What makes her that way? How does her personality complicate her life? What role does her giftedness play? What can happen to people like this as they become adults? What keeps Louise from turning into a prickly adult? If you could talk to Louise as a teenager, what advice would you give her?

Using ability. Why is Louise able to make use of her intelligence? What is the turning point for her? What could other possible turning points be for someone like Louise? How might the book have ended so that Louise would take more command of her own future?

Peck, Robert Newton. *A Day No Pigs Would Die.* Random, 1994.

Robbie tells of his thirteenth year growing up in a Shaker family in Vermont, and especially of his father, who was both illiterate and wise. Rather than a plot, Peck offers a series of vignettes that reveal the daily concerns of a rural community in which a Shaker family is even more traditional than most.

Rob grows up knowing that he is different and valuing his own family even as he sees the disadvantages of their way of life. Rob is different because of his religion, not because of giftedness, but the principle is the same: to recognize and value both his strengths and those of his family, and to be able to accept both himself and his father in spite of their differentness.

Differentness. What factors help Rob accept his and his family's differentness? Is this story outdated, or is it relevant today? How so? Generalize: What are the advantages and disadvantages of being different? How can people decide how and when to accept being different?

Identity. How is growing up a Shaker an advantage to Rob? How is it a disadvantage? Will he overcome the disadvantages? How? What does Rob admire in his father? What do you admire in Rob? In his place, what would you have done differently? Would you have rebelled? At what point, and why then? Was Rob wrong not to?

Rand, Ayn. *Anthem.* Signet, 1996.

In a future collectivist society, Equality 7-2521 is out of place because he is more intelligent than most. Assigned to be a Street Sweeper, he discovers a tunnel that becomes a hiding place for him, and in which he writes and experiments, eventually discovering electricity. When he presents his discovery to the Scholars, they reject him, and he flees to the Uncharted Forest, finding there an abandoned house from the Unmentionable Times (the 20th century). Here he finds manuscripts and reads in them his heritage, including the forbidden lost word: ego, I. Recognizing the possibilities of individualism, he resolves to begin a new life and a new political order.

This novel was written for the purpose of extolling individualism over collectivism. Middle school students with lively intellectual interests are enthusiastic about it. They understand the political message, see a need for balance between the individual and the community, and identify with Equality's urge to know and his frustration at being repressed.

Differentness. How can people who are different cope in our society without leaving, as Equality did?

Identity. Does anything like the Scholars' rejection of Equality's idea ever happen to students in school or to teenagers at home? How do they react?

Moral concerns. How can people like Equality, who are different from or brighter than others, manage to be themselves and yet fit into a community?

Relationships with others. Do you agree with Equality that "we have no need of our brothers"? Under what conditions might Equality recognize the need for other people?

Using ability. Can you explain why Equality so strongly wants to study and to experiment? What personal qualities make him able to do so, while others cannot, although they may wish to do so?

Sebestyen, Ouida. *Words by Heart.* Bantam, 1996.

Lena's Papa has high hopes for his daughter, so he moves his family from the post-Reconstruction South to the more open West, where a black family may have a better chance. But Papa's willingness to work brings resentment from Mr. Haney, who loses his job to Papa, and Lena learns that not everyone rejoices with her when she wins the scripture-reciting contest. It is clear that prejudice here is merely subtler than it is in the South, and the family will still need extraordinary fortitude to survive.

Racial prejudice is the theme of this book, with Lena's giftedness adding emphasis to the need of blacks for opportunities to grow and develop. Talented blacks can see a version of their own struggle in Lena's story, and all talented students can recognize Lena's and her father's acceptance of the responsibility to use one's gifts, even against difficult odds.

Differentness. What does Papa teach Lena that will help her survive? What else do you think she will need to get through the next few years?

Identity. If you were in Lena's position, do you think you could make it? What would be your greatest asset? your greatest liability?

Using ability. What did Papa teach Lena, both by what he said and by the way he lived? Is there anything in that which could be useful to you? If your own life is easier than Lena's, how might that make it more of a challenge for you to grow up to be a productive person, making full use of the abilities you have? How are you doing so far?

Speare, Elizabeth George. *The Witch of Blackbird Pond.* Laurel Leaf, 1978.

Kit Tyler grew up with her grandfather in Barbados, but upon his death in her sixteenth year, she sails to Connecticut to live with an aunt whom she has never met. Kit does not fit in with the Puritan Connecticut of 1687, but she finds a few kindred spirits: Nat, first mate of the ship on which she sailed; Prudence, a downtrodden child hungry to learn; and Hannah, the outcast Quaker who lives by Blackbird Pond and who is thought to be a witch. Kit's friendship with Hannah leads to the accusation that Kit herself is a witch.

Characterization is excellent in this book. Kit is accepted if not understood by her Puritan relatives, and she comes to respect her stern uncle's fairness and sense of justice. Several characters— Kit, her uncle, Hannah, Nat, the young minister-in-training, and even Prudence—provide examples of standing alone for their own beliefs and the consequences (both the difficulties and the rewards) of doing so. The book also offers examples of ways in which people need and support each other.

Differentness. Consider each of the people who take a stand for their beliefs. What characteristics do they have that put them in this position? How do they find the strength or courage they need? What sustains them?

Drive to understand. This book is often read simply for the insight it gives into the lives of the New England colonists.

Moral concerns. How would this story have been different if the people of the village had asked questions of Hannah before deciding that she was a witch? How can we avoid similar pre-judging—that is, prejudice?

Relationships with others. Consider instances in which one person supports another even without liking what that person is doing. Have you ever seen someone offer that kind of support to another? Why do people do this? Have you ever done it yourself? Can you think of an opportunity to do so? What would be the consequences, both positive and negative?

Spiegelman, Art. *Maus: A Survivor's Tale.* Pantheon, 1986.

Spiegelman, Art. *Maus: A Survivor's Tale, II: And Here My Troubles Began.* New York: Pantheon, 1991.

In his first book, this son of survivors of Auschwitz tells the story of his parents' meeting and the early years of their marriage in Poland, up until the time they arrived at Auschwitz and were separated. The second volume continues the story with their experiences in Auschwitz and after the war, including insights into long-term psychological effects of the Holocaust on one survivor, Vladek Spiegelman, and on his relationship with his son. (Spiegelman's mother, Anja, committed suicide in 1968, leaving no note.)

Spiegleman bases his story on taped discussions with his father and tells it in cartoon form, drawing Jews as mice, Nazis as cats, Poles as pigs, and Americans as dogs. The scene alternates between Poland in the 1930s and 40s and Rego Park, New York, where Art interviews his aging father and tries to maintain their uneasy relationship. The harrowing wartime experiences of Polish Jews, combined with evidence of the lasting impact on Vladek Spiegelman's personality, told with simple words and cartoon illustrations create a vivid impression of the terror of those years like no other literature of the period.

Drive to understand. What new information or feelings about the Holocaust do you gain from this story? What part does the cartoon treatment play in your new understanding?

Moral concerns. Does the cartoon format trivialize the subject matter? Why or why not?

Relationships with others. Describe Vladek Spiegelman in a brief character sketch. Why is he so complex a person? How did Vladek's experiences affect his personality, which affected his relationship with his son, which affected his son's personality? Relate this domino concept to other intergenerational relationships you know.

Stewart, Mary. *The Crystal Cave.* Ballantine, 1990.

For those who love the Arthurian legends, here is Mary Stewart's story of one of the more mysterious characters: Merlin the magician, who took the infant Arthur and reared him, safe from the turmoil of the court. This novel begins well before Arthur's birth, telling of the childhood and youth of Merlin, whose mother, the daughter of a king, would not reveal who Merlin's father was. Merlin grew up ignored as a bastard in his grandfather's court until he escaped during a period of strife and found himself in a position to change the course of British history.

Stewart paints a picture of the education of Merlin as a young man gifted with the Sight, the ability to see what will come. But Merlin does not control his gift. It comes when it will; he can only prepare. We see in Merlin a lonely boy who learns how to learn from everyone he meets. We also gain an understanding of the struggle between the native Britons and the invading Saxons, and of a time when three religions competed for the loyalty of the people who became the English. The historical background of this story is made clear in Stewart's explanation of place names we can find on today's maps.

Drive to understand. Readers may want to find other versions of the Arthurian stories, or nonfiction accounts of the search for the historical Arthur. How does Stewart's version of the story help us see why an historical Arthur might have become a legend?

Identity. Describe how Merlin feels about his gift and how he talks about it to others. What can a person with intellectual or artistic gifts learn from Merlin's example?

Using ability. What kind of life must Merlin lead in order to make the most of the Sight? How does he learn this? What does he do to make it happen? What environment do you need to make the best use of your abilities?

Sullivan, Charles, ed. *Imaginary Gardens: American Poetry and Art for Young People.* Abrams, 1989.

This is a collection of poems by American poets, illustrated with paintings, drawings, and photographs by American artists. The book covers all of American history, from the colonial to the modern period. Some of the poets included are Benet, Bly, Dickinson, Eliot, and Silverstein—a range of writers—and the artists include Audubon, Benton, Calder, O'Keeffe, and Wyeth. Altogether they present a rich panorama of American artists, both literary and graphic, to give young readers an idea of the work of people whose names they may have heard—or will hear in the future.

Drive to understand.

Sutcliff, Rosemary. *Flame-Colored Taffeta.* Econo-Clad, 1999.

Although she is best known for her fiction of early medieval England, Sutcliff writes here of the 18th century—specifically, of a time of smugglers and intrigue revolving around the efforts to crown Bonnie Prince Charlie. Twelve-year-old Damaris lives on a farm near England's coast, and when she finds a wounded smuggler—or spy—she and her friend Peter must contrive to keep him hidden and safe while, with the help of old Genty, the Wise Woman, they nurse him back to health.

The plot is well-constructed and suspenseful; this book really is hard to put down. Discussion could focus on the historical events surrounding Bonnie Prince Charlie and on other literary—and musical—treatments of the same story. Or it could lead to other fiction set in the 18th century, such as Leon Garfield's books, *Smith* and *The Sound of Coaches*.

Drive to understand. What differences do you see between the rural world Sutcliff presents and Garfield's urban settings? What similarities do you see? Analyze differences in the authors' writing styles, and assess the suitability of each style for their subjects. What emotional effect does each writer's work have on the reader?

Sutcliff, Rosemary. *The Sword and the Circle.* Puffin, 1994.

For her retelling of the Arthurian legends, Sutcliff draws stories from several sources and weaves them into a whole—a collection of stories of Arthur and Guenever, Lancelot, Gawain, Tristan and Iseult, Merlin, and others, all of the Fellowship of the Round Table. Sutcliff has written often of this period and others in British history, and her sense for language and place enhances the tales to create an experience of wonder and imagination for sensitive readers.

Drive to understand. The author's note will intrigue readers who want to know more about the origins of these tales—who was the historical Arthur, for instance? Her stories come from history, poetry, and legend; some readers may want, now or later, to read the earlier versions. Especially inquisitive readers may also want to compare Sutcliff's retelling of the Arthurian legends with others.

Sutcliff, Rosemary. *Sword Song.* Farrar, Straus and Giroux, 1998.

At 17, Bjarni Sigurdson is banished from Rafnglas, the Viking settlement that has been his home since he and his older brother left Norway. Out of impulsive anger, he has committed a murder, and Rafn, the chief of this settlement on the west coast of Britain, gives him a sword and orders him to be on the merchant ship leaving for Dublin in the morning. For the next five years, Bjarni must find his own way in the constantly shifting fortunes of the Viking Age. He becomes a mercenary, hiring out his sword arm to one chieftain after another. His impulsiveness carries him into trouble more than once, as leaders such as Onund Treefoot and the wise Lady Aud watch, correcting and encouraging him with care and concern. Finding adventure as soldier and sailor, gradually he proves his fierce loyalty to his chief, and he grows from boy to man during his banishment. On his return to Rafnglas, alone after leaping from a ship in a storm, he faces his greatest challenge: protecting a young woman who is struggling to keep her ancestral farm from those who believe her to be a witch.

Sword Song is Sutcliff's last book, left in second draft when she died suddenly in 1992. Because her language is true to the time, her vocabulary full of words that the people of the British Islands used before Chaucer, it is both challenging and fascinating to read. Sutcliff provides insight into the hardships of daily life, the ever-present danger of sudden death, and the mingling of cultures and religions as Vikings meet Picts and Christianity meets the old religion of the Norsemen. Her research is trustworthy; this is a fine example of how history can be learned through fiction.

Drive to understand. Much discussion could be built around the Vikings' way of life. As we would expect, Sutcliff depicts them as warlike, but what else does she show us that does not fit the stereotype? For example, despite language barriers and constant warfare, the different peoples of the Scottish islands attempt to understand each other's customs and strive not to offend. Why was this important to them? Why is it important to us?

Temple, Frances. *The Ramsay Scallop.* HarperTrophy, 1995.

Fourteen years old at the dawn of the 14th century, Elenor is the orphaned daughter of an English lord and lady, betrothed to Thomas, who is away on a Crusade. When the Crusaders return to Ramsay Castle, Thomas is quiet and introspective. The Crusade had not been as glorious as the men had been led to believe it would be when they set out, and they feel guilty for deeds that, it seems now, would have been better left undone. The women, for their part, have managed things quite well, but there will be a period of adjustment. Elenor, in particular, has no wish to marry, and Thomas is too disillusioned and sick at heart to consider it. The community requires healing, and it is important to all that Thomas and Elenor, the future rulers, find friendship and trust for each other. Pondering all of this, the wise Father Gregory sets Thomas' penance for sins committed on the Crusade: on behalf of all of the folk of Ramsay, Thomas (with Elenor, who agrees) will go on a pilgrimage to Santiago de Compostela, the shrine of Saint James in Spain. To Elenor's relief, they will travel as chaste companions, not consummating their marriage until the pilgrimage is completed.

Gregory's charge requires Elenor and Thomas to be together for many months, facing increasing hardship, offering compassion to strangers and receiving help from others, observing and learning to value the strengths in each other. It also provides the reader a rich experience of life in the Middle Ages—its squalor, its beauty, and its focus on Christianity—ranging from religious fanaticism to scholarly philosophy, leaving the reader with much to consider after the reading is done.

Drive to understand. What secular and religious values of the Middle Ages were expressed by the Crusades? How did the Crusades play a part in establishing those values? What role did pilgrimages play in establishing values? What traditions in our culture play the same roles?

Moral concerns. What guidelines do Elenor and Thomas have for making decisions, for distinguishing right from wrong? How does this compare with the experience of young adults in the early 21st century?

Whelan, Gloria. *Goodbye, Vietnam.* Random, 1993.

Thirteen-year-old Mai and her family live in the Mekong Delta of Vietnam in the early 1990s, after the conflict there. Life for them is difficult under the new government, even after the return of her father, who had been taken away by the police many months before. Mai has been out of school for two years because her family needs her to work to keep them from starving. Much of the rice harvest is taken by the government, food prices rise daily, and now Mai's grandmother will be taken away soon because she will not give up the old ways of healing. But Mai's uncle and his family have escaped by boat to Hong Kong; they send a card saying they hope to get to Chicago.

One day, Mai's mother tells her that they will be leaving their village, the home of their ancestors, to try to find a new life elsewhere. They walk for two nights through swamps and forests, then find passage on a small and vastly overcrowded boat—thanks to the fact that her father has a secret skill as a mechanic, and the boat's old engine needs constant attention. During the thousand-mile voyage, both Mai and her father act quickly to save other refugees; in each case, the people they have saved bring talents that are beneficial to all. When they arrive in Hong Kong, they spend weeks in a crowded refugee camp, hoping that they will not be among those sent back to Vietnam.

Whelan's story is well researched, full of detail, and sparely written. Without sentimentality, she leaves the reader newly aware of the strength of the human spirit—in facing hardship, danger, fear, and sickness, bolstered by courage and by the determination to find a better life—and of the interdependence that characterizes the human condition.

Drive to understand. Mai's story sheds light on a particular moment in history, but her family's experience in general is that of refugees in many times and places. Why do people become refugees? Should other countries accept them, even if there are no jobs? What solutions are there to this problem?

Moral concerns. In fleeing without the proper papers and in bribing the police officer with a duck, Mai's family is doing something illegal. What is your response to this? If it is all right in their situation, why is that so? How can you decide a question like this?

Relationships with others. Why is it so important that the people crowded onto the boat get along with each other? How do they manage to do so, even under such difficult conditions? How does their culture help them? How would what you have been taught help you?

Using ability. Both the grandmother and *Bac si* Hong are willing to risk arrest to use their knowledge of healing. Why is it so important to them? What do you think might be that important to you, under circumstances like theirs? What would you have to offer?

White, Ruth. *Belle Prater's Boy.* Yearling, 1998.

When Gypsy Leemaster's Aunt Belle suddenly and mysteriously disappears, her cousin Woodrow—Belle Prater's boy—comes to live with their grandparents, next door to Gypsy in a Virginia mining town, and Gypsy and Woodrow become best friends. Woodrow has lived in a shack in the hills, he has few clothes, and his eyes are crossed; but he is well liked immediately for his cleverness with stories, his humor, and his warmth toward people of every age. In contrast, Gypsy is the beautiful daughter of a beautiful mother, living in one of the nicest homes in Coal Station. Her strongest wish is to be able to cut her long blonde hair, because she believes that people see only her hair, not the person underneath it—but her mother promised her father before he died that she would never let Gypsy cut her hair. While Woodrow tries to explain to himself why his mother left, Gypsy's anger over her father's death gradually comes to the surface. Together they learn the story they have not been told, and together they are able to transcend the tragedies of their parents' leaving.

This Newbery Honor Book is full of humor, of wisdom about the value of seeing through appearances to the person underneath, and about the truth that there is no escape from pain even for people who seem to have everything. Setting her story in the 1950s, White has created warm parental figures in the children's grandparents, in Gypsy's mother and stepfather, and in the townspeople. Both the characterization and setting are masterfully handled. Young readers will remember Gypsy's hunger to be known for more than her beauty, and Woodrow's expert way of dealing with people, for a long time.

Identity. What is behind Gypsy's desire that others see who she is, and not just her hair? Without saying anything about her physical appearance, how would you describe Gypsy? How would people describe you? How might you be misjudging someone you know because of a physical feature, whether it is beautiful like Gypsy's hair or unfortunate like Woodrow's eyes?

Relationships with others. What draws Woodrow and Gypsy together, beyond the fact that they are cousins? How do they help each other reach an understanding of what has happened to their parents? Consider the specific things they each do to help cheer up the other. What similar idea have you had to help a friend?

Wojciechowska, Maia. *Shadow of a Bull.* Aladdin, 1992.

Manolo's father was once the greatest bullfighter in Spain, and everyone expects Manolo to be just like him. When Manolo is almost 12—the age at which his father first fought a bull—a group of men who have been watching him since his father's death begin training him to become a toreador. Manolo is not sure that he wants to be a bullfighter, and he assumes that his fear means that he lacks courage. He sets for himself the task of learning to be brave. Two people, though, help clarify his hopes for the future: Juan, who passionately longs to become a bullfighter, and the doctor who has spent his life repairing bodies broken in the bullring.

Manolo is trapped by the expectations of others, and he is confused by his own definition of courage. The decision that he eventually makes reflects both self-knowledge and moral courage.

Drive to understand. This well-written story conveys with respect the historical tradition behind bullfighting, but it also raises inevitable questions, without giving any definitive answers. Manolo's answer, as it should be, is for only himself, leaving room for discussion.

Identity; Intensity. How does Manolo feel about himself? How would you describe him to someone else? How does Manolo define courage? How does he show it? How would you have defined it before reading the book? How about after reading the book? Do you see examples of moral courage in others? In yourself?

Moral concerns. What was your opinion of the custom of bullfighting before you read this book? Has it changed? If so, in what ways, and why? Under what circumstances (if any) do you think killing an animal is justified?

Using ability. What advice would you give Manolo? Manolo's mother says that what his father did was "for himself, most of all for himself." Is that all right, or is it selfish? Why? What does Manolo do for himself? Is it selfish? What do you do for yourself that is not selfish?

Yep, Laurence. *Dragonwings.* HarperTrophy, 1989.

Born in China, eight-year-old Moon Shadow travels to the "demon land"—America—in 1903 to join his father, Windrider, who has lived and worked in the Chinese community in San Francisco since before Moon Shadow was born. Life for the Chinese men working in California is uncertain and dangerous, as they struggle to learn a new language and new ways, sending much of their income home to their families in China. Moon Shadow works with his father in a Chinatown laundry, then moves to another neighborhood when his father takes a job with one of the demons. Windrider is a kitemaker whose imagination is caught by the Wright brothers' experiment with flying, and Moon Shadow is carried along on his father's dream of building an aeroplane. Despite setbacks and danger, and with the help of both Chinese and "demon" friends, they succeed for a moment.

Looking at the San Francisco of those years through Moon Shadow's eyes is sometimes jolting and always instructive, illuminating American and Chinese cultures at once. The plot, based on the story of a Chinese immigrant who built a flying machine in 1909, gives Yep ample opportunity to explore the lives and struggles of the Chinese who came to America in the early years of the 20th century.

Differentness. In this book, we recognize how much more people are alike than different, and yet Moon Shadow is constantly faced with his differentness. Often, he expresses his opinion that the demon ways are wrong. Why do American ways seem wrong to him? On what basis can he—and we—judge when another is "wrong" or "right"? How does he know that he is doing the right thing, even though he is different? How can you adapt that to your own experience?

Drive to understand. Examine any stereotypical pictures you may have had about Chinese workers in America. What have you learned from reading *Dragonwings* that might alter those pictures?

Relationships with others. Describe Moon Shadow's friendship with Robin. How is she different? Look at the friendship from her point of view. What does she bring to it, and what does she gain from it?

Using ability. In learning to get along in a new country, the Chinese immigrants had to use every personal resource they could muster. What were some of the qualities they displayed, good and bad? How many of those qualities do you have? What qualities or abilities might you develop further if you were challenged to survive as much as they were? How can you develop those qualities even if your survival is not an issue?

Senior High (Grades Nine – Twelve)

Adderholdt, Miriam and Jan Goldberg. *Perfectionism: What's Bad about Being Too Good?* Illustrated by Caroline Price Schwert. Free Spirit, 1999.

Many gifted teenagers are victims of perfectionism, harboring so strong a desire to do everything perfectly that they consider second place or a grade of "B" a failure. Some go so far as to avoid risking that failure by refusing to accept new challenges or to take advanced courses.

Perfectionism speaks to these students, describing its effects on the mind, body, and relationships and then prescribing practical steps toward becoming more realistic about expectations. Counselors, teachers, and librarians will find the book a useful tool for school-based discussions on giftedness, and parents can use it effectively at home. The insights it offers are as important for adults working with gifted youngsters as for the students themselves.

This book can be used independently by students in the middle grades or in senior high. For younger students, parents can gather ideas from the book and present them to their children in whatever way seems appropriate.

Perfectionism; Using ability.

Auel, Jean. *The Clan of the Cave Bear.* Bantam, 1984.

This popular novel features several characters who stand out in their prehistoric clan because of their special abilities. The medicine woman of the Clan of the Cave Bear cares for a five-year-old girl from an unknown clan who was orphaned when an earthquake swallowed her home. As the young girl grows, the differences between the Cro-Magnon Ayla and the Neanderthal Clan people become apparent. The Clan is deeply traditional, relying on a mixture of instinct and knowledge from past ages. Ayla displays flexibility, intelligent curiosity, a drive toward individuality, and a willingness to take risks—all of which puts her at odds with the Clan people.

These differences between Ayla and the people who surround her are analogous to the differences a highly talented student may sense between himself and many of the people around him. Understanding how Ayla feels and seeing her responses to the situation should help him understand and respond constructively to his own situation.

Identity. How does Ayla come to recognize her differences? How does she feel about them? What is her self-concept, and how does it affect her behavior? How does it change as she learns more about herself?

Relationships with others. How does Ayla compromise her abilities in order to fit in with the Clan, and how does she decide when not to compromise? What mistakes does she make? Can you go on from this to draw a set of criteria to determine when compromise is adaptive and when it is nonproductive? What would be Ayla's definition of personal integrity? What is yours?

Bauer, Marion Dane, ed. *Am I Blue? Coming Out from the Silence.* HarperTrophy, 1995.

This is a collection of 16 original stories, each from a different perspective on the experience of growing up gay or lesbian, or loving someone who is gay or lesbian. They include Lois Lowry's "Holding," about how Will finally tells his best friend that his father is gay; William Sleator's "In the Tunnels," told from the point of view of a young gay Vietnamese soldier; Francesca Lia Block's "Winnie and Tommy," in which Tommy comes out to his girlfriend; Nancy Garden's "Parent's Night," about Karen's struggle to tell her parents that she is lesbian and their courage in supporting her; and M. E. Kerr's "We Might as Well All Be Strangers," describing how Alison discovers that the person in her family who understands her best is her grandmother, who remembers the Holocaust. In "Michael's Little Sister" by C. S. Adler, Michael struggles against the recognition that he is gay until his little sister, Becky, relates Michael's difference to her own sense of being different—in her case, because she is more interested in learning about nature than about "silly parties and TV shows."

The award-winning authors, some gay or lesbian and some not, reach across boundaries of color, class, nationality, and religion. In every story, the focus is on the primary importance of relationship—and for the young people in these stories, how that is affected by sexual orientation. For gifted children, the primary focus is the same: how their relationships are affected—for them, by having exceptional talent. The underlying question in *Am I Blue?*, although it is about a different way of being different, is the fundamental question gifted children have, spoken or not: "Can I be myself and still have friends?" "Will lack of understanding— my own and others'—defeat the relationships I value?" And the answer, repeated often in this book, is the same: "You are not alone."

Discussion of these stories will depend in large part on whether the leader assumes the students in the group are gay or lesbian, or straight, or some of each. The following questions, only a beginning, as always, are designed to discuss the book as a whole. Answers may be based on any story that seems relevant to the discussion.

Differentness. How do the characters in these stories respond to the feeling of being different? How are their responses similar to those of people who are different in other ways, such as heightened intellectual curiosity or special talent or interests?

Drive to understand. For students who know little about the issues gay or lesbian teenagers must struggle with, this book is a multi-faceted source of information and fresh awareness. *Am I Blue?* could be used simply for this purpose, as a resource for the exploration of homophobia.

Identity. While determining one's sexual identity is a theme in many of the stories, other forms of identity-seeking are here, too: ethnic identity, role in one's family, individuality within the group. What others can you add from your own experience, based on having an unusual talent or interest? How do these many identity issues relate to each other? Notice how in many of the stories the answer to the character's identity questions are left open at the end. Why is that? Answer in general terms, considering all the kinds of identity search that have been mentioned.

Relationships with others. Consider the stories in which the tone of an important relationship shifts with the revelation that someone is gay or lesbian. When love or friendship deepens, what factors cause that result? When distance enters the relationship, why is that so? What universal factors can you think of that cause relationships to either deepen or fall apart as individuals define themselves more clearly in regard to issues other than sexual orientation?

Becker, Jurek. *Bronstein's Children.* Translated by Leila Vennewitz. University of Chicago Press, 1999.

Hans was an East German Jew just finishing at the gymnasium and preparing for the university when he discovered his father and two other men torturing a former Nazi concentration camp guard they had captured. The book alternates in time between the present, as Hans recalls the events leading up to his father's death, and flashbacks to the two-week period when the guard was held captive, a year earlier. The small cast of characters includes Hans's girlfriend Martha and her parents, who take Hans in after his father dies; and his sister Elle, who is in a mental institution due to sudden violent outbursts dating back to the Nazi period.

The story line is deceptively simple, the structure demanding, the mood somber. The questions raised are serious ones. They can be asked in relation to the Nazi period only, or they can be asked in broader terms, as they apply to victims in other situations—perhaps even to readers' own lives.

Aloneness. Hans is lonely, alienated, and left to work out his solution by himself. How does he do it? Why does it take so long?

Identity. Who are the victims? How long does one remain a victim? How does one stop being a victim, and how much control does one have over this?

Moral concerns. How does one gain control over one's own life and destiny? How does one gather the strength and courage to act?

Bradbury, Ray. *Fahrenheit 451.* Ballantine, 1996.

In Bradbury's imagined future, firemen have become those who create fire—the censors who burn books (which have a conflagration point of 451 degrees Fahrenheit). In doing so, they are merely carrying out the will of the majority, who long ago scorned books, turning to the pseudo-world of television instead. Books, after all, cause dissension, since they don't agree with each other, and in any case, the populace is more docile when kept in the state of intellectual numbness induced by video.

But Montag is a fireman who questions. After his wife attempts suicide (a common occurrence in this world), he brings down the books he has hidden in the attic and begins to read them, looking for answers and meaning. In due time, the firemen arrive to burn his house and books, and Montag becomes a fugitive. As the war that has threatened throughout the story descends upon the city, Montag finds himself welcomed by a group of other questioners and dissidents, each carrying the treasure of a remembered book in his brain.

The "Author's Afterword" is a protest against publishers' attempts to remove passages thought to be offensive from Bradbury's works as they were considered for use in high school anthologies—effectively censoring this book on censorship. The Ballantine Del Rey edition of 1979 restored lost sections and printed the Afterword—all of which is worth discussion in itself. Here, in addition to censorship, Bradbury anticipates the rampant growth of restrictions on thinking, speaking, and writing that resulted from the move toward "politically correct" expression.

Drive to understand. Follow Beatty's history of the end of books. What looks familiar? How far have we gone toward the future Bradbury predicts? Did the end of the Cold War (which Bradbury did not foresee) change any of his forecasts?

Moral concerns. What is the role, the danger, and the future face of censorship in our time? What are the differing roles of the public and the government? How does censorship affect the development and appropriate use of your abilities? What are sources of censorship in your life? What is your personal responsibility regarding censorship?

Finally, have you read the works the men have memorized? They make a good reading list.

Chatwin, Bruce. *Utz.* Penguin, 1999.

Kaspar Utz, the only surviving descendant of his wealthy grandmother, is able to bear life in Prague under Communism rather well. Through various understandings with the authorities, Utz retains and even augments his collection of Meissen porcelain. The narrator, an English historian of the Northern Renaissance, meets Utz on a research trip to Prague in 1967, just before the "Prague Spring" of 1968—that brief period when there was hope of relief from the Communist regime. He returns in the late 80s, years after Utz's death (but before the collapse of the Iron Curtain) to learn the fate of the Meissen collection. He pieces together more of Utz's story, especially the role of his servant Marta, but the reader is left to conjecture about the Meissen.

Written by an English writer and based on Eastern European history and culture, this book will prove a serious challenge to American high school students, but it is worth the effort. Some background reading on August the Strong, the history of Meissen porcelain, and Dresden will add to the pleasure and will enable motivated readers to follow the story easily, preparing them to consider the philosophical questions raised in this brief novel.

Drive to understand. Consider the aspects of Western society that disgusted Utz. What causes the difference between his attitude and that of those who wanted to emigrate? How does his attitude toward the Western world square with his passion for porcelain? What is Chatwin saying about materialism? What implications, if any, do you see for the blending of Eastern and Western European (and American) culture after the events of 1989? What do you think happened to the Meissen collection? What *should* have happened to it? Why?

Moral concerns. Utz says that the collection ruined his life. If so, in what way? Is Utz's fascination with porcelain a form of idolatry in your view?

Cole, Brock. *Celine.* Farrar, Strauss and Giroux, 1993.

Celine is a junior in a Chicago high school, an artist living with her 22-year-old stepmother while her irresponsible father is on a European lecture tour. Jake is a young boy in the apartment across the hall, whose artist father is separated from his mother. Celine copes with these disparate people as well as with typical high school problems—the paper on Holden Caulfield, the friend who uses Celine as a cover to attend a forbidden party, the unwelcome boyfriend—with a sense of humor tinged with a fine edge of irony and devastatingly clear self-awareness.

It is the writing rather than the plot that will appeal to mature readers of *Celine*. Cole provides a sample of the thinking of a talented high school girl as she deals gamely, without pretension or illusions, with the realities of daily living, including the shortcomings of herself and others. Despite the distractions, we know Celine will prevail, if only because of her clear sense of herself as an artist.

Identity. Questions might include inquiry into the role art plays in integrating the different aspects of Celine's life. What, if anything, does or could play such a role in your life?

Using ability. Explore the importance of knowing that there is something we do well, of pursuing something outside ourselves that helps us keep perspective, as art does for Celine. What other qualities in Celine help her stay on top of things? What pursuits and qualities in you help you in the same way?

Cole, Brock. *The Goats*. Farrar, Straus and Giroux, 1992.

They are called goats because they are scapegoats, the brunt of a cruel trick at an exclusive but poorly supervised summer camp. Left alone at night on an island, the boy and girl make their way to the mainland and to an empty cabin. They determine never to return to the camp, and for three days they avoid the searchers. During this time, they fall in with a group at another summer camp, and these campers treat them with kindness and understanding. They learn to care for and depend on each other, building feelings of trust that neither has known before.

They see themselves as "socially retarded" for their age, as the girl puts it, because they do not fit in. But in a short time, they learn to relate well to each other—proving to themselves and demonstrating to the reader that those who don't fit in with the crowd do very well if they can find just one person to whom they can talk freely.

Aloneness. To build an understanding of why some people are isolated by the cruelty of others, discuss scapegoating. Why is it that some people are "goats"? What causes a group—a neighborhood, school, or nation—to find goats? What characteristics make individuals vulnerable, likely to become goats? Consider the consequences of scapegoating: What characteristics of scapegoated individuals might make them valuable to society? What effect will this incident have on Laura and Howie as they grow older, and in their adult lives? What changes will have occurred in them? How will it affect their personalities, if at all? What effect will it have, if any, on what they choose to contribute to society? To discuss scapegoating at a personal level, inquire: Do you know any goats? Can you see beneath the surface to the qualities they have to offer? Do you ever see yourself as a goat? How can you grow beyond it?

Relationships with others. To use this book to help children discover ways of coping with being alone, ask: Are some people "socially retarded" for their age, as Laura says she is? If so, how does this happen, and what can one do about it? What was the difference that made the second set of campers kind to Laura and Howie? What did Laura and Howie learn that would help them get along better with others?

Cormier, Robert. *I Am the Cheese.* Laurel Leaf, 1991.

Adam Farmer tells the story of a bicycle ride from Massachusetts to Vermont in search of his father. Interspersed between chapters about the ride are documents recording a therapist's interviews with Adam, during which his memories slowly tell the story of his childhood in a happy family with a terrible shadow looming over it. Adam's father, a reporter, had provided information on organized crime to the government, and since then, his family's life has been ruled by the governmental agency that protects witnesses who have put their lives in danger. They have been given a whole new identity. Adam discovers that he isn't even Adam Farmer, that he was actually born Paul Delmonte. Finally he realizes that Brint, his "therapist," is trying to cause him to remember further information, information that Adam's father never gave him. It becomes impossible to know whom to trust—and the chilling sense that this is so grows until by the end of the novel, it is the point of the story.

This book is recommended for good readers because it is challenging—with flashbacks, alternating settings, and shifting loyalties—and because it presents new ideas and information that raise questions about the role of government in citizens' private lives. It lends itself to conjectural discussion.

Moral concerns. Should Adam's father have given the information? What is Brint's motive? Mr. Gray's? How could the system be handled better?

Crutcher, Chris. *Ironman.* Laurel Leaf, 1996.

Bo Brewster is an Ironman, a triathlete, who uses intense training in swimming, cycling, and running to help cope with the strained relationship between him and his father. Bo's coach and English teacher, Mr. Redmond, is much like his father, and angry outbursts at Coach Redmond result in Bo's forced membership in the Nak Pack, an anger management group of troubled boys (and one girl) who meet with Mr. Nakatani every morning before school. Feeling that he really doesn't belong in this group, Bo slowly learns the sources of the others' anger and begins to understand his own. He tells his story with growing insight and pointed humor in the form of unsent letters to radio and TV talk show host Larry King, who, he reasons, listens to everyone, no matter how unlikely the story.

Recently published nonfiction books (*Real Boys* and *A Fine Young Man*) discuss some of the destructive ways adults sometimes choose to try to turn boys into men. Crutcher's book addresses this in fiction, and does it well. Bo's manner is brash and flippant at first; his gradual move toward emotional awareness and vulnerability is always balanced by the extreme physical demands he places on himself as a triathlete, and he remains believable. Readers find much to think about, particularly regarding the line between someone else's problem and one's own problem. Crutcher tells this story about introspection with a rapid pace and plenty of action.

Drive to understand. One point that Crutcher makes in *Ironman* is that everyone has a story, and that most people use various kinds of defenses to hide their story from others. What examples of this do you see around you? How does it change your feelings toward a person when you consider the story behind his or her actions? Does the story excuse destructive actions or merely explain them? What is your role in these situations?

Relationships with others. Mr. Nak tells Bo that it doesn't need to be okay with Bo that Mr. S. is gay; it needs to be okay with Mr. S. What, then, is Bo's role? Does his relationship with Mr. S. change? By the end of the book, how has Bo's relationship with his father changed? What will happen in the future? Why? What will Bo's role be?

Curie, Eve. *Madame Curie.* Translated from the French by Vincent Sheean. DaCapo, 1986.

Gathering letters, family stories, and her own memories, Marie Curie's daughter wrote this biography shortly after her mother's death. She tells of Marie's childhood in Russian-occupied Poland and of her intellectual isolation while she worked as a governess to send her sister to medical school in Paris. When she was 24, Marie was finally able to go to Paris for her own studies. The book tells of her marriage to Pierre Curie, of their partnership in the discovery of radium, of the lonely years of dedicated work after his death, and of the honors she at last endured, having no talent for the life of the celebrity.

The book is a rich source for high school students whose interests are intellectual in nature. It presents the different worlds of well-educated children growing up in Poland and of the life of scientists in Paris at the turn of the century. Most stimulating for many readers is the glimpse of the excitement of intellectual life in Europe at that time; it made demands on Marie and Pierre that they gladly met. Marie's life is a ringing statement of the connection between hard work and accomplishment, as well as of the passionate absorption of a gifted adult in her work. Both she and Pierre were happiest in their laboratory, but they also had warm relationships with family and colleagues.

Drive to understand. This book is listed here because of the picture it provides of intellectual life in both Eastern and Western Europe before and after World War I. For gifted students whose only experience with meeting their intellectual needs and interests has been the contemporary American high school, this view of Europe can be both stimulating and inspiring.

Intensity. Discuss the contrast between play during Marie's youth in Poland and work during her adulthood in Paris. Did she make a bad choice, in your view? Why or why not?

Using ability. How did Marie's childhood and youth prepare her for her life's work? How did specific incidents lead her to her career choice? How important was the influence of her family?

Dickinson, Peter. *Eva.* Laurel Leaf, 1990.

Eva Adamson is 14, living in a future in which the burgeoning population has resulted in an almost complete take-over of the earth by humans, who are crowded into high rise buildings in sprawling cities and who rarely see a tree or an animal. Her father does research on the few remaining chimpanzees, all in captivity, and when Eva is critically injured in an accident, her parents consent to an experimental attempt to save her life—transplanting Eva's brain into the body of a chimpanzee named Kelly. Her human mind survives but receives some of Kelly's genetic memory, and Eva becomes more comfortable in social groupings of chimps than of humans. Convinced that humans are giving up—social systems are failing, no one is going into research, long-term planning has lost its viability—a brilliant young rebel arranges for Eva and a group of chimps to escape to one of the few remaining natural tropical forests.

Several controversial and discussable themes permeate this disturbing book, including: the effects of overpopulation on the earth's ecology, the ethical questions of the use of animals in research, the impact of the media on human initiative, and the loss of will to communal progress.

Drive to understand. The basic question of the book concerns what it means to be human. Have we somehow gone beyond the best that is human, to our detriment? Has the human race peaked?

Moral concerns. If we could start over again, as Eva's chimps may, what changes would you make in history? In human nature? In what ways do we have the potential to make these changes? How can we prevent, even now, the future Dickinson projects?

Douglass, Frederick. *Narrative of the Life of Frederick Douglass, an American Slave.* Signet, 1997.

Born a slave in Maryland in 1818, Frederick Douglass escaped to the north 20 years later. He had taught himself how to read and write but was otherwise uneducated. Nevertheless, leaders of the abolitionist movement recognized his intelligence and eloquence, and by 1841, he was a public speaker for their cause. Later he became Recorder of Deeds for the District of Columbia and United States Minister to Haiti. Written in 1845, this narrative is the story of his years in slavery. He tells of being passed from one owner to another, how and why he was beaten, what happened to his family and friends, and how a kind mistress taught him the alphabet and a few words before her husband forbade her to continue, saying that reading would make him unfit to be a slave— thereby firing in Frederick the determination to learn to read. The fact that he gives no details of his escape, fearing that the information would close the route to freedom for fellow slaves, creates for the modern reader a startling sense of immediacy and authenticity.

Drive to understand; Moral concerns. The contrast between the appalling descriptions of slavery on the one hand and, on the other, the clear evidence of Frederick's sensitivity, intellect, and ability to articulate experiences and feelings is deeply moving. The book is valuable both for understanding slavery and as the autobiography of a gifted writer who fought against overwhelming odds to realize his capacities.

Eco, Umberto. *The Name of the Rose*. Translated from the Italian by William Weaver. Harcourt, 1995.

Set in a 14th-century monastery in northern Italy, this acclaimed mystery novel is told by Adso of Melk, a Benedictine novice assigned to serve William of Baskerville, a Franciscan monk whose mission it is to arrange talks between emissaries of the two popes—one in Rome and one in Avignon. This mission, however, is merely the background for the more immediate problem Brother William faces: finding the causes of the mysterious deaths, one each day, of the monks in the Italian abbey where the talks are to take place. This mystery centers on the library, where manuscripts are kept in a labyrinth forbidden to all but a few, and which William and Adso must therefore explore by night.

Eco is a philosopher, historian, aesthetician, and semioticist, and his story is laced with discussions that range over all of these fields. In addition to unraveling the mystery, then, the reader's mind is challenged by the theology, the logic, and the politics of the 14th century, amid the confusion of Italian civil and ecclesiastical intrigue just after Dante's time.

Drive to understand. Readers may wish to discuss questions that are raised or implied in the text. For example, Adso comments, "I had always believed logic was a universal weapon, and now I realized how its validity depended on the way it was employed" (p. 262). In a discussion of the allegorical value of the legend of the unicorn, he says, "Higher truths can be expressed while the letter is lying" (p. 316). In Adso's final discussion with William, they consider the role of laughter, and of evil as a perversion of good (p. 491-2). If both leader and readers note such quotations as they read, they will gather plenty of material for discussion when they meet.

Elyé, Beatrice. *JumpStart: Ideas to Move Your Mind*. Great Potential Press (formerly Gifted Psychology Press), 2000.

A teacher, Elyé bases her book on a series of discussion-starters she developed for her gifted students. Each chapter embraces a different topic, all of them relevant issues for bright teens.

Examples are time management, conversational skills, organizing meetings, health, success, solitude, and mentors. In other words, this book encourages and guides young people to delve into a series of topics vital to their emotional, intellectual, and social development.

Each chapter begins with an essay on the topic and then goes on to suggest questions and activities the reader may pursue. Each chapter closes with "Words of Wisdom" (quotations from an astounding array of people, including Janis Joplin, Abraham Lincoln, Katherine Mansfield, Eleanor Roosevelt, and Lucille Ball— to take a few from the chapter on self-esteem) and two blank pages for notes.

The reader can roam through the book, selecting topics that appeal in any order, but the first chapter on "Personal Notebooks" might be a good place to begin. The remaining chapters will surely generate ideas that will fill several journals.

Faulkner, William. *The Sound and the Fury.* Random House, 1990.
This "tale told by an idiot" is related in four parts, the first told by Benjy, the mentally handicapped son of an old Mississippi family. Subsequent narrators are Benjy's brothers: Quentin, who tells of the day he committed suicide, and Jason, whose meager (and partly ill-gotten) savings are stolen by the brothers' niece, last of the family, when she runs off with a sideshow pitchman. The story, then, is of the decline and ultimate demise of a family that traced its lineage to a Civil War general and a governor.

The book is technically complex, employing not only multiple narrators but shifting time sequences and Faulkner's stream-of-consciousness writing style. An American classic, it challenges and rewards good readers. It is worth reading if only for the pleasure of recognizing fine literature—some sentences are brilliant jewels describing internal experience. Beyond seeing it as a work of art, however, thoughtful high school students will find that it helps focus questions of value and of what is to be done with one's life.

Drive to understand. The Sound and the Fury can be recommended to college-bound students with an interest in literature as an example of Faulkner's writing.

Using ability. Consider each of the major characters: Jason III and Caroline; their children, Quentin, Candace, Jason IV and Benjy; Candace's daughter, Quentin; and the cook, Dilsey. What are the elements of familial decay, and what are their origins? What elements work against decay, nudging the family instead toward maintenance or even advancement of its viability? Which are inevitable, and over which do individuals have some measure of control? In your own life, can you identify negative and positive forces that may determine your future? Do you have any control? How are you using the opportunities you have to make the most of your circumstances?

Fleischman, Paul. *Whirligig.* Holt, 1998.

Obsessed with doing just the right thing to gain popularity in his new school, Brent sets off a chain of events that concludes with the death of an 18-year-old girl. For atonement, her mother asks that Brent bring joy to the world, as Lea would have. She asks him to build four whirligigs, placing one in each corner of the United States. Though Brent is unaware of the results of his work, the reader learns how his whirligigs change the lives of a schoolgirl in Maine, a streetsweeper in Miami, a parent in Washington, and a teenager in San Diego. Brent, too, is changed by his experience. He learns the meaning of karass, a group of people linked without knowing it, perhaps never knowing who is in their karass or why.

Fleischman begins his story with a picture that will be all too familiar to young readers, as Brent agonizes over what to wear and how to behave at a party. The rest of the book moves forward and backward in time, shifting from Brent's travels around the country to the stories of people affected by his whirligigs. One connecting thread is the story of Brent's gradual movement toward recovery from the tragedy. The vignettes from the four corners of the country also tie the narrative together.

Identity. Contrast Brent's knowledge of himself before and after the accident. How can one gain self-knowledge without the intervention of tragedy? How would Brent have dealt with the party after his journey?

Relationships with others. The Miami streetsweeper comments, "People are always in a group.... And whenever there's a group there's fighting.... That's how life is." Do you agree? If you know of a group with no fighting, explain how they make that happen. Should we try to stop the fighting, or accept it as the streetsweeper does?

Frankl, Viktor E. *Man's Search for Meaning: An Introduction to Logotherapy.* Translated from the German by Ilse Lasch. Beacon, 2000.

The first part of this book tells of Frankl's experience in Auschwitz and other concentration camps, where he spent three years as a slave laborer. A psychiatrist, he focuses on the psychological reactions he observed in himself and in fellow prisoners. From his experiences came logotherapy, sometimes called the Third School of Viennese Psychiatry, after Freud and Adler. (Frankl speaks of the will to meaning, in contrast to Freud's will to pleasure and Adler's will to power.) The final third of the book gives a brief explanation of logotherapy.

This will be a useful book for young adults concerned with developing a philosophy of life, and it may be especially helpful for those who experience existentialist depression. Here are a few ideas that may be particularly intriguing: While existentialist philosopher Jean-Paul Sartre says that we invent ourselves, Frankl asserts that we do not invent the meaning of our existence, we detect it. He speaks of the existential vacuum that often manifests itself in boredom. And he speaks of the need for each person not to ask the meaning of life but to ask the meaning of his or her own life: "to life [we] can only respond by being responsible." In contrast to Maslow, Frankl believes that the pinnacle of human existence is self-transcendence rather than self-actualization.

(There is some evidence showing that Maslow would have added self-transcendence to his pyramid had he lived longer.)

Drive to understand. There is much material here for thought and discussion; the book can be read again years later for more depth. Adolescents will respond to those ideas for which they are ready. Leaders may do well to let them pose the questions for discussion.

Fuller, Iola. *The Loon Feather*. Harcourt Brace, 1967.

Oneta, daughter of Tecumseh, grows up on Mackinac Island, at the confluence of Lakes Michigan and Huron, in the early years of the 19th century, when Mackinac was a fur-trading center at which French and Indian cultures met. Her French stepfather sends her to school in Quebec, and when Oneta returns to Mackinac at age 24, she has learned to see the best in each culture and to understand the reasons for the conflicts between them. Eventually, she chooses to return to her Indian heritage, but she does so by serving as a bridge for her people from the old ways to the new.

In the person of Oneta, this unusual book gently compels the reader to look at two conflicting cultures with respect and understanding for each. Fuller masterfully evokes the natural beauty and atmosphere of a specific place, and the story is set in an accurately depicted historical period. Nevertheless, the theme of accepting the differences of others is a universal human challenge, which Oneta and others meet with dignity and a sustaining sense of self. The book is recommended for its challenge to readers to hold two conflicting views at once, stretching their minds and their sympathies.

Drive to understand. What qualities do you admire in Oneta? In Martin Reynolds? What knowledge of American Indians have you gained from this book? Have any of your attitudes changed as a result of reading *The Loon Feather*? Which ones, and how? What new understanding have you gained of other historical clashes of cultures? What applications to your own life can be found here?

Galbraith, Judy and Jim Delisle. *The Gifted Kids Survival Guide: A Teen Handbook.* Ed. by Pamela Espeland. Illustrated by Harry Pulver, Jr. Free Spirit, 1996.

This is the "revised, expanded, and updated edition" of a title that has been popular since 1983, written to and for teens and providing information about every aspect of giftedness that can be useful to them as they grow up gifted. After taking plenty of time to explain definitions of giftedness, intelligence, and testing, the authors discuss ways students can take charge of their own education. The final chapter, "On Being a Teenager," discusses adolescence in general, drugs and sex, and suicide among gifted teens, with suggestions for prevention.

The authors are veterans in the field of gifted education, and the conversational tone of the book attests to their knowledge and comfort with gifted adolescents.

Arrogance. In discussing how students can ask for appropriate educational programs, sample conversational ploys are presented that can be generalized to help young people understand how they can avoid sounding arrogant.

Perfectionism. A segment on perfectionism offers suggestions for mastering this potentially destructive characteristic.

Relationships with others. A chapter devoted to relationships includes helpful information on finding friends, handling teasing, developing conversational strategies, and getting along with parents.

Golding, William. *The Lord of the Flies.* Penguin, 1999.

A group of British boys is stranded on a coral island during an atomic war. Two leaders emerge immediately: the fair-minded Ralph, whose efforts focus on keeping a fire going to attract rescuers, and the militant Jack, who becomes a hunter and scorns efforts toward rescue. There is also the thoughtful Piggy, who is not a natural leader but whose insight guides Ralph. As the days wear on, memories of civilization fade, and the boys adopt primitive ways related to the hunt, painting their faces for camouflage and dancing to stir up blood lust. Horrible accidents occur as these practices continue unrestrained, and the boys gradually divide themselves into followers of Ralph or of Jack, with the majority following Jack. The boys—and the reader—long for adult supervision, but of course, the world's adults are busy destroying each other. Rescue comes at last, but not before the author's point about the dark side of human nature has been made.

Nevertheless, this is not a depressing book. However overwhelmed they are by the greater numbers in Jack's group, Ralph and Piggy never give up their faith in the group process or their search for what is right. Therefore, the human spirit is not destroyed by the reversion to savagery of the other boys—one independent spirit can make all the difference.

Arrogance. What role does arrogance—the assumption of one individual that he is superior to others—play in this story?

Moral concerns. How does Ralph keep going in the final hunt? Why does he not align himself with Jack to save himself? What less dramatic examples do you see of the same behavior around you, or in the newspaper? Have you ever kept going when you were alone but right? What enabled you to do so?

Relationships with others. Describe and analyze Piggy's attitude toward being teased. How is it useful to him? How could you use his example to encourage an elementary school child to cope with teasing? (This question can be used to help high school students find a way to understand and accept painful teasing remembered from their own childhoods.)

Greene, Bette. *The Drowning of Stephan Jones.* Laurel Leaf, 1997.

Living in a small Arkansas town, Carla Wayland has been raised to be an independent thinker and to oppose injustice. But now, what she most wants is to continue being the girlfriend of good-looking, popular Andy Harris. For a long time, she tries to overlook the dark side of Andy, which includes his blind hatred of Frank and Stephan, a peaceful gay couple who live in the next town. Andy is the leader when he and two friends attack Stephan one day, and he follows the attack with a series of harassing late-night telephone calls to Stephan and Frank, Carla all the while playing the adoring girlfriend—sometimes protesting, but all too gently. A Christian, and naively certain that a man of God will have compassion, Stephan persuades Frank that they should seek help from the minister of Andy's church. The meeting goes well at first, but when the Rev. Roland Wheelwright realizes the two men are gay, his demeanor alters completely, and he angrily shouts that there is no compassion for them.

By spring, Frank and Stephan have their shop well lighted and their phone tapped, so the attacks and telephone calls cease. Carla wants to believe that Andy has changed. But late on prom night, when Andy and Carla and four friends are driving home late and drunk, they meet Frank and Stephan walking home after their car has broken down. The boys get out of the car, and an appalling attack on Stephan follows. Carla is a witness; the book ends with her return to her primary values as she testifies at the trial.

While Greene (the author of *Summer of My German Soldier*, found in the Middle School section of this bibliography), has written on controversial topics in the past, her topic for this book carries more emotional charge for today's readers. She gives religious fundamentalists a spokesperson for their point of view, both through Rev. Wheelwright and through Andy, who has learned much from his minister as well as from his father. In contrast, Carla's voice is timid, limited for the most part to silent wondering and to quiet questioning of Andy's motives and actions. Frank and Stephan do nothing to provoke attack; it is clear that they are simply hated for what they are. At this stage in our national awareness of minority rights, this is an important book for thoughtful young people to read.

Aloneness. In addition to the newcomers, Frank and Stephan, Carla's mother Judith has often felt alone in Rachetville. How has she found the courage to defend her beliefs? How do you feel about her decision to move away?

Differentness. On page 2, we learn that Carla feels different— why does she? How does her feeling of differentness influence her actions? How is the experience of students who are different because they are gifted similar to the experience of students who are different because they are gay?

Drive to understand. What do you learn from this book? Do you feel that Greene has painted an accurate picture of the town? Of the situation? Why or why not? In what way might the situation have changed since Greene wrote the book, which was first published in 1991?

Moral concerns. Choose any character other than the victims and consider how that person could have prevented the drowning of Stephan Jones. What support would that person have needed to help him or her do so? Where can such support be found? If the people of Rachetville decide that they do not want something like this to happen again, what steps should they take? What is your own community doing to prevent such hate crimes? What are you doing?

Relationships with others. Trace Carla's relationships with others from the beginning of the book to the end. What has changed? What has changed within Carla? How will the events in the story affect her future relationships with others?

Hesse, Hermann. *Demian: The Story of Emil Sinclair's Youth.* HarperCollins, 1999.

As the subtitle suggests, *Demian* is really not so much about Max Demian as it is about Emil Sinclair. Beginning with an incident that occurred when he was 10 years of age, Sinclair recounts the "steps that I took to reach myself," ending with his first year of university and the beginning of World War I. In the intervening years, there are long periods when he has no contact with Demian at all, but each renewal of the friendship is highly significant for Sinclair's development. One other person, the musician and religious seeker Pistorius, is also important, both for what he teaches and for the fact that Sinclair must grow beyond him.

This psychologically-oriented account of the growing up of a highly sensitive, introspective boy has appealed to thoughtful young people since its first appearance. Sinclair is tormented by issues of right and wrong, good and evil; he tries desperately to understand how to live his life. "I wanted only to try to live in accord with the promptings which came from my true self. Why was that so very difficult?" In a time when it is difficult even to learn to *hear* the promptings from one's true self over the raucous demands of advertising and peer pressure, this book can be both a stimulus and a solace for those who march to their own drumbeat.

Aloneness. Why does Sinclair separate from his parents, even though it was a loving home? In what way does he return? How does this apply to you?

Identity. Such a personal book calls forth responses on a very personal level. Several themes may be drawn out in discussion: What is your interpretation of the "mark of Cain"? What is your experience of a *daemon* or fate? What objections might others raise to these concepts? How would you discuss them with those who might consider them elitist? Why was Pistorius not suitable as a long-term mentor? How does Sinclair's story help you understand yourself?

Intensity; Introversion; Sensitivity. Students who give evidence of these characteristics may enjoy this book because they see themselves in Sinclair.

Moral concerns. What is your interpretation of Demian's assertion that "Others sense their own laws within them; things are forbidden to them that every honorable man will do any day in the year and other things are allowed to them that are generally despised"?

Using ability. Sinclair says, "Each man had only one genuine vocation—to find the way to himself." Do you agree? How might this pertain to career choice?

Hesse, Hermann. *Steppenwolf.* Holt, 1990.

Harry Heller, a lonely intellectual of 47, calls himself the Steppenwolf—wolf of the steppes—in acknowledgment of the uncivilized, animal part of his nature. Loneliness and existential suffering have become the dominant forces in his life, bringing him to the point of suicide. Then he meets Hermine, a beautiful young woman who takes him in hand, teaches him to dance, and introduces him to the life of the dance halls in the Germany of the 1920s. The story culminates in a masked ball, reminiscent of a Faustian revelry, which becomes mystical and symbolic. Harry emerges with a resolve to re-enter the game of life, this time to learn to laugh.

Even at 47, Harry still struggles to balance his intellectual interests—writing, classical music, and political theory—with more common concerns such as dancing, jazz, people, and laughter. The two parts of the story represent extremes: the mood is sober and depressed until Harry meets Hermine, then happy and wild to the point of unreality. Suicide, loneliness, and Harry's inability to fit in are themes throughout the book, yet the overall impact is not depressing because Harry learns that neither intellectualism nor socializing is sufficient in itself. There must be a balance, and he will continue to try to find it.

Steppenwolf is not easy reading and should be recommended for older, mature, high-potential students who are likely to be dealing with similar issues. Ask students to identify themes they would like to discuss as they read the book.

Drive to understand. Themes for mind-expanding discussion include the concept that some people are "the suicides," or "those who see death and not life as the releaser"; Harry's dream of his interview with Goethe; his view of the bourgeoisie and of the immortals; Pablo's opinions on music versus Harry's; and Hermine's last talk with Harry, summarizing the views of both of them.

Identity. Consider with students the implication that Harry takes himself too seriously, that he needs to laugh at himself. If they have seen the film "Amadeus," compare and contrast Harry and his idol, Mozart, concerning laughter and taking oneself and one's work too seriously.

Introversion. Discuss Steppenwolf's search for balance between his natural introversion and his need to be with people.

Relationships with others. How can others be helpful to Steppenwolf? How might they be damaging? How should he act to make the most of relationships with other people?

Howe, James. *The Watcher.* Aladdin, 1999.

The summer Margaret is 13, her parents rent a cottage at the beach, the first time they have taken a month-long vacation. She does not play on the beach, but instead sits at the top of the steps leading down to the sand, watching. Chris, the lifeguard, is aware that she is watching, as is Evan, the older child in the family Margaret likes to watch most. She believes Evan's family is the perfect family, quite unlike her own. Spinning a romantic fairy-tale, Margaret imagines that she is part of this perfect family, but she cannot stay with them, because every night she must return to the beast and the enchanted doll. In shifting scenes, Howe provides glimpses of Chris's and Evan's worlds, until finally they intersect with Margaret's real and imagined worlds in a powerful, fast-paced, and satisfying conclusion.

We see Margaret only through the eyes of others and through the imaginative story she weaves, until the very end. By then we have developed an understanding of Evan and Chris. The shifting narrations, including Margaret's fantasy world, require holding several stories in mind at once. In addition, Howe makes good use of metaphor, so that although the reading level is not difficult, fully understanding the story will stretch some readers.

Aloneness. Each of the three main characters—Margaret, Evan, and Chris—has reason to feel alone; each needs to find someone to talk to. They respond to this need in different ways. What are these ways? Are these the best ways available to them?

Arrogance. Evan assumes that Margaret stays by herself because she thinks she's better than everyone else, but his mother has a different insight. Why is it easy to make the assumption Evan does? In what situations is it best to look further and be more understanding?

Differentness. Evan struggles with feeling different—"not cool." What is it about him that makes him feel this way? What ways do you know to deal with this feeling?

Relationships with others. Evan's mother says that we think we are entitled to perfection, and that we think there is something wrong with us if we settle for less. How does this assumption affect our choice of friends? Our ability to be a friend?

Using ability. Jenny tells Chris more than once that he has more ability than he is using. What has kept Chris from realizing his potential? Will that change as a result of the role he plays in helping Margaret? What more will he need?

Hunt, Irene. *The Lottery Rose.* Berkley, 1992.

When seven-year-old Georgie wins a rosebush in a grocery store lottery, it brings to life the beautiful gardens in books, which represent to Georgie a safe haven from his alcoholic mother and her boyfriend's beatings. When the neighbors finally call the police to stop a beating and Georgie is sent to a residential school, he takes his precious lottery rose with him. Georgie knows that Mrs. Harper's lovely garden across the street from the school is the perfect home for his rosebush, but when he plants it there without permission, Mrs. Harper is so angry that he fears her, even though he learns to love her father, Mr. Collier, and her mentally handicapped son, Robin. Georgie's old school file labels him "retarded," "destructive," and "incorrigible," but in the accepting environment of the new school, with Mr. Collier teaching him to read and Robin looking up to him as a friend, Georgie begins to relax, and he begins to give as well as receive love and trust. Eventually, Georgie learns to trust Mrs. Harper, and then a tragedy brings them even closer together.

With a background in psychology, Hunt writes with knowledge and sensitivity about the strong and conflicting feelings of a victim of child abuse. Robin is depicted with love and respect, and Mrs. Harper's anger and grief are shown in ways that young readers can understand. No one in the book enjoys a perfect life, but the story shows how interdependence can lift people above the limitations of circumstance.

Relationships with others. What does Georgie need from other people? What does he give to them? Ask the same questions for Robin and Mrs. Harper. Why is it hard to ask others for that which we need? Who in the story gives without being asked? Do you know someone who does this? Do you know what it is that you need from other people? That you give to others?

Using ability. Why does Georgie think he will never be able to read? Why can he learn so much more easily at his new school than at the old one? What factors, other than intelligence, affect how well children do in school? (For broader understanding, encourage children to name more influences on success in school than those in this story.) Do you know anyone who is not doing as well in school as he or she could? What does he or she need to be able to do his or her best?

Hunt, Irene. *William.* Ace, 1984.

Eight-year-old William and his sisters Amy and Carla would have been left alone when Mama died if she had not established a bond with Sarah, a teenager who has come to live in her aunt's house until her baby is born. Then the three children and baby Elizabeth become a family headed by Sarah—but the arrangement is threatened when Amy and Sarah quarrel. Through it all, William grows and matures, and when Sarah has the opportunity to study art in Chicago, he is able to accept her departure.

Though told from the point of view of William, this book is at least equally interesting for Sarah's story. An artist and an unmarried teenage mother, burdened with too many responsibilities, and distrustful of the conventional world, she nevertheless plays her role well, providing essential support to the younger children while using this period of several years to gather her own forces.

Using ability. Discuss Sarah's reasons for not wanting to go to art school. Why does she finally decide to go? What would you have done? What has she gained from her time in Florida? In what ways is she conventional and in what ways is she unconventional? Where do you fall on this scale? How does Sarah's position on the conventional-unconventional continuum affect her potential to use her talent? How does your position affect yours?

Kerr, Barbara. *Smart Girls: A New Psychology of Girls, Women, and Giftedness.* Gifted Psychology Press, 1997.

This is nonfiction, a report of a research study done by Kerr as the result of a high school reunion. The gifted women in her class asked her to find out why they were pursuing typical careers or homemaking instead of being the world leaders they had been told they would be.

In a readable style, Kerr discusses the developmental history of the typical gifted girl, the barriers to intellectual achievement, the family-career conflict, and ways in which gifted girls can be helped to aim higher. She includes several short biographical sketches of eminent women that illustrate her findings.

Gifted teenage girls should read this book as part of their task of recognizing what effects their intelligence can have on their choices over the next few critical years. It may make them uneasy about choices they have already made that could limit their futures, and it will be quite natural for them to set the book aside unless they talk with women who are old enough to give living examples of what Kerr is describing.

Identity. Where in the book do you see yourself? Your friends? Your mother or other older relatives? What changes would you like to see in the pattern? What obstacles do you see? What suggestions would you have for young women who want to overcome these obstacles?

Using ability. What critical decisions will you be making in the next few years that may determine whether you can make maximum use of your abilities? What planning can you do to keep your options open as long as possible? What are the patterns of decision-making by gifted women that you should be aware of in yourself?

Klass, David. *California Blue*. Point, 1996.

John Rodgers is a junior, growing up in a mill town in northern California. His father's high school football record has not been broken, and John's older brothers were football stars. The youngest in his family, John is a serious runner on the track team but not a star. He is also a serious student with a particular interest in butterflies, and during one run through old-growth forest, he finds an unusual chrysalis which he takes home. When it hatches into a brilliant blue butterfly he cannot identify, he takes it to his biology teacher, who alerts her professor at Berkeley. John's discovery is an unknown species whose habitat in the company forest threatens his father's job and the life of the little milltown. The uneasy relationship between father and son is strained to the breaking point, just as his father is undergoing treatment for leukemia.

While he has always felt very different from the people of his town, these events precipitate a crisis, forcing John to choose between what he knows and a future he cannot even imagine. For the first time, he begins to understand who he is, separate from his family and his town. His biology teacher, the Berkeley professor, and an environmental activist provide glimpses of very different ways of looking at the world. Father and son are reconciled by the end of the book, and John's future is wide open.

John could be a role model for young people whose interests and intensity set them apart from those around them. Although it is not comfortable for him to feel so different, he chooses being himself over fitting in with the crowd. The reader senses how clean and right that feels to John.

Differentness. John is very different from many people in this story, but he is quite similar to a few. What decisions can he make that will allow him to benefit from the friendship of those few?

Intensity. How do you think John has discovered and maintained his interest in butterflies in the absence of support from family and friends? Do you know of other examples, in books or in real life, of people with this kind of intensity? How does it affect their lives? What are some advantages of being so interested in a particular thing?

Moral concerns. How do you feel about John's determination not to break the law and about what follows? What would your decision have been? At what point in the story would you have made it?

Relationships with others. John's issues with his family, with peers, and with teachers make his life very complex during the time of this story. How can he sort it all out over the next few years?

Lagerkvist, Par. *Barabbas.* Translated by Alan Blair. Vintage Books, 1989.

Swedish intellectual Par Lagerkvist has written a fictional account of the life of Barabbas after he was selected to be freed and Jesus crucified in his stead. Stunned and inarticulate, Barabbas listens to Peter describe the crucifixion from his point of view, then goes to the tomb on Easter morning to see the stone rolled away. He finally leaves Jerusalem to rejoin his band of thieves, but finds that he no longer belongs. Years of slavery follow, and when he is taken to Rome, he becomes aware of the Christians there. Still inarticulate, he is drawn toward them and finally joins them in his own way, without their knowledge or consent; he remains alone to the end.

This fine book demands the best of the reader and offers a journey inward. It can lead to discussion on many levels. One useful approach is the question of Barabbas's aloneness, so fundamental as to put the loneliness most of us experience in a different perspective. Also important is the potential the book has to help focus the religious questions many inquisitive people begin to raise in the senior high years.

Drive to understand. It might be helpful to talk of Barabbas not as a person but as an archetype: the Barabbas story. What is universal here? How does he represent—potentially—the experience of all of us? What does his story tell us about being human? Is the Barabbas story a necessary part of the Jesus story? How? What do we learn of our own potential in pondering the Barabbas story?

Introversion; Moral concerns. These two categories, too, might be useful points of departure for discussion, depending on the students and the context.

Lasky, Kathryn. *Beyond the Burning Time.* Pointe, 1996.

In 1692, Mary Chase is helping her widowed mother work the farm while her brother, Caleb, is apprenticed to a master ship builder in nearby Salem. That winter, several girls in Salem Village begin acting strangely, seeing spectral figures and having fits. Seeking causes, some people come to believe that they are afflicted by the devil. In the theocracy of Massachusetts—tightly run by Puritan ministers but without a civil government—it is not long before some are crying witchcraft, and the afflicted girls are encouraged to name the witches. Mary watches in growing fear as more pious church members are arrested as witches, while her mother fiercely but calmly assures her that the charges are nonsense. Then the inevitable happens: Goody Chase, too, is arrested and taken to prison. Caleb takes Mary to Boston, finding work for her in an inn, before she herself is accused. Then brother and sister begin a desperate search for a way to save their mother.

This work is extensively researched historical fiction. Many of the characters in the book—but not the Chase family—are historical figures. In addition to documenting the background of mass hysteria and ignorance, Lasky points out how the residents of Salem Village (now Danvers, near Salem) were divided along lines of family and property ownership, and how the families of many of the accusers stood to gain through the disappearance of rival landowners. In an author's note, she clarifies how the vacuum in government, left when a former governor of Massachusetts revoked the colony's Charter in 1684, jeopardized titles to land and left property ownership open to question, setting the stage for the uncertainty and lawlessness that erupted seven years later. This book has a large scope, many characters, and much historical detail; it could easily prove overwhelming for many high school readers, but will provide thought-provoking challenge for gifted students.

Aloneness. Consider the different ways in which people experienced being alone during the witch trials in Salem. How do they compare to ways in which people feel alone in our present society? Which of them have affected you? How have you responded?

Drive to understand. What does this event in our history tell us about the importance of the separation of church and state?

Moral concerns. What does Mary's metaphor of the sun and the moon and the eclipse mean to her? How did she change, and what brought about those changes? How can you explain the story of Mary Esty's appearances after her death, and her search for vengeance? Are Mary and Caleb guilty of causing the death of Constable Dewart?

Levitin, Sonia. *The Return.* Atheneum, 1987.

In the early 1980s, drought and famine made life hard for all Ethiopians, and the persecution of Ethiopian Jews grew so threatening that some fled. In 1984-1985, a secret airlift transported thousands of Ethiopian Jews to Israel. Based on that event, Levitin tells the story of Desta, her brother Joas, her sister Almaz, and her betrothed, Dan. As part of a larger group, they flee on foot into the Sudan in the hope of reaching Jerusalem. Desta becomes the leader of the group. Through loss, suffering, and endurance, her courage grows.

The Return is recommended for thoughtful readers for several reasons. Writing in the first person, Levitin captures the rhythm of her characters' speech and thought, and maintains it. She smoothly depicts the development from girl to young woman, as Desta considers her responsibility to her family, grows in self-awareness, and faces the conflict between education and early marriage. The major characters—Desta, Dan, and Aunt Kibret—are well-rounded, showing real complexity. The book fosters an awareness of the larger world, as Desta meets with fortitude difficulties most readers will never know. In fact, most readers will not have known of the historical event—the airlift—on which the book is based. By the end of the story, Desta and her family have shown us real people behind the starvation-dulled faces we see on television.

Drive to understand. Learn more about Ethiopian Jews. What is their history in Ethiopia? How have they fared since 1985? Learn more about the drought areas in Africa, and how war plays into drought as a cause of starvation.

Moral concerns. Discuss Hagos, the boy who has grown up without family in the refugee camp, and the importance of knowing that one is part of a family, a community, or a religious group that embraces common values. Even when separated from all that is familiar, Desta and the others find that their background of common values imparts the essence of humanity. What values would you take to a POW or refugee camp?

Lipsyte, Robert. *The Contender.* Carousel, 1991.

Alfred Brooks has dropped out of school. He lives with a widowed aunt and her daughters and works in a small grocery store in Harlem. His best friend, James, is using drugs and spending time with older boys who jeer Alfred about his dead-end job. Only Henry, crippled from polio, has a kind word: Henry suggests that Alfred come to the gym where Henry works to learn to box. After James and his new friends are caught attempting to break into the grocery store, Alfred does go to the gym, where Mr. Donatelli begins by telling Alfred what is ahead of him: no guarantees of championship, but a great deal of hard work before he can even be a contender. "Everybody wants to be a champion. That's not enough. You have to start by wanting to be a contender." Despite discouragement and threats from James's new friends, Alfred does become a contender, and then uses his new self-confidence and self-discipline to reach out to others.

Drive to understand. This award-winning book is tightly written, offering in brief vignettes a picture of the difficulties of growing up in a ghetto.

Using ability. What are the positive influences in Alfred's life? The negative? Why does he choose in favor of the positive? What events discourage him, and what keeps him going? How is boxing helpful to him? In what areas would you like to be a champion? Are you a contender yet? If not, what steps can you take to become one? What might discourage you, and how will you keep yourself going in spite of it? Who are your models and possible mentors? And whom can you help?

Moliere, Jean Baptiste Poquelin. *The Misanthrope.* Dover, 1992 (written in 1666).

Set in Moliere's contemporary and fashionable 17th-century Paris, this drama is one of the masterpieces of the great French comedian. Alceste values sincerity in communication with others so highly that he is uncomfortable with the flattery that is considered good manners in courtly drawing rooms. He becomes quite fanatical about it, ignoring and hurting well-meaning friends and finally resolving to withdraw from society altogether because in his eyes it is so dishonest.

Moliere's genius is to draw the comedic and the serious very close together; as a result, this comedy offers a wealth of material for thoughtful discussion. However, high school students may need some background to understand the excesses of the French court at that time. If the play is only read, the comedy will not come through nearly as poignantly as it does on the stage.

Arrogance. What role does, or should, tolerance for human weakness play in establishing our expectations of others?

Intensity. How far can one sensibly go in standing up for one's values? How much is Alceste losing by being such an absolutist about his?

Perfectionism. What standards do you feel very strongly about? In what ways do you compromise? Should you?

Relationships with others. Is Alceste justified in hurting others in the name of standing up for his beliefs? How do we know whether and when to sacrifice honesty for politeness? How might Alceste have avoided the outcome that occurs at the play's end?

Oneal, Zibby. *The Language of Goldfish.* Puffin, 1990.

For someone who resists change, adolescence can be a frightening time. Carrie Stokes is frightened, but she doesn't know why. She is most comfortable on Saturday mornings in her art teacher's home, but when confronted with symbols of growing up, such as junior dancing class, she has brief spells of dizziness. Finally, she loses touch with reality to such an extent that her concerned parents arrange for her to meet with a psychiatrist. The combination of her talks with him and her continuing pursuit of her art work—plus her acceptance of an unexpected change in her art teacher—bring Carrie to an acceptance of change in herself.

Gifted in math as well as in art, Carrie has the advantage of being in the advanced math class; nevertheless, she feels out of step. The critical times come when she is forced to do something she is not ready for by people who expect her to act 13 before she is ready to. She must be herself and must have some control over her own rate of growth.

The book offers several insights into the pressures placed on young people to grow up at the rate society dictates into the necessity of being oneself despite external pressures, and into the experience of psychotherapy—something about which young people probably need more information than they presently have. It also brings out the fact that people respond to the same situation in different ways for entirely legitimate reasons.

Aloneness; Introversion. Why does Carrie withdraw from friends at school? How does she spend the time by herself that she gains by withdrawing? Is withdrawing or the wish to be alone good for her? What are your reasons for your answer?

Differentness; Identity. Why did Carrie respond the way she did to the pressures of growing up? Can Carrie's story help you be more tolerant of responses that you may not understand in people around you? In yourself? What does Carrie learn about herself? What does she do to help herself get better? Which of her strengths help her cope with being different? Which of your strengths help you?

Relationships with others. How do other people help Carrie get better? What does Carrie do to allow them to help her? Have you ever been in a situation in which others could have helped if you had allowed it? Why is it difficult to accept help? What are the rewards for people who can help?

Peck, Richard. *Remembering the Good Times.* Laurel Leaf, 1986.

At 16, Buck Mendenhall looks back over the past four years to tell the story of his friendship with Kate Lucas and Trav Kirby. Coming from different backgrounds, they are brought together by the transformation of their rural area into an affluent suburb. Together they face the stresses of adolescence in a too-rapidly changing world. It is Trav, the brilliant and wealthy one, who finally cannot cope with the combination of pressure at home and mediocrity and neglect in the new school.

This book is rich in characters, relationships, and issues for discussion, but paramount is the suicide of bright, intense, sensitive Trav. Discussion of suicide is difficult, but worth the effort. Leaders should be prepared with their personal answers to the questions they ask, however incomplete those answers may be.

Identity. Trav and Kate both have talent. What are the differences that make Kate stronger? Do you share Kate's sentiments when she says: "I'll never trust anything again. I'll never believe in anything or anybody. You can count on that"?

Using ability. Why did Trav kill himself? Whose "fault" was it? How might it have been prevented? What could Trav have done to prevent it? How do you answer the questions he raised about "deteriorating conditions" and the lack of challenge in school?

Pirsig, Robert M. *Lila: An Inquiry into Morals.* Bantam, 1992.

The author of *Zen and the Art of Motorcycle Maintenance* continues to state his Metaphysics of Quality in the form of a novel. The story line in *Lila* has Phaedrus sailing down the Hudson River, hoping to get to Florida before winter. In a bar in Kingston he meets Lila, who joins him and becomes a focus for some of his metaphysical musings. In this book, it is Lila who slips toward insanity, as Phaedrus watches with concern.

The real stuff of the book is the wide-ranging philosophy, and *Lila* is suitable only for those who will be intrigued by that—the story line is too slight to hold interest by itself. But those who would like an informal glimpse of philosophy at work can watch Phaedrus's mind roam as he explores such topics as the state of anthropology, Indian versus Victorian morals, European values versus late-20th-century American values, and religion and science.

Drive to understand. Phaedrus's musings provide plenty of discussion starters. To avoid too much leader domination, readers could be asked to jot down page numbers when they find a discussion they would like to pursue with the leader. Or they might be encouraged to follow one theme—the Victorian, or the anthropological, for example—throughout the book. Victorians specialized in manners, 20th-century intellectuals in causes. What might be next? Another recurring topic is the opposing roles of society and the intellect. How does this conflict affect you? How does your response to it compare with Pirsig's? He says intellectual patterns have won. Do you agree?

Moral concerns. Are Victorian moral codes returning? If we do not return to Victorian values, what might ultimately replace them?

Pullman, Philip. *The Golden Compass.* Knopf, 1995.

In this first book of a fantasy trilogy, Pullman introduces Lyra Belacqua, growing up in Jordan College, Oxford. Her education from the scholars is spotty at best, but she is a scrapper and a born leader, and she learns much by playing with the town children and the gyptians who travel through, as well as from her daemon familiar, Pantalaimon. Her comfortable life dissolves abruptly when her uncle, Lord Asriel, returns from a journey to the North with news of mysterious experiments involving children and their daemons. It is clear to the reader—though not to Lyra—that she is destined to play a pivotal role in world-changing events.

The Golden Compass will challenge the best middle school readers and intrigue adults. The language is on the high level we seek for good readers, and mystery is drawn through the novel— not really settled by the end of this volume but continuing on to the sequels, *The Subtle Knife* and *The Amber Spyglass* (the trilogy is called *His Dark Materials*). Lyra is uneducated, but she is curious, intelligent, and highly intuitive; through her, the story invites conjecture about this world and possible others. The scope of the trilogy is huge, and leaders will want to bring their own responses to the creating of discussion questions. Following are only a few initial possibilities.

Arrogance. Can Lord Asriel's arrogance be defended? What is the role of arrogance when one is pursuing a great idea? Is it a positive or a negative trait? Why do you think so?

Intensity. Compare the intensity of Lord Asriel with that of Lyra.

Moral concerns. Consider questions for the whole trilogy, including such topics as religion versus science, and the value of research (for example, does the end justify the means)? Is it acceptable for Lyra to lie her way through her adventures as she does? Why or why not? Whose motives are evil? By what standard? What is the source of the evil in this book?

Relationships with others. How does Mrs. Coulter's manipulative nature differ from Lyra's? Is one worse or better than the other? Why do you think so?

Reade, Charles. *The Cloister and the Hearth.* AMS Press, 1970.

Erasmus, the great Dutch humanist, scholar and theologian, was born circa 1466, apparently out of wedlock. The 19th-century British writer Charles Reade wove a long and carefully-researched novel around the imagined lives of Erasmus's parents. In Reade's fiction, the young Gerard Eliasson and Margaret a Peter are cruelly separated after an interrupted marriage ceremony, and Gerard, a gifted scribe and illustrator, flees Holland to seek his fortune in Italy, home of the arts. When he is told, falsely, that Margaret has died, he turns to the priesthood in despair. The real love story unfolds later, after Gerard returns to Holland and, finding Margaret and their son there, relives the anguish of separation, this time caused by his status as a priest. The young Erasmus grows up knowing both parents, though Margaret and Gerard continue to live separate lives, caring for each other from a distance and working together in providing for the poor people in their community.

This is a long book (913 pages in the Modern Library edition), to be read not for a deadline, not to finish the book, but for the pleasure gained in the reading—a summer book, with much food for thought. Wonderfully versatile, Reade writes equally convincingly of the raw danger in medieval foot travel and of subtle psychological change, of theological reflection and domestic strife, and of friendship among men and among women. The language he employs is an early form of modern English, sprinkled with bits of Latin, Greek, French, and German, in sentences graced by rhythm and framed in long cadences—a luxuriant style in refreshing contrast to the short, choppy sentences of many modern novels. There is humor, based on understatement, as well as controlled outrage at the social injustices of the day. Altogether, this is a compelling picture of conditions in the late medieval period, bringing the 15th century to life in the reader's imagination. Highly recommended, *The Cloister and the Hearth* is both a challenge and a pleasure. It may be available only in libraries or in a multi-volume collection of Reade's works, but is worth the effort of ordering on interlibrary loan if necessary.

Drive to understand. Erasmus appears in the book, but only as a child. A follow-up might be to read about Erasmus, read something by Erasmus, and then look for foreshadowing—has Reade attributed to Gerard any stirrings of ideas which Erasmus brought to fruition, perhaps in his correspondence with Martin Luther?

Moral concerns. Can we separate the 15th-century attitudes Reade describes from the 19th-century attitudes in which he was steeped—attitudes toward women, toward the Church, and toward German, French, Italian, and Dutch people?

Reynolds, Sheri. *The Rapture of Canaan.* Thorndike, 1997.

Ninah Huff lives in the South, in a large extended family headed by her grandfather, founder and preacher of The Church of Fire and Brimstone and God's Almighty Baptizing Wind. Driven by the teaching that declares that when the rapture comes and the righteous go to heaven, sinners will be left behind, each member of the family strives to follow Grandpa's rules. However, Ninah sometimes questions, as does Grandpa's wife Leila, Ninah's beloved Nanna. When Ninah finds herself pregnant, Nanna is her support, and when Grandpa declares that Ninah's baby is the new Messiah, Nanna—along with others in the community—shares Ninah's doubt. The Church of Fire and Brimstone changes as Grandpa's control diminishes, but Ninah emerges as an independent thinker, bolstered by her own faith.

The author balances her presentation, conveying the love and nurturing of the close-knit family along with the strong element of punishment in Grandpa's religion. For Ninah, her church's version of Christianity both guides and complicates her life during the normal turmoil of adolescence. Always questioning, she becomes defiant, but only after much thought and experience. She personifies the adolescent struggling to become herself against unusually difficult odds.

Aloneness. What are the sources of Ninah's strength? How does her religion help her? How do other people help? Why is weaving so important to Ninah? Is there some art or other activity in your life that is important to you in the same way?

Drive to understand. What are the advantages of growing up in this community? What are the disadvantages? There is a great disparity between these advantages and disadvantages; what effect does this have on the community? Assuming that Reynolds has accurately depicted some religious groups in her story of Fire and Brimstone, how has she modified your previous picture of what life would be like in such a community? What do you imagine happens when Ninah and Canaan return to the group at the end of the book?

Identity. Ninah says, "It made me crazy how James went back and forth between believing what he'd been taught and believing his own instincts." How does one decide between the two? How do you make that distinction for yourself?

Relationships with others. In the relationship between Ninah and James, who is the leader? If James, what makes that so? If Ninah, what makes that so? What motivates Ninah's friendship with Ajita Patel?

Richter, Hans Peter. *Friedrich.* Translated from the German by Edite Kroll. Puffin, 1987.

This story is told through a series of vignettes about the friendship between the narrator, a Christian boy, and Friedrich, a Jewish boy, in Germany from 1925 to 1942. Friedrich's family lives in the apartment above the narrator's, and the two families are distant friends. As pressure against Jews builds, the landlord arranges an attack on Friedrich's family, and his mother dies as a result. Eventually, his father is arrested, and Friedrich finds a hideout elsewhere. Seeking a picture of his parents, he returns to the narrator's family's apartment just as the air raid siren sounds, but the landlord will not allow Friedrich into the air raid shelter. When they return to the house, they find Friedrich sitting on the stoop. He has been shot and killed.

From the early picture of joy and spontaneous fun between Friedrich and his mother as they play in the snow, the book moves relentlessly to the final scene, bringing the enormity of the Holocaust down to one family and one boy. This is an excellent example of the growing body of literature written to acquaint young people with the events of World War II in Germany, but it is different from many others (and thus more representative of reality) in that Friedrich is not a survivor. The value of this literature lies in the importance of educating a new generation of leaders about these events and, insofar as they can be understood, the structures that allowed them to occur.

Drive to understand; Moral concerns. This story in itself will not provide enough information for a full discussion. Rather, it provides the emotional impact that prepares students to look at the situation from both sides. Discuss the growing reluctance of the narrator's family to help Friedrich's family. Include discussion of similar hostilities elsewhere in the world. Aim for some understanding of circumstances that might cause, or prevent, a recurrence in any country.

Sagan, Carl. *The Dragons of Eden: Speculations on the Evolution of Human Intelligence.* Ballantine, 1989.

High school students who enjoy conjecture may be interested in this popularized version of our understanding of brain structure and function. For example, they might find challenge in—or wish to challenge—Sagan's suggestions regarding the link between the development of the neocortex and the Genesis story. As the subtitle points out, Sagan is here presenting "speculations" rather than hard science, and the book must be read in that spirit. However, the book is sufficiently grounded in science to hold the interest of a reader open to questioning.

Drive to understand. Discussion could easily be based on questions and responses to Sagan's speculations that occur to the reader while reading. Suggest that readers note questions and comments as they read, and bring them to the discussion.

Smith, Huston. *The World's Religions.* Harper San Francisco, 1992.

The son of missionaries to China and a professor of philosophy at Massachusetts Institute of Technology, Huston Smith has written descriptions of seven great religions: Hinduism, Buddhism, Confucianism, Taoism, Islam, Judaism, and Christianity. His aim is to convey "the meaning these religions carry for the lives of their adherents." Accordingly, he writes little of doctrine and less of history (both of which are to be found in a good adult encyclopedia), but reveals for each of these religions "why and how they guide and motivate the lives of those who live by them."

In the final chapter, he presents a sound argument for accepting the validity of each faith for the people who follow it.

Drive to understand. Senior high students who are beginning their personal religious search find this book useful, especially appreciating Smith's objectivity, which frees them to reach their own conclusions. The objectivity is balanced by a respect for each religion and its people—a human perspective that prevents the material from ever becoming intellectualized or dry. Thoughtful young people seeking meaning for their lives will find here seven different broad approaches to the question of meaning which have stood the test of time. Moreover, while acknowledging the triviality and violence to which religion can descend, Smith describes each religion in its highest, most intellectually and spiritually challenging form. Readers will find stimulus for thought in each of these religions, and they will also gain a greater understanding of their followers.

Storr, Anthony. *Solitude: A Return to the Self.* Ballantine, 1989.

A Clinical Lecturer in Psychiatry at Oxford, Anthony Storr suggests that post-Freudian psychological theories place too much emphasis on interpersonal relationships as a sole foundation of human happiness. He argues instead that, especially for the creatively gifted, solitude may be essential to a contented, productive life. Certainly, the desire for solitude is not to be thought of as pathological. "If it is considered desirable to foster the growth of the child's imaginative capacity, we should ensure that our children...are given time and opportunity for solitude" (p. 17). "The capacity to be alone...becomes linked with self-discovery and self-realization" (p. 21). Storr explores the role of solitude in learning, thinking, creativity, and self-knowledge, as well as in grief work and religious insight, and he suggests that individuals can find life's meaning in interests and ideas, as well as in intimate relationships. Indeed, for some gifted individuals at some times, ideas may be more important than relationships.

Chapters on solitude and creativity late in life may not appeal to teenage readers, but Storr's extensive use of biographical material to illustrate his point undoubtedly will. The book should prove reassuring to those unusual students—the highly gifted in particular—who are more comfortable alone than with others.

Aloneness; Introversion. How do you feel about alone time? How do those around you feel about it? How well do you use it? If you need more, how might you get it?

Relationships with others. In your own life, what is the present balance between interests and relationships? Are you happy with this balance? How would you change it?

Using ability. What implications does this idea of balance between ideas or interests and interpersonal relationships have for your career choice?

Strasser, Todd. *The Wave.* Laurel Leaf, 1981.

Based on a real incident in a California high school in 1969, this is the story of a teacher's attempt to demonstrate to a history class how it felt to live in Germany under Nazism. Within a short time, the students and even the teacher are caught up in The Wave, their experimental totalitarian organization, which requires its members to obey their leaders without questioning. It spreads to include students outside the history class until the teacher realizes that it has gained a momentum of its own and must be stopped somehow. It is clear that this will hurt some of the students, especially Robert, an underachiever who is rebelling against his brother's success, and for whom The Wave is a born-again experience. The story is told largely from the point of view of Laurie, an "A" student and editor of the student paper, who questions the group and finally writes an editorial exposing its dangers.

Strasser does well at presenting The Wave from various points of view so that the reader begins to understand how such a group can be attractive, and to whom. The saving grace is Laurie's insistence on thinking for herself and her mother's support as she stands alone for what she sees as right.

Aloneness. How does Laurie keep fighting, even after David and Amy desert her? What qualities does that take? Do you have these qualities? How can one develop them?

Identity. What is happening to the teacher during the course of the experiment? What is happening to Robert? In what way is Laurie different from the others in the book, leading her to respond differently to the situation? How does all of this relate to a sense of identity?

Moral concerns. Why does Laurie take the Hitler film "too seriously"? Why and how do good people like David become involved in a group like The Wave? How could that involvement be avoided?

Relationships with others. What role does the need to belong play in this story? Why does Robert become so deeply involved so easily? How can young people work to develop healthier relationships with friends?

Using ability. What characteristics does Laurie have that make it logical for her to fight The Wave? Why is it important for her to use those characteristics? What would have happened to The Wave and to her if she had not fought it?

Thomas, Elizabeth Marshall. *Reindeer Moon.* Pocket Books, 1991.

Set in Siberia 20,000 years ago, this novel of prehistory tells the story of Yanan, who is 13 years old when the story begins. Gathered in family groups of about a dozen people, traveling on foot, following the animals to summer and winter hunting grounds, and subject always to sudden death through injury, illness, or childbirth—or slow death through starvation—Yanan's people focus first on finding food and second on the complex social fabric of their lives. Thomas depicts well the dependence of these hunter-gatherers on the animals of the plains they roam—the lions, tigers, horses, deer, wolves, and mammoths—and assumes that there is a consequent intimacy between the spiritual lives of animals and people. Much of the novel focuses on the spiritual lives of the people, and the interweaving of personal and spiritual relationships creates an absorbing story line, despite the repetition of the relentless search for food.

Courageous, headstrong, and alone, Yanan comes of age without her parents' guidance, and she makes some fatal errors in judgment. Readers will recognize the impatience, impetuosity, and moodiness of adolescence, despite the millennia that separate Yanan and today's young people—who face essentially the same questions.

Drive to understand. What gives meaning to the lives of Yanan's people? What can we learn from this fictional version of paleolithic life that might help us define what is essentially human? From this perspective, discuss the role of material goods in defining what it is to be human. In the same light, consider the role of knowledge, which has increased so much since then; the role of developments in religion since 18,000 B.C.E.; and the changes in our relationship to animals.

Thomas, Joyce Carol. *Marked by Fire.* Avon, 1999.

Growing up in the black community of an Oklahoma town, Abby Jackson learns wisdom and strength from her mother, from Mother Barker, from the rural rhythm of nature and the sudden devastation of a tornado, and from the cruelty of some of her neighbors. After an assault, she stops using her lovely singing voice. Mother Barker and her mother help her gradually regain her sense of self, and she reaches adulthood with a deep, sure sense of her own uniqueness, and with a commitment to using her healing abilities, as well as her voice, for others.

The style moves imperceptibly between prose and poetry. Evocations of the rhythms of speech in the singing and story-telling of the women of the community are especially powerful. There is a haunting quality in the writing style and in the person of Abby herself that makes this a beautiful book to read.

Identity. Abby's parents are Patience and Strong. How does Abby develop and use these qualities? Why are they especially useful for a sensitive person like Abby? Are you aware of using or developing these qualities in your own life? How do you know when to use which?

Relationships with others. What examples are there in the book of acceptance of human failings? Is it a strength or a weakness to be so accepting? Why? How is acceptance of human failings related to Abby's acceptance of her special talents?

Using ability. Will Abby become a doctor? Should she? Why or why not?

Thomas, Rob. *Rats Saw God.* Aladdin, 1996.

Leaving his father's house in Houston after a disastrous junior year, Steve York continues his use of drugs as he begins his senior year in San Diego. But it is being named a National Merit Finalist, not substance abuse, that lands him in the office of counselor Jeff DeMouy. Steve cannot graduate unless he makes up his failing grade in English III, and DeMouy offers him a way to do that while avoiding summer school: write a 100-page paper. The alternating chapters of *Rats Saw God* track Steve's senior year in San Diego, interspersed with his paper about his sophomore and junior years in Houston. Gradually, we learn why Steve moved to his mother's house, and we watch as he works out a new vision of his future in his writing. (We also learn how the title makes sense.)

Thomas writes as Steve would think, beginning with a swaggering, in-your-face style designed to impress observers with his intelligence and cynicism. It slowly evolves into a still-intelligent but more straightforward style as Steve becomes more comfortable with himself and with his father, whom he calls "the astronaut"—because he is one, and because he is more astronaut than father in Steve's eyes. The author clearly knows teens and sees past their hairstyles and body-piercings to the anxiety and potential lying underneath. Characterization is excellent, and the narrative commands attention as the plot unfolds chapter by chapter. The end is bittersweet, but like the rest of the book, it is also realistic.

Arrogance. Is Steve arrogant? How would he appear to be so to most students at both of his schools? What purpose does this attitude serve for him? When and why does it diminish?

Relationships with others. What qualities does Steve seek in friends? What part does intelligence play in this search, either consciously or otherwise? How would you answer these questions for yourself?

Using ability. What are Steve's strengths? How well does he use them in high school? How might that change in the future? How did you feel about his not choosing Harvard?

Tillich, Paul. *The Dynamics of Faith.* HarperCollins, 1986.

Tillich examines the phenomenon of faith—objectively, analytically, and apart from specific doctrinal content, so that although he is one of this century's great Christian theologians, followers of other religions, too, can read this book for greater understanding of their experience of their own faith. Defining faith as "ultimate concern," he considers what faith is and what it is not. He also looks at the symbols of faith and at different types of faith. Sections on mythology and humanism as they relate to faith may be of particular interest to gifted high school students.

Drive to understand. This book is suggested for questioning young people as an introduction to religious thinking at its highest and most challenging—and therefore potentially most interesting—level. Whether the readers are among those who take religion seriously, those who question whether religion has any value at all, or those who read simply for exposure to a new field, interested high school students would do well to meet Tillich. This book is a good introduction to his thought.

Tolan, Stephanie S. *A Good Courage.* Beech Tree, 1998.

Ty (short for Tie-Dye Rainey) and his mother, Jasmine, are on their way to Florida for yet another new start when a TV ad for the Kingdom, a religious community, catches her attention. They join the group, and Jasmine fits in immediately. Ty, on the other hand, is skeptical but unconcerned, since he feels sure that her interest in the Kingdom will flag in a few weeks, as it always has before in similar situations. But here, parents and children are separated, and in the few moments he has to talk with his mother, Ty realizes that she is settling in for longer than he can bear to. Children are carefully controlled, and while they are not beaten, there are enough incidents of unhealthy treatment and danger-ous punishment that Ty finally escapes and goes to the police to complain of child abuse. The police return with Ty to the King-dom, where the leader, Brother Daniel, acts his part so smoothly that Ty's story is not believed. Help comes from an unexpected source, however, and Ty escapes again, this time with his new friend Samarah. An old friend, a father-figure, meets them and takes them back to the Home Place, the commune where Ty and Jasmine had most recently stayed.

Tolan has the courage to write on controversial topics, and she treats them with an even hand. As our empathy with Ty and the other children grows, the sense of being trapped causes revul-sion but not too much fear. Characters are well-rounded; even Brother Daniel, who could be portrayed as a dictator, is seen in a softer light by the end of the book. Religion is treated with respect.

Aloneness. How is Ty required to stand alone in the Kingdom? In what areas does he change his thinking while maintaining a core of self?

Identity. Distinguish between physical and mental control. How does Ty retain his own way of thinking? What is the source of his strength? Why is his mother so easily swayed? In what ways does Ty grow and change? What does he learn?

Tolan, Stephanie. *Welcome to the Ark.* HarperTempest, 2000.

Varying family circumstances bring four child prodigies together at a residential home for disturbed children in upstate New York. Elijah, Taryn, Miranda, and Doug range in age from six to 17 and in talent from clairvoyance to extraordinary abilities in math and languages. Selected for a new program called the

Ark, the four children move to a family setting in a group home, joining two psychologists who want to learn whether, through computer networking, they can help other child prodigies around the world. The networking soon surpasses computer capabilities, as the four prodigies become so attuned to one another that they dream the same dreams and experience each other's memories, eventually concluding that they share a quest, the exact nature of which they must determine. Sharing also a horror of violent acts, they begin testing ways in which, with their psychic abilities, they might end violence peacefully. As their networking reaches out to children in other countries, the director of the residential home fears losing control and closes the Ark, separating the children. Eight years later, Taryn, Miranda, and Doug meet again, apparently by coincidence. The sense that they share a quest returns as the book ends.

Welcome to the Ark is the first book of a projected science-fiction trilogy. Like Susan Cooper's *Dark Is Rising* fantasy sequence for younger readers, Tolan's book explores the response of children with special talents to the forces of evil, and it raises the question of whether these children bear some responsibility to combat these forces. The sense that they may have such a responsibility gives meaning to the lives of the gifted children, overcoming the pain that their gifts have brought to them in the past.

Aloneness; Introversion. Considering Elijah, Taryn, Miranda, and Doug each in turn, what role does time alone play in the lives of each of them? When is it healthy, and when is it not—or is it always healthy?

Identity. Again considering each of the main characters in turn, how aware are they of being gifted? How does this awareness affect their decisions? How has their gift been a negative in the past, and how have they dealt with that?

Moral concerns; Using ability. What is the connection between the abilities of the children of the Ark and their quest? In your view, do they have a responsibility to pursue their quest? Why or why not? What would be the consequences of a decision to pursue their quest? What would be the consequences of their deciding *not* to pursue it?

Relationships with others. A major theme of this book is that highly gifted people often appear to others to be misfits, even mentally unbalanced. What is your response to this? What can be done to increase understanding?

Voigt, Cynthia. *Building Blocks.* Scholastic, 1994.

Brann Connell has grown up believing that his father is weak, indecisive, and ineffectual. In a time-warp experience, he spends a day with his father as a boy, seeing his father's childhood home and family and watching how 10-year-old Kevin coped with a very difficult situation regarding his own father. Brann returns to his own time with a better understanding not only of his father, but also of his father's traits, which represent a strength Brann lacks.

Voigt reveals a sensitivity to different personality styles that can help gifted children recognize—even look for—something of value in people they have not previously been able to understand. This book suggests that, for those who look below the surface and are open to another's experience, there is much to know about other people.

Identity. How are Brann and Kevin different? What strengths of Kevin does Brann discover? What caused Kevin to become the person he is now? Choose one of Kevin's traits and discuss how it can look like a weakness from one angle and a strength from another. Do you know anyone like Kevin, with a characteristic that can be both bad and good? Do you have any such traits?

Relationships with others. How will Brann's experience change his future relationship with his father? Can you choose someone you have difficulty understanding or with whom you are impatient and imagine a story like this told about that person? How does it change your feeling about him or her? How does Brann's experience help him understand himself better?

Voigt, Cynthia. *Izzy, Willy-Nilly*. Aladdin, 1995.

Izzy is a sophomore—a pretty, popular cheerleader—when she accepts Marco's invitation to a party, not because she especially likes him, but because he is a senior. Marco drinks too much, and the accident on the way home results in the amputation of Izzy's right leg. As she recuperates, Izzy watches her friendships change. Marco never calls, even to apologize. Lauren, who plans to be a model, withdraws from Izzy, overwhelmingly appalled at physical imperfection. Suzy's habit of lying becomes a too-familiar brand of false friendliness. Even Izzy's strong and loving parents, who deal efficiently with the practical aspects of her handicap, are not available to recognize her emotional vulnerability. Only Roseamunde, who is seen as weird and is rejected by Izzy's popular group, comes forward as a friend who can accept and reflect what Izzy is experiencing, though she does so awkwardly at first. The daughter of an artist, Roseamunde is more intellectual than the others and is different in her own right—and she says exactly what she feels, a trait that enables her to reach Izzy in her isolation. When Izzy returns to school, she finds that she is still popular, but now she is on her way to becoming an individual.

Voigt offers an absorbing story line with a psychological depth that continues to merit thought and discussion long after the reading is done. A teacher, she records the high school atmosphere accurately, and even the weaker characters are sympathetically drawn. Roseamunde, with the social awkwardness combined with the sensitivity, maturity, penetrating insights, and direct honesty characteristic of many bright and introspective people, is especially memorable.

Identity. What does Izzy learn about herself from Roseamunde? From the accident? In what other ways can high school students become individuals beyond the high school scene? Why is it so important to Izzy that Roseamunde is so direct? Why does Roseamunde seem rough, and Izzy smooth, in being honest? Why is Roseamunde more developed as an individual by the age of 15 than Izzy is?

Relationships with others. What did Roseamunde see in Izzy that led her to believe that she could be a friend? What do Roseamunde and Izzy have in common with each other that they do not share with Lisa, Lauren, and Suzy? What can they continue to learn from each other?

Voigt, Cynthia. *Jackaroo.* Point, 1995.

Gwyn is a 16-year-old innkeeper's daughter—in medieval Wales, to judge from the names. Times are hard, and although the innkeeper is prosperous and his family better off than most, Gwyn feels intense sympathy for the poor, so distant from the concerns of the ruling lords. In this hard winter, a lord and his son stop at the inn, and when they leave suddenly, they request a servant for each of them. Gwyn and the manservant Burl attend them, but the four are separated in a blizzard, and Gwyn and the lordling spend many days snowbound in an abandoned stone cabin. Gradually they become friends, despite the awkwardness of the lord/servant relationship, and the lordling teaches Gwyn to read. Cleaning the cupboards of the stone cabin one day, she finds an old pair of thigh-high leather boots, a plumed hat, and a tunic—the costume worn by the legendary Jackaroo, who rides to aid the people in difficult times. Gwyn has never believed the legends, but she finds the costume useful. In its disguise, she is able to dispense some of the gold pieces given to her by the lord when she returned his son safely to him to people who desperately need help. However, riding as Jackaroo enables Gwyn to feel fully her strength and independence, and she realizes that she can no longer follow the narrow choices open to her at the inn or in the nearby village.

Voigt captures language patterns and medieval mores and restrictions well, describing vividly the lives of common people living in a period most literature depicts only through the eyes of the nobility. Many readers will identify with Gwyn's sensitivity to the needs she sees around her, and with the sense of differentness it engenders. The love story of Gwyn and Burl is slow and subtle, a long friendship developing before Gwyn recognizes it as love.

Differentness; Sensitivity. Why is Gwyn so much more aware of others' needs than most people are in this story? Why is Burl aware? What restrictions did medieval living patterns impose on "different" people, such as Gwyn and Burl? If the Earl had not intervened, what could they have done? What restrictions do present living patterns and unwritten rules impose on people like them? What options do such people have now?

Identity. How did playing Jackaroo help Gwyn clarify her own identity? Why was doing what she did dangerous? What was Win warning her about? How would you have advised her about marriage? Why?

Voigt, Cynthia. *The Runner.* Point, 1997.

In this prequel to *Homecoming*, Voigt tells the story of Bullet—Samuel Tillerman—a 17-year-old high school junior in 1967. The war in Vietnam is a distant struggle, not nearly as threatening as the conflict in Bullet's home, where his father's tight control has already sent Bullet's older brother and sister away for good. Only Bullet and his mother are left—she to endure, and Bullet to mark time until he, too, can leave. The discipline of running hardens Bullet—but running also brings him into contact with Tamer, an older black student. Tamer and Bullet's boss insist that he look at himself with the same insistence on truth that he turns on the rest of the world. The book is beautifully written and demands much of the reader. Those who have read *Homecoming*, *Dicey's Song*, and *A Solitary Blue* will gain greater understanding of the children's grandmother, Abigail Tillerman, in this book. Those who have not read any of Voigt's *Homecoming* series will want to start here.

Drive to understand. What is Bullet's major inner conflict? Leaving his mother? Coaching Tamer? Facing his prejudice? Why do you choose the one you do?

Identity. Of the men Bullet knows, which is the best mentor for him, and why? What qualities make him a good mentor?

Moral concerns. Why would Bullet urge Tamer to stay out of Vietnam, but not do so himself?

Vonnegut, Kurt. *Slaughterhouse Five.* Delta, 1999.

Twenty-four years after the city of Dresden, "the Florence of the Elbe," was firebombed by the Allied Powers, Vonnegut published this novel based on his experiences as a prisoner of war and survivor of that massacre. As is fitting for an event too awful to look at straight on, the narrative dances around the bombing, foreshadowing the terrible event we know is coming, but then glancing off to focus instead on the story of Billy Pilgrim, the chaplain's assistant who plays Vonnegut's role. Billy is a time-traveler; his consciousness shifts easily from awareness of the present to past and future scenes of his own life. His understanding of time as a continuum (whatever has been always is) rather than as made up of discreet moments is enhanced when he is kidnapped and taken to the planet Tralfamadore to be exhibited in a zoo. His story parallels the events leading up to the firebombing, setting it in a context of confusion and chaos.

The form of this novel is a kaleidoscopic mix of events, places, and people, not a chronological narrative at all—emphasizing the impossibility of comprehending Dresden through a logical, linear approach. It can only be approached sideways, out of the corner of one's eye. Today's students may need to be reminded that the book first appeared during another event that challenged comprehension: the Vietnam conflict.

Differentness. Discuss Billy's differences in seeing what others do not see, and how he copes with that.

Drive to understand. Vonnegut's method of telling the story could be considered now in light of new insights about left brain/right brain or random versus sequential thinking. What does this approach tell us that a historical chronology would not? For what other subjects would this style be appropriate? What do you consider sequentially, and what holistically or spatially? Why?

Moral concerns. What does the historical event of Dresden have in common with other 20th-century massacres? How does it differ? What have we learned?

Webb, James T., Elizabeth A. Meckstroth, and Stephanie S. Tolan. *Guiding the Gifted Child.* Gifted Psychology Press, 1989.

Although this book is subtitled *A Practical Source for Parents and Teachers,* it is such a clear explanation of the major emotional difficulties a gifted child faces that teenagers are able to gain much self-understanding from it. Stephanie Tolan's "Open Letter to Parents, Teachers and Others: from Parents of an Exceptionally Gifted Child" is especially recommended for highly gifted young adults. If they identify with RJ, they may begin to understand why they felt as they did in elementary school. This acceptance of their younger selves can be a cathartic experience for them and can mark the beginning of a new level of self-acceptance and understanding.

Teenagers and adults can read this book separately, each noting page and paragraph numbers they would like to consider further, and then meet for discussion.

Achievement; Identity; Intensity; Moral concerns; Perfectionism. Each of these issues is mentioned in this book.

Aloneness. The chapter on depression should interest people who are concerned about aloneness in the life of a gifted child.

Identity. The first three chapters will help young people develop a better understanding of their identities as gifted persons.

Relationships with others. The chapters on communication of feelings, peer relationships, sibling relationships, and parent relationships all offer information that will promote discussion of getting along with others.

Using ability. Chapters that relate to making maximum use of potential are those on motivation, stress management, and discipline.

Wolfe, Tom. *Bonfire of the Vanities*. Bantam, 1988.

Sherman McCoy is a Wall Street whiz of the high-flying '80s, a junk bond Master of the Universe, until he stumbles over the belief that he deserves to have ever more. An accident in the Bronx with his mistress in his car brings Sherman devastating publicity—which transforms inexorably into notoriety—and acquaints him with a reality that is as harsh as his upbringing has been privileged.

Wolfe skillfully draws a wide range of characters and requires the reader to remember each throughout the long novel as he pulls the cast closer together toward the final court scene. Sherman undergoes psychological changes that provide a good beginning for discussion.

Arrogance. How does the tone of the book change after Sherman is stripped of arrogance? What is the effect of this on you as the reader?

Identity. Sherman is a decent person who shrinks from anything he considers to be ill-bred. What acts are moral or immoral in his view? Where is the line between morality and a good upbringing?

Moral concerns. Why does Sherman have difficulty regarding the tapes? Would you? Why or why not? How could this theme be treated with someone such as yourself as the main character? What temptations could cause you to rise so high and fall so far?

Using ability. In order to have become a "Master of the Universe," Sherman must be of above-average intelligence. Why then does he get into so much trouble? What are the uses and limits of high intelligence as a guide for living?

Wolff, Tobias. *This Boy's Life: A Memoir*. Grove Press, 2000.

Prize-winning fiction author Tobias Wolff turns to nonfiction for this story of his boyhood, which is also the story of the masking and creating of an identity. Born in Alabama in 1945, he moved with his mother to Washington State after his parents separated when he was 10. "Jack," as he calls himself, spends most of his teenage years in Seattle and then in a small mountain town, now with a volatile stepfather. He is a discipline problem, his friends are unsavory, and an almost schizophrenic split develops between who he believes he is and how others see him. A very strong core of undeveloped self-knowledge enables him to avoid being defeated by the difficult circumstances of his life; he is also aided by a renewed contact with his older brother, who had stayed with their father when the family separated. We do not see the completion of his growing up in this book, but we do see a major act of deception (which stops short of self-deception) that gives him an escape from the limitations of his early years.

This Boy's Life raises questions about who we are, who we think we are, who others think we are, and who we may become. One of Wolff's achievements is to make it possible for us to see with unusual clarity the lines between those four facets of self-understanding and self-creation. Evidence of the dichotomies in his self-perception appears throughout the book; toward the end of the book, we see introspection directly related to this theme.

Achievement. How does high potential complicate Wolff's boyhood?

Identity. Describe Wolff as he is, as he thinks he is, as others see him, and as a potential adult. Now do the same for yourself, and then for some other person you would like to understand better. How do the circumstances of your life make the development of your identity a different task from Wolff's? How does the book help you understand someone you know?

Moral concerns. Reread the paragraphs that deal with Jack's relationship with Arthur in the story of the grudge fight on pages 217-218. How does he use the words "citizen" and "outlaw"? What prevents Wolff from "trying to be a citizen"? Which is the better route, and what is the cost of each? How are you choosing, and why?

Index

1984, 99

A

Abilities, use of in gifted children, 29-36
Ability grouping and gifted children, 48, 54, 55, 64, 168
Abrahamson, R. F., 84-85, 102, 223
Abuela, 205
Academy of Educational Development, 191
Across Five Aprils, 71, 139, 199
Adams, Adrienne, 233
Adams, P. J., 167, 192
Adderholdt, M., 33, 38
ADHD (*see also* attention deficit/hyper activity disorder), xviii, 10, 39
Adoff, A., 250
The Adventures of High John the Conqueror, 234
Adventuring with Books: A Booklist for Pre-K – Grade 6., 254
African literature, 204, 205, 231, 233
Age-appropriate books. *See* Reading Guidance
The Age of Chivalry, 99
Alderson, B., 234
Alexander and the Terrible, Horrible, No Good, Very Bad Day, 205
Alexander, D., 161, 192
Alexander, Lloyd, 237, 240-241, 256
Alice's Adventures in Wonderland, 87
Aliki, 235
Aliteracy, 61
Aloneness, 258, 260, 276. *See also* Loneliness
Alvino, James, 178, 192

American Federation of Teachers, 89-90
American Library Association, 148, 179, 185, 253-255
American literature, 234
Amidon, S. R., 48, 64
Amos and Boris, 202
Anansi the Spider, 204
Andersen, Hans Christian, 239
Andromeda Strain, 242
Angelou, Maya, 248
Animal Farm, 242
Anne of Green Gables, 87
Anno's Journey, 206
Anno's Medieval World, 131
Anthem, 158, 208
Anthony, Piers, 242
Anti-intellectualism, 7, 42
Applebee, A., 171, 192
The Arabian Nights, 234
Arabic literature, 234
Arbuthnot, M. H., 252
Architecture: The Natural and the Manmade, 99
The Arm of the Starfish, 157
Arrogance in gifted children, 21
Ashley Bryan's African Tales, Uh-Huh, 233
Ashley, L. F., 251
Asimov, Isaac, 242
Associated Press, 89
Asynchrony, 14-15
At the Back of the North Wind, 239
Attention deficit/hyperactivity disorder (ADHD), xviii, 10, 39
Attention needs in gifted children, 20

Atwell, N., 175, 192
Auel, Jean, 208
Authentic biography, 225
Avi, 71
Avid readers, 10, 20, 88, 91-92, 95, 97, 98, 129, 176, 206, 225

B

Babbitt, Natalie, 242
Babies Need Books, 75, 102
Baby Sitters Club series, 87
Baker, Jeannie, 204
Barzun, Jacques, 161-162, 192
Basal readers, 163, 166
Basalization, 164
Baskin, B. H., 83, 102
The Bat-Poet, 208
Bates, M., 18, 38
Bauer, M. D., 177, 192
Beauty, 240
Becoming a Nation of Readers, 163
Beers, K., 61, 64, 102, 192, 212, 256
Begin Here: The Forgotten Conditions of Teaching and Learning, 161, 192
Bernstein, J. E., 113, 148
Best Books for Children; Preschool through Grade 6, 253
Best Books for Junior High Readers, 253
Best Books for Young Adults: The History, the Selections, the Romance, 254
The Best of Bookfinder, 81, 102
Bettelheim, B., 230, 256
Bibliotherapeutic discussions. *See also* Intellectual book discussions
    at home, 178
    at school, 108
    capping technique, 139
    children in, 123-125
    confidentiality in, 139
    leading discussions, 122, 130, 139
    literature for, 125-127, 128
    motivation of readers in, 129-130, 137
    place and time for, 127, 129, 170
    planning for, 131

Bibliotherapy
    and mental health professionals, 107
    clinical, 107-108
    definition of, 106
    developmental, 107-108
    goals of, with gifted children, 141
    literature for, 120-122
    process of, 114
    qualifications for, 113-114
    strengths of, 146
    studies of, 110-112
Bibliotherapy: A Clinical Approach for Helping Children, 108
Bibliotherapy: The Interactive Process: A Handbook, 113
Billington, James H., 59, 64
Biographical fiction, 225-227
Biography, 225
    criteria for selecting, 226-227
    for gifted readers, 121, 228
    in bibliotherapy, 228
Blake, William, 246
Blishen, Edward, 207
Bloom, Benjamin, 155, 192
Bloom's Taxonomy of Educational Objectives, 155, 174-175
Blue Highways, 100
The Blue Sword, 241
Blueberries for Sal, 218
Book clubs, 100, 128, 148
Book discussions. *See* Bibliotherapeutic discussions; Intellectual book discussions
The Book of Three , 236-237, 240
Booklist, 125, 128, 212, 224
Books. *See also* Literature
    for emotional development, 37
    for intellectual development, 152
    for older children, 206
    picture books, 70, 79, 201-203, 216, 220, 253, 257, 261
Books for the Gifted Child, 93, 102, 211
Books for the Gifted Child, Volume 2, 96, 103, 211
The Borrowers, 93, 239

Boston, Lucy M., 239
The Boy Who Had Wings, 200
Boys, 20, 38, 73-74, 82, 83, 88, 103, 148
Bradbury, Ray, 242
Brain development, 56-57, 58
Brave New World, 242
Bridge to Terabithia, 131, 170
Brown, Marcia, 203
Bruchac, Joseph, 234
Bryan, Ashley, 233
Buescher, T., 3-4, 38
Burgess, Anthony, 242
Burningham, John, 206
Butler, D. , 75, 78, 102

C

Caddie Woodlawn 71, 200
Caduto, Michael J., 234
Caldecott Award, 257, 277
Call It Courage, 155, 199, 209
The Call of Stories: Teaching and the Moral Imagination, 121, 148
Calliope (magazine), 211
Campbell, Joseph, 100
Career decisions in gifted children, 34-35
Carlsen, G. R., 82, 84, 102
Carroll, Lewis, 246
Carry On, Mr. Bowditch, 201, 228
Carter, B., 82, 84-85, 102, 223, 254, 256
Castiglione, L. V., 173, 192
The Cat Ate My Gymsuit, 199
Catcher in the Rye, 117
Catharsis in bibliotherapy, 116
Cather, Willa, 71
Celtic literature, 234
Celtic Myths, 234
Cendrars, Blaise, 203
The Center for Gifted Studies (University of Southern Mississippi), 53
Chall, Jeanne, 162-163, 192
Characteristics and needs of gifted children, 11, 15, 47-52, 87-88
    performance, 51-52
    thought-processing, 50-51

verbal, 49-50
Characterization in discussions, v, 98
Charlotte's Web, 87, 239
Chase, Richard, 234
Cheaper by the Dozen, 201
Children and Books, 252
Children in Crisis, 121,
The Children of Green Knowe, 239
Children's literature, reference books on, 252-255
"The Children's Literature Web Guide", 167
The Child's Developing Sense of Theme: Responses to Literature, 171, 193
Choosing Books for Children: A Common sense Guide, 211
Christabel, 100
Christopher, John, 242
Cianciolo, P. J., 253
"City", 177
The Clan of the Cave Bear, 208
Clark, B., xviii, 49, 53, 62, 64, 74, 77, 102, 168, 192
Classics in literature, 83-86, 144
Clay, M., 75, 78, 102
Cleary, Beverly, 79, 245
Climb into the Bell Tower, 256
A Clockwork Orange, 242
Cobblestone (magazine), 211
Colangelo, N., 38, 52, 54, 65, 65
Coles, R., 115, 121, 148
Colhoun, A., 189-191, 192
College decisions in gifted students, 6
College of William and Mary, Center for Gifted Education, 9, 42
Colum, Padraic, 233, 235
Communicating through Young Adult Books, 181, 193
Computers. *See* Library skills
Concrete operational stage, 171
Confidentiality in discussions, 139
Cook, Elizabeth, 236, 256
Coolidge, Olivia, 235
Cooney, Barbara, 233
Cooper, Susan, 241

Cooperative learning, 54-55, 65
Cornett, C. E., 106, 148
Cornett, C. F., 106, 148
Counselors. *See* Psychologists
Courlander, Harold, 234
Creative Home Schooling for Gifted Children,
    65, 178, 193
Crichton, Michael, 242
The Cricket in Times Square, 93
Cry, The Beloved Country, 72
Cullinan, B., 165, 192
cummings, e. e., 248
Curie, Eve, 226

D

Dabrowski, K., 45-46
Dailey, S., 231, 256
Davis, G. A., 34, 38, 52, 54, 64, 65
A Day No Pigs Would Die, 201
"Dear America" series, 218
A Death in the Family, 72
Definitive biography, 225-226
Delisle, J., 117, 148
Demian, 207
Depression in gifted children, 94, 119-120
    existential, 143
The Description of Wales, 99
Detracking, 53, 54, 55
Developing imagination in gifted children,
    10-12, 51
Developmental bibliotherapy, 107-108
Developmental stages, 109
Didactic fiction, 122, 126
Discussion groups. *See* Bibliotherapeutic
    discussions; Intellectual book discussions
Dobyns, S. M., 121, 148
Dodson, Shireen, 128, 148
Dole, J. A., 167, 192
Doll, B., 107, 113, 148
Doll, C., 107, 113, 148
Donelson, Kenneth, 252
Dr. Seuss, 76, 205, 248
Dragonslayer: The Story of Beowulf, 231, 234
Dreyer, Sharon, 81, 102

Drive to understand in gifted children, vii,
    44, 46, 106, 198
Dune, 242

E

Earthfasts, 208, 240
Earthsea trilogy, 241
Education of gifted children, 38, 42. *See also*
    Schools
    economic barriers, 52-53
    funding for, 52-53, 56, 164-165
Egoff, S., 251
Ehrlich, V. Z., 49, 64
Elementary children, early (grades K-2)
    bibliotherapy goals for, 141-142
    curriculum for gifted, 34, 192, 216, 223
    fantasy and science fiction for, 239-244
    in discussions123-125
    K-6 literature curriculum for, 216
    library skills of, 185
    poetry for, 244-250
    reading interests of, 79-80
    reading patterns of, 73
    traditional literature for, 229-236
Elementary children, upper (grades 3-5)
    bibliotherapy goals for, 142-143
    curriculum for gifted, 34, 192, 216, 223
    fantasy and science fiction for, 239-244
    in discussions, 123, 125
    K-6 literature curriculum for, 216
    library skills of, 185
    poetry for, 244-250
    reading interests of, 80-82
    reading patterns of, 73
    traditional literature for, 229-236
Eliot, T. S., 100
Emotional development in gifted children
    and establishing identity, 7-15
    and multipotentiality, 34-35
    and perfectionism, 32-33
    and psychosocial needs in adolescents,
    3-4, 38
    and relationships with others, 23-28
    and risk-taking, 30-31

and the drive to understand, 44, 46
and the need for time alone, 16-20
and using abilities, 29-31
criteria for selecting books for, 197-211
Emotional overexcitability, 9-10, 23
Encyclopedia Brown books, 79
Endangered Minds: Why Children Don't Think, 56, 64, 193
Engels, D, W., 111, 149
Epics, 216, 229, 240
Escape literature, 71, 125, 154, 237
Essentials of Children's Literature, 193, 252
Estell, D., 86, 102, 254
Evan's Corner, 217
Expectations of gifted children
external, 35
internal, 35-36
Eyeopeners: How to Choose and Use Children's Books about Real People, Places, and Things, 253
Eyeopeners II: Children's Books to Answer Children's Questions about the World around Them, 253

F

Fahrenheit 451, 242
Fairy tales, 73, 80, 88, 229-230
Fantasy
criteria for selecting, 242-243
for gifted readers, 237-238
when to introduce, 238-241
Fantasy Literature for Children and Young Adults: An Annotated Bibliography, 254
Far Eastern literature, 234-235
Farming, 75
The Farthest Shore, 241
Father's Arcane Daughter, 139, 209
Federal Office of Gifted and Talented, 52
Ferraro, S., 219, 256
Fiction
criteria for selecting, 217-219
in bibliotherapy, 121-122
Fictionalized biography, 225-226
Fiedler, E. D., 55, 64

Finn, C. E., 41, 65
Fitting in, attempts at in gifted children, 20, 23, 30-31
Flack, J., 166-167, 192, 226, 256
The Fledgling, 74
Folktales, 205, 216, 230-231, 256
Forbes, Esther, 218
Ford, Richard, 100
Formal operational stage, 172
Free Fall, 205
Freehill, M., 208, 212
Freeman, J., 90, 102
Freud, S., 100
Frey, D., 3, 38
Friendship skills, 21-22
Fritz, Jean, 74
From the Mixed-up Files of Mrs. Basil E. Frankweiler, 209
Funding
for gifted programs, 52, 53, 56
for reading programs, 164-165
Future of an Illusion, 100
Future Problem Solving, 42

G

Galda, L., 165, 193
Garfield, Leon, 71, 207
Garner, Alan, 240
Gates of Excellence, 251
Gender differences in reading interests, 73-74
Gerald of Wales, 99
Gibbons, Gail, 75
Giff, Patricia Reilly, 87
Gifted children. *See also* Characteristics and needs of gifted children
Differentness in, 8-9
Emotional characteristics of, 114, 198-201
Emotional development of, 3-7, 37, 38-39, 42, 105-106
Emotional needs of, 28, 43, 206, 127
Intellectual characteristics of, 48, 49, 61, 168
Intellectual development of, 42, 47-48, 151

Intellectual needs of, 41, 43, 48, 49, 214, 217

Intellectual peers of, 49, 51, 55, 152, 153, 161, 180

Gifted Children and Legal Issues: An Update, 53

Gifted readers, special characteristics of, 87-89

Giftedness

    ambivalence toward the label of, 9

    definition of, xviii

    discussing with children, 142

    identification of, 7

Gillespie, John T., 253

The Gingerbread Boy, 74, 230

A Girl Called Al, 124, 135

Girls, 20, 34, 38, 73-74, 82-83, 88, 103, 121

The God Beneath the Sea , 207

Goldberg, J., 33, 38

The Golden Fleece, 233, 235

The Golden Hoard: Myths and Legends of the World, 235

A Golden Treasury of Poetry, 247, 250

Gone with the Wind, 168

A Good Courage, 145

Good Night, Moon, 218

Good Reading: A Guide for Serious Readers, 100, 211

Gordon, Ruth, 250

The Grapes of Wrath , 168

Greek and Roman literature, 80, 207, 231, 235

Greek Myths, 235

Greenaway, Kate, 233

Greene, Constance C., 135

Grimm brothers, 230, 238

Guest, Charlotte, 241

Guiding Gifted Readers, vi, 111

Guiding the Gifted Child 28, 39

H

Hall, S. L., 75, 78, 102

Halsted, J. W., 46, 64

Hardy Boys series, 71

Harlem, 250

Harris, K. H., 93, 102, 211

Harrison, Michael, 250

Harry Potter series, 80, 239

Harter, M. R. , 57

Hauser, P., 93, 96, 103, 211

Hawkins, S. , 88, 102

Haynes, C., 74, 102

Healy, J. M., 56-58, 60, 64, 163, 193

Hearne, Betsy Gould, 211

Hebert, T. P., 112, 148

Heidi, 87

Helping Gifted Children Soar, 56, 66

Herald, D. T., 82, 85, 103

Herbert, Frank, 242

The Hero and the Crown, 241

Hesse, Herman, 207

Hey! Get Off Our Train, 206

Hierarchy of needs, 29, 36

High fantasy, 216, 237, 239, 241

    when to introduce, 240-241

Higher levels of thinking 64, 173

Historical fiction, 71, 80, 82, 217-218, 227

Hitchcock, Alfred, 71

Hoban, Tana, 204

The Hobbit, 241

Homesick: My Story, 74

Home schooling, 62, 65. *See also* Parents and book discussions, 128

    effectiveness of, 62

    websites for, 166, 178

Hopkins, Lee Bennett, 177

House of Stairs, 242

"The House that Jack Built", 76

Howe-Cousar, C., 175-176, 193

Howley, A. A., 23, 38

Howley, C. B., 23, 38

Hughes, Langston, 177

Hunter, Mollie, 115, 148

Huxley, Aldous., 242

Hynes, A. M., 113, 146, 148

Hynes-Berry, M., 113, 146, 148

I

I, Robot, 242

Identification in bibliotherapy, 114-115

Identity, establishment of in gifted children, 4, 7-10

The Idiot, 99

If the Owl Calls Again; A Collection of Poems, 250

Illustrations, 76, 201, 204-207, 221-222, 233, 253

Image in poetry, 244, 246-249

"In Just-", 248

Incubation time, 18, 51

    need for in children, 159, 180

    use of by discussion leaders, 132-133

Independent readers, 79-80, 89, 158, 218

Individual pacing, 152, 158, 180

Informational Picture Books for Children, 253

Insight in bibliotherapy, 116-117

The Institute for Law and Gifted Education, 53

Intellectual book discussions, 175

Intellectual development

    and books for older children, 152, 206-210

    and picture books, 202-206

    and thinking effectively, 153-155

    and using intellect effectively at home, 90

    as an emotional need, 43

    criteria for selecting books for, 258

    need for in gifted children, 42, 44

    traits of optimal, 45, 47-48, 202

Intellectual overexcitability, 9, 44

Intellectual peers in discussions, 49, 51, 55, 152, 161, 180

Internet. *See also* Library skills

    and databases, 184, 189-190, 191

    and search engines, 189-190, 191

Introversion, 17-18, 94, 159, 259

Izzy, Willy-Nilly, 208

J

The Jack Tales, 234

Jacob Have I Loved, 138, 145

Janeczko, Paul B., 250

Janos, P. M., xix, xxi

Jarrell, Randall , 208

Jarvis, J., 20, 38, 59, 64, 97, 103

Jarvis, R., 20, 38, 59, 64, 97, 103

Jennifer, Hecate, Macbeth, William McKinley and Me, Elizabeth, 199

Johnny Tremain, 71, 218

Johnson, N. J., 176, 193

The Journey through Wales, 99

Jude the Obscure, 99

Julie of the Wolves, 116-117

The Jungle Books , 239

Junior Great Books, 175

Jupiter Communications, 189

Jurassic Park, 242

Just as Long as We're Together, 199

K

Kaplan, J. S., 108, 148

Karnes, F. A., 53, 64, 65

Kearney, K., 55, 65

Keepers of the Earth: Native American Stories and Environmental Activities for Children, 234

Kerr, B. A. , 20, 24, 33, 34, 35, 38, 48, 65

Kiersey, D., 18, 38

Kindergarten. *See* Elementary children, early

Kipling, Rudyard, 239

Kobrin, B., 253

Konigsburg, E. L., 139, 209

L

Lack, C. R.108, 148

Lahr, S. S., 171-172, 193

Lange, R. E., 55, 64

Langerman, D., 74, 103

Langton, Jane, 74

Language development in children, 74, 75-77, 83, 162-164

Language in literature, 164, 202-208

The Last Lion, 101
Latham, Jean Lee, 201
Lawson, Robert, 239
Leadership, 11, 13
Lear, Edward, 246
Legal action for gifted programs, 53
Legends, 80, 216, 229, 230, 234-235, 236, 240-241
The Legends of Charlemagne, 99
LeGuin, Ursula, 241
L'Engle, Madeleine, 200, 242
Lerner, A. 115, 148
Levy, J., 57
Lewis, C. S., 80, 240
Librarians
    in schools, 70-72, 76, 97, 107, 122, 128, 215, 219
    training of, 108, 110, 113, 165, 184-185
Libraries
    public, research in, 187-188
    resources of, 183-184
    school, evaluation of, 183-185
    staffing of, 184-185
Library skills
    and the Internet, 183-184, 186, 189-191
    teaching of, 185, 186-187
The Limits of Art, 99-100
Lind, S., ix, 9, 38
The Lion, the Witch, and the Wardrobe, 240
Literature. *See also* Books
    about children's literature, 70-72, 76, 251-252
    biography, 225-229
    curriculum, 81, 216
    fantasy, 236-244
    fiction, 121, 216-219
    nonfiction, 220-225
    poetry, 244-251
    science fiction, 236-244
    traditional literature, 229-236
    understanding of in discussion, 115, 122-126
Literature-based reading curriculum, 81, 164

Literature circles, 165, 169, 175-176, 193
Literature for Today's Young Adults, 252
The Little Red Hen, 76, 230
Little Women, 87
Livingston, Myra Cohn, 245-246, 249-250, 256
"Lone Dog", 248
Loneliness, 228, 229. *See also* Aloneness
The Loon Feather, 156
The Lord of the Rings , 241
Lovecky, D., 96, 103
Lynch-Brown, C., 164, 193, 237, 252
Lynn, R. N., 254

M

Mabinogion, 240-241
Macbeth, 99
MacDonald, George, 239
MacLachlan, Patricia, 87
Madame Curie, 72, 226
The Magic Bookshelf, 20, 38, 59, 64, 97, 103
The Magic Treehouse series , 218
Magical Tales from Many Lands, 235
Mahlendorf, U. R., 115, 148
Manchester, William, 101
Marked by Fire, 208
Marquardt, R. G., 53, 64, 65
Martin, C. E., 81, 103
Mary Poppins, 239
Maslow, Abraham, 16, 29, 36, 38
Mature readers, 73, 98-101
May, J. P., 241, 256
May, Rollo, 231, 256
Mayne, William, 240
Mayo, Margaret, 235
McBratney, Sam, 234
McCaffrey, Anne, 241
McCaughrean, Geraldine, 235
McCord, David, 247
McDermott, Gerald, 204
McKinley, Robin, 240
McLeod, Irene Rutherford, 248
Meckstroth, E. A., 28, 38, 49, 66
The Merry Adventures of Robin Hood, 234

The Microbe Hunters, 228
Middle school students (grades 6-8)
  bibliotherapy goals for, 143-144
  curriculum for gifted, 98-99, 216
  fantasy and science fiction for, 238-242
  fiction for, 83-84
  library skills of, 86, 87
  nonfiction for, 84, 85
  poetry for, 245-248
  reading patterns of, 83
  traditional literature for, 233-236
Millions of Cats, 218
Milliot, J., 85, 103
Milne, A. A., 239
Moats, L. C., 75, 78, 102, 162-163, 193
Mockett, S., 203, 212
Montgomery, L. M., 87
Moon, W. L. H., 100
Moral issues, awareness of in gifted
  children, 11
Morelock, M. J., 14, 38
Moses, H. A., 149
The Mother-Daughter Book Club, 128, 148
Mother Goose rhymes, 70, 76, 244, 248
Motivation to learn in gifted children, 82,
  85, 129
Mrs. Frisby and the Rats of NIMH, 137, 140
Multipotentiality in gifted children, 34-35,
  144
My Name Is Aram, 72
My Name Is Not Angelica, 201
Myers, Walter Dean, 250
Mythology
  for gifted children, 231, 233, 243-244

N

Narnia series, 80. 240
A Nation at Risk, 54
National Council of Teachers of English,
  163, 254
*National Excellence: A Case for Developing
  America's Talent,* 42, 65

Nelson, Gail A., 93, 96, 103, 211
*The New Oxford Treasury of Childrens'
  Poems* , 247, 250
Newbery Award, 257
Newman, B. M., 172, 193
Newman, P. R., 172, 193
Nilsen, A. P., 252
Nodelman, P., 242, 256
Noe, K. L. S., 175, 193
Nonfiction, 220, 224-225
  criteria for selection, 220-223
  for gifted readers, 70, 73-75, 84, 98, 223
  in bibliotherapy, 120-121
Nordheimer, J., 53, 65
Norse literature, 231, 235, 240
Norton, D. E., 252
Norton, Mary, 93, 239
Nye, Naomi Shihab, 250

O

Obermiller, T., 58, 65
O'Brien, Robert C., 239
O'Dell, Scott, 71, 201
Odin's Family: Myths of the Vikings, 235
Odyssey (magazine), 211
Odyssey of the Mind, 42
Office of Educational Research and
  Improvement, 42, 65
Old Ramon, 90
Omnivore, 242
On the Road, 100
*Only Connect: Readings in Children's
  Literature,* 251
Open-endedness in nonfiction, 221, 223
The Ordinary and the Fabulous, 236, 256
Orwell, George, 242
Outstanding Books for the College Bound,
  255
Over Sea, Under Stone, 241
Overexcitability , 9-10, 23, 38, 44-45
The Owl Service, 240

P

Paley, V., 58

Pardeck, J. A., 108, 148

Pardeck, J. T., 108, 148

Parents. *See also* Reading aloud; Reading
  guidance
  and gifted children, 61-62
  and libraries, 184-185, 187-188
  and resistant readers, 94-95, 97
  and school programs for gifted
  children, 62, 151
  as bibliotherapeutic discussion leaders,
  128-129
  as intellectual book discussion leaders,
  178, 179
  in finding friends for gifted children,
  24-25
  introducing poetry, 244-248
  meeting intellectual needs of gifted
  children, 61-62, 178, 179

Part-time Boy, 199

Paterson, Katherine, 167, 170, 198, 212, 251

Pearce, Philippa, 239

Peck, Robert Newton, 201

Peers, need for in gifted children, 24, 26-27

Pendarvis, E. D., 23, 31, 38

People, 204

Perfectionism in gifted children, 32-33.
  See also Using abilities

*Perfectionism: What's Bad about Being Too
  Good?*, 33, 38

Perry, H. K., 194

Peter Pan, 87

The Phantom Tollbooth, 207

Philip, Neil , 235

Piaget, Jean, 171

Picard, Barbara Leonie, 235

"The Pickety Fence", 247

Picture books
  criteria for selection, 202-206
  for gifted children, 212, 216, 253

Picture Books for Gifted Children, 212

Piechowski, M. M., 9, 38, 44-46, 65

Pierce, K. M., 254

*Pierced by a Ray of Sun: Poems about the
  Times We Feel Alone*, 250

Phonics, 162-164

*The Place My Words Are Looking For: What
  Poets Say about and through Their
  Work*, 250

Plot in discussions, 133, 138, 171-172, 177,
  182, 183, 205

Poe, Edgar Allan, 71

Poetry, 244-250
  criteria for selecting, 248-250
  introducing , 245-247

The Power of Myth, 100

Prelutsky, Jack, 249

Pre-operational stage, 171

Preschool children
  bibliotherapy goals for, 141-142
  literature for, 230, 253
  reading patterns, 73-76
  teaching to read, 77-79

Problem novels, 81-82

Probst, R., 176, 193

Psychologists, 108, 118-120, 203

R

Rabbit Hill, 239

Rackham, Arthur, 233

The Rainbow People, 235

Rakow, Susan R., 84, 103

Ravitch, D. , 7, 38, 41, 54, 65, 162, 163, 193

The Read-aloud Handbook, 90, 103

Readers. *See* Avid readers; Independent
  readers; Mature readers; Resistant readers

Reading aloud, 74-76, 89-90

Reading Begins at Home, 75, 78, 102

Reading, brain development and, 57

Reading guidance
  age-appropriate books, 73-86
  for avid readers, 91-94
  for mature readers, 98-101
  for resistant readers, 94-98
  fundamentals of, 70-73
  with gifted readers, 69-73

Reading Lists for College-Bound Students, 86, 102
Reading log, 96, 183
Reading patterns, 73-74
    gender differences in, 73-74
    in early elementary students, 79-80
    in gifted students, 87-88
    in middle school students, 82-85
    in preschool children, 74-76
    in senior high students, 85-86
    in upper elementary children, 80-82
Reading, teaching of. *See also* Basal readers; Basalization; Literature circles
    curricula, 42, 166-167
    for gifted students, 78, 89, 166, 167
    look-say method of, 163
    phonics in, 162-164
    whole language in, 162-165
Reading to Heal 137, 149
Reading too much, 93
Reading wars, 162-163
Reading workshops, 175
Reference materials in children's literature, 252-255
Re-Forming Gifted Education: Matching the Program to the Child, 54, 55, 66
Reis, S. M., 121, 148, 166, 167, 193
Relationships with others in gifted children, 17, 22, 23-29
Renzulli, J. S., 166, 167, 193
Research skills. *See* Library skills
Resistant readers, 94-97, 100
    at home, 97, 129
    at school, 96
Rimm, S. B., 34, 38, 39, 54, 59, 64, 65, 178, 193
Riordan, R. J., 112, 148
Risk-taking in gifted children, 4, 11, 30-32
Rivero, L., 62, 65, 178, 193
Robinson, A., 55, 65
Robinson, D. , 131, 149
Rogers, K.B., 54-56, 66
Rosenberg, B. 241-242, 256
Russell, D. , 88, 103

S

Samuels, B. G., 63, 83-85, 102-103, 192
Sanfield, Steve, 234
Satchwell, M. L., 86, 102, 254
Saunders, J. , 178, 193
Scales, P. , 181, 193
Scarry, Richard, 204
Schaefer, Jack, 90
School Library Journal, 125, 128
Schools
    curricula for gifted children, 42-43
    discussion groups at, 122-127
    K-6 literature curriculum, 215-216
Schrank, F. A., 111, 149
Science fiction
    criteria for selecting, 242-243
    for gifted readers, 88, 237-238
    when to introduce, 238-241
Scully, Vincent, 99
Selden, George, 93
Selection of books, 8, 208, 211
Self-actualization, 30, 31, 36, 147
Self-Consciousness, 86, 103
Self-esteem, 29, 30, 36, 119
Sendak, Maurice, 204
Senior high students
    bibliotherapy goals for, 144-145
    biography for, 226, 228
    college-bound reading for, 86, 99, 102
    library skills of, 187-188
    needs of, xviii, 34, 35
    poetry for, 248, 250
    reading patterns of, 85-87
Seredy, Kate, 230
Series fiction books, 217, 218-219
The Serpent's Tongue: Prose, Poetry, and Art of the New Mexico Pueblos, 234
Sesame Street, 57
Setting in discussions, 120, 130, 182, 209
Shadow , 203
Shadow of a Bull, 145
Shadows and Reflections, 204
Shrodes, Carolyn, 114

Silverman, L. K., 10, 39, 43, 66, 96, 103

Silverstein, Shel, 246, 248, 249

Sir Cedric, 201

Sitting Bull and His World, 227

Slake's Limbo, 209

Slaughterhouse Five, 209

Slavson, S. R., 114, 149

Sleator, William, 242

Slow Dance Heart Break Blues, 250

Slower processing, 158, 159

Smith, 208

Smutny, J. F., 47, 64, 66

Social conditions, 56-57

The Space between Our Footsteps, 250

Spache, G. D., 116, 149

Speare, Elizabeth George, 71

Spiegel, D. L., 165, 193

Spier, Peter, 204

Sports, 26, 81, 89, 217

The Sportswriter, 100

The Spying Heart: More Thoughts on Reading and Writing Books for Children, 212, 251

Stanley, J., 137, 149

Steig, William, 202

Steindorf, S., 178, 194

Step Lightly: Poems for the Journey, 250

Stevenson, Robert Louis, 246, 247

Story, emotional response to, 76, 133, 170

The Story of King Arthur and His Knights, 234

Strachey, Lytton, 226

Straight Talk about Reading, 75, 78, 102, 193

A String in the Harp, 207

Strip, C., 56, 66

Stubbs, G. T., 251

Stuart-Clark, Christopher, 247, 250

Suicide, 117, 120, 148

Summer of the Swans, 200

Sutcliff, Rosemary, 231, 234, 235

Sutherland, Z., 252

Swanton, S. I., 80, 103

"The Swing", 247

Swinger, A. K., 87, 103

Sylvester and the Magic Pebble, 202

Symbol in poetry, 208, 246, 249

T

Tales of the Mabinogi, 99

Tales of the Norse Gods, 235

Taxonomy of Educational Objectives, 155, 174, 175, 192, 212

Taylor, C. J., 235

Teachers

and gifted children, 20-25, 28-29

and resistant readers, 96

Television's effect on intellectual growth, 57-59

Textbooks in children's literature, 164, 233, 251

This Boy's Life, 100

Thomas, Joyce Carol, 208

Thought-processing characteristics and needs of gifted children, 50-51

The Three Billy Goats Gruff, 76

The Three Little Pigs, 230

Through the Eyes of a Child, 252

Tillman, C. E., 111, 149

The Tiger's Whisker and Other Tales and Legends from Asia and the Pacific, 234

Time alone, need for in gifted children, 4, 5, 16-20

A Time to Fly Free, 200

Tolan, Stephanie, 28, 39, 49, 66, 145

Tolkien, J. R. R., 239, 241

Tom Jones, 99

The Tombs of Atuan , 241

Tomlinson, C. M., 164, 193, 237, 252

Tom's Midnight Garden, 239

Too Late the Phalarope, 72

Traditional literature

criteria for selecting, 232-236

when to introduce, 230-232

Travers, P. L., 239

Trelease, Jim, 90, 103

The True Confessions of Charlotte Doyle, 74

The Trumpet of the Swan, 93

Tuck Everlasting, 242

"TV, Video Games and the Growing Brain", 60-61

U

Underachievement in gifted children, 34, 39, 59, 109
Universalization in bibliotherapy, 114, 117
University of Chicago Laboratory Schools, 58
Untermeyer, Louis, 247, 250
Updike, John, 86, 103, 248
The Upstairs Room , 156
U.S. News and World Report, 99
Using abilities, 29-36
Using Literature to Help Troubled Teens Cope with Identity Issues, 108

V

VanTassel-Baska, J., 172, 173, 194
Veenker, K., 47, 66
Veenker, S., 47, 66
Verbal characteristics and needs of gifted children, 49-50
Video games' effect on intellectual growth, 57, 59
The Village by the Sea, 209
Visual-motor integration, 59
Vonnegut, Kurt, 209

W

Wait time, 173
Waldhorn, Arthur, 211
Walker, S. Y., 178, 194
The Wanderings of Odysseus: The Story of the Odyssey, 235
Wartes, J., 62, 65
Watership Down, 239
Webb, J. T., 10, 28, 39, 43, 49, 66
Weber, Olga S., 211
Wells, Rosemary, 202, 203, 212
Welton, A., 203, 212
What Do Our 17-Year-Olds Know? , 41, 65

Where the Forest Meets the Sea, 204
White, E. B., 93
The White Mountains , 242
The White Stag, 230
Whitehead, R. J., 88, 103
Whitmore, J. R., 34, 39
Whole language, 162-165
Who's in Rabbit's House?, 205
Why Johnny Can't Read, 162, 193
Wilder, Laura Ingalls, 71
Willard, Nancy, 250
Williams, R., 17, 39
Wilson, L. S., 112, 148
The Wind in the Willows, 239
Wind, Sand and Stars, 72
Winebrenner, S., 55, 64
Winn, M., 59, 66
Winnie-the-Pooh, 131, 239
Winner, E., xix, xxi, 17, 34, 39
The Witch of Blackbird Pond, 92, 201
Withdrawal in gifted children, 21
A Wizard of Earthsea, 241
The Wolfling, 131, 199
Wood, Nancy, 234
Words by Heart, 156
Wright, P. S., 86, 102, 254
A Wrinkle in Time, 242
Writing style
    in discussions, 182
    in literature, 222

Y

Yep, Laurence, 235
Yolen, Jane, 200
Young adult literature, 82-85, 144, 145, 254

Z

Zaccaria, J., 108, 149
Zeiger, Arthur, 211
Zen and the Art of Motorcycle Maintenance, 117

Annotated Bibliography: Index of Categories

Preschool (Up to Four Years Old)

Aloneness
Amanda Pig on Her Own, 288
Where Does the Trail Lead?, 276

Arrogance
I'm Terrific, 286

Creativity
Frederick, 283

Developing Imagination
Frederick, 283
I Spy: An Alphabet in Art, 285
In the Small, Small Pond, 269
James and the Rain, 272
Louhi, Witch of North Farm, 279
My Grandma Lived in Gooligulch, 277
Sir Cedric, 280
Something from Nothing, 281
Sun Song, 284
Time of Wonder, 285
Time to Sleep, 269
Where Does the Trail Lead?, 276
Where's Waldo?, 282

Differentness
Frederick, 283

Drive to Understand
Anno's Counting Book, 277
Fortune Tellers, The, 276
Guess Who?, 273
Hey! Get Off Our Train, 279
I Spy: An Alphabet in Art, 285
Little Island, The, 284
Louhi, Witch of North Farm, 279
Shrinking Mouse, 282
Something from Nothing, 281
Sun Song, 284

Identity
Amanda Pig on Her Own, 288
Complete Tales of Winnie-the-Pooh, The, 286
Empty Pot, The, 280
Frederick, 283
I'm Terrific, 286
Owl Babies, 275
Titch, 283
Turtle Knows Your Name, 278

Introversion
Frederick, 283

Moral Concerns
Empty Pot, The, 280
Hey! Get Off Our Train, 279

503

Perfectionism
Empty Pot, The, 280

Relationships with Others
Complete Tales of Winnie-the-Pooh, The, 286
Friends, 282
I'm Terrific, 286
Owl Babies, 275
Shrinking Mouse, 282

Stevie, 287
Titch, 283

Sensitivity
In the Rain with Baby Duck, 271

Using Ability
Frederick, 283

Kindergarten to Grade Two

Aloneness
Evan's Corner, 307
Feelings, 289
Man Who Lived Alone, The, 305
Silver Pony, The, 370

Creativity
Ben's Trumpet, 309
Cinder-Eyed Cats, The, 316
Daniel's Duck, 294
Man Who Lived Alone, The, 305
Ramona the Brave, 299
Silver Pony, The, 370
What Happened to Patrick's Dinosaurs?, 298

Developing Imagination
Abuela, 301
Cinder-Eyed Cats, The, 316
Dawn, 291
Free Fall, 322
If at First You Do Not See, 294
On Market Street, 312
Outside Over There, 317
Owl Moon, 324
Peboan and Seegwun, 311
Shadow, 298
Shadows and Reflections, 308
Tomas and the Library Lady, 315
Tomie de Paola's Book of Poems, 301
What Happened to Patrick's Dinosaurs?, 298
Where the Forest Meets the Sea, 290

Who Came Down that Road?, 312

Differentness
Ben's Trumpet, 309
Daniel's Duck, 294
Hannah, 321
Henry Hikes to Fitchburg, 309
Knots on a Counting Rope, 313
Man Who Lived Alone, The, 305
Ramona the Brave, 299

Drive to Understand
Abuela, 301
Anansi the Spider: A Tale from the Ashanti,
    314
Anno's Journey, 290
Bears, 303
Bird Watch: A Book of Poetry, 324
Boston Coffee Party, The, 315
Castle on Hester Street, The, 307
Dandelions, 295
Dawn, 291
Eleventh Hour, The, 292
Elfwyn's Saga, 323
Evan's Corner, 307
Island Boy, 300
Legend of the White Buffalo Woman, The,
    304
Old Turtle, 323
Ox-Cart Man, 306
Peboan and Seegwun, 311

Red Leaf, Yellow Leaf, 301
Sign of the Seahorse, The, 293
Stay Away from Simon!, 297
Story of Holly and Ivy, The, 305
Tomas and the Library Lady, 315
What Are You Figuring Now? A Story about Benjamin Banneker, 302
Where the Forest Meets the Sea, 290
Who Came Down that Road?, 312

Identity
Feelings , 289
Ida and the Wool Smugglers, 289
Island Boy, 300
Knots on a Counting Rope, 313
Little Red Lighthouse and the Great Gray Bridge, The, 318
Man Who Could Call Down Owls, The, 296
Outside Over There, 317
Sylvester and the Magic Pebble, 317

Intensity
Ben's Trumpet, 309
Daniel's Duck, 294
What Are You Figuring Now? A Story about Benjamin Banneker, 302

Introversion
Evan's Corner, 307
Man Who Lived Alone, The, 305
Silver Pony, The, 370

Moral Concerns
Boston Coffee Party, The, 315
Sign of the Seahorse, The, 293
Where the Forest Meets the Sea, 290

Perfectionism
Daniel's Duck, 294

Relationships with Others
Alexander and the Terrible, Horrible, No Good, Very Bad Day, 319
Best Friends, 310
Evan's Corner, 307
Everett Anderson's Friend, 299
Feelings, 289
Hannah, 321
Henry Hikes to Fitchburg, 309
Iktomi and the Berries, 303
Ramona the Brave, 299
Red Leaf, Yellow Leaf, 301
Rosie and Michael, 320
Sign of the Seahorse, The, 293
Stay Away from Simon!, 297
Who Will Be My Friends?, 308

Sensitivity
Daniel's Duck, 294
Hannah, 321
Old Turtle, 323
Sylvester and the Magic Pebble, 317

Using Ability
Daniel's Duck, 294
Little Red Lighthouse and the Great Gray Bridge, The, 318
Tye May and the Magic Brush, 291
What Are You Figuring Now? A Story about Benjamin Banneker, 302
What Happened to Patrick's Dinosaurs?, 298

Grades Three to Five

Achievement

Freaky Friday, 363

Girl Called Al, A, 341

Aloneness

Bridge to Terabithia, A, 361

Girl Called Al, A, 341

Jennifer, Hecate, Macbeth, William McKinley, and Me, Elizabeth, 351

Time to Fly Free, A, 369

Train to Somewhere, 329

Arrogance

Harriet the Spy, 336

Racso and the Rats of NIMH, 330

Ronia the Robber's Daughter, 354

Summer of the Swans, 330

Creativity

Silver Pony, The, 370

Differentness

Boy Who Had Wings, The, 375

Bridge to Terabithia, A, 361

Caddie Woodlawn, 328

Gammage Cup, The, 347

Girl Called Al, A, 341

Harriet the Spy, 336

Jennifer, Hecate, Macbeth, William McKinley, and Me, Elizabeth, 351

Mrs. Frisby and the Rats of NIMH, 360

Nothing's Fair in Fifth Grade, 332

Time to Fly Free, A, 369

Wrinkle in Time, A, 352

Drive to Understand

Birchbark House, The, 334

Bridge to Terabithia, A , 361

Brothers of the Heart: A Story of the Old Northwest 1837-1838, 327

Brown Honey in Broomwheat Tea, 368

Cathedral: The Story of Its Construction, 357

Danny the Champion of the World, 331

Death of the Iron Horse, 340

Don't Feed the Monster on Tuesdays!, 359

From the Mixed-up Files of Mrs. Basil E. Frankweiler, 350

Go Fish, 367

Golem, 372

Half-a-Moon Inn, The, 337

Hiroshima, 373

Home Place, 333

Iron Ring, The, 326

Maid of the North, The: Feminist Folk Tales from Around the World, 362

Maps and Globes, 349

Mermaid Summer, The, 345

Miranda's Last Stand, 370

Phantom Tollbooth, The, 346

Seedfolks, 338

Sign of the Beaver, The, 364

Summer of the Swans, 330

Talking to the Sun: An Illustrated Anthology of Poems for Young People, 350

Train to Somewhere, 329

Usborne Illustrated Guide to Norse Myths and Legends, 336

Visit to William Blake's Inn, A: Poems for Innocent and Experienced Travelers, 371

Where Do You Think You're Going, Christopher Columbus?, 339

Whisper of Glocken, The, 348

Wrinkle in Time, A, 352

Identity

Anastasia Krupnik, 356

Anne of Green Gables, 358

Arthur, for the Very First Time, 357

Birchbark House, The, 334

Boy Who Had Wings, The, 375

Bridge to Terabithia, A, 361

Brothers of the Heart: A Story of the Old Northwest 1837-1838, 327

Brown Honey in Broomwheat Tea, 368

Caddie Woodlawn, 328
Call It Courage, 365
Don't Feed the Monster on Tuesdays!, 359
Ella Enchanted, 353
First Two Lives of Lukas-Kasha, The, 325
Freaky Friday, 363
From the Mixed-up Files of Mrs. Basil E. Frankweiler, 350
Gammage Cup, The, 347
Gifted Kids Survival Guide for Ages 10 and Under, The, 339
Girl Called Al, A, 341
Harriet the Spy, 336
Heads, I Win, 343
Iron Ring, The, 326
Jennifer, Hecate, Macbeth, William McKinley and Me, Elizabeth, 351
Love You, Soldier, 343
Miranda's Last Stand, 370
Mrs. Frisby and the Rats of NIMH, 360
Nothing's Fair in Fifth Grade, 332
Racso and the Rats of NIMH, 330
Shiloh, 359
Stick Up for Yourself! Every Kid's Guide to Personal Power and Positive Self-Esteem, 347
Time to Fly Free, A, 369
Wrinkle in Time, A, 352

Intensity
Birchbark House, The, 334
Caddie Woodlawn, 328
Time to Fly Free, A, 369

Introversion
Bridge to Terabithia, A, 361
Silver Pony, The, 370
Time to Fly Free, A, 369

Moral Concerns
Caddie Woodlawn, 328
Danny the Champion of the World, 331
Death of the Iron Horse, 340
Ella Enchanted, 353

First Two Lives of Lukas-Kasha, The, 325
Golem, 372
Hiroshima, 373
Iron Ring, The, 326
Miranda's Last Stand, 370
Mrs. Frisby and the Rats of NIMH, 360
Ronia the Robber's Daughter, 354
Seedfolks, 338
Shiloh, 359
Train to Somewhere, 329

Perfectionism
Don't Feed the Monster on Tuesdays!, 359
Iron Ring, The, 326
Perfectionism: What's Bad about Being Too Good?, 431

Relationships with Others
Best-laid Plans of Jonah Twist, The, 344
Birchbark House, The, 334
Bridge to Terabithia, A, 361
Dog on Barkham Street, A, 366
Don't Feed the Monster on Tuesdays!, 359
Ella Enchanted, 353
Gammage Cup, The, 347
Gifted Kids Survival Guide for Ages 10 and Under, The, 339
Girl Called Al, A, 341
Golem, 372
Harriet the Spy, 336
Heads, I Win, 343
Jennifer, Hecate, Macbeth, William McKinley, and Me, Elizabeth, 351
Kid Next Door and Other Headaches, The: Stories about Adam Joshua, 364
Later, Gator, 374
Miranda's Last Stand, 370
Nothing's Fair in Fifth Grade, 332
Philip Hall Likes Me. I Reckon Maybe, 341
Racso and the Rats of NIMH, 330
Ronia the Robber's Daughter, 354
Seedfolks, 338

Stick Up for Yourself! Every Kid's Guide to Personal Power and Positive Self-Esteem, 347
Summer of the Swans, 330
Train to Somewhere, 329
Zebra Wall, The, 342

Sensitivity

Bridge to Terabithia, A, 361
Later, Gator, 374

Using Ability

Anne of Green Gables, 358
Boy Who Had Wings, The, 375
Bridge to Terabithia, A, 361
Brown Honey in Broomwheat Tea, 368
Dog on Barkham Street, A, 366

Freaky Friday, 363
Go Fish, 367
Harriet the Spy, 336
Perfectionism: What's Bad about Being Too Good?, 377
Phantom Tollbooth, The, 346
Philip Hall Likes Me. I Reckon Maybe, 341
Pippi Longstocking, 354
Stick Up for Yourself! Every Kid's Guide to Personal Power and Positive Self-Esteem, 347
Time to Fly Free, A, 369
Visit to William Blake's Inn, A: Poems for Innocent and Experienced Travelers, 371
Where Do You Think You're Going, Christopher Columbus?, 339

Grades Six to Eight

Achievement

Midwife's Apprentice, The, 393
Yolonda's Genius, 396

Aloneness

Cat Ate My Gymsuit, The, 394
Daphne's Book, 401
Lemming Condition, The, 379
My Name Is Not Angelica, 415
String in the Harp, A, 385
Summer of My German Soldier, 400
View from Saturday, The, 406
Watsons Go to Birmingham—1963, The, 391

Arrogance

Folk Keeper, The, 383
Gifted Kids Survival Guide, The: A Teen Handbook, 398
True Confessions of Charlotte Doyle, The, 382
View from Saturday, The, 406

Creativity

Bat-Poet, The, 404
Dragonsong, 412
View from Saturday, The, 406
Yolonda's Genius, 396

Differentness

Anthem, 418
Bat-Poet, The, 404
Day No Pigs Would Die, A, 418
Dragonwings, 430
Folk Keeper, The, 383
Jacob Have I Loved, 417
Lemming Condition, The, 379
Nothing but the Truth, 381
Reach for the Moon, 376
Summer of My German Soldier, 400
View from Saturday, The, 406
Watsons Go to Birmingham—1963, The, 391
Witch of Blackbird Pond, The, 420
Words by Heart, 419

Drive to Understand

Across Five Aprils, 403
Carry On, Mr. Bowditch, 409
Crystal Cave, The, 422
Dark Is Rising, The, 387
Dawn of Fear, 387
Don't Feed the Monster on Tuesdays!, 359
Dragonsong, 412
Dragonwings, 430
Fighting Ground, The, 380
Flame-Colored Taffeta, 423
Goodbye, Vietnam, 426
Imaginary Gardens: American Poetry and Art for Young People, 423
Maus: A Survivor's Tale, 421
Maus: A Survivor's Tale, II: And Here My Troubles Began, 421
Microbe Hunters, 395
Midwife's Apprentice, The, 393
My Name Is Not Angelica, 415
Ramsay Scallop, The, 425
Shadow of a Bull, 429
Sitting Bull and His World, 411
Smith, 399
String in the Harp, A, 385
Summer of My German Soldier, 400
Sword and the Circle, The, 424
Sword Song, 424
True Confessions of Charlotte Doyle, The, 382
Trumpeter of Krakow, The, 405
Watsons Go to Birmingham—1963, The, 391
Westmark (trilogy), 377
Witch of Blackbird Pond, The, 420
Wolfling, The, 414

Identity

And This Is Laura, 386
Anthem, 418
Belle Prater's Boy, 428
Carry On, Mr. Bowditch, 409
Cat Ate My Gymsuit, The, 394
Chasing Redbird, 389
Come Sing, Jimmy Jo, 416

Crystal Cave, The, 422
Dawn of Fear, 387
Don't Feed the Monster on Tuesdays!, 359
Day No Pigs Would Die, A, 418
Father's Arcane Daughter, 406
Folk Keeper, The, 383
Gifted Kids Survival Guide: A Teen Handbook, The, 398
Jacob Have I Loved, 417
Lemming Condition, The, 379
Nothing but the Truth, 381
Shadow of a Bull, 429
Sitting Bull and His World, 411
Stick Up for Yourself! Every Kid's Guide to Personal Power and Positive Self-Esteem, 347
String in the Harp, A, 385
True Confessions of Charlotte Doyle, The, 382
View from Saturday, The, 406
Walk Two Moons, 390
Watsons Go to Birmingham—1963, The, 391
Westmark (trilogy), 377
Words by Heart, 419
Yolonda's Genius, 396

Intensity

Bat-Poet, The, 404
Dragonsong, 412
Shadow of a Bull, 429
Westmark (trilogy), 377
Yolonda's Genius, 396

Introversion

Chasing Redbird, 389
View from Saturday, The, 406

Moral Concerns

Anthem, 418
Arm of the Starfish, The, 410
Dragonsong, 412
Fighting Ground, The, 380
Goodbye, Vietnam, 426
Kid's Guide to Social Action, The, 410
Maus: A Survivor's Tale, 421

Maus: A Survivor's Tale, II: And Here My Troubles Began, 421
My Name Is Not Angelica, 415
Nothing but the Truth, 381
Ramsay Scallop, The, 425
Shadow of a Bull, 429
Sitting Bull and His World, 411
Summer of My German Soldier, 400
Trumpeter of Krakow, The, 405
Watsons Go to Birmingham—1963, The, 391
Westmark (trilogy), 377
Witch of Blackbird Pond, The, 420

Planet of Junior Brown, The, 402
Stick Up for Yourself! Every Kid's Guide to Personal Power and Positive Self-Esteem, 347
True Confessions of Charlotte Doyle, The, 382
View from Saturday, The, 406
Village by the Sea, The, 398
Walk Two Moons, 390
Watsons Go to Birmingham—1963, The, 391
Witch of Blackbird Pond, The, 420
Yolonda's Genius, 396

Perfectionism

Don't Feed the Monster on Tuesdays!, 359
Gifted Kids Survival Guide: A Teen Handbook, The, 398
Midwife's Apprentice, The, 393
Perfectionism: What's Bad about Being Too Good?, 431
View from Saturday, The, 406

Relationships with Others

Across Five Aprils, 403
And This Is Laura, 386
Anthem, 418
Belle Prater's Boy, 428
Cat Ate My Gymsuit, The, 394
Chasing Redbird, 389
Daphne's Book, 401
Dawn of Fear, 387
Don't Feed the Monster on Tuesdays!, 359
Dragonwings, 430
Father's Arcane Daughter, 406
Folk Keeper, The, 383
Gifted Kids Survival Guide: A Teen Handbook, The, 398
Goodbye, Vietnam, 426
Jacob Have I Loved, 417
Kid's Guide to Social Action, The, 410
Maus: A Survivor's Tale, 421
Maus: A Survivor's Tale, II: And Here My Troubles Began, 421
Nothing but the Truth, 381

Sensitivity

Bat-Poet, The, 404
Chasing Redbird, 389
View from Saturday, The, 406
Watsons Go to Birmingham—1963, The, 391

Using Ability

Across Five Aprils, 403
And This Is Laura, 386
Anthem, 418
Arm of the Starfish, The, 410
Carry On, Mr. Bowditch, 409
Crystal Cave, The, 422
Come Sing, Jimmy Jo, 416
Dragonsong, 412
Dragonwings, 430
Father's Arcane Daughter, 406
Folk Keeper, The, 383
Gifted Kids Survival Guide: A Teen Handbook, The, 398
Goodbye, Vietnam, 426
Jacob Have I Loved, 417
Kid's Guide to Social Action, The, 410
Microbe Hunters, 395
Midwife's Apprentice, The, 393
Native American Doctor: The Story of Susan LaFlesche Picotte, 397
Nothing but the Truth, 381
Perfectionism: What's Bad about Being Too Good?, 377
Planet of Junior Brown, The, 402

Reach for the Moon, 376
Shadow of a Bull, 429
Stick Up for Yourself! Every Kid's Guide to Personal Power and Positive Self-Esteem, 347
True Confessions of Charlotte Doyle, The, 382

Trumpeter of Krakow, The, 405
View from Saturday, The, 406
Westmark (trilogy), 377
Wolfling, The, 414
Words by Heart, 419

Grades Nine to Twelve

Achievement
Guiding the Gifted Child, 486
This Boy's Life, 487

Aloneness
Beyond the Burning Time, 461
Bronstein's Children, 435
Demian, 452
Drowning of Stephan Jones, The, 450
Goats, The, 438
Good Courage, A, 478
Guiding the Gifted Child, 486
Language of Goldfish, The, 465
Rapture of Canaan, The, 470
Solitude: A Return to the Self, 473
Watcher, The, 455
Wave, The, 474
Welcome to the Ark, 479

Arrogance
Bonfire of the Vanities, 487
Gifted Kids Survival Guide: A Teen Handbook, The, 398
Golden Compass, The, 467
Lord of the Flies, 449
Misanthrope, The, 464
Rats Saw God, 477
Watcher, The, 455

Differentness
Am I Blue?, 433
California Blue, 459
Drowning of Stephan Jones, The, 450
Jackaroo, 483
Language of Goldfish, The, 465

Slaughterhouse-five, 485
Watcher, The, 455

Drive to Understand
Am I Blue?, 433
Barabbas, 460
Beyond the Burning Time, 461
Cloister and the Hearth, The, 468
Contender, The, 463
Dragons of Eden, The: Speculations on the Evolution of Human Intelligence, 472
Drowning of Stephan Jones, The, 450
Dynamics of Faith, The, 478
Eva, 442
Fahrenheit 451, 435
Friedrich, 471
Ironman, 440
Lila: An Inquiry into Morals, 466
Loon Feather, The, 448
Madame Curie, 441
Man's Search for Meaning; An Introduction to Logotherapy, 447
Name of the Rose, The, 444
Narrative of the Life of Frederick Douglass, An American Slave, 443
Rapture of Canaan, The, 470
Reindeer Moon, 475
Return, The, 462
Runner, The, 484
Slaughterhouse-five, 485
Sound and the Fury, The, 445
Steppenwolf, 453
Utz, 436
World's Religions, The, 472

Identity

Am I Blue?, 433
Bonfire of the Vanities, 487
Bronstein's Children, 435
Building Blocks, 481
Celine, 437
Clan of the Cave Bear, The, 432
Demian, 452
Good Courage, A, 478
Guiding the Gifted Child, 486
Izzy, Willy-Nilly, 482
Jackaroo, 483
Language of Goldfish, The, 465
Marked by Fire, 476
Rapture of Canaan, The, 470
Remembering the Good Times, 466
Runner, The, 484
Smart Girls: A New Psychology of Girls, Women, and Giftedness, 458
Steppenwolf, 453
This Boy's Life, 487
Wave, The, 474
Welcome to the Ark, 479
Whirligig, 446

Intensity

California Blue, 459
Demian, 452
Golden Compass, The, 467
Guiding the Gifted Child, 486
Madame Curie, 441
Misanthrope, The, 464

Introversion

Barabbas, 460
Demian, 452
Language of Goldfish, The, 465
Solitude: A Return to the Self, 473
Steppenwolf, 453
Welcome to the Ark, 479

Moral Concerns

Barabbas, 460
Beyond the Burning Time, 461
Bonfire of the Vanities, 487
Bronstein's Children, 435
California Blue, 459
Cloister and the Hearth, The, 468
Demian, 452
Drowning of Stephan Jones, The, 450
Eva, 442
Fahrenheit 451, 435
Friedrich, 471
Golden Compass, The, 467
Guiding the Gifted Child, 486
I Am the Cheese, 439
Lila: An Inquiry into Morals, 466
Lord of the Flies, 449
Narrative of the Life of Frederick Douglass, An American Slave, 443
Return, The, 462
Runner, The, 484
Slaughterhouse-five, 485
This Boy's Life, 487
Utz, 436
Wave, The, 474
Welcome to the Ark, 479

Perfectionism

Gifted Kids Survival Guide: A Teen Handbook, The, 398
Guiding the Gifted Child, 486
Misanthrope, The, 464
Perfectionism: What's Bad about Being Too Good?, 377

Relationships with Others

Am I Blue?, 433
Building Blocks, 481
California Blue, 459
Clan of the Cave Bear, The, 432
Drowning of Stephan Jones, The, 450
Gifted Kids Survival Guide: A Teen Handbook, The, 398
Goats, The, 438

Golden Compass, The, 467
Guiding the Gifted Child, 486
Ironman, 440
Izzy, Willy-Nilly, 482
Language of Goldfish, The, 465
Lord of the Flies, 449
Lottery Rose, The, 456
Marked by Fire, 476
Misanthrope, The, 464
Rapture of Canaan, The, 470
Rats Saw God, 477
Solitude: A Return to the Self, 473
Steppenwolf, 453
Watcher, The, 455
Wave, The, 474
Welcome to the Ark, 479
Whirligig, 446

Sensitivity

Demian, 452
Jackaroo, 483

Using Ability

Bonfire of the Vanities, 487
Celine, 437
Contender, The, 463
Demian, 452
Guiding the Gifted Child, 486
Lottery Rose, The, 456
Madame Curie, 441
Marked by Fire, 476
*Perfectionism: What's Bad about Being Too
   Good?,* 377
Rats Saw God, 477
Remembering the Good Times, 466
*Smart Girls: A New Psychology of Girls,
   Women, and Giftedness,* 458
Solitude: A Return to the Self, 473
Sound and the Fury, The, 445
Watcher, The, 455
Wave, The, 474
Welcome to the Ark, 479
William, 457

Index for All Ages

The following books can be used with
   various age groups:

Anno's Journey, 290
Bat-Poet, The, 404
Boy Who Had Wings, The, 375
Eleventh Hour, The, 292
Empty Pot, The, 280
Frederick, 283
*Gifted Kids Survival Guide, The: A Teen
   Handbook,* 398
*Gifted Kids Survival Guide for Ages 10 and
   Under, The,* 339
Guiding the Gifted Child, 486
I Spy: An Alphabet in Art, 285
*Imaginary Gardens: American Poetry and
   Art for Young People,* 423
Legend of the White Buffalo Woman, The, 304
*Maid of the North, The: Feminist Folk Tales
   from Around the World,* 362

Man Who Could Call Down Owls, The, 296
Maus: A Survivor's Tale, 421
*Maus: A Survivor's Tale, II: And Here My
   Troubles Began,* 421
My Grandma Lived in Gooligulch, 277
*Perfectionism: What's Bad about Being Too
   Good?,* 377
Reach for the Moon: What Once Was White,
   376
Silver Pony, The, 370
*Talking to the Sun: An Illustrated Anthology
   of Poems for Young People,* 350
Tye May and the Magic Brush, 291
Who Came Down That Road?, 312
William, 457

Annotated Bibliography: Index of Authors

Abeel, Samantha. *Reach for the Moon*, 376

Adderholdt, Miriam and Jan Goldberg. *Perfectionism: What's Bad about Being Too Good?*, 325

Albert, Burton. *Where Does the Trail Lead?*, 276

Alderson, Sue Ann and Ann Blades. *Ida and the Wool Smugglers*, 289

Alexander, Lloyd. *The Beggar Queen*, 377

Alexander, Lloyd. *The First Two Lives of Lukas-Kasha*, 325

Alexander, Lloyd. *The Fortune Tellers*, 276

Alexander, Lloyd. *The Iron Ring*, 326

Alexander, Lloyd. *The Kestrel*, 377

Alexander, Lloyd. *Westmark*, 377

Aliki. *Feelings*, 289

Anno, Mitsumasa. *Anno's Counting Book*, 277

Anno, Mitsumasa. *Anno's Journey*, 290

Arkin, Alan. *The Lemming Condition*, 379

Auel, Jean. *The Clan of the Cave Bear*, 432

Avi. *The Fighting Ground*, 380

Avi. *Nothing but the Truth*, 381

Avi. *The True Confessions of Charlotte Doyle*, 382

Baker, Jeannie. *Where the Forest Meets the Sea*, 290

Bang, Molly. *Dawn*, 291

Bang, Molly Garrett. *Tye May and the Magic Brush*, 291

Barton, Byron. *Bones, Bones, Dinosaur Bones*, 267

Base, Graeme. *The Eleventh Hour*, 292

Base, Graeme. *My Grandma Lived in Gooligulch*, 277

Base, Graeme. *The Sign of the Seahorse*, 293

Bauer, Marion Dane, ed. *Am I Blue?*, 433

Becker, Jurek. *Bronstein's Children*, 435

Billingsley, Franny. *The Folk Keeper*, 383

Blos, Joan W. *Brothers of the Heart: A Story of the Old Northwest 1837-1838*, 327

Bond, Nancy. *A String in the Harp*, 385

Bradbury, Ray. *Fahrenheit 451*, 435

Brett, Jan. *The Hat*, 267

Bridwell, Norman. *Clifford's Bathtime*, 263

Brink, Carol Ryrie. *Caddie Woodlawn*, 328

Brown, Deni. *What Can You Find Around the House?*, 264

Brown, Margaret Wise. *Goodnight, Moon*, 264

Brown, Margaret Wise. *The Runaway Bunny*, 268

Brown, Ruth. *If at First You Do Not See*, 294

Bryan, Ashley. *Turtle Knows Your Name*, 278

Bulla, Clyde Robert. *Daniel's Duck*, 294

Bunting, Eve. *Dandelions*, 295

Bunting, Eve. *The Man Who Could Call Down Owls*, 296

Bunting, Eve. *Train to Somewhere*, 329

Burningham, John. *Hey! Get Off Our Train*, 279

Byars, Betsy Cromer. *Summer of the Swans*, 330

Carle, Eric. *The Very Busy Spider*, 264

Carrick, Carol. *Stay Away from Simon!*, 297

Carrick, Carol. *What Happened to Patrick's Dinosaurs?*, 298

Cendrars, Blaise. *Shadow*, 298

Charlip, Remy and Lilian Moore. *Hooray for Me*, 268

Chatwin, Bruce. *Utz*, 436

Cleary, Beverly. *Ramona the Brave*, 299

Clifton, Lucille. *Everett Anderson's Friend*, 299

Cole, Brock. *Celine*, 437

Cole, Brock. *The Goats*, 438

Conford, Ellen. *And This Is Laura*, 386

Conly, Jane Leslie. *Racso and the Rats of NIMH*, 330

Cooney, Barbara. *Island Boy*, 300

Cooper, Susan. *The Dark Is Rising*, 387

Cooper, Susan. *Dawn of Fear*, 387

Cooper, Susan. *Greenwitch*, 387

Cooper, Susan. *The Grey King*, 387

Cooper, Susan. *Over Sea, Under Stone*, 387

Cooper, Susan. *Silver on the Tree*, 387

Cormier, Robert. *I Am the Cheese*, 439

Creech, Sharon. *Chasing Redbird*, 389

Creech, Sharon. *Walk Two Moons*, 390

Crews, Donald. *Carousel*, 268

Crews, Donald. *Freight Train*, 268

Crutcher, Chris. *Ironman*, 440

Curie, Eve. *Madame Curie*, 441

Curtis, Christopher Paul. *The Watsons Go to Birmingham—1963*, 391

Cushman, Karen. *The Midwife's Apprentice*, 393

Dahl, Roald. *Danny the Champion of the World*, 331

Danziger, Paula. *The Cat Ate My Gymsuit*, 394

de Paola, Tomie. *Tomie de Paola's Book of Poems*, 301

DeClements, Barthe. *Nothing's Fair in Fifth Grade*, 332

de Gerez, Toni. *Louhi, Witch of North Farm*, 279

de Kruif, Paul. *Microbe Hunters*, 395

Demi. *The Empty Pot*, 280

Dickinson, Peter. *Eva*, 442

Dorros, Arthur. *Abuela*, 301

Douglass, Frederick. *Narrative of the Life of Frederick Douglass, an American Slave*, 443

Dragonwagon, Crescent. *Home Place*, 333

Eastman, P. D. *Are You My Mother?*, 264

Eco, Umberto. *The Name of the Rose*, 444

Ehlert, Lois. *Red Leaf, Yellow Leaf*, 301

Elyé, Beatrice. *JumpStart: Ideas to Move Your Mind*, 444

Erdrich, Louise. *The Birchbark House*, 334

Evans, Cheryl and Anne Millard. *Usborne Illustrated Guide to Norse Myths and Legends*, 336

Faulkner, William. *The Sound and the Fury*, 445

Fenner, Carol. *Yolonda's Genius*, 396

Ferris, Jeri. *Native American Doctor: The Story of Susan LaFlesche Picotte*, 397

Ferris, Jeri. *What Are You Figuring Now? A Story about Benjamin Banneker*, 302

Fitzhugh, Louise. *Harriet the Spy*, 336

Fleischman, Paul. *The Half-a-Moon Inn*, 337

Fleischman, Paul. *Seedfolks*, 338

Fleischman, Paul. *Whirligig*, 446

Fleming, Denise. *In the Small, Small Pond*, 269

Fleming, Denise. *Time to Sleep*, 269

Fox, Paula. *The Village by the Sea*, 398

Frankl, Viktor E. *Man's Search for Meaning: An Introduction to Logotherapy*, 447

Fritz, Jean. *Where Do You Think You're Going, Christopher Columbus?*, 339

Fuller, Iola. *The Loon Feather*, 448

Gag, Wanda. *Millions of Cats*, 269

Galbraith, Judy and Jim Delisle. *The Gifted Kids Survival Guide: A Teen Handbook*, 398

Galbraith, Judy. *The Gifted Kids Survival Guide for Ages 10 and Under*, 339

Garfield, Leon. *Smith*, 399

Gerrard, Roy. *Sir Cedric*, 280

Gibbons, Gail. *Farming,* 270

Giganti, Paul. *How Many Snails? A Counting Book,* 270

Gilks, Helen. *Bears,* 303

Gilman, Phoebe. *Something from Nothing,* 281

Goble, Paul. *Death of the Iron Horse,* 340

Goble, Paul. *Iktomi and the Berries: A Plains Indian Story,* 303

Goble, Paul. *The Legend of the White Buffalo Woman,* 304

Godden, Rumer. *The Story of Holly and Ivy,* 305

Golding, William. *Lord of the Flies,* 449

Greene, Bette. *The Drowning of Stephan Jones,* 450

Greene, Bette. *Philip Hall Likes Me. I Reckon Maybe,* 341

Greene, Bette. *Summer of My German Soldier,* 400

Greene, Constance C. *A Girl Called Al,* 341

Hahn, Mary Downing. *Daphne's Book,* 401

Hall, Donald. *The Man Who Lived Alone,* 305

Hall, Donald. *Ox-Cart Man,* 306

Hamilton, Virginia. *The Planet of Junior Brown,* 402

Handforth, Martin. *Where's Waldo?,* 282

Heine, Helme. *Friends,* 282

Heller, Linda. *The Castle on Hester Street,* 307

Henkes, Kevin. *The Zebra Wall,* 342

Hermes, Patricia. *Heads, I Win,* 343

Hesse, Hermann. *Demian,* 452

Hesse, Hermann. *Steppenwolf,* 453

Hest, Amy. *In the Rain with Baby Duck,* 271

Hest, Amy. *Love You, Soldier,* 343

Hill, Elizabeth Starr. *Evan's Corner,* 307

Hill, Eric. *Spot in the Garden,* 265

Hill, Eric. *Where's Spot?,* 265

Hoban, Tana. *Black on White,* 265

Hoban, Tana. *Colors Everywhere,* 265

Hoban, Tana. *Red Blue Yellow Shoe,* 266

Hoban, Tana. *Shadows and Reflections,* 308

Hoff, Syd. *Who Will Be My Friends?,* 308

Honeycutt, Natalie. *The Best-laid Plans of Jonah Twist,* 344

Howe, James. *The Watcher,* 455

Hunt, Irene. *Across Five Aprils,* 403

Hunt, Irene. *The Lottery Rose,* 456

Hunt, Irene. *William,* 457

Hunter, Mollie. *The Mermaid Summer,* 345

Hutchins, Pat. *Rosie's Walk,* 271

Hutchins, Pat. *Shrinking Mouse,* 282

Hutchins, Pat. *Titch,* 283

Isadora, Rachel. *Ben's Trumpet,* 309

Jarrell, Randall. *The Bat-Poet,* 404

Johnson, D. B. *Henry Hikes to Fitchburg,* 309

Juster, Norton. *The Phantom Tollbooth,* 346

Kauffman, Gershen, Lev Raphael, and Pam Espeland. *Stick Up for Yourself! Every Kid's Guide to Personal Power and Positive Self-Esteem,* 347

Kellogg, Steven. *Best Friends,* 310

Kelly, Eric P. *The Trumpeter of Krakow,* 405

Kendall, Carol. *The Gammage Cup,* 347

Kendall, Carol. *The Whisper of Glocken,* 348

Kerr, Barbara. *Smart Girls: A New Psychology of Girls, Women, and Giftedness,* 458

Klass, David. *California Blue,* 459

Knowlton, Jack. *Maps and Globes,* 349

Koch, Kenneth and Kate Farrell. *Talking to the Sun: An Illustrated Anthology of Poems for Young People,* 350

Konigsburg, E. L. *Father's Arcane Daughter,* 406

Konigsburg, E. L. *From the Mixed-up Files of Mrs. Basil E. Frankweiler,* 350

Konigsburg, E. L. *Jennifer, Hecate, Macbeth, William McKinley and Me, Elizabeth,* 351

Konigsburg, E. L. *The View from Saturday,* 406

Krauss, Ruth. *The Carrot Seed,* 272

Kuskin, Karla. *James and the Rain,* 272

Lagerkvist, Par. *Barabbas,* 460

Larry, Charles. *Peboan and Seegwun,* 311

Lasky, Kathryn. *Beyond the Burning Time,* 461

Latham, Jean Lee. *Carry On, Mr. Bowditch,* 409

L'Engle, Madeleine. *The Arm of the Starfish,* 410

L'Engle, Madeleine. *A Wrinkle in Time,* 352

Levine, Gail Carson. *Ella Enchanted,* 353

Levitin, Sonia. *The Return,* 462

Lewis, Barbara A. *The Kid's Guide to Social Action,* 410

Lindgren, Astrid. *Pippi Longstocking,* 354

Lindgren, Astrid. *Ronia the Robber's Daughter,* 354

Lionni, Leo. *Frederick,* 283

Lipsyte, Robert. *The Contender,* 463

Lobel, Arnold. *On Market Street,* 312

Lowrey, Janette Sebring. *The Poky Little Puppy,* 272

Lowry, Lois. *Anastasia Krupnik,* 356

Lyon, George Ella. *Who Came Down that Road?,* 312

Macauley, David. *Cathedral: The Story of Its Construction,* 357

MacDonald, Golden. *The Little Island,* 284

MacLachlan, Patricia. *Arthur, for the Very First Time,* 357

Marrin, Albert. *Sitting Bull and His World,* 411

Martin, Bill and John Archambault. *Knots on a Counting Rope,* 313

Marzollo, Jean. *Sun Song,* 284

McCaffrey, Anne. *Dragonsong,* 412

McCloskey, Robert. *Blueberries for Sal,* 273

McCloskey, Robert. *Time of Wonder,* 285

McDermott, Gerald. *Anansi the Spider: A Tale from the Ashanti,* 314

Micklethwaite, Lucy. *I Spy: An Alphabet in Art,* 285

Miller, Margaret. *Guess Who?,* 273

Milne, A. A. *The Complete Tales of Winnie-the-Pooh,* 286

Moliere, Jean Baptiste Poquelin. *The Misanthrope,* 464

Montgomery, L. M. *Anne of Green Gables,* 358

Mora, Pat. *Tomas and the Library Lady,* 315

Moser, Adolph. *Don't Feed the Monster on Tuesdays,* 359

Naylor, Phyllis Reynolds. *Shiloh,* 359

North, Sterling. *The Wolfling,* 414

O'Brien, Robert C. *Mrs. Frisby and the Rats of NIMH,* 360

O'Dell, Scott. *My Name Is Not Angelica,* 415

Oneal, Zibby. *The Language of Goldfish,* 465

Opie, Iona. *My Very First Mother Goose,* 274

Paterson, Katherine. *A Bridge to Terabithia,* 361

Paterson, Katherine. *Come Sing, Jimmy Jo,* 416

Paterson, Katherine. *Jacob Have I Loved,* 417

Peck, Richard. *Remembering the Good Times,* 466

Peck, Robert Newton. *A Day No Pigs Would Die,* 418

Phelps, Ethel Johnston. *The Maid of the North: Feminist Folk Tales from Around the World,* 362

Piper, Watty. *The Little Engine that Could,* 274

Pirsig, Robert M. *Lila: An Inquiry into Morals,* 466

Pullman, Philip. *The Amber Spyglass,* 468

Pullman, Philip. *The Golden Compass,* 467

Pullman, Philip. *The Subtle Knife,* 468

Rand, Ayn. *Anthem,* 418

Rappaport, Doreen. *The Boston Coffee Party,* 315

Reade, Charles. *The Cloister and the Hearth,* 468

Reynolds, Sheri. *The Rapture of Canaan,* 470

Richter, Hans Peter. *Friedrich,* 471

Rodgers, Mary. *Freaky Friday,* 363

Rohmann, Eric. *The Cinder-Eyed Cats,* 316

Ross, Katharine. *The Little Quiet Book,* 266

Sagan, Carl. *The Dragons of Eden: Speculations on the Evolution of Human Intelligence,* 472

Scarry, Richard. *Richard Scarry's Best First Book Ever,* 275

Sebestyen, Ouida. *Words by Heart,* 419

Sendak, Maurice. *Outside Over There,* 317

Seuss, Dr. *The Foot Book,* 266

Sharmat, Marjorie Weinman. *I'm Terrific*, 286

Shaw, Charles G. *It Looked Like Spilt Milk*, 266

Smith, Huston. *The World's Religions*, 472

Smith, Janice Lee. *The Kid Next Door and Other Headaches: Stories about Adam Joshua*, 364

Speare, Elizabeth George. *The Sign of the Beaver*, 364

Speare, Elizabeth George. *The Witch of Blackbird Pond*, 420

Sperry, Armstrong. *Call It Courage*, 365

Spiegelman, Art. *Maus: A Survivor's Tale*, 421

Spiegelman, Art. *Maus: A Survivor's Tale, II: And Here My Troubles Began*, 421

Steig, William. *Sylvester and the Magic Pebble*, 317

Steptoe, John. *Stevie*, 287

Stewart, Mary. *The Crystal Cave*, 422

Stolz, Mary. *A Dog on Barkham Street*, 366

Stolz, Mary. *Go Fish*, 367

Stone, Erika. *Baby Talk*, 266

Storr, Anthony. *Solitude: A Return to the Self*, 473

Strasser, Todd. *The Wave*, 474

Sullivan, Charles, ed. *Imaginary Gardens: American Poetry and Art for Young People* 423

Sutcliff, Rosemary. *Flame-Colored Taffeta*, 423

Sutcliff, Rosemary. *The Sword and the Circle*, 424

Sutcliff, Rosemary, *Sword Song*, 424

Swift, Hildegarde H. and Lynd Ward. *The Little Red Lighthouse and the Great Gray Bridge*, 318

Temple, Frances. *The Ramsay Scallop*, 425

Thomas, Elizabeth Marshall. *Reindeer Moon*, 475

Thomas, Joyce Carol. *Brown Honey in Broomwheat Tea*, 368

Thomas, Joyce Carol. *Marked by Fire*, 476

Thomas, Rob. *Rats Saw God*, 477

Tillich, Paul. *The Dynamics of Faith*, 478

Tolan, Stephanie S. *A Good Courage*, 478

Tolan, Stephanie S. *A Time to Fly Free*, 369

Tolan, Stephanie S. *Welcome to the Ark*, 479

Tresselt, Alvin. *Hide and Seek Fog*, 287

Van Leeuwen, Jean. *Amanda Pig on Her Own*, 288

Viorst, Judith. *Alexander and the Terrible, Horrible, No Good, Very Bad Day*, 319

Viorst, Judith. *Rosie and Michael*, 320

Voigt, Cynthia. *Building Blocks*, 481

Voigt, Cynthia. *Izzy, Willy-Nilly*, 482

Voigt, Cynthia. *Jackaroo*, 483

Voigt, Cynthia. *The Runner*, 484

Vonnegut, Kurt. *Slaughterhouse-five*, 485

Waddell, Martin. *Owl Babies*, 275

Ward, Lynd. *The Silver Pony*, 370

Webb, James T., Elizabeth A. Meckstroth, & Stephanie S. Tolan. *Guiding the Gifted Child*, 486

Weisner, David. *Free Fall*, 322

Whelan, Gloria. *Goodbye, Vietnam*, 426

Whelan, Gloria. *Hannah*, 321

Whelan, Gloria. *Miranda's Last Stand*, 370

White, Ruth. *Belle Prater's Boy*, 428

Willard, Nancy. *A Visit to William Blake's Inn: Poems for Innocent and Experienced Travelers*, 371

Wisniewski, David. *Elfwyn's Saga*, 323

Wisniewski, David. *Golem*, 372

Wojciechowska, Maia. *Shadow of a Bull*, 429

Wolfe, Tom. *Bonfire of the Vanities*, 487

Wolff, Tobias. *This Boy's Life*, 487

Wood, Douglas. *Old Turtle*, 323

Yep, Laurence. *Dragonwings*, 430

Yep, Laurence. *Hiroshima*, 373

Yep, Laurence. *Later, Gator*, 374

Yolen, Jane. *Bird Watch: A Book of Poetry*, 324

Yolen, Jane. *The Boy Who Had Wings*, 375

Yolen, Jane. *Owl Moon*, 324

Annotated Bibliography: Index of Titles

Abuela. Dorros, 301

Across Five Aprils. Hunt, 403

Alexander and the Terrible, Horrible, No Good, Very Bad Day. Viorst, 319

Am I Blue? Bauer, 433

Amanda Pig on Her Own. Van Leeuwen, 288

Amber Spyglass, The. Pullman, 468

Anansi the Spider: A Tale from the Ashanti. McDermott, 314

Anastasia Krupnick. Lowry, 356

And This Is Laura. Conford, 386

Anne of Green Gables. Montgomery, 358

Anno's Counting Book. Anno, 277

Anno's Journey. Anno, 290

Anthem. Rand, 418

Are You My Mother? Eastman, 264

Arm of the Starfish, The. L'Engle, 410

Arthur, for the Very First Time. MacLachlan, 357

Baby Talk. Stone, 266

Barabbas. Lagerkvist, 460

Bat-Poet, The. Jarrell, 404

Bears. Gilks, 303

Beggar Queen, The. Alexander, 377

Belle Prater's Boy. White, 428

Ben's Trumpet. Isadora, 309

Best Friends. Kellogg, 310

Best-laid Plans of Jonah Twist, The. Honeycutt, 344

Beyond the Burning Time. Lasky, 461

Birchbark House, The. Erdrich, 334

Bird Watch: A Book of Poetry. Yolen, 324

Black on White. Hoban, 265

Blueberries for Sal. McCloskey, 273

Bones, Bones, Dinosaur Bones. Barton, 267

Bonfire of the Vanities. Wolfe, 487

Boston Coffee Party, The. Rappaport, 315

Boy Who Had Wings, The. Yolen, 375

Bridge to Terabithia, A. Paterson, 361

Bronstein's Children. Becker, 435

Brothers of the Heart: A Story of the Old Northwest 1837-1838. Blos, 327

Brown Honey in Broomwheat Tea. Thomas, 368

Building Blocks. Voigt, 481

Caddie Woodlawn. Brink, 328

California Blue. Klass, 459

Call It Courage. Sperry, 365

Carousel. Crews, 268

Carrot Seed, The. Krauss, 272

Carry On, Mr. Bowditch. Latham, 409

Castle on Hester Street, The. Heller, 307

Cat Ate My Gymsuit, The. Danziger, 394

Cathedral: The Story of Its Construction. Macauley, 357

Celine. Cole, 437

Chasing Redbird. Creech, 389

Cinder-Eyed Cats, The. Rohmann, 316

Clan of the Cave Bear, The. Auel, 432

Clifford's Bathtime. Bridwell, 263

Cloister and the Hearth, The. Reade, 468

Colors Everywhere. Hoban, 265

Come Sing, Jimmy Jo. Paterson, 416

Complete Tales of Winnie-the-Pooh, The. Milne, 286

Contender, The. Lipsyte, 463

Crystal Cave, The. Stewart, 422

Dandelions. Bunting, 295

Daniel's Duck. Bulla, 294

Danny the Champion of the World. Dahl, 331

Daphne's Book. Hahn, 401

Dark Is Rising, The. Cooper, 387

Dawn. Bang, 291

Dawn of Fear, Cooper, 387

Day No Pigs Would Die, A. Peck, 418

Death of the Iron Horse. Goble, 340

Demian. Hesse, 452

Dog on Barkham Street, A. Stolz, 366

Don't Feed the Monster on Tuesdays. Moser, 359

Dragons of Eden, The: Speculations on the Evolution of Human Intelligence. Sagan, 472

Dragonsong. McCaffrey, 412

Dragonwings. Yep, 430

Drowning of Stephan Jones, The. Greene, 450

Dynamics of Faith, The. Tillich, 478

Eleventh Hour, The. Base, 292

Elfwyn's Saga. Wisniewski, 323

Ella Enchanted. Levine, 353

Empty Pot, The. Demi, 280

Eva. Dickinson, 442

Evan's Corner. Hill, 307

Everett Anderson's Friend. Clifton, 299

Fahrenheit 451. Bradbury, 435

Farming. Gibbons, 270

Father's Arcane Daughter. Konigsburg, 406

Feelings. Aliki, 289

Fighting Ground, The. Avi, 380

First Two Lives of Lukas-Kasha, The. Alexander, 325

Flame-Colored Taffeta. Sutcliff, 423

Folk Keeper, The. Billingsley, 383

Foot Book, The. Seuss, 266

Fortune Tellers, The. Alexander, 276

Freaky Friday. Rodgers, 363

Frederick. Lionni, 283

Free Fall. Weisner, 322

Freight Train. Crews, 268

Friedrich. Richter, 471

Friends. Heine, 282

From the Mixed-up Files of Mrs. Basil E. Frankweiler. Konigsburg, 350

Gammage Cup, The. Kendall, 347

Gifted Kids Survival Guide: A Teen Handbook, The. Galbraith and Delisle, 398

Gifted Kids Survival Guide for Ages 10 and Under, The. Galbraith, 339

Girl Called Al, A. Greene, 341

Go Fish. Stolz, 367

Goats, The. Cole, 438

Golden Compass, The. Pullman, 467

Golem. Wisnieski, 372

Good Courage, A. Tolan, 478

Goodbye, Vietnam. Whelan, 426

Goodnight, Moon. Brown, 264

Greenwitch. Cooper, 387

Grey King, The. Cooper, 387

Guess Who? Miller, 273

Guiding the Gifted Child. Webb, Meckstroth, & Tolan, 486

Half-a-Moon Inn, The. Fleischman, 337

Hannah. Whelan, 321

Harriet the Spy. Fitzhugh, 336

Hat, The. Brett, 267

Heads, I Win. Hermes, 343

Henry Hikes to Fitchburg. Johnson, 309

Hey! Get Off Our Train. Burningham, 279

Hide and Seek Fog. Tresselt, 287

Hiroshima. Yep, 373

Home Place. Dragonwagon, 333

Hooray for Me! Charlip and Moore, 268

How Many Snails? A Counting Book. Giganti, 270

I Am the Cheese. Cormier, 439

I Spy: An Alphabet in Art. Micklethwaite, 285

Ida and the Wool Smugglers. Alderson and Blades, 289

If at First You Do Not See. Brown, 294

Iktomi and the Berries: A Plains Indian Story. Goble, 303

I'm Terrific. Sharmat, 286

Imaginary Gardens: American Poetry and Art for Young People. Sullivan, 423

In the Rain with Baby Duck. Hest, 271

In the Small, Small, Pond. Fleming, 269

Iron Ring, The. Alexander, 326

Ironman. Crutcher, 440

Island Boy. Cooney, 300

It Looked Like Spilt Milk. Shaw, 266

Izzy, Willy-Nilly. Voigt, 482

Jackaroo. Voigt, 483

Jacob Have I Loved. Paterson, 417

James and the Rain. Kuskin, 272

Jennifer, Hecate, Macbeth, William McKinley and Me, Elizabeth. Konigsburg, 351

JumpStart: Ideas to Move Your Mind. Elyé, 444

Kestrel, The. Alexander, 377

Kid Next Door and Other Headaches, The: Stories about Adam Joshua. Smith, 364

Kid's Guide to Social Action, The. Lewis, 410

Knots on a Counting Rope. Martin and Archambault, 313

Language of Goldfish, The. Oneal, 465

Later, Gator. Yep, 374

Legend of the White Buffalo Woman, The. Goble, 304

Lemming Condition, The. Arkin, 379

Lila: An Enquiry into Morals. Pirsig, 466

Little Engine that Could, The. Piper, 274

Little Island, The. MacDonald, 284

Little Quiet Book, The. Ross, 266

Little Red Lighthouse and the Great Gray Bridge, The. Swift and Ward, 318

Loon Feather, The. Fuller, 448

Lord of the Flies. Golding, 449

Lottery Rose, The. Hunt, 456

Louhi, Witch of North Farm. de Gerez, 279

Love You, Soldier. Hest, 343

Madame Curie. Curie, 441

Maid of the North, The: Feminist Folk Tales from Around the World. Phelps, 362

Man Who Could Call Down Owls, The. Bunting, 296

Man Who Lived Alone, The. Hall, 305

Man's Search for Meaning: An Introduction to Logotherapy. Frankl, 447

Maps and Globes. Knowlton, 349

Marked by Fire. Thomas, 476

Maus: A Survivor's Tale. Spiegelman, 421

Maus: A Survivor's Tale, II: And Here My Troubles Began. Spiegelman, 421

Mermaid Summer, The. Hunter, 345

Microbe Hunters. de Kruif, 395

Midwife's Apprentice, The. Cushman, 393

Millions of Cats. Gag, 269

Miranda's Last Stand. Whelan, 370

Misanthrope, The. Moliere, 464

Mrs. Frisby and the Rats of NIMH. O'Brien, 360

My Grandma Lived in Gooligulch. Base, 277

My Name Is Not Angelica. O'Dell, 415

My Very First Mother Goose. Opie, 274

Name of the Rose, The. Eco, 444

Narrative of the Life of Frederick Douglass, an American Slave. Douglass, 443

Native American Doctor: The Story of Susan LaFlesche Picotte. Ferris, 397

Nothing but the Truth. Avi, 381

Nothing's Fair in Fifth Grade. DeClements, 332

Old Turtle. Wood, 323

On Market Street. Lobel, 312

Outside Over There. Sendak, 317

Over Sea, Under Stone. Cooper, 387

Owl Babies. Waddell, 275

Owl Moon. Yolen, 324

Ox-Cart Man. Hall, 306

Peboan and Seegwun. Larry, 311

Perfectionism: What's Bad about Being Too Good? Adderholdt and Goldberg, 377, 431

Phantom Tollbooth, The. Juster, 346

Philip Hall Likes Me. I Reckon Maybe. Greene, 341

Pippi Longstocking. Lindgren, 354

Planet of Junior Brown, The. Hamilton, 402

Poky Little Puppy, The. Lowrey, 272

Racso and the Rats of NIMH. Conly, 330

Ramona the Brave. Cleary, 299

Ramsay Scallop, The. Temple, 425

Rapture of Canaan, The. Reynolds, 470

Rats Saw God. Thomas, 477

Reach for the Moon. Abeel, 376

Red Blue Yellow Shoe. Hoban, 266

Red Leaf, Yellow Leaf. Ehlert, 301

Reindeer Moon. Thomas, 475

Remembering the Good Times. Peck, 466

Return, The. Levitin, 462

Richard Scarry's Best First Book Ever. Scarry, 275

Ronia the Robber's Daughter. Lindgren, 354

Rosie and Michael. Viorst, 320

Rosie's Walk. Hutchins, 271

Runaway Bunny, The. Brown, 268

Runner, The. Voigt, 484

Seedfolks. Fleischman, 338

Shadow. Cendrars, 298

Shadow of a Bull. Wojciechowska, 429

Shadows and Reflections. Hoban, 308

Shiloh. Naylor, 359

Shrinking Mouse. Hutchins, 282

Sign of the Beaver, The. Speare, 364

Sign of the Seahorse, The. Base, 293

Silver on the Tree. Cooper, 387

Silver Pony, The. Ward, 370

Sir Cedric. Gerrard, 280

Sitting Bull and His World. Marrin, 411

Slaughterhouse-five. Vonnegut, 485

Smart Girls: A New Psychology of Girls, Women, and Giftedness. Kerr, 458

Smith. Garfield, 399

Solitude: A Return to the Self. Storr, 473

Something from Nothing. Gilman, 281

Sound and the Fury, The. Faulkner, 445

Spot in the Garden. Hill, 265

Stay Away from Simon! Carrick, 297

Steppenwolf. Hesse, 453

Stevie. Steptoe, 287

Stick Up for Yourself! Every Kid's Guide to Personal Power and Positive Self-Esteem. Kauffman, Raphael, and Espeland, 347, 404

Story of Holly and Ivy, The. Godden, 305

String in the Harp, A. Bond, 385

Subtle Knife, The. Pullman, 468

Summer of My German Soldier. Greene, 400

Summer of the Swans. Byars, 330

Sun Song. Marzollo, 284

Sword and the Circle, The. Sutcliff, 424

Sword Song. Sutcliff, 424

Sylvester and the Magic Pebble. Steig, 317

Talking to the Sun: An Illustrated Anthology of Poems for Young People. Koch and Farrell, 350

This Boy's Life. Wolff, 487

Time of Wonder. McCloskey, 285

Time to Fly Free, A. Tolan, 369

Time to Sleep. Fleming, 269

Titch. Hutchins, 283

Tomas and the Library Lady. Mora. 315

Tomie de Paola's Book of Poems. de Paola, 301

Train to Somewhere. Bunting, 329

True Confessions of Charlotte Doyle, The. Avi, 382

Trumpeter of Krakow, The. Kelly, 405

Turtle Knows Your Name. Bryan, 278

Tye May and the Magic Brush. Bang, 291

Usborne Illustrated Guide to Norse Myths and Legends. Evans and Millard, 336

Utz. Chatwin, 436

Very Busy Spider, The. Carle, 264

View from Saturday, The. Konigsburg, 406

Village by the Sea, The. Fox, 398

Visit to William Blake's Inn, A: Poems for Innocent and Experienced Travelers. Willard, 371

Walk Two Moons. Creech, 390

Watcher, The. Howe, 455

Watsons Go to Birmingham—1963, The. Curtis, 391

Wave, The. Strasser, 474

Welcome to the Ark. Tolan, 479

Westmark. Alexander, 377

What Are You Figuring Now? A Story about Benjamin Banneker. Ferris, 302

What Can You Find Around the House? Brown, 264

What Happened to Patrick's Dinosaurs? Carrick, 298

Where Do You Think You're Going, Christopher Columbus? Fritz, 339

Where Does the Trail Lead? Albert, 276

Where the Forest Meets the Sea. Baker, 290

Where's Spot? Hill, 265

Where's Waldo? Handforth, 282

Whirligig. Fleischman, 446

Whisper of Glocken, The. Kendall, 348

Who Came Down that Road? Lyon, 312

Who Will Be My Friends? Hoff, 308

William. Hunt, 457

Witch of Blackbird Pond, The. Speare, 420

Wolfling, The. North, 414

Words by Heart. Sebestyen, 419

World's Religions, The. Smith, 472

Wrinkle in Time, A. L'Engle, 352

Yolonda's Genius. Fenner, 396

Zebra Wall, The. Henkes, 342

About the Author

Judith Wynn Halsted, M.S. has been involved with gifted children for over 35 years—as an educator, librarian, counselor, parent, and grandparent. A former director of gifted programs at Pathfinder School in Traverse City, MI, she also founded—along with her husband, psychologist David W. Halsted, Ph.D.—Halsted Academic Advisors. Judy now works as an educational consultant helping gifted children and their families develop educational plans particularly aimed toward higher education opportunities.

Other Books from Great Potential Press

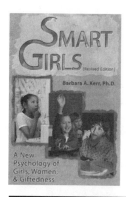

Smart Girls: A New Psychology of Girls, Women, and Giftedness
by Barbara A. Kerr, Ph.D.
Over 80,000 copies sold!
Why do so many talented girls often fail to realize their potential as adults? Dr. Kerr investigates this question and also offers practical advice to parents, teachers, and smart women about ways to help gifted girls continue to grow and succeed.
ISBN 0-910707-26-X / 270 pp. / paperback / $24.00

Helping Gifted Children Soar: A Practical Guide for Parents and Teachers
by Carol A. Strip, Ph.D. with Gretchen Hirsch
(winner, 2001 Glyph Award)
This user-friendly guidebook educates parents and teachers about gifted issues such as working together, choosing curriculum, meeting emotional needs, and finding support. A must-read to establish a solid foundation for gifted education.
ISBN 0-910707-41-3 / 288 pp. / paperback / $18.00
Also available in Spanish!

Guiding the Gifted Child: A Practical Source for Parents and Teachers
by James T. Webb, Ph.D., Elizabeth A. Meckstroth, M.S.W., and Stephanie S. Tolan, M.A.
Over 100,000 copies sold!
Called the Dr. Spock book for parents of gifted children, this award-winning book covers important information on the unique social and emotional concerns regarding gifted children. Chapters focus on motivation, discipline, relationships, peers, stress, and depression.
ISBN 0-910707-00-6 / 266 pp. / paperback / $18.00

To order materials or to request a free catalog, please write, call, email, or visit our Web site:

Great Potential Press, Inc.
P.O. Box 5057 Scottsdale, AZ 85261
Toll-free 1.877.954.4200 fax 602.954.0185
giftedbook@earthlink.net
www.giftedbooks.com

Other Videos from Great Potential Press

Parenting Successful Children
featuring James T. Webb, Ph.D.
Internationally acclaimed speaker, Dr. James Webb, describes over two dozen practical strategies to help parents set limits, avoid power struggles, minimize sibling rivalry, and enhance family relationships.
ISBN 0-910707-36-7 / VHS / 52 minutes / $28.00

Is My Child Gifted? (If so, what can I expect?)
featuring James T. Webb, Ph.D.
Dr. Webb discusses the most common characteristics of giftedness in children and different types of gifted children. He also addresses the trials of educating and parenting gifted children in today's world.
ISBN 0-910707-45-6 / VHS / 45 minutes / $25.00

Do Gifted Children Need Special Help?
featuring James T. Webb, Ph.D.
Gifted children see the world through their own eyes and often get criticized for the very characteristics that make them who they are. Dr. Webb explores the reactions and challenges that gifted children often experience because of their unique traits, and gives helpful suggestions.
ISBN 0-910707-44-8 / VHS / 45 minutes / $25.00

To order materials or to request a free catalog, please write, call, email, or visit our Web site:

Great Potential Press, Inc.
P.O. Box 5057 Scottsdale, AZ 85261
Toll-free 1.877.954.4200 fax 602.954.0185
giftedbook@earthlink.net
www.giftedbooks.com